The One Year® Book of Bible Trivia for Kids

Katrina Cassel

the one year book of **Bible Trivia** for kids

Tyndale House Publishers, Inc.
Carol Stream, Illinois

Visit www.cool2read.com.

TYNDALE, Tyndale's quill logo, *The One Year,* and *One Year* are registered trademarks of Tyndale House Publishers, Inc. The One Year logo is a trademark of Tyndale House Publishers, Inc.

The One Year Book of Bible Trivia for Kids

Copyright © 2013 by Katrina Cassel. All rights reserved.

Cover illustration © doodlemachine/iStockphoto. All rights reserved.

Illustration of girl copyright © doodlemachine/iStockphoto. All rights reserved.

Designed by Jacqueline L. Nuñez

Edited by Erin Gwynne

Unless otherwise indicated, all Scripture quotations are taken from the *Holy Bible*, New Living Translation, copyright © 1996, 2004, 2007, 2013 by Tyndale House Foundation. Used by permission of Tyndale House Publishers, Inc., Carol Stream, Illinois 60188. All rights reserved. (Some quotations may be from the previous edition of the NLT, copyright © 2007.)

Scripture quotations marked NIV are taken from the Holy Bible, *New International Version*,® *NIV*.® Copyright © 1973, 1978, 1984, 2011 by Biblica, Inc.™ Used by permission of Zondervan. All rights reserved worldwide. www.zondervan.com. (Some quotations may be from the previous edition of the NIV, copyright © 1984.)

Scripture quotations marked "ICB" are taken from the International Children's Bible.® Copyright © 1986, 1988, 1999 by Thomas Nelson, Inc. Used by permission. All rights reserved.

Printed in the United States of America

ISBN 978-1-4143-7160-3

19 18 17 16 15 14 13
7   6   5   4   3   2   1

To

Rick: best friend for life

Tyler: firstborn

Jessica: firstborn princess

Jeff: my first Haitian sensation

Adam: compassionate warrior

Jasmine: my joy and song

Kaleb and Kayla: chosen ones

Acknowledgments

A special thank you to the Tyndale team, from Katara Patton, who saw the possibilities for the book, to Erin Gwynne, whose touch transformed the devotions, to Jackie Nuñez, whose design gave the pages kid appeal. Also thank you to Teresa Cleary for her suggestions and corrections.

January 1

A Light to Guide You

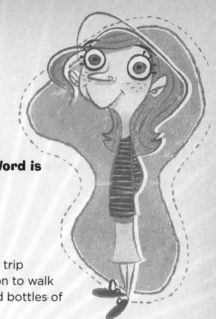

Q: Which book of the Bible says God's Word is a light for your path?
a. Hebrews
b. Psalms
c. Proverbs

Imagine this. You and a friend are on a camping trip with your parents. The two of you get permission to walk along a nearby nature trail. You pack snacks and bottles of water in your backpacks, and you start off.

You are having fun and forget to pay attention to the time. The sun is setting quickly, and you realize you'd better head back to the campsite. You know you just have to cut through the woods to get back.

"Which way?" you ask your friend.

"I don't know. What do you think?" Your friend looks around.

"I'm not sure. Everything looks different in the dark."

"Wait a minute. I think I have a flashlight in my backpack." Your friend digs around for a few seconds and pulls out a flashlight. The flashlight gets clicked on, and a bright beam of light cuts through the darkness.

"Point it over there," you say. "I think that's the way back."

Your friend shines the light where you point. Sure enough, your campsite is straight ahead. The flashlight has saved the day.

God says his Word will be a light for your path, just like the flashlight lights the path in the story above. The Bible tells you how to live, and it helps you make decisions. It's important to become familiar with the Bible so you can use it as your guide for life. Read from the Bible each day, and ask yourself how the Scripture applies to you.

For You

When it comes to life's questions, you don't need to feel around in the dark, trying to find your way. You already have a light—the Bible. God's Word can guide you in making the right decisions and knowing what to do when you aren't sure of the way. Take time to read a few verses of Scripture every day.

Answer: b
Your word is a lamp to guide my feet and a light for my path. Psalm 119:105

January 2

Make No Mistake

Q: Which word means "without error"?
a. *infallible*
b. *inspired*
c. *inflatable*

Have you ever been at a family gathering where your parents, grandparents, aunts, and uncles were telling stories about their past, but no one could agree on the details? Your dad starts telling about the time he borrowed the car to take your mom on their first date. But your grandfather corrects him about what kind of car it was. Then your mother tells your dad they didn't go to the restaurant he named for their date. It takes quite a while to get the details worked out, and it's possible not everyone agrees on the story.

The Bible contains many stories, but all of their details agree because God is the author of the Bible. He used around 40 different men to do the actual writing from their own personalities and experiences. But the message is always the same: humans have a problem—sin. God has the answer—salvation. That's amazing when you consider the Bible was written over a time period of around 1,500 years. And the men who wrote it were from three different continents and had various jobs—shepherd, tax collector, doctor, fisherman, and more.

The Bible doesn't contain mistakes, because God is the true author of the Bible. Although he used humans to record his words, the message is his.

For You

There may be times when you're reading the Bible and it doesn't seem to match up. When that happens, ask a parent or a leader at church to help you find out why. Sometimes we may not understand the Bible, but God's message is always right.

Answer: a
Although the word *infallible* isn't used in the Bible, the Bible tells us that it's the Word of God and that God never makes mistakes.

All Scripture is inspired by God and is useful to teach us what is true and to make us realize what is wrong in our lives. It corrects us when we are wrong and teaches us to do what is right. 2 Timothy 3:16

Old Testament: Books of Law

January 3

The Void

Q: How many days did God take to create the world and everything in it?
a. 1
b. 6
c. 7

Did your parents ever watch any of the *Star Trek* shows? If so, they might remember the *Star Trek: Voyager* episode called "Night." In it, the starship *Voyager* has been traveling through a black void for several weeks. There are no planets, stars, or other ships to be seen. The crew is feeling depressed by the constant darkness. Of course, by the end of the episode, the *Voyager* crew is back in an area of space teeming with stars, planets, and other species, and all is well.

That same kind of nothingness might be what you would have seen if you had been around when God started his work of creation. Then God spoke the heavens and earth into existence. But it wasn't earth like you now know it. Can you imagine darkness everywhere you look? No sun or moon. No trees, plants, or flowers. No fish or birds. Not even a mosquito. Just a dark, empty planet.

Thankfully God didn't leave the earth like that. He created light to shine on the earth. He separated the waters in the earth from the sky. He moved the waters together so there would also be dry land to live on. He filled the earth with trees and plants, and then he hung the sun, moon, and stars in the sky. He filled the seas with fish and the sky with birds. Then he created other animals to dwell on earth. What fun he must have had creating the elephant's long nose and the zebra's black-and-white stripes.

God created the earth and filled it with plants and animals. It was all ready for God's final act of creation—man.

For You

God created earth with mankind in mind. He wanted to create a place for his people to live and worship him. Everything he made was for you to enjoy. Take time this week to notice God's handiwork around you in the things he created.

Answer: b
Then God looked over all he had made, and he saw that it was very good! And evening passed and morning came, marking the sixth day. Genesis 1:31
(The Whole Story: Genesis 1)

January 4

Adam and Eve

Q: What did God use to make Adam and then Eve?
a. He made them both from nothing.
b. Adam was made from dust, and Eve was made from Adam's rib.
c. Adam was made from God's rib, and Eve was made from Adam's rib.

Have you ever read suspense books? These are books where a main character is in trouble, and you don't know what's going to happen next. One Christian suspense author writes about scientists who create a group of what appears to be perfect humans. The problem is God didn't create them, so they have no souls. They become ruthless killers. The good guys have to figure out how to track them down and destroy them—or the good guys will be destroyed!

God created the first man from the dust of the ground and breathed life into him. God placed the man in a beautiful garden filled with fruit trees. It was the perfect place to live, but Adam was alone and needed companionship. God put Adam to sleep, and then God formed Eve from one of Adam's ribs.

Now God's work of creation was complete. Only God can create humans and breathe life into them, and only God can give humans a spirit and soul so they can tell the difference between right and wrong.

For You

God created Adam and Eve in his own image. That doesn't mean they physically looked like God, but they could share some of his characteristics. God created you in his image too. He wants you to be like him in your thoughts and actions. Take a look at your life and consider ways in which you resemble your heavenly Father.

Answer: b
The LORD God formed the man from the dust of the ground. He breathed the breath of life into the man's nostrils, and the man became a living person. . . . While the man slept, the LORD God took out one of the man's ribs. . . . Then the LORD God made a woman from the rib, and he brought her to the man.
Genesis 2:7, 21-22
(The Whole Story: Genesis 2:7-23)

January 5

Downtime

Q: What did God do on the seventh day of Creation?
a. He rested from all his work.
b. He created the angels.
c. He visited his creation.

God did his work of creation in six days, and then he rested. Genesis 2:3 says, "God blessed the seventh day and declared it holy, because it was the day when he rested from all his work of creation." Some people refer to this day of rest as the Sabbath.

Did God need to rest? No. He could have created a million more worlds and still kept going, but he chose to declare a day of rest. He probably did this to set an example for us. He knew things would become so busy that people wouldn't slow down and take time to think about him.

Some people declare Saturday as the Sabbath and worship God then. Others worship on Sunday because Jesus rose from the dead on the first day of the week. The important thing is to have a day of the week that's different from the others. This is the day you attend church and maybe spend more time with your family.

That might bring up the question, What about people who have to work on the Sabbath and can't go to church? People like doctors, police officers, and fire-fighters are often needed on that day. There is no easy answer to that question, but since God knows people's hearts—and their schedules—he knows if they take time to honor him, even if it's not on the day they'd normally go to church.

The important thing is to set aside time to honor God and to gather with other believers one day a week. And honoring God shouldn't happen just one day a week; it should be an everyday thing.

For You

It's good to think about God, read your Bible, and pray on the Sabbath. But it's important to do those same things every day, not just one day a week. God needs people who don't just go to church, then come home and forget about God the rest of the week. He needs people who will put him first every day. Those are the people he can use to do his work.

Answer: a
On the seventh day God had finished his work of creation, so he rested from all his work. And God blessed the seventh day and declared it holy, because it was the day when he rested from all his work of creation. Genesis 2:2-3
(The Whole Story: Genesis 2:1-3)

January 6

Sin Enters the World

Q: What kind of fruit did Eve take from the tree of the knowledge of good and evil?
a. a pear
b. an apple
c. We don't know.

God made a beautiful garden home for Adam and Eve. He told them they could eat from any tree except the tree of the knowledge of good and evil. One day Satan, who was disguised as a serpent, approached Eve in the Garden. The conversation went like this:

Serpent: "Did God really say you must not eat the fruit from any of the trees in the garden?"

Eve: "Of course we may eat fruit from the trees in the garden. It's only the fruit from the tree in the middle of the garden that we are not allowed to eat."

Serpent: "God knows that your eyes will be opened as soon as you eat it, and you will be like God, knowing both good and evil."

Eve fell for the lie and ate fruit from the forbidden tree, and then Adam did the same. When they ate the fruit, things changed. Sin entered the world, and everyone who has lived since that time is born with the tendency to sin. Adam and Eve were banished from their Garden home, and they could no longer walk and talk personally with God in the Garden as they had before.

Although Adam and Eve were punished for their sin, God already had a plan in place. He knew one day he'd send his Son to die on the cross to pay the penalty so people could be forgiven of their sins.

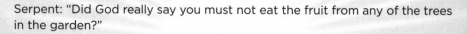

For You

First Corinthians 10:13 promises that God will help you find a way out of every temptation. You just have to ask him. The next time you're tempted to do something wrong, ask God for help. You might need to walk away from a situation.

Answer: c
The woman was convinced. She saw that the tree was beautiful and its fruit looked delicious, and she wanted the wisdom it would give her. So she took some of the fruit and ate it. Then she gave some to her husband. Genesis 3:6
(The Whole Story: Genesis 3)

Anger Is Destructive

Q: What did Cain do after God accepted Abel's offering but rejected his?
a. brought a new offering
b. killed his brother
c. cried out to God

Cain was a farmer, and Abel was a shepherd. Cain brought a gift of his crops to God, and Abel brought the best of the firstborn of his lambs. God accepted Abel's offering but not Cain's.

Why did God reject Cain's offering? We aren't told exactly, but there are three possibilities. One is that it wasn't the kind of offering God required. At times God asked for a blood offering. We don't know if that's what was required here or not. The Bible doesn't say.

Another possibility is the offering was inferior. The Bible says Abel gave the best of the firstborn of his lambs, but it doesn't say Cain gave his best.

The third possibility is that Cain's heart was wrong. "We must not be like Cain, who belonged to the evil one and killed his brother. And why did he kill him? Because Cain had been doing what was evil, and his brother had been doing what was righteous" (1 John 3:12). Cain was not living a life pleasing to God, and that may have been why his offering was rejected.

God told Cain he would be accepted when he did what was right, but Cain didn't want to change his ways, so he turned his anger on his brother. One day when they were in the field, Cain attacked Abel and killed him. God banned Cain from his homeland. You can read about it in Genesis 4.

Cain's heart was wrong, and it led to anger, jealousy, and finally murder. How much better it would have been for Cain to turn from his sin and live a righteous life so God could accept and bless him.

For You

God wants you to live a life that pleases him. Ask him to show you anything in your life that needs to be fixed, and then do whatever it takes to correct it.

Answer: b
One day Cain suggested to his brother, "Let's go out into the fields." And while they were in the field, Cain attacked his brother, Abel, and killed him.
Genesis 4:8
(The Whole Story: Genesis 4:1-16)

January 8

God's Plan Continues

Q: What child did Eve say was given to her to replace Abel after his death?
a. Seth
b. Reuben
c. Lamech

The first two brothers to ever walk this earth were opposites. Abel loved and obeyed God. Cain didn't. Rather than turning to God, Cain let anger and jealousy consume him, and he committed the first murder.

God had promised a Savior who would come from Adam's family tree. But Abel, who loved God and would have been the one in Jesus' family tree, was dead. So God replaced Abel with Seth. That doesn't mean Seth was just like Abel. It means Seth was chosen to be the ancestor of Jesus in Abel's place.

It was only because Seth loved God, just as Abel had, that God was able to use him in this special way. In fact the Bible tells us, "When Seth grew up, he had a son and named him Enosh. At that time people first began to worship the LORD by name" (Genesis 4:26). Seth passed his love for God on to his children.

God's plan to walk and talk with Adam and Eve in the Garden was ruined by their sin. The plan for Abel to be an ancestor of Jesus was ruined by Cain's sin. But Seth's obedience turned things around.

For You

God has a plan for you just as he did for Abel and Seth—and even as he did for Cain, although Cain chose not to fulfill God's plan. If you try to do the things you know God wants you to do each day, he will be able to use you to do important things for him. You face a lot of decisions every day. Make each choice one that pleases God, and live in a way that allows God to use you however he chooses. It's an adventure you don't want to miss.

Answer: a
[Eve] gave birth to another son. She named him Seth, for she said, "God has granted me another son in place of Abel, whom Cain killed." Genesis 4:25
(The Whole Story: Genesis 4:25-26)

January 9

Praise God with Music

Q: What instruments did Jubal play?
a. harp and flute
b. trumpet and guitar
c. trumpet and drums

Do you play a musical instrument? Perhaps you are in your school's band. Did you know that people in Bible times played instruments? David played the harp to calm King Saul, but he wasn't the first to play an instrument.

Jubal, mentioned in Genesis, played the flute and harp. Some Bible translations say he played the lyre and pipe, or harp and organ. He's the first person mentioned in the Bible who played instruments. Was there music around before Jubal? There isn't any mention of it, but it's a possibility. Perhaps God gave Adam and Eve the gift of music.

Praising God with music is a good idea. The Bible says,

Praise the LORD with melodies on the lyre; make music for him on the ten-stringed harp. Sing a new song of praise to him; play skillfully on the harp, and sing with joy.
   (Psalm 33:2-3)

I will sing a new song to you, O God! I will sing your praises with a ten-stringed harp.
   (Psalm 144:9)

It isn't just the psalmist who talks about praising God with music. The New Testament encourages believers to sing to the Lord. Check out what Ephesians 5:18-20 says to you: "Be filled with the Holy Spirit, singing psalms and hymns and spiritual songs among yourselves, and making music to the Lord in your hearts. And give thanks for everything to God the Father in the name of our Lord Jesus Christ."

For You

Music, whether played on an instrument or sung, is a good way to praise God. Does the music you sing, play, or listen to do that? If not, it might be time to make some changes in your music.

Answer: a
Jubal [was] the first of all who play the harp and flute. Genesis 4:21
(The Whole Story: Genesis 4:20-21)

January 10

A Job to Do

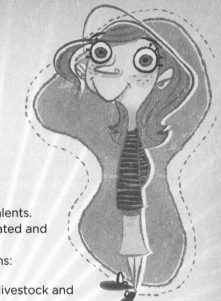

Q: What material did Tubal-cain work with?
a. silver and gold
b. gold and copper
c. bronze and iron

People in Bible times had many abilities and talents. Sometimes we think of them as being uneducated and lacking skills, but that's not so.

Lamech, a descendant of Cain, had three sons:

Jabal, "who was the first of those who raise livestock and live in tents" (Genesis 4:20)
Jubal, "the first of all who play the harp and flute" (Genesis 4:21), who was talked about in yesterday's devotion
Tubal-cain, who knew how to melt metals and make armor, weapons, and other utensils and objects (see Genesis 4:22)

Even though Lamech didn't follow God, the Lord blessed him with children who were gifted in different areas. One son had herds so large he had to take them to other places to graze, and he invented some sort of tent as a way to have shelter during those times (see Genesis 4:20). Another son was a musician. The third brother made things of metal and taught others to do the same.

Which of these was the most important? None was more or less important than the others. God gives each person talents and abilities, and the Lord uses those to accomplish his work here on earth. God needs some people to be musicians and others to be electricians or plumbers. He needs some to preach and others to be doctors or missionaries.

God has a job for you, too. He needs you to do that job to fulfill what he has planned for you to accomplish. God may not show you all at once what he wants you to do, but he'll lead you step-by-step along the way.

For You

Look for one thing you can do today to accomplish something for God.

Answer: c
Lamech's other wife, Zillah, gave birth to a son named Tubal-cain. He became an expert in forging tools of bronze and iron. Tubal-cain had a sister named Naamah. Genesis 4:22
(The Whole Story: Genesis 4:17-24)

January 11

Believing God

Q: A large school bus is about 45 feet long. How many buses would you have to line up end to end to equal the length of the ark?

a. 4

b. 8

c. 10

God created Adam and Eve. Adam and Eve had children. Then their children had children. As more people filled the earth, they began doing wicked things. It got worse and worse until one day God looked down from heaven at his creation, and everywhere he looked, people were disobeying him. They'd forgotten how to live in a way that would please God. This made God very sad.

Then God saw Noah and his family, like a light in the darkness. God decided to destroy the whole world and start over with Noah and his family. God asked Noah to build a boat that was 450 feet long, 75 feet wide, and 45 feet high. That was no easy job. There were no home improvement stores from which they could buy lumber and nails. Noah and his sons had to do it all by hand.

Building the ark wasn't hard just because of the manual labor; it was hard because people were likely making fun of the Noah family. Noah insisted God was going to destroy the world with a huge flood, but people had never seen rain before. They didn't believe Noah, and they thought he was crazy. But no matter what people said or did, Noah kept building the ark. He believed God, and his trust in God saved him and his family.

For You

Sometimes God might ask you to do things that are hard. You may have to stand alone at times. But, like Noah, you can obey God without knowing the end result. Just trust that the Lord knows what he's doing and that things will turn out the way he plans.

Answer: c

[God said to Noah,] "Build a large boat from cypress wood and waterproof it with tar, inside and out. Then construct decks and stalls throughout its interior. Make the boat 450 feet long, 75 feet wide, and 45 feet high." Genesis 6:14-15
(The Whole Story: Genesis 6)

January 12

The Ark Provides Salvation

Q: The ark represents what Jesus did for us in providing salvation.
True
False

You've probably heard Noah's story many times. Because people became so wicked, God decided to destroy the world and start over with Noah's family and pairs of each kind of animal. After Noah and his sons completed the ark, the animals and Noah's family got on board, and God closed the ark door. Then it began to rain. It rained for 40 days and 40 nights. Everything on the earth, except Noah's family and the animals on the ark, was destroyed.

The story of Noah's ark is similar to the story of Jesus. Just like the ark saved Noah, his family, and the animals from the Flood, Jesus can save us from the punishment of our sins. Ephesians 2:8-9 tells us, "God saved you by his grace when you believed. And you can't take credit for this; it is a gift from God. Salvation is not a reward for the good things we have done, so none of us can boast about it."

God told Noah, "Build a large boat from cypress wood and waterproof it with tar" (Genesis 6:14). The Hebrew word translated as "tar" in that verse is *kaphar*. It is the same word that is translated other places in the Bible as "atonement."

Why is that important? To atone for something is to make up for the wrong done. We all sin and disobey God. But when Jesus died on the cross, he made it possible for us to be right with God. That's atonement. And that's the same word that's used for the tar that covered the ark—*kaphar*. The ark is a symbol of Jesus.

Noah and his family found salvation in the ark. You can find salvation in Jesus and eternal life in heaven.

For You

Noah had to step out in faith and believe what God said was true. He was saved because of his faith. You can be saved because of your faith too.

Answer: True. Even though the Bible doesn't say that the ark is like Jesus, they both provided salvation.

The LORD said to Noah, "Go into the boat with all your family, for among all the people of the earth, I can see that you alone are righteous." Genesis 7:1

(The Whole Story: Genesis 7)

January 13

God's Promises

Q: God placed the rainbow in the sky to
a. add color to the new world.
b. be a memorial for all the animals who died.
c. be a sign of his promise never to flood the entire earth again.

God gives many promises in the Bible. God promised as far back as Adam and Eve that he'd send a Savior. God promised Abraham and Sarah they would have a son in their old age. God promised he'd lead his people out of slavery in Egypt. God promised David his kingdom would be established forever. These are only a few examples of God's promises to people in the Bible.

Did you know God has given you promises too? God promises you

a room in heaven (see John 14:1-3);
new strength when you trust in him (see Isaiah 40:31);
his presence all the time (see Hebrews 13:5);
peace when you leave your problems with him (see Philippians 4:6-7);
forgiveness when you confess your sins (see 1 John 1:9); and
an escape from temptation (see 1 Corinthians 10:13).

Can you think of more promises God has given you? There are hundreds in the Bible. God gave Noah a promise too. He promised he would never again destroy the world with a flood. God put a rainbow in the sky as a sign of that promise.

Sometimes friends make promises without thinking. They might promise to come to your house or to call you. They may promise to lend you a movie or help you with your history report. While these promises may be made with good intentions, they are often broken.

This isn't true with God. Read 2 Samuel 22:31: "God's way is perfect. All the LORD's promises prove true. He is a shield for all who look to him for protection." Isn't that a good verse to remember? Why not memorize it today?

For You

What promise from God do you think is most special to you? Why? Share that promise with someone today.

Answer: c
[God said to Noah,] "I have placed my rainbow in the clouds. It is the sign of my covenant with you and with all the earth." Genesis 9:13
(The Whole Story: Genesis 8:20–9:17)

January 14

Building Monuments to Yourself

Q: What structure did the people build to show their importance?
a. Mount Moriah
b. the tower of Babel
c. an Egyptian pyramid

Years after the Flood, the world was full of people who all spoke the same language. They decided to build a large tower that would reach into the heavens to show how great they were. The people said, "Come, let's build a great city for ourselves with a tower that reaches into the sky. This will make us famous and keep us from being scattered all over the world."

The people planned on showing their importance by building a huge monument to themselves, but God wasn't impressed by the people or by their tower. So God mixed up their language. One minute they were all talking and laughing together, and the next minute they couldn't understand each other. They must have been so confused!

Slowly people divided into groups based on what language they spoke, and the groups moved away from each other. In that way, God scattered the people across the world. They found out the hard way that they were not as important as they thought they were.

Sometimes people today think they are more important than they are. They may not build a tower like the people in the book of Genesis, but they may do other things to show their importance. People you know may do things to show how important they think they are. Can you think of some of the ways they do that?

For You

Have you ever done anything to pretend you are more important than others? Maybe you won't go to someone's house because you think your house is nicer. Or maybe you only wear a certain brand of clothes because it's popular. Those are ways of trying to look important. Ask God to point out to you attitudes you may need to change in your life.

Answer: b
That is why the city was called Babel, because that is where the LORD confused the people with different languages. In this way he scattered them all over the world. Genesis 11:9
(The Whole Story: Genesis 11:1-9)

January 15

By Faith

Q: How many days did God tell Abraham it would take to move?
a. 7
b. 1
c. God didn't tell Abraham where he was going or how long it would take to get there.

When your family is getting ready to go somewhere, your parents probably like to be sure of the directions and exactly how long the trip will take. They may use an Internet map program, their GPS, or an app on their phone. Or they may pull out an atlas and figure out the directions and travel time for themselves.

Abraham, a Bible character also known as Abram, didn't have that option. Not only were electronic maps unavailable, but God didn't tell him where he was going! He just told Abraham, "Leave your native country, your relatives, and your father's family, and go to the land that I will show you."

Like Noah, Abraham chose to believe God and step out in faith. He packed up his family, household goods, and animals and set out simply following God. That was a huge step of faith, and God rewarded Abraham for it. He chose Abraham to be the father of his special people, the Jews, also sometimes called the Israelites or the Hebrews.

It may have been easier for Abraham to stay where he was rather than move his family to an unknown place, but Abraham chose to follow God's plan. Sometimes today it is easier for people to go their own way rather than listen to God and follow his leading, but when people do that, God can't bless them as he blessed both Noah and Abraham.

For You

Do you try to listen to God each day and do things his way? God's way is the best way because he knows the special plan he has for your life, and he'll lead you down the right path step-by-step. Ask him to show you what he wants you to do today.

Answer: c
The LORD had said to Abram, "Leave your native country, your relatives, and your father's family, and go to the land that I will show you." Genesis 12:1
(The Whole Story: Genesis 12)

January 16

Abraham and Lot

Q: How many trained men who were part of his household did Abraham take with him to rescue Lot from the enemy army?
a. 18
b. 318
c. 1,018

Abraham (or Abram) was an unselfish man who loved and served God. Abraham's nephew, Lot, moved with him to the new land God led Abraham to. Both Abraham and Lot had many family members and livestock: cattle, sheep, and goats. They couldn't live close together because there wasn't enough room for all the animals and people. So Abraham told Lot to choose which half of the land he wanted, and Abraham would take the other.

But Lot was selfish. He thought of himself first, and most of his decisions were based on what was best for him. Lot saw the fertile plains of the Jordan Valley and chose the whole valley for himself.

Abraham allowed Lot to have the best land. Not only that, but Abraham looked out for Lot even after they separated. One day some invaders captured Lot and took everything he owned. Abraham could have ignored the problem, but he gathered together 318 trained men from his household and rescued Lot and all his possessions. Abraham thought of others more than himself.

For You

Abraham was unselfish and looked out for others. Lot was selfish and took the best for himself. Who are you most like—Abraham or Lot? Do you always want the best choice, or do you let others have the best choice sometimes? Do you consider others' feelings and needs as well as your own? If you are more like Lot, ask God to help you learn to be unselfish and giving.

Answer: b

When Abram heard that his nephew Lot had been captured, he mobilized the 318 trained men who had been born into his household. Then he pursued Kedorlaomer's army until he caught up with them at Dan. Genesis 14:14
(The Whole Story: Genesis 13:1–14:16)

January 17

Getting Ahead of God

Q: When Sarah became angry with Hagar, where did Hagar flee to?
a. her own home
b. the wilderness
c. a new land

Sarah, also known as Sarai, didn't think she would ever have a baby. So she decided Abraham (or Abram) should have a child with her maid, Hagar. Then Sarah and Abraham would raise him as their son. This was done a lot in early Old Testament times, but it's not something God approved of.

When Hagar found out she was pregnant with Abraham's child, she started to look down on Sarah. She acted as though she were better than Sarah because she could have a child and Sarah couldn't.

Sarah became angry and was mean to Hagar. Hagar fled to the wilderness, but an angel met her there and sent her back to Sarah. Hagar returned to Abraham's household, and she gave birth to a son named Ishmael.

Later, Isaac was born to Sarah, and Abraham held a big feast (see Genesis 21:1-13). During this celebration, Sarah saw Hagar and her son, Ishmael, making fun of Isaac. Sarah demanded that Abraham send Hagar and Ishmael away. This made Abraham sad, because Ishmael was his son too. God promised Abraham he'd make a great nation from Ishmael, but Ishmael was not the child God had promised Abraham would have.

There was a lot of drama between Sarah and Hagar because of jealousy and rivalry. If Sarah had been willing to believe God and wait to have her own child, the drama could have been avoided. Sometimes we don't wait for God to take action, but we try to do things ourselves. That never works out very well.

For You

Sometimes God wants you to go ahead and do something, but other times he may want you to wait. Pray about your plans, and God will give you peace about your actions if they are the right ones.

Answer: b

Abram replied, "Look, she is your servant, so deal with her as you see fit." Then Sarai treated Hagar so harshly that she finally ran away. The angel of the LORD found Hagar beside a spring of water in the wilderness. Genesis 16:6-7
(The Whole Story: Genesis 16)

January 18

Waiting

Q: What did Sarah do when God told her she'd have a baby?
a. rejoice
b. laugh
c. pray

John is used to getting everything he wants. Each birthday and Christmas he gets the latest expensive gadget. But he quickly becomes bored with his gift and searches for something more exciting.

Mikayla lives with her grandmother in a one-bedroom apartment. Mikayla sleeps on the couch each night and stores her bedding in the closet during the day. Mikayla wants a ten-speed bicycle, so she's found jobs walking pets, pet sitting, or babysitting. She works most afternoons and all day on Saturdays to earn enough money for a bike.

Which one is most appreciative of what he or she has: John or Mikayla? It might seem John would be because he has more, but in reality, Mikayla probably is because she worked for the bike and had to wait longer before she could get it. It was something she wanted enough to invest her own time and effort into getting.

God promised that Abraham's family would become a great nation, but Abraham didn't have any children. Sarah couldn't have a baby. Years went by without the promised child being born. Finally when Sarah was past the age of having a baby, God told her she would give birth to a son. Sarah laughed. How could that be? It was humanly impossible. But it wasn't impossible with God.

Why did God make Abraham and Sarah wait? Maybe so that, like Mikayla, they'd appreciate their gift more. Or maybe so they'd learn to trust God more. Perhaps they had to wait so God would get the credit for this miracle baby.

Have you asked God to do something he hasn't done yet? That may not mean he'll never do it. It might mean he's waiting so you'll appreciate it more when it happens.

For You

Have you ever waited a long time to get something or worked to buy something yourself? How do you think waiting changed your feelings toward what you received or bought?

Answer: b
Abraham and Sarah were both very old by this time, and Sarah was long past the age of having children. So she laughed silently to herself and said, "How could a worn-out woman like me enjoy such pleasure, especially when my master—my husband—is also so old?" Genesis 18:11-12
(The Whole Story: Genesis 18:1-15)

January 19

Don't Look Back

Q: Lot's wife looked back at the city they'd left and was turned into what?
a. stone
b. salt
c. sand

Have you ever gone to church camp? Often there is a bonfire at the end of camp. The campers may throw a stick into the fire to symbolize their desire to follow God while all the other campers and leaders sing a song about following God. It would have been good if Lot's wife had felt the same way.

Lot and his wife lived in Sodom. It was a wicked city, so God decided to destroy it. God sent two angels to tell Lot to get his whole family out of the city before it was too late. Lot wasn't following God like he should have been, but he did believe the angels.

Lot tried to warn his daughters' fiancés, but they thought he was joking. Only Lot, his wife, and their two daughters left the city. The angels told them not to look back or stop until they reached safety.

But Lot's wife couldn't resist the urge to look back. God turned her into a pillar of salt! That may seem like a harsh punishment, but God's way is always right. Perhaps God knew her heart was as wicked as the other Sodom residents'. Or maybe it was a sign she didn't want to follow God and leave the wickedness behind.

God wants us to look ahead to what he has for us, not look back and long for something else.

For You

Are you looking toward God and seeking his plan for you, or are you distracted by other things? Keep looking ahead and determine to go God's way, not your own.

Answer: b
But Lot's wife looked back as she was following behind him, and she turned into a pillar of salt. Genesis 19:26
(The Whole Story: Genesis 19:1-29)

Can God Count on You?

Q: God said Abraham's descendants would be like what two things?
a. stars in the sky and sand on the beach
b. birds in the air and fish in the sea
c. flowers and bees in the field

Abraham was a friend of God (read James 2:23), and God made a lot of promises to him. God told Abraham, "I will make you into a great nation. I will bless you and make you famous, and you will be a blessing to others. I will bless those who bless you and curse those who treat you with contempt. All the families on earth will be blessed through you" (Genesis 12:2-3).

God promised to

- make Abraham's descendants a great nation;
- bless Abraham with wealth;
- protect Abraham by blessing those who liked him and cursing those who treated him with contempt; and
- bless all families through him.

God chose to bless Abraham this way because Abraham believed in God, and God knew he could count on him.

There are people you count on every day. Your parents provide your meals, wash your clothes, and make sure you have what you need. You know there will be food on the table and clean clothes to wear. Your parents count on you for things too. Maybe it's your job to take the trash out or to wash the dishes. If you do your jobs well, your parents will see how dependable you are.

How about God? Can he count on you? God needs people today who will hear his voice and follow him just as he needed people to hear and follow him in Abraham's day. Are you one of them?

For You

Are you faithful in reading your Bible and praying each day? Are you dependable in following God's rules and trying to live the way he wants you to? If you are, God will be able to count on you like he counted on Abraham.

Answer: a
I will certainly bless you. I will multiply your descendants beyond number, like the stars in the sky and the sand on the seashore. Your descendants will conquer the cities of their enemies. Genesis 22:17
(The Whole Story: Genesis 12:2-3; 22:15-18)

January 21

What Will You Give Up for God?

Q: What did God ask Abraham to sacrifice on the altar in Moriah?
a. his best lamb
b. his son
c. the firstborn of his flock

Abraham and Sarah rejoiced because God kept his promise and gave them a son—Isaac. But then the Lord asked Abraham to do something difficult. God asked Abraham to take a trip to Moriah and sacrifice Isaac on an altar there.

God again asked Abraham to step out in faith, but this time God was asking him to give up the child he'd waited so long for. Did God really want Abraham to kill his own son? No. God is against human sacrifices. But Abraham was willing to sacrifice his son for God, and that's what God wanted. God wanted to know that Abraham loved him more than his own son. When God saw how much Abraham loved him, he sent an angel. "'Don't lay a hand on the boy!' the angel said. 'Do not hurt him in any way, for now I know that you truly fear God. You have not withheld from me even your son, your only son.'"

Abraham had set out on that journey very sad and full of grief. He had expected to come home alone. But God provided a ram for the sacrifice. God had a special plan in mind for Isaac because, like Abraham, Isaac also had complete faith in God.

God wanted to know that Abraham was willing to give up his only son for him, and Abraham didn't hold back. Are there things in your life God might want you to give up for him? Are you willing to do it?

- -

For You

What things are most important to you? Friends? Sports? Popularity? Money? Are any of those things more important to you than God? If so, it might be time to rethink what is most important to you.

- -

Answer: b

[God said to Abraham,] "Take your son, your only son—yes, Isaac, whom you love so much—and go to the land of Moriah. Go and sacrifice him as a burnt offering on one of the mountains, which I will show you." Genesis 22:2
(The Whole Story: Genesis 22:1-19)

January 22

Finding a Wife for Isaac

Q: How did Abraham find a wife for Isaac?
a. He didn't. Isaac found one himself.
b. He sent his servant to his homeland to find a wife.
c. He threw dice.

Isaac, the promised son, had grown up and was ready to be married. Marriage worked differently back then. Often marriages were arranged. When it was time for Isaac to get married, Abraham didn't want him to marry a woman from Canaan, where they lived. The Canaanites didn't believe in God, and Abraham wanted Isaac to have a wife who shared his faith.

Abraham sent his trusted servant, Eliezer, back to Abraham's homeland to find a bride for Isaac. This was a big responsibility for Eliezer, so he asked God for help: "This is my request. I will ask one of them, 'Please give me a drink from your jug.' If she says, 'Yes, have a drink, and I will water your camels, too!'—let her be the one you have selected as Isaac's wife. This is how I will know that you have shown unfailing love to my master."

Before Eliezer had even finished praying, Rebekah arrived at the well with her jug. She not only gave the servant water to drink, but she gave his camels water to drink too. A marriage was arranged, and Rebekah traveled with the servant back to Canaan.

One day Rebekah was getting water from the well for her family, and the next she was on her way to a new land to marry Isaac. God knew she would be the perfect wife for Isaac.

God's plans are always best because he knows each of us and what we are capable of. He works things out to bring the right people together to accomplish the plans he has.

For You

God knows what your future holds. You might make your own plans, but he already has the perfect plan worked out for you. Be open to his leading so you don't miss the adventure.

Answer: b
[Abraham said to his servant,] "Go instead to my homeland, to my relatives, and find a wife there for my son Isaac." Genesis 24:3-4
(The Whole Story: Genesis 24)

January 23

Twins

Q: Which Bible mom gave birth to twins?
a. Sarah
b. Rachel
c. Rebekah

There is something special about twins. If you have friends who are twins, you may have found that they are alike in many ways, but they are also different in many ways. Even identical twins have different likes and dislikes.

Rebekah, Isaac's wife, gave birth to twins. They were both boys, but they weren't identical. In fact, they were quite different in both looks and personality. Esau, born first, was red and hairy. Jacob had smooth skin, unlike his brother.

Esau loved to be outdoors, and he became a hunter. He was Isaac's favorite child. Isaac loved to eat the meat Esau brought home. Jacob preferred to be indoors, and he was his mother's favorite. The parents each having a favorite son caused problems you'll read about in future devotions.

God had a unique plan for each of Rebekah's twin sons, but a lot of events kept things from happening as they should have. It didn't catch God by surprise, though. He knows that we tend to take matters into our own hands instead of waiting for him to work. God is able to take our messes and work them out for his good.

For You

You may not think one incident can change the course of events much, but the decisions you make each day have an impact on your future. Be open to what God has for you each day and follow his prompting when you feel him speaking to you in your heart.

Answer: c
Isaac pleaded with the LORD on behalf of his wife, because she was unable to have children. The LORD answered Isaac's prayer, and Rebekah became pregnant with twins. Genesis 25:21
(The Whole Story: Genesis 25:19-28)

Caring about What's Important

Q: Esau sold his birthright (the privileges he received for being the firstborn) to his brother Jacob in exchange for what?
a. pieces of silver
b. seven sheep
c. a bowl of stew

In Old Testament times, being the firstborn son was an honor. He received a double portion of the land and money, as well as the right to be the leader of the family and the spiritual leader when the father died. For Jacob and Esau, it meant the older one would carry on God's promises to Abraham to become a great nation, dwell in the land of Canaan, and be an ancestor of Jesus.

One day Esau came home very hungry from hunting. He wanted some of the stew Jacob was making. Jacob asked for Esau's birthright in exchange for it. Esau gave him all the privileges of being the firstborn for a bowl of stew.

It was a great honor to be the firstborn, but Esau was just thinking about how hungry he was in the moment. The future blessings and the role of being the spiritual leader didn't seem important to him. Those things meant a lot to Jacob, though, and that's why he asked for the birthright.

Esau didn't seek after God. He didn't desire the things God wanted to give him. He gave away his birthright for something he could have right then. That is something we still do today. Sometimes we don't think about what is really important, only about what we want right now. But when we choose that, we may miss out on something much better.

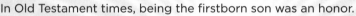

For You

Do you look for God's plan and make good choices for yourself, or do you mostly choose what you want right now? Ask God to help you make good decisions for yourself instead of giving in to your desires.

Answer: c
"Look, I'm dying of starvation!" said Esau. "What good is my birthright to me now?" But Jacob said, "First you must swear that your birthright is mine." So Esau swore an oath, thereby selling all his rights as the firstborn to his brother, Jacob. Genesis 25:32-33
(The Whole Story: Genesis 25:27-34)

January 25

Deceiving Isaac

Q: What did Jacob cover his skin with to make his father think he was Esau?
a. goatskin
b. red paint
c. cloth

Rebekah liked to get things done. Jacob made the most of opportunities. Rebekah's get-things-done personality and Jacob's habit of making the most of opportunities were good character traits when they were used to help others, but they weren't good when they were used to scheme against others. This was the case when it came time for Isaac, then old and blind, to give his final blessing to Esau.

Isaac sent Esau to hunt wild game and cook it for him. Then Isaac would give Esau a blessing as the firstborn. Rebekah overheard this, and she planned to deceive Isaac and gain the blessing for Jacob. She prepared two young goats to taste the same as the dish Esau was going to make with the wild game. Rebekah covered Jacob's smooth skin with a goatskin and had him dress in Esau's clothing, which smelled of the outdoors.

Things went as Rebekah planned. Jacob took the food to Isaac, claiming to be Esau, and Isaac said a special blessing over him. (You can read the blessing in Genesis 27:28-29.) All was well until Esau took his meat to Isaac. Then Esau found out Jacob had tricked their father into giving Jacob the blessing intended for him.

God had already told Rebekah before her twins were born that her older son would serve his younger brother, but she didn't wait to let God work. She made her own plans, and it caused angry feelings and divided the family.

Running ahead of God isn't a good idea. If you pray about your plans, God will give you a peace about going ahead with them if it's what he wants. Otherwise it's better to wait and see how God works.

 For You

If you need to make a decision, pray and ask God to guide you. If you aren't sure what he wants you to do, talk to a parent, Sunday school teacher, or pastor for guidance.

Answer: a
[Rebekah] covered [Jacob's] arms and the smooth part of his neck with the skin of the young goats. Genesis 27:16
(The Whole Story: Genesis 27)

The Consequence of Sin

Q: What did Jacob see in his dream?
a. Esau chasing him in a chariot
b. angels going up and down a stairway
c. manna falling from heaven to feed him

Jacob bought Esau's birthright with a bowl of stew. Later Rebekah and Jacob plotted together to deceive Isaac and steal the blessing from Esau. Esau was angry and decided he would kill Jacob after their father died. Rebekah found out about his plan and told Jacob to flee to her brother Laban's house many miles away in Haran (see Genesis 27:41-43).

Jacob traveled all day. Then he slept using a large stone for a pillow! He dreamed angels were going up and down a stairway from earth to heaven. God was at the top of the stairway, and he told Jacob the ground he was lying on would belong to Jacob and his descendants. God promised to be with Jacob and protect him wherever he went. He promised Jacob that one day Jacob would return to this land.

In the morning, Jacob set up the stone that he had been sleeping on as a memorial pillar to show what had happened there.

Jacob was wrong to deceive Isaac and take the blessing meant for Esau. Jacob's act caused pain for Esau and increased the animosity between the brothers. Even though Jacob chose to do the wrong thing, God still had a plan for him and still promised to bless him and watch over him.

Sometimes we act without thinking about consequences. Doing a certain thing might not seem so bad at the time, but it may harm someone else or you in ways you didn't plan. It's important to listen for God's leading in your life so you can avoid the harmful effects of sin.

For You

Think before acting, and ask God to point out to you things in your life that are harmful to yourself and others.

Answer: b
As [Jacob] slept, he dreamed of a stairway that reached from the earth up to heaven. And he saw the angels of God going up and down the stairway.
Genesis 28:12
(The Whole Story: Genesis 28:10-22)

January 27

Working Toward a Goal

Q: How many years did Jacob work for Laban for the privilege of marrying Rachel?
a. 1
b. 7
c. 14

Jacob fled from home and traveled to Haran. He arrived in time to move the heavy stone from the mouth of a well and help his cousin Rachel water her father's flocks.

After Jacob had lived with his uncle for about a month, Laban asked him what wages he wanted for the work he was doing. Jacob wanted to marry Rachel. (Back then cousins could marry.) He agreed to work seven years in order to marry Rachel. Jacob was so in love with Rachel that it didn't seem like a long time to him. But Jacob received a big surprise later when he found out he'd married Rachel's sister, Leah, who was covered by a veil at the wedding. Jacob, who had helped deceive his brother, had now been deceived by his uncle!

Laban told Jacob the oldest daughter had to marry first. He promised Jacob that once his wedding week was over, he could marry Rachel, too. But he had to stay and work another seven years after that to pay for her.

Jacob was willing to work hard for what he wanted and not give up. He worked fourteen years for Rachel. That is a long time, but Jacob pressed on and accomplished his goal.

For You

Sometimes it seems hard to wait or to work toward a goal that is a long way off, but when you achieve the goal, you have a sense of accomplishment for sticking with it. Is there something you want? Are you willing to work for it? Ask God and your parents to help you set a goal for yourself and take one step each day toward reaching it.

Answer: c

"It's not our custom here to marry off a younger daughter ahead of the firstborn," Laban replied. "But wait until the bridal week is over, then we'll give you Rachel, too—provided you promise to work another seven years for me." So Jacob agreed to work seven more years. Genesis 29:26-28
(The Whole Story: Genesis 29:1-30)

Jacob Leaves Laban's House

Q: What did Rachel steal from her father when she left his home?
a. his idols
b. his money
c. his best cattle

Jacob married both Leah and Rachel, and they had many children. Jacob decided it was time to go back to his homeland. He asked to take all the speckled, spotted, or black goats for all the work he'd done for Laban. Jacob was smart about breeding animals, and when it was finally time for Jacob and his family to leave, he had a large, strong flock of animals.

Jacob packed up his family and animals, and they set out while Laban was away shearing sheep. What Jacob didn't know was that Rachel had stolen Laban's idols.

Laban went after Jacob and asked why he'd left without allowing Laban to say good-bye to Rachel and Leah. He asked Jacob why he had stolen the idols. Laban searched through all the tents but didn't find the idols. Rachel had hidden them in her camel saddle, which she was sitting on.

We don't know why Rachel took the idols. She may have taken them to keep her father from worshiping them or as keepsakes of home or perhaps for their value. She may have considered them her inheritance.

Rachel grew up in a home with idols, but Jacob taught her about God and his laws. She chose to follow Jacob and God's way over her father's way (see Genesis 35:2-4). Each person must choose to follow God for himself or herself.

For You

You may be surrounded by people who don't believe in God or who have chosen not to live his way. It may be hard to stand alone, but God will give you the strength to follow him even if no one else is.

Answer: a
At the time they left, Laban was some distance away, shearing his sheep. Rachel stole her father's household idols and took them with her. Jacob outwitted Laban the Aramean, for they set out secretly and never told Laban they were leaving.
Genesis 31:19-20
(The Whole Story: Genesis 30–31)

January 29

A New Name

Q: When Jacob wrestled with God,
a. he got a broken arm and stitches.
b. he got knocked out in the first round.
c. he got his hip wrenched out of its socket.

Jacob was on his way home, but he wasn't alone like he had been when he fled many years earlier. Now he had two wives, servants, and many children. He had a large number of goats, sheep, donkeys, and camels. Even so, he was still fearful about seeing his brother, Esau, again after his hasty departure and years of separation (see Genesis 27:41-44).

One night during his journey home, Jacob sent the others ahead, and he camped alone. A man came and wrestled him all through the night. At the end, the man wrenched Jacob's hip out of its socket. The man said, "Let me go, for the dawn is breaking!"

Jacob knew this was no ordinary man. He told the man he wouldn't let him go unless the man blessed him. The man told him, "Your name will no longer be Jacob. From now on you will be called Israel, because you have fought with God and with men and have won."

Jacob had changed since the days when he got both his brother's birthright and his blessing. Jacob had learned it was better to do things God's way than his own. God gave Jacob a new name to reflect the changes in Jacob's heart.

When you become a believer in Jesus, you become a new person inside. You are a child of God, and your heart changes. And you have a new name too—Christian.

For You

Jacob's heart changed, and God changed his name, too. The old Jacob was known for his trickery and deceit, but the new, improved Jacob was known for his faith in God. How do others see you? What are you known for?

Answer: c
When the man saw that he would not win the match, he touched Jacob's hip and wrenched it out of its socket. Genesis 32:25
(The Whole Story: Genesis 32:22-32)

Jacob and Esau Meet Again

Q: How many times did Jacob bow before his brother?
a. 2
b. 7
c. 10

Jacob wasn't sure how his brother would feel about seeing him again, so Jacob sent his servants ahead to tell Esau he was coming. The men returned with the news that Esau was on his way with 400 men. Jacob feared for his family, so he divided them into two groups. That way if Esau's men attacked one group, the other group could escape.

Then Jacob began selecting gifts for Esau. What gifts would you give someone who might still be angry with you after many years? Jacob chose 200 female goats, 20 male goats, 200 ewes, 20 rams, 30 female camels with their young, 40 cows, 10 bulls, 20 female donkeys, and 10 male donkeys. He sent his servants ahead with the gifts.

The next day Jacob saw Esau coming toward him. Jacob bowed to the ground seven times in front of him. Jacob didn't need to worry about Esau being angry with him. Esau was happy to see him.

Jacob had assumed that Esau was still angry with him, but Esau had changed just as Jacob had. Esau had forgiven Jacob and let go of the bitterness he felt toward his brother years earlier.

It's natural to feel angry when someone wrongs you, but God wants you to forgive. Holding a grudge doesn't help anyone. You can only find peace when you let go of the anger and make the decision to forgive the other person. Forgiving someone means you let go of the right to be angry or to get even. That's what God asks of you.

For You

Are you angry with someone for wronging you? Ask God to help you let go of the anger and decide that you will forgive the person, even if that person isn't sorry. You will have peace instead of bitterness in your heart.

Answer: b
As he approached his brother, [Jacob] bowed to the ground seven times before him. Genesis 33:3
(The Whole Story: Genesis 32:6-16; 33)

January 31

Sibling Rivalry

Q: How old was Joseph when he tattled to his father about his brothers' wrong behavior?
a. 10
b. 17
c. 20

Jacob had 12 sons who had several different mothers. Jacob loved Joseph the best because he was the oldest son of Jacob's favorite wife, Rachel. Unfortunately Rachel died giving birth to her second son, Benjamin.

The brothers were jealous of Joseph. It didn't help that Joseph tattled to their dad about the brothers' bad behavior. To make things worse, Joseph had two dreams about himself and his brothers, which he shared with them. In the first dream, he and his brothers were in the field tying up bundles of grain. Joseph's bundle stood up, and the brothers' bundles bowed down to it. In the second dream the sun, moon, and 11 stars bowed down to Joseph. This was too much for the brothers. Anger filled their hearts, and they made plans to harm Joseph.

Does it seem like Joseph's brothers had good reason to hate Joseph? After all, parents aren't supposed to have favorites. While it was normal for the brothers to be jealous, the way they handled it was wrong. Allowing jealousy to turn to hatred hurt everyone.

It's hard to watch someone else be favored or get what you want. If you aren't on guard, you'll end up having bad feelings toward the other person even if that person isn't at fault. Ask God to rid you of bad feelings and give you wisdom to know what to do.

For You

One way to defeat jealousy is to look at what you have, rather than at what someone else has that you don't. Developing a spirit of thankfulness is one of the best cures for envy. Think of 10 good things in your life and write them down. Thank God for each of them.

Answer: b

When Joseph was seventeen years old . . . Joseph reported to his father some of the bad things his brothers were doing. Jacob loved Joseph more than any of his other children because Joseph had been born to him in his old age. So one day Jacob had a special gift made for Joseph—a beautiful robe. Genesis 37:2-3
(The Whole Story: Genesis 37:1-11)

Joseph's Brothers' Plans

Q: How did Joseph's brothers get rid of him?
a. They killed him and said a wild animal did it.
b. They left him in a well.
c. They sold him to traders for 20 pieces of silver.

Have you ever wished you could get rid of a pesky younger brother or sister? It might have crossed your mind, but you'd never really do it. That wasn't the case with Joseph's older brothers.

One day Jacob sent Joseph to check on his older brothers, who were taking care of their father's flocks. When the brothers saw him coming, they plotted against him. Some of the siblings wanted to kill him and then tell their father a wild animal had killed him. Reuben, the oldest, suggested they throw him into a well and let him die there. He secretly planned to return later and rescue Joseph.

The brothers took Joseph's coat off of him and put him in the deep well. When they saw a group of travelers approaching, the brothers decided to sell Joseph to the travelers for 20 pieces of silver. The brothers killed a goat and dipped Joseph's coat in the blood. Then they took it to their father and led him to believe his favored son was dead. Jacob was very sad.

Have you noticed something about Abraham's descendants? While they all had faith in God, family members plotted against and tricked other family members. Yet God still used them and called them his chosen people. Imagine how much more he could have blessed them if they had followed him completely rather than dealing in dishonesty so many times.

For You
Abraham's family suffered because of dishonesty. Determine you will live with integrity. That means doing the right thing even if no one knows, because, of course, God always knows.

Answer: c
[Judah said to his brothers,] "Instead of hurting him, let's sell him to those Ishmaelite traders. After all, he is our brother—our own flesh and blood!" And his brothers agreed. Genesis 37:27
(The Whole Story: Genesis 37:18-36)

February 2

Trusting God in Good Times and Bad

Q: Whose lie caused Joseph to be put in prison?
a. the cupbearer's
b. Potiphar's wife's
c. Pharaoh's

Joseph's brothers sold him to traders, who took him to Egypt. In Egypt Joseph was sold to Potiphar, the captain of the guard for Pharaoh. (Pharaoh was the king of Egypt.) Joseph ended up in the palace, and God made Joseph successful in everything he did.

This success didn't go unnoticed. Potiphar put Joseph in charge of his household and everything he owned. Things went well. The household ran smoothly. The crops grew abundantly, and the animals were well cared for.

Potiphar wasn't the only one who noticed how successful Joseph was. Mrs. Potiphar was watching Joseph closely too. She liked Joseph and wanted to have a relationship with him. Joseph knew this was wrong because Mrs. Potiphar had a husband.

Joseph refused to have a wrong relationship with Mrs. Potiphar, and this made her angry. She was used to getting her own way. One day she grabbed Joseph by his cloak, but he fled, leaving the garment behind. Mrs. Potiphar showed it to her husband. She lied and said Joseph had attacked her.

Potiphar was angry when he saw the cloak and heard his wife's story. He put Joseph into the jail where the king's prisoners were held.

Joseph must have wondered why God allowed this, but he didn't complain or become bitter. He had faith in God and trusted the Lord with his future.

For You

It's easy to trust God in good times, but it's not always easy in bad times. When you face problems or are wrongly accused of something, let Joseph be your example. Handle it without complaining or becoming bitter. Watch for God to work.

Answer: b

"That Hebrew slave you've brought into our house tried to come in and fool around with me," she said. "But when I screamed, he ran outside, leaving his cloak with me!" Genesis 39:17-18
(The Whole Story: Genesis 39)

February 3

Pharaoh's Dreams

Q: What animals did Pharaoh see in his dream?
a. cows
b. pigs
c. vipers

Joseph was in prison because Mrs. Potiphar lied, but God blessed Joseph. The prison warden noticed Joseph's good character and put him in charge of the other prisoners.

One day two prisoners had dreams. God told Joseph what the dreams meant, and Joseph told the prisoners. One of the prisoners was released. He forgot how Joseph had told him what his dream meant—until Pharaoh had two dreams no one could explain. Then the man told Pharaoh about Joseph's ability to interpret dreams.

Pharaoh sent for Joseph and told him about the dreams. In the first dream, seven fat cows were grazing. Seven sickly looking cows ate them. In the second dream, seven full heads of grain were growing on a single stalk. Seven shriveled heads of grain ate the seven healthy heads of grain.

God told Joseph the dreams meant there would be seven years when crops would grow well and food would be plentiful. Then there would be seven years of famine when food would be scarce.

Pharaoh put Joseph in charge of gathering and storing food during the plentiful years so there would be enough during the famine. Again God gave Joseph success; the people in his land had food, while the people in other countries didn't. They had to travel to buy food from Joseph.

In good times and bad, God was with Joseph and gave him success in all he did.

For You

The hard times Joseph faced strengthened his faith in God, and the Lord blessed him more because of it. You can't avoid difficulties, but you can control how they affect you. Keep reading your Bible and praying so you will be strong in your faith when hard times come.

Answer: a
In his dream [Pharaoh] saw seven fat, healthy cows come up out of the river and begin grazing in the marsh grass. Then he saw seven more cows come up behind them from the Nile, but these were scrawny and thin. These cows stood beside the fat cows on the riverbank. Then the scrawny, thin cows ate the seven healthy, fat cows! Genesis 41:2-4
(The Whole Story: Genesis 40–41)

February 4

Joseph's Brothers Need Food

Q: When Joseph's brothers came to buy food, he accused them of being
a. spies.
b. murderers.
c. betrayers.

God used Pharaoh's dreams to show a famine was coming, so Joseph planned ahead and stored food. Soon people in other countries were running out of food and traveling to Egypt to buy it.

One day Jacob sent his 10 oldest sons to buy food. He kept Benjamin at home because he'd never gotten over losing Joseph. He didn't want to lose his youngest son. Benjamin was the only other child Rachel had given birth to.

When the brothers arrived in Egypt, Joseph recognized them, but they didn't know who he was. Joseph said, "You are spies! You have come to see how vulnerable our land has become."

The brothers protested, "We, your servants, are all brothers, sons of a man living in the land of Canaan. Our youngest brother is back there with our father right now, and one of our brothers is no longer with us."

Joseph said he'd keep one brother in prison. The rest had to go home and return with the youngest brother to prove their story was true. Joseph gave them grain and had their money put in the bags of grain too. He gave them supplies for their journey and sent them on their way, except for Simeon, who stayed behind to prove they'd return.

Jacob refused to let the brothers take Benjamin to Egypt. But the food ran out again, and they made the long trip back with Benjamin.

Joseph's brothers mistreated him, but God made sure Joseph was in the right place to help his family survive the famine. Sometimes what is difficult at the time becomes a good thing later.

For You

When someone treats you unfairly or unkindly, it's easy to want to get even. But be like Joseph and determine to do what is right. Let God take care of the rest.

Answer: a
[Joseph] remembered the dreams he'd had about [his brothers] many years before. He said to them, "You are spies! You have come to see how vulnerable our land has become." Genesis 42:9
(The Whole Story: Genesis 42:1–43:15)

The Final Test

Q: What did Joseph have placed in his youngest brother's sack?
a. extra grain
b. pieces of gold
c. Joseph's silver cup

When Joseph's brothers returned to Egypt for more food during the famine (see yesterday's devotion), Joseph had a test for them. He told his palace manager to put his silver cup, and the money paid for Benjamin's grain, in the top of Benjamin's sack. The brothers left early the next day not knowing it was there.

After they'd traveled awhile, Joseph sent his manager after them. The manager stopped them and demanded to know who had Joseph's silver cup and the money. That person would remain in Egypt as a slave.

When the cup and money were found in Benjamin's sack, all the brothers returned to Joseph. Judah pleaded to become a slave in Benjamin's place. He knew his father couldn't bear it if Benjamin didn't return home. Judah's offer showed Joseph that his brothers had changed. They were no longer the cruel siblings they'd once been. Joseph told his brothers who he was.

The brothers went home and packed up their possessions. Then they moved with their families and their father to Egypt to be with Joseph and have food.

When the brothers sold Joseph years earlier, they never dreamed one day he'd save them from famine. Joseph was able to repay kindness for their evil. He could only do that because of his faith in God.

For You

Joseph's silver cup was important because it was a sign of his authority. Sometimes these cups were used to tell the future. Joseph didn't need his cup for that reason. God was in charge of his future. The Lord sees the whole plan for our lives, but he reveals it to us one piece at a time. Trust God to guide you day by day as Joseph did.

Answer: c
When his brothers were ready to leave, Joseph gave these instructions to his palace manager: "Fill each of their sacks with as much grain as they can carry, and put each man's money back into his sack. Then put my personal silver cup at the top of the youngest brother's sack, along with the money for his grain."
So the manager did as Joseph instructed him. Genesis 44:1-2
(The Whole Story: Genesis 44–45)

February 6

God Intended It for Good

Q: Joseph's brothers were afraid that after their father's death Joseph would do what?
a. get revenge on them for selling him
b. move back to their homeland
c. raise the price of grain

Joseph's family moved to Egypt, where he continued working for Pharaoh during the great famine. Jacob was happy to find out Joseph wasn't dead after all, and Jacob was able to spend his last years with Joseph before dying.

Joseph's brothers were getting nervous, though. Everything seemed to be going well, but they were afraid that after their father died, Joseph would get revenge on them for selling him. They couldn't believe he'd really forgiven them and wasn't planning to get even.

Many events in his life could have caused Joseph to be bitter and unforgiving. His brothers sold him into slavery, Mrs. Potiphar lied about him, he spent time in prison, and there was a famine taking place. Joseph trusted God and continued to do right in spite of the things that happened to him and around him. That allowed God to work in amazing ways. Joseph became an important man in Egypt and made plans that saved not only his own family but countless others who would have died during the famine.

People may do evil to others, but God can overrule the wickedness and use bad circumstances for his own good.

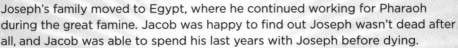

For You

Romans 8:28 says, "We know that God causes everything to work together for the good of those who love God and are called according to his purpose for them." God uses hard times for his own good. How is God using hard times in your life right now?

Answer: a
After burying Jacob, Joseph returned to Egypt with his brothers and all who had accompanied him to his father's burial. But now that their father was dead, Joseph's brothers became fearful. "Now Joseph will show his anger and pay us back for all the wrong we did to him," they said. Genesis 50:14-15
(The Whole Story: Genesis 50:14-26)

February 7

Two Brave Women

Q: What order did Pharaoh give Shiphrah and Puah?
a. kill all the Israelite baby boys
b. collect taxes from all the Israelites
c. gather straw to make bricks

Four hundred years had passed since Joseph moved his father, Jacob, and the rest of his family to Egypt. His brothers and their families had stayed there, and the family grew in number as new generations were born. Now there were millions of Jacob's descendants living in Egypt.

Of course by now Joseph and the pharaoh who valued his help (see Genesis 41) were long gone. The pharaoh who now ruled was alarmed by how many Israelites (Hebrews) were living in Egypt. He was afraid they'd take over the land, so he made them all slaves. He thought that would keep them from growing in number, but it didn't.

Pharaoh called for Shiphrah and Puah. They were women who helped deliver babies. He ordered them to kill all the Hebrew baby boys as they were born. The women couldn't do that. They knew it was wrong.

Pharaoh found out they weren't obeying his order. They told him, "The Hebrew women are not like the Egyptian women. They are more vigorous and have their babies so quickly that we cannot get there in time."

Shiphrah and Puah lied to Pharaoh. There might have been a better way to handle the situation, but God blessed them for sparing the babies in spite of the lie. The women knew Pharaoh could have them killed for disobeying his order, but they did it anyway. They wanted to do the right thing and save the Hebrew babies.

Doing the right thing takes courage. Shiphrah and Puah acted bravely, and it saved the lives of many babies.

► For You
Doing right takes more courage than going along with the crowd. Do you have the bravery it takes to do the right thing even when others aren't?

Answer: a
Pharaoh, the king of Egypt, gave this order to the Hebrew midwives, Shiphrah and Puah: "When you help the Hebrew women as they give birth, watch as they deliver. If the baby is a boy, kill him; if it is a girl, let her live." But because the midwives feared God, they refused to obey the king's orders. Exodus 1:15-17
(The Whole Story: Exodus 1)

February 8

Baby Afloat

Q: Into what river did Moses' mother place him in his floating basket?
a. Euphrates
b. Colorado
c. Nile

When you were little, you may have had a float ring you sat in when you were at a pool. You could safely float around, watching the older kids play. Moses' mother, Jochebed, set him afloat, but it wasn't the same situation at all.

Moses was born during the time Pharaoh was killing the Hebrew baby boys. Jochebed hid Moses in her house for three months, but it became too difficult to hide him any longer. Someone was sure to hear him crying.

Jochebed made a tiny floating boat from reeds that grew in the swampy area along the Nile River. She coated it with tar and pitch to make it waterproof. Then she set Moses afloat. His big sister, Miriam, watched over Moses from a distance.

When Pharaoh's daughter went to the Nile to bathe, she saw the basket and sent her servant to get it. Miriam offered to find someone to nurse the baby until he was old enough to be weaned. Then the child would be taken to live with Pharaoh's daughter at the palace.

God had a plan. Just as God used the difficult times in Joseph's life to put him in the right place at the right time (as we read about in the February 1–6 devotions), God used Pharaoh's desire to kill the Hebrew infants to put Moses in Pharaoh's own palace. One day, Moses would return to the palace to help free his own people from slavery.

Try as they might, people cannot ruin God's plans. God puts people in the right place at the right time to carry out his work.

For You

God may not show you exactly what he has planned, but he will use you to do his work if you are willing. You may be in exactly the right place to do something for God just as Joseph and Moses were.

Answer: c
When she could no longer hide him, she got a basket made of papyrus reeds and waterproofed it with tar and pitch. She put the baby in the basket and laid it among the reeds along the bank of the Nile River. Exodus 2:3
(The Whole Story: Exodus 2:1-10)

February 9

God Chooses Moses

Q: After Moses killed a man for beating an Israelite (Hebrew), where did he hide the body?
a. in a lake
b. in the sand
c. in a cave

Sometimes you might think you're too young, too ugly, too shy, too loud, or too inexperienced to do much for God. But the people God used to do his work in the Bible—including Moses—were far from perfect.

One day Moses was watching the Hebrew slaves working hard and being treated poorly. When Moses saw an Egyptian beating a slave, he looked to see if anyone was watching. Then he killed the Egyptian and buried him in the sand. He thought no one had seen.

Someone had seen, though, and word got back to Pharaoh. Moses fled from Egypt to Midian. While he was sitting by a well, seven daughters of a Midianite priest, Jethro (also known as Reuel), came to get water. Some shepherds came by and made them leave, but Moses came to their rescue and watered their flocks for them.

When Jethro heard about Moses' kindness, he sent his daughters to invite Moses to eat with them. Moses stayed with the family and eventually married Zipporah, one of the seven daughters.

Time passed, and the pharaoh who wanted to kill Moses died, but the Hebrews were still slaves in Egypt. God chose Moses to be their deliverer. There were stronger and wiser men God could have chosen, but he picked Moses. God chooses unlikely people so everyone can see it is God doing the work, not people.

For You

Don't worry that you don't have enough talent to serve God. He is looking for your willingness, not your abilities. God created you, so he knows what you are capable of. If he chooses you for a job, it's because you are the perfect person for it.

Answer: b
Many years later, when Moses had grown up, he went out to visit his own people, the Hebrews, and he saw how hard they were forced to work. During his visit, he saw an Egyptian beating one of his fellow Hebrews. After looking in all directions to make sure no one was watching, Moses killed the Egyptian and hid the body in the sand. Exodus 2:11-12
(The Whole Story: Exodus 2:11-25)

February 10

God Gets Moses' Attention

Q: What did Moses see burning?
a. grass
b. a bush
c. a house

Moses grew up as an Egyptian prince. His every need was met, and everything was done for him. He was well known throughout the land. Yet that didn't prepare him for the job God had in mind for him.

After killing an Egyptian, Moses had fled to Midian (see yesterday's devotion). Now Moses was a lowly shepherd living in the desert. This was his training ground for God's work of leading the slaves out of Egypt and into the wilderness.

One day Moses was taking care of the flock when he saw a bush that was on fire but never burned up. Moses approached it for a closer look. God called to Moses and told him to remove his sandals because he was standing on holy ground. God told Moses he'd chosen him to deliver the Israelites from slavery. Moses was to tell Pharaoh to let the Israelites go free.

Moses was reluctant. He didn't think Pharaoh would listen to him. But God already had that under control. He had special signs for Moses to show that the Lord was with him. God told Moses to throw his shepherd's staff to the ground. When he did, it became a snake! That got Moses' attention—he ran from the snake. God told Moses to pick up the snake by the tail, and it became his staff again.

God used a burning bush to get Moses' attention. This was something unusual he knew Moses would investigate. Then he used Moses' shepherd's staff as a sign of God's power. Both the bush and the shepherd's staff were ordinary things, but God used them to do something extraordinary.

God often works through the ordinary things in our lives, but with his touch, those things become anything but ordinary.

For You

God can take the everyday things in your life and use them to accomplish amazing things. For Moses it was a bush and a shepherd's staff. What might God use in your life?

Answer: b
"This is amazing," Moses said to himself. "Why isn't that bush burning up? I must go see it." Exodus 3:3
(The Whole Story: Exodus 3:1–4:9)

February 11

Life Gets Harder for the Israelites

Q: When the Israelites were slaves in Egypt, what were they forced to make?
a. bricks
b. houses
c. cotton cloth

Kyle scooped another shovelful of snow from the driveway. He wanted to go on an amusement park trip with his church during spring break, but he didn't have enough money. His parents said they'd pay him to shovel each time it snowed, and they'd pay for half the trip if he earned half. To take his mind off how cold he was, Kyle thought about how much fun the trip would be.

The Hebrews in Egypt had to work hard day after day, but there was no end in sight for them. They didn't have anything special to look forward to. God was planning a big trip for them—a journey to freedom—but they didn't know that. In fact, things got worse before they got better.

After Moses and his brother, Aaron, went to talk to Pharaoh about freeing the Israelites, Pharaoh told the slave drivers to stop providing the straw the Hebrews needed to make the bricks they were forced to make. He said they had to find their own straw but still make the same number of bricks each day!

The Israelites were angry with Moses because life got harder after he talked to Pharaoh. Moses didn't understand why God had allowed that to happen. But God wasn't finished yet. He knew the whole plan, while the Israelites could only see the daily hardship they faced. Even though it seemed God was ignoring their problems, he'd already set his plans in motion.

For You

Sometimes it's hard to see beyond everyday problems—the difficult math homework, the bully who targets you, and the arguing between you and your siblings. But these things are temporary and only a small part of your life. Stay faithful and remind yourself: God is at work even when you can't see it.

Answer: a
[Pharaoh said,] "Do not supply any more straw for making bricks. Make the people get it themselves! But still require them to make the same number of bricks as before. Don't reduce the quota. Exodus 5:7-8
(The Whole Story: Exodus 5)

February 12

God Gets Pharaoh's Attention

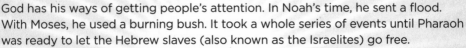

Q: God sent several plagues to get Pharaoh to let the slaves go free. Which plague was first?
a. hail
b. water in the river turning to blood
c. locusts covering Egypt

God has his ways of getting people's attention. In Noah's time, he sent a flood. With Moses, he used a burning bush. It took a whole series of events until Pharaoh was ready to let the Hebrew slaves (also known as the Israelites) go free.

After the first time Moses talked to Pharaoh, things got worse for the slaves. Moses asked God why this had happened. God answered, "Now you will see what I will do to Pharaoh. When he feels the force of my strong hand, he will let the people go. In fact, he will force them to leave his land!" (Exodus 6:1).

God had a whole series of plagues planned for Egypt. You can read about them in Exodus 7:14–12:30, but here's a quick summary.

First, the Nile River turned to blood. After that plague, frogs covered the whole land. Ground dust turned to gnats. The land was filled with flies. All the horses, donkeys, camels, cattle, sheep, and goats died. The Egyptians and their animals broke out with horrible sores. Hail killed every unprotected person and animal and ruined most of the crops. Locusts arrived and ate everything not destroyed in the hailstorm. Total darkness covered the land.

Even after all these disasters took place, Pharaoh would still not allow the slaves to go free. God had one more thing planned, and it was the worst of all. You'll read about it in the next devotion.

God is a God of second, third, fourth, and even tenth chances. But Pharaoh's heart was hardened against God and the Israelites. In the end, God got Pharaoh's attention.

For You
Keep your heart open to God. If he is asking you to do something, do it.

Answer: b
As Pharaoh and all of his officials watched, Aaron raised his staff and struck the water of the Nile. Suddenly, the whole river turned to blood! Exodus 7:20
(The Whole Story: Exodus 7:14–10:29)

February 13

Saving the Firstborns

Q: What were the Israelites to do to save their firstborn males?
a. put blood on the tops and sides of the doorframes
b. keep all doors and windows closed all night
c. wrap the firstborn children in linen

God used a series of plagues to get Pharaoh's attention. He sent frogs, flies, gnats, darkness, and more to convince Pharaoh to let the slaves go free (see Exodus 7:14–10:29). God could have just forced Pharaoh to let the Israelites go free, but that's not how he works.

God told Moses that he, the Lord, was going to kill every firstborn male child and animal in the land. God gave instructions about what the Israelites had to do in order for their firstborns to be spared. They were to kill a one-year-old male goat or lamb and smear the blood on the sides and tops of the doorframes of their houses. They were also given instructions on how to prepare the animal for their meal.

The angel of death would pass by any home with blood on the doorframe, and that family would be spared. But without the blood, the firstborn male would die. There was great sorrow in Egypt that night as families discovered their firstborn sons had died.

Pharaoh sent for Moses and Aaron during the night. "Get out!" he ordered. "Leave my people—and take the rest of the Israelites with you!"

No family without the blood of the lamb or goat on their doorframe was spared. This was a symbol of what Jesus would do later. His blood was shed on the cross so we might be spared the penalty of sin.

For You

Jesus has already paid the penalty for sin so you don't have to. If you haven't yet accepted Jesus as your Savior, now is a good time to talk to someone about it. If Jesus is already your Savior, share the Good News with someone today.

Answer: a
The LORD will pass through the land to strike down the Egyptians. But when he sees the blood on the top and sides of the doorframe, the LORD will pass over your home. He will not permit his death angel to enter your house and strike you down. Exodus 12:23
(The Whole Story: Exodus 11:4-5; 12:1-42)

February 14

God's Guidance

Q: How did God lead the Israelites through the wilderness?
a. with his voice
b. with fire and ice
c. with a cloud and fire

Kaitlyn dropped her backpack on the car floor and arranged her pillow so she could sleep on the long trip to Grandma's. Her dad backed the car out of the garage. Instead of turning onto the road they always took, he drove past it.

"Where are you going?" Kaitlyn asked. "This isn't the road we take."

"This will get us to the highway. It's a little longer, but there's a lot less traffic."

Kaitlyn adjusted her pillow and prepared to sleep. She'd leave the driving to her dad.

It was time for God's people to leave Egypt. They'd been there 430 years—ever since Joseph had moved his family there to have food during the famine. The shortest route from Egypt to the Promised Land led through Philistine country. Instead of going that way, God led the Israelites around the Philistines. He knew if the Israelites had to battle the Philistines, they might give up and return to Egypt.

During the day, God led the people with a cloud. At night he led them with a pillar of fire to give them light. That way they could travel either by day or night, and they'd always know God was with them.

Sometimes it might seem God is leading you the long way to reach a goal. Don't complain or give up. Just follow. He has a reason for what he does. Just as he led the Israelites around the Philistines to avoid a war, he may be leading you another way because he knows what each path holds, and he's choosing what's best for you.

For You
Have you been trying to accomplish something without making progress? God might be leading you a different way. Ask God to show you what to do. You will feel peace in your heart when you make the right choice.

Answer: c
The LORD went ahead of [the Israelites]. He guided them during the day with a pillar of cloud, and he provided light at night with a pillar of fire. This allowed them to travel by day or by night. Exodus 13:21
(The Whole Story: Exodus 13:17-22)

February 15

Another Miracle

Q: The Israelites crossed what sea on dry land?
a. China Sea
b. Red Sea
c. Mediterranean Sea

The Israelites had their freedom, but Pharaoh was regretting the decision to let them go, so he went after them. As the Israelites journeyed toward the Promised Land, 600 war chariots swooped down on them. Other chariots followed. The Israelites were trapped between the mountains and the sea.

Even though the Israelites had seen the way God delivered them from Pharaoh once already, they were terrified. "Why did you bring us out here to die in the wilderness? It's better to be a slave in Egypt than a corpse in the wilderness!" they said.

Moses told them, "Don't be afraid. Just stand still and watch the LORD rescue you today. The Egyptians you see today will never be seen again. The LORD himself will fight for you. Just stay calm."

Moses was right. God had a plan. The Lord told Moses to hold his shepherd's staff over the Red Sea. The sea divided, and God sent a strong wind to dry a path through the sea so the Israelites could walk right across! They had never seen anything like it. When the Egyptians tried to follow, Moses held his staff out again, and God let the water crash down on the enemy. Not one Egyptian survived.

God had once again delivered his people in a miraculous way—despite their lack of faith and their complaining. He continued to be with them during their journey, although they quickly forgot his miraculous works and grumbled often.

For You

At the first sign of trouble, the Israelites started to complain instead of remembering how God had delivered them from Pharaoh once already. When things go wrong in your life, remind yourself of all the things God has done for you in the past, and ask him to help you through the troublesome times.

Answer: b
The people of Israel walked through the middle of the sea on dry ground, with walls of water on each side! . . . Pharaoh's chariots and army he has hurled into the sea. The finest of Pharaoh's officers are drowned in the Red Sea.
Exodus 14:22; 15:4
(The Whole Story: Exodus 13:17–14:31)

February 16

Singing Praises to God

Q: What instrument did Miriam play to praise the Lord?
a. drum
b. cymbal
c. tambourine

In the 1980s there was a popular Christian song that said, "The horse and rider thrown into the sea." Someone had set these words to a new tune, but it wasn't a new song. Moses, Miriam, and the Israelites first sang similar words after God sent the Red Sea crashing down on the Egyptians who were pursuing them.

Miriam, Moses' sister, played the tambourine, and all the women followed her with tambourines, dancing and singing, "Sing to the LORD, for he has triumphed gloriously; he has hurled both horse and rider into the sea."

Moses and Miriam knew the parting of the Red Sea was a miracle God used to show he was looking out for the Israelites. They wanted to praise him, and singing was an important part of praise. It was also a way to remember God's works and pass them down the generations. Some think this song of Moses' is the oldest written song. People sang before this, but no one may have written down any of the words. With all the people singing to God along with Miriam and the other women playing tambourines and dancing, this was an event that would be long remembered.

Churches today often begin their services by singing praises to God. This is a good way to focus on what he's done for us and to prepare our hearts for the pastor's message.

For You

Singing praises to God after a time of trouble—or even during trials—is a good way to keep your focus on God and off of yourself. You can also make singing or listening to worship music part of your daily time with God. Why not try it this week?

Answer: c
Miriam the prophet, Aaron's sister, took a tambourine and led all the women as they played their tambourines and danced. Exodus 15:20
(The Whole Story: Exodus 15:1-21)

February 17

Don't Complain

Q: What did God have Moses do to make the water drinkable?
a. add sugar
b. boil it
c. throw a piece of wood into it

The Israelites were complainers. You'd think they'd lived a grand life in Egypt the way they complained about having to leave it. When the 600 chariots were chasing them, they grumbled and complained to Moses (see Exodus 14:10-12). God miraculously delivered them, but now, only a short while later, they were complaining again.

The Israelites had traveled three days in the desert without finding water. Finally they reached Marah, where there was water, but they were dismayed to find it was too bitter to drink. Instead of turning to God, they grumbled at Moses because there wasn't drinkable water.

Moses asked God what to do, and the Lord showed him a piece of wood. When Moses threw it into the water, the water became sweet. God had met the Israelites' needs again.

As you read about the Israelites, one thing you'll notice is any time something went wrong, they forgot about God's previous miracles and provisions for them. Instead of asking him for help, they would complain. How much better it would have been if they'd remembered to turn to God first and ask him for help. Are you like the Israelites, or do you look to God to meet your needs?

For You

When things go wrong in your life, look to God. Feeling sorry for yourself will make you a complainer like the Israelites. Instead, be like Moses and turn to God for the answers.

Answer: c
Moses cried out to the LORD for help, and the LORD showed him a piece of wood. Moses threw it into the water, and this made the water good to drink.
Exodus 15:25
(The Whole Story: Exodus 15:22-27)

February 18

God Meets the Israelites' Needs

Q: What did God provide for the Israelites to eat on their journey?
a. fish and loaves of bread
b. unleavened bread and honey
c. quail and manna

On their way to the Promised Land, the Israelites camped at Elim, where there were springs of water and palm trees. Then the Israelites set out again, and as their tendency had been since leaving Egypt, they began complaining. Once again they turned on Moses and cried out, "If only the LORD had killed us back in Egypt. There we sat around pots filled with meat and ate all the bread we wanted. But now you have brought us into this wilderness to starve us all to death."

The people had been delivered from slavery and were on the way to a special land God had promised them. They didn't look ahead to that, though. And they didn't look back at the miracles God had done to get them this far. They only saw the immediate problem.

The desert they were in was not a fruitful place. The sand and stone environment was barren of natural resources, but God hadn't failed them. In the evening, God provided meat from quail. In the morning, God rained down bread from heaven for them. They were to gather it daily and take only what they needed for that day. The sixth day was the only day the people were supposed to take extra so they wouldn't have to gather food on the Sabbath.

God met the Israelites' needs each day. Their job was to obey and trust him.

For You

God met the Israelites' daily needs. He didn't give them food ahead of time because he wanted them to learn to trust him. You can trust God to meet your daily needs too. He may not give you all you want, but he will give you what is best for you.

Answer: c

That evening vast numbers of quail flew in and covered the camp. . . . The Israelites called the food manna. It was white like coriander seed, and it tasted like honey wafers. Exodus 16:13, 31
(The Whole Story: Exodus 16)

February 19

Life-Giving Water

Q: Where did Moses get water for the Israelites to drink?
a. from a pond
b. from a rock
c. from the sky

As you read about in the devotionals on February 17 and 18, the Israelites were struggling in their travels to the Promised Land. In Marah the water was too bitter to drink, so God showed Moses a piece of wood to throw into the water. When Moses did, the water turned sweet. Then the Israelites didn't have food and God provided that for them. Now the Israelites were camped at Rephidim, and there was no water at all.

If God could part the Red Sea—hold the waters back and dry a path for the Israelites—certainly he could provide drinking water for them. He was just waiting for them to ask. But once again, they turned on Moses and asked why he'd brought them out of Egypt just to die of thirst.

God led Moses to a rock and told him to strike it with his staff. If he did this, water would come out. It happened just as God said, and the people had enough to drink. God provided water to meet the Israelites' physical needs, but they would soon be thirsty again. People need water to live.

In the New Testament, Jesus talked with a woman by a well. He told her, "Anyone who drinks this water will soon become thirsty again. But those who drink the water I give will never be thirsty again. It becomes a fresh, bubbling spring within them, giving them eternal life" (John 4:13-14).

Just as a person's body gets hungry and thirsty, so does his or her soul. Moses gave the people water for their physical bodies, but only Jesus can give spiritual water that satisfies our souls.

For You

Just as you eat so you aren't hungry, you should feed your soul so you won't be spiritually empty. Fill yourself with God's Word each day.

Answer: b
[The Lord said to Moses,] "I will stand before you on the rock at Mount Sinai. Strike the rock, and water will come gushing out. Then the people will be able to drink." So Moses struck the rock as he was told, and water gushed out as the elders looked on. Exodus 17:6
(The Whole Story: Exodus 17:1-7)

The Amalekites Defeated

Q: The Israelites were winning against the Amalekites as long as
a. Moses held his staff up.
b. the sun was high in the sky.
c. a sacrifice was burning on an altar.

While the Israelites were camped at Rephidim, where God gave them water from a rock, the Amalekite warriors attacked. Moses called for Joshua and put him in charge of the battle. Moses said he would stand at the top of the hill and hold up his staff. This was the same staff he'd used to part the Red Sea and to bring forth water from the rock. So while Joshua and some men went to fight, Moses climbed to the top of the hill, along with his brother, Aaron, and their friend Hur.

As long as Moses held his staff up, the Israelites were winning. When he lowered it, the Amalekites began to win. If you've ever tried to hold your arms up over your head for very long, then you know the problem with that. Moses' arms became tired. Aaron and Hur found a rock for Moses to sit on. Then they held his arms up for him. The fighting went on until sunset, when the Israelites finally defeated the Amalekites.

It might seem like Moses' staff had special powers, but the power was really God's. The staff was a reminder that God was with them, and that the Lord has the power over any enemy. Moses couldn't continue to hold the staff by himself, but with the help of two friends he was able to hold it up until the Israelites were victorious.

For You

Even though God called Moses to be a leader, Moses still needed help. It's important to have Christian friends to pray for you, offer you encouragement, and help you as you try to live the way Jesus wants you to live each day. You can do the same for them. Can you think of two friends who would support you like Aaron and Hur did for Moses?

Answer: a
As long as Moses held up the staff in his hand, the Israelites had the advantage. But whenever he dropped his hand, the Amalekites gained the advantage.
Exodus 17:11
(The Whole Story: Exodus 17:8-16)

February 21

Jethro's Suggestion

Q: What did Moses' father-in-law suggest Moses do?
a. stone the complaining Israelites
b. travel more hours during the day
c. appoint people under him as leaders to take some of the responsibility off of himself

Moses had a lot of responsibility in leading the millions of Israelites who had left Egypt under his care. People would come to him for advice and to settle their disputes. Moses would try to solve the people's problems and teach them about God and God's laws at the same time.

Jethro, Moses' father-in-law, came to visit him. He saw Moses was under a lot of stress trying to solve everyone's problems from morning to night. He gave Moses some advice. Jethro told Moses to choose honest and capable men to be in charge of groups of people. They could solve the minor problems for the people they were in charge of and only bring the most serious problems to Moses.

This plan worked well, and Moses was able to concentrate on being the right kind of leader for the people without feeling so stressed.

It's easy for those in charge to try to do everything themselves, but Jethro's advice was good. Things go better if you share the work with other capable people. This worked for Moses, and it still works today.

For You

It's easy to try to do too much even if you're not in a leadership position like Moses was. If you feel stressed or under pressure, take a look at all you're trying to accomplish. See if there are changes you need to make. You, like Moses, might need some help.

Answer: c
Select from all the people some capable, honest men who fear God and hate bribes. Appoint them as leaders over groups of one thousand, one hundred, fifty, and ten. They should always be available to solve the people's common disputes, but have them bring the major cases to you. Let the leaders decide the smaller matters themselves. They will help you carry the load, making the task easier for you. Exodus 18:21-22
(The Whole Story: Exodus 18)

February 22

God's Ten Rules

Q: Where was Moses when he received the Ten Commandments?
a. Mount Sinai
b. Mount Moriah
c. Mount Everest

God was making a new nation of his chosen people, and he had some laws that would help the Israelites live the way they should. As the Israelites followed these rules, they would become more holy. There were many laws given, but God gave Moses tablets with 10 special ones we call the "Ten Commandments" written on them.

The first law God gave them was "You must not have any other god but me." The Israelites had just come from Egypt, a land with many gods. The Egyptians worshiped several false gods in hopes of being blessed or prosperous in many areas of life.

The first four commandments of God's ten special rules talk about a person's relationship with God. The next six talk about a person's relationship with other people.

Here is what they say to us today:

1. Only worship God.
2. Don't let anyone or anything take God's place.
3. Do not use God's name as a swear word.
4. One day of the week should be set apart to worship God.
5. Respect your parents.
6. Do not kill another person.
7. Be faithful to your spouse when you marry.
8. Do not take something that belongs to someone else.
9. Do not lie about anyone or anything.
10. Do not want for yourself what others have.

For You

Although these rules were given to Moses on Mount Sinai for the Israelites, they are still good rules for today. How are you doing with obeying them? Which rules do you need to work on?

Answer: a
The LORD came down on the top of Mount Sinai and called Moses to the top of the mountain. So Moses climbed the mountain. Exodus 19:20
(The Whole Story: Exodus 19:20–20:21)

February 23

Aaron Gives In

Q: After Moses had been up on the mountain for a long time, what did the people talk Aaron into doing?
a. moving on without Moses
b. making a golden calf
c. throwing a surprise party for Moses

Has anyone talked you into doing something you didn't want to do? Jenna's friends decided they didn't like another sixth grade girl, and they said mean things to her. They told Jenna if she wanted to be their friend, she had to say something unkind too. Jenna did it, but she felt sick inside later thinking about the look on the girl's face.

Moses' brother, Aaron, gave in to what other people wanted him to do. Moses had been up on Mount Sinai for a long time. The people got tired of waiting for him, so they asked Aaron to make them a new god to serve. Aaron, who had witnessed many miracles of God, should have been the one to say no and remind the people of all God had done for them. But he melted down gold the people had brought to him and shaped it as a calf.

God sent Moses back down the mountain to deal with the wayward Israelites. Moses was angry. He destroyed the idol, and God sent a plague on the people for what they'd done.

The people had seen God's miracles, but they quickly turned to an idol. Aaron went along with them even though he should have acted as their spiritual leader. If Aaron had been willing to say no to the plan, the story might have had a different ending.

For You

Decide you will do what's right even when friends try to talk you into doing something wrong. If your friends do that very often, it might be time to look for some new friends.

Answer: b
All the people took the gold rings from their ears and brought them to Aaron. Then Aaron took the gold, melted it down, and molded it into the shape of a calf. When the people saw it, they exclaimed, "O Israel, these are the gods who brought you out of the land of Egypt!" Exodus 32:3-4
(The Whole Story: Exodus 32)

February 24

A Place to Worship

Q: What was the name of the place where the Israelites went to worship?
a. the church
b. the Tabernacle
c. the tent

During the last few days, we've learned that the book of Exodus is about the Israelites' escape from slavery in Egypt and their journey to the Promised Land. On their journey, they built a place they could go to worship God. This place was called the Tabernacle. It was very important to the Israelites.

There are different kinds of church buildings today. Some churches are made of wood, and others are made of brick. Some have stained-glass windows; others have clear windows. Some churches have a cross on top; others have a bell. What a church looks like isn't as important as what the church is used for—worshiping God.

The Tabernacle that Moses and the people worshiped in was a mobile tent with portable furniture. God gave instructions for how it should be made, and it traveled with the people on their journey to the Promised Land.

The Tabernacle was a symbol that God was with his people. A cloud settled over the Tabernacle, and the glory of the Lord filled the place. At night a fired burned in the cloud. When the cloud lifted, the people traveled, but if the cloud covered the Tabernacle, they stayed. This was the way God led them throughout their whole journey.

For You

The Tabernacle was important to the Israelites because it showed God's presence was with them. You have the Holy Spirit as a sign God is with you. The Holy Spirit guides you through your conscience. He uses that to tell you when you've done wrong and to give you peace when you are living right.

Answer: b
[The Lord said to Moses,] "You must build this Tabernacle and its furnishings exactly according to the pattern I will show you." Exodus 25:9
(The Whole Story: Exodus 25–27; 40)

February 25

The Priests

Q: Who served as priests for the Israelites?
a. Moses and Aaron
b. the oldest men from each tribe
c. Aaron and his sons

The Tabernacle was built according to certain regulations. This was to ensure it was a good place for God to meet with his people. God gave them rules we wouldn't think about today. One of the rules was that the people were to bring pure oil for the lamps, and the lamps should be burning in the Lord's presence at all times (see Exodus 27:20-21).

There needed to be special people in charge of the sacrifices made in the Tabernacle. God told Moses to set apart his brother, Aaron, and Aaron's sons, Nadab, Abihu, Eleazar, and Ithamar as priests.

The priests had rules about how they could act and what they should wear. The special chestpiece, ephod, robe, tunic, turban, and sash they wore identified them as priests.

There were two sacred rooms in the Tabernacle. One was the Holy Place, and the other one was called the Most Holy Place. The Holy Place was where the priests would talk with God and tend to the Tabernacle. Only the high priest could go into the Most Holy Place, and he could only go in once a year on the Day of Atonement (see Leviticus 16). That's when he would offer a sacrifice for the sins of the nation.

A curtain separated the Most Holy Place from the Holy Place (see Exodus 26:33). In Jesus' time, the Tabernacle had been replaced with the Temple, but sacrifices were still offered. When Jesus died on the cross, the curtain in the Temple tore from top to bottom (see Mark 15:38). That was a sign that people no longer needed the priests to offer sacrifices for sins. Jesus had just paid the full price for sin.

For You

You don't have to have a priest offer sin sacrifices for you or talk to God on your behalf. Jesus is your priest so you can ask forgiveness for your own sins or pray anytime you want.

Answer: c
[The Lord said to Moses,] "Call for your brother, Aaron, and his sons, Nadab, Abihu, Eleazar, and Ithamar. Set them apart from the rest of the people of Israel so they may minister to me and be my priests." Exodus 28:1
(The Whole Story: Exodus 28:1-5)

February 26

Grain Offerings

Q: Grain offerings were seasoned with what as a reminder of God's eternal covenant?
a. salt
b. herbs
c. blood

Offerings were an important part of the Israelites' lives. There were burnt offerings, grain offerings, peace offerings, sin offerings, and guilt offerings. These were for the forgiveness of sins, honoring God, and showing thankfulness. There were very strict rules regarding how the offerings were to be prepared and presented.

The grain offering was an offering people could choose to give to honor God. The grain offering was to be seasoned with salt—in order to remind the Israelites of God's promise to always be with them.

Salt is useful in other ways too. Have you heard the saying "salt in the wound"? Salt in a wound stings, so if someone says you poured salt in his or her wound, it means you said or did something that made it hurt worse. But salt in a wound also helps defeat infection, just as God's work in us helps defeat sin.

Salt is also used as a seasoning. Mark 9:50 says, "Salt is good for seasoning. But if it loses its flavor, how do you make it salty again? You must have the qualities of salt among yourselves and live in peace with each other." God wants his people to be salt in the world. Because of the hope we have in Jesus, we can make a difference to those around us by what we say and do.

For You

In what ways can you be salt to others? Do one thing today that will make a difference to those around you.

Answer: a
Season all your grain offerings with salt to remind you of God's eternal covenant. Never forget to add salt to your grain offerings. Leviticus 2:13
(The Whole Story: Leviticus 2)

February 27

Aaron's Family

Q: During the ordination of the priests, Aaron and his sons
a. tried hard to keep all of God's rules.
b. kept all but one of God's rules.
c. kept all of God's rules.

Do you know what a reputation is? Your reputation is what other people think of you. Usually you earn a reputation by your actions. For instance, if you are always the first one to pick up trash in the cafeteria, fold the clothes from the dryer at home, or pass out papers in your class at church, you'll earn a reputation for being helpful. But if you grab the first cookies out of the oven, dominate the television to make sure you get to watch your favorites, or always make sure you're first in line, you'll earn a reputation of being selfish.

Many times someone's outward behavior reflects who he or she is inside. Sometimes people can fool others, though. A person might be the kindest and friendliest person at church but then act hateful and selfish at home. That person has two reputations, one at church and one at home. Sometimes a person can fool everyone, and then people are shocked when the truth comes out.

When God says something about a person, he is always right. That's because he can see a person's heart. That person may fool his or her family, friends, or coworkers, but not God.

The Bible says, "Aaron and his sons did everything the LORD had commanded through Moses." This verse is specifically talking about keeping the rules for the ordination of the priests, but that was a lot of rules. Things had to be done exactly as commanded, and there were a lot of things to remember.

Sadly, later two of Aaron's sons became careless about following God's rules, and God destroyed them with a blast of fire (see Leviticus 10:1-2). Aren't you glad he doesn't do that when we fail to keep his rules?

For You

What's your reputation with God? Can he count on you to keep his rules, or are other things more important? Don't become lazy like Aaron's sons. Be strong in your faith every day.

Answer: c
Aaron and his sons did everything the LORD had commanded through Moses.
Leviticus 8:36
(The Whole Story: Leviticus 8)

February 28

The Festivals

Q: What festival called for a day of complete rest?
a. Festival of Firstfruits
b. Festival of Harvest
c. Festival of Trumpets

Do you look forward to days off school for holidays? Even if you're home-schooled, you probably have time off at Thanksgiving, Christmas, or during the spring. The Israelites had special times of celebration too. They were called feasts or festivals. There were many festivals—Passover, Unleavened Bread, First-fruits, Harvest, Trumpets, Day of Atonement, and Shelters. Each one had a different purpose, different foods, and different ways of being celebrated, and they lasted either one or seven days.

The Festival of Trumpets took place on the first day of the seventh month. For the Israelites, that was September or October. The sound of the trumpet was associated with this day, which was to be a day of complete rest. Some of the festivals were times of celebration as the Israelites remembered certain past events, but the Festival of Trumpets was a time of repentance and forgiveness.

Can you think of another time the trumpet is mentioned in the Bible? In 1 Thessalonians 4:16-17 it is written that "the Lord himself will come down from heaven with a commanding shout, with the voice of the archangel, and with the trumpet call of God. First, the Christians who have died will rise from their graves. Then, together with them, we who are still alive and remain on the earth will be caught up in the clouds to meet the Lord in the air. Then we will be with the Lord forever."

Just as the trumpet marked the Festival of Trumpets, a trumpet blast will sound at the return of Christ. Are you ready?

For You
Do you have times of celebration at your house? Christmas and Easter are celebrations of Jesus' birth and resurrection. How do you make those days special?

Answer: c
The LORD said to Moses, "Give the following instructions to the people of Israel. On the first day of the appointed month in early autumn, you are to observe a day of complete rest. It will be an official day for holy assembly, a day commemorated with loud blasts of a trumpet. You must do no ordinary work on that day. Instead, you are to present special gifts to the LORD."
Leviticus 23:23-25
(The Whole Story: Leviticus 23)

March 1

Count Them

Q: The number of fighting men among the Israelites after they left Egypt was about
a. 100,000.
b. 600,000.
c. 1,000,000.

A year after the Israelites left Egypt to go to the Promised Land, God told Moses to count the men 20 years old and older who were able to fight. The Levites weren't counted because their tribe was in charge of carrying the Tabernacle and all its furnishings when they traveled. The Levites would set up the Tabernacle when the Israelites stopped traveling and rested.

The number of men who were able to fight added up to 603,550. God also had Moses list all the males from the tribe of Levi who were one month old or older. There were 22,000 of them.

God had different jobs for different people. There were men who were to fight and others who were to carry the Tabernacle and serve as priests. Even the different clans in the tribe of Levi had different Tabernacle duties. Some would pack and carry the loads. Others cared for the sacred objects in the Tabernacle (see Numbers 3–4).

God didn't need Moses to count the people. He already knew the number. The census was for Moses' sake. God wanted Moses to know how many men there were in each tribe and organize them by jobs.

God still knows how many people are available to do his work. Unfortunately not all of those who are able are willing. Can God count you among the ones who are ready to work for him?

For You

There are all kinds of jobs you can do for God. You can help a parent or teacher with a task. You can help a friend with homework. You can sit by someone who is alone. You can help a younger brother or sister with a tough task. Just look around you. Find one thing to do for God today.

Answer: b
They were registered by families—all the men of Israel who were twenty years old or older and able to go to war. The total number was 603,550.
Numbers 1:45-46
(The Whole Story: Numbers 1)

March 2

Pay It Back

Q: According to the book of Numbers, if a person took something from another person, he was to return it plus an additional ____.
a. 4 percent
b. 10 percent
c. 20 percent

There was a story on the news about a pet scam. A man advertised free pets—all people had to do was pay for the shipping. A few hours after people wired the money for the flight, the man contacted them again, pretending to be an airport official. He told them that their pet needed flight insurance or a new crate to make the second half of its flight. The people were asked to send more money. Sometimes people were so excited about the new pet, they sent the money without checking into it. One lady spent $3,000 before she found out her two Siberian huskies not only weren't on their way, but they didn't even exist.

According to the law God gave Moses, that pet scammer would need to make restitution. Restitution means giving back, repaying, or making right the wrong that was done. Under the law given to Moses, the man would be required to repay the original $3,000 and 20 percent more. That would be an extra $600.

We don't live under Old Testament law anymore, but making restitution is still a good idea. If you accidentally break your brother's earphones, buy him a new pair even if you have to clean the garage to earn the money. If you steal your sister's candy and eat it, replace it—along with giving an apology.

The first step in making something right is to confess it to God. The second step is to make restitution.

For You
God doesn't require you to add an additional 20 percent when making restitution, but it's important to make things right when you hurt or wrong someone. Is there someone you need to make things right with today?

Answer: c
The LORD said to Moses, "Give the following instructions to the people of Israel: If any of the people—men or women—betray the LORD by doing wrong to another person, they are guilty. They must confess their sin and make full restitution for what they have done, adding an additional 20 percent and returning it to the person who was wronged." Numbers 5:5-7
(The Whole Story: Numbers 5:5-8)

The Nazirites

Q: People who took the vow of a Nazirite must not
a. drink wine or other alcohol, eat or drink anything that comes from the grapevine, cut their hair, or be near a dead body.
b. drink wine or alcohol, get married, or be a Tabernacle helper.
c. cut their hair, get married, or eat or drink anything that comes from the grapevine.

Some people in the Bible chose to be totally set apart for the Lord. They agreed to follow special rules. These people were called Nazirites. (You might also see it spelled *Nazarite*.) While becoming a Nazirite was voluntary and would only last a certain period of time, there are three times in the Bible when a child was chosen from birth to be a Nazirite. Those three children were Samuel, Samson, and John the Baptist.

There were special rules for the Nazirites. One was that they could not drink wine or any fermented drink. They weren't even allowed to eat grapes or raisins. They were not allowed to cut their hair during the time they were under the Nazirite vow. And they couldn't go near a dead body because by Jewish law, it would make them ceremonially unclean. You can read the full list of rules in Numbers 6:2-8.

Even though we no longer live under Old Testament law, God calls us to be separate from the world just as the Nazirites chose to be set apart. Romans 12:1-2 says, "Dear brothers and sisters, I plead with you to give your bodies to God because of all he has done for you. Let them be a living and holy sacrifice— the kind he will find acceptable. This is truly the way to worship him. Don't copy the behavior and customs of this world, but let God transform you into a new person by changing the way you think. Then you will learn to know God's will for you, which is good and pleasing and perfect."

For You

God wants Christians to live in a different way. He calls us to be set apart by living his way, not the way our culture lives. Can you think of ways you act differently because you are Christian?

Answer: a
As long as they are bound by their Nazirite vow, they are not allowed to eat or drink anything that comes from a grapevine—not even the grape seeds or skins.
Numbers 6:4
(The Whole Story: Numbers 6:1-21)

March 4

Bless You

Q: Fill in the blanks: "May the LORD bless you and _____ you. May the LORD _____ on you and be gracious to you. May the LORD show you his _____ and give you his _____."
a. protect, smile, favor, peace
b. see, look, strength, power
c. keep, look, might, strength

Blessings were important in Old Testament times. Jewish parents said blessings over their children from birth into adulthood.

Do you remember the story of Rebekah and Jacob tricking Isaac into giving Jacob the blessing of the firstborn? Isaac said this blessing over Jacob: "From the dew of heaven and the richness of the earth, may God always give you abundant harvests of grain and bountiful new wine. May many nations become your servants, and may they bow down to you. May you be the master over your brothers, and may your mother's sons bow down to you. All who curse you will be cursed, and all who bless you will be blessed" (Genesis 27:28-29).

Years later, Jacob blessed Joseph's two sons: "The people of Israel will use your names when they give a blessing. They will say, 'May God make you as prosperous as Ephraim and Manasseh'" (Genesis 48:20). Today some Jewish families still bless their sons with the words, "May God make you as prosperous as Ephraim and Manasseh."

In the New Testament, parents brought their children to Jesus to be blessed. They knew the blessing was more than happy words. The blessing spoken over a child was real and would come to pass.

Perhaps your family could adopt Moses' words as your own special blessing, "May the LORD bless you and protect you. May the LORD smile on you and be gracious to you. May the LORD show you his favor and give you his peace."

For You

We don't think about blessings today, but they are still part of the Jewish culture and faith. In Old Testament times, the father's words had the power to come true. Do you think God still honors blessings today?

Answer: a
May the LORD bless you and protect you. May the LORD smile on you and be gracious to you. May the LORD show you his favor and give you his peace.
Numbers 6:24-26
(The Whole Story: Numbers 6:22-27)

Hearing God

Q: When Moses entered the Tabernacle, he always heard the voice of God coming from where?
a. the lamps
b. between the two cherubim above the Ark's cover
c. the altar of burnt offering

Has God ever spoken to you? He probably has, but not in the same way he spoke to Moses. When Moses went into the Tabernacle to talk with God, he heard God's voice speaking to him out loud. The voice came from between two cherubim above the Ark of the Covenant.

That was the way God spoke to Moses, but how does he speak to you now? God might speak through his Word, the Bible. He might speak to you through the pastor's message at church or through your parents' advice. God might also speak to you through the Holy Spirit and your conscience.

The important thing is to listen to God. And if you aren't sure something is from God, check it against the Bible. God will never ask you to do something he speaks against in his Word. So if you think you're hearing God say it's okay to lie or steal in a certain situation, that's not God. The Bible says those things are sin. Another way to know if you're hearing God is to ask a more mature Christian, such as a parent, pastor, or Sunday school teacher, for advice.

God spoke to Moses aloud, but today he often speaks in the stillness of our hearts through his Holy Spirit or his Word.

For You

If you don't hear God speaking to you, you might not be listening. You should feel guilt when you do something wrong. That's the Holy Spirit letting you know what you did was wrong. You may also feel a prompting to fix a problem or situation while reading your Bible. That's God speaking to you too. Slow down and spend time each day reading your Bible and giving the Lord time to speak to you.

Answer: b
Whenever Moses went into the Tabernacle to speak with the LORD, he heard the voice speaking to him from between the two cherubim above the Ark's cover—the place of atonement—that rests on the Ark of the Covenant. The LORD spoke to him from there. Numbers 7:89
(The Whole Story: Numbers 7:89)

March 6

Calling the People Together

Q: What did God tell Moses to use in order to call the people together?
a. a ram's horn
b. two silver trumpets
c. a large drum

How do you know when it's time for school to start? If you are homeschooled, your mom or dad tells you it's time to begin. If you go to a public or private school, there's a bell that signals the start of school. There may be a tardy bell to let you know you didn't make it in time too.

Moses had a bigger challenge than signaling the start of school. He had to let millions of Israelites know when it was time to gather for an informational meeting or to pack up and move out. One trumpet blast meant only the leaders of the clans of Israel were to assemble at the entrance of the Tabernacle. Two blasts meant everyone should gather.

There was a different signal that meant pack up and move. When the signal blew the first time, the tribes east of the Tabernacle would break camp and move forward. When the signal blew again, the tribes on the south would move. The trumpets were also sounded for war, at festivals, at the beginning of each month, and when offerings were given to God.

The trumpets were an important part of the Israelites' journey. It would be hard to get the attention of so many people in order to give instructions. This was the way God instructed Moses to do it.

For You

Today God gives us instructions through his Word and through the people in authority in our lives. Maybe sometimes it would be easier to understand what God wants if he'd use trumpet signals, but if you try to do the things you already know God wants you to do and tune in to him, it will be easier to understand the other things he plans for you to do.

Answer: b
The LORD said to Moses, "Make two trumpets of hammered silver for calling the community to assemble and for signaling the breaking of camp."
Numbers 10:1-2
(The Whole Story: Numbers 10:1-10)

March 7

The Right Abilities for the Job

Q: Because of his skill, Moses' brother-in-law, Hobab, did what?
a. read the Scriptures to the people
b. built wagons for traveling
c. served as a wilderness guide

God blesses different people with different skills. Moses was a gifted leader. Aaron was the spokesman. Miriam sang and led praise. Each of these three siblings brought different abilities to the journey to the Promised Land.

The Israelites were still in Sinai, but the cloud had lifted, and after about 11 months of being camped there, it was time to move on. The Tabernacle was taken down and prepared for travel. The tribes packed and lined up in order. Hobab, Moses' brother-in-law (his wife's brother), had been with Moses while they were camped. Now he prepared to go back to his own family and people.

Moses wanted Hobab to travel with the Israelites. Hobab knew the area they were in and would have been able to give them advice about where to camp and find water. Hobab knew the dangers and problems, and he could offer good counsel to Moses.

It isn't known whether Hobab journeyed with the Israelites to Canaan or returned home. Even though Moses valued Hobab's skills and wanted him to travel with them, God was ultimately guiding the people by using the cloud to show them where and when to go.

For You

God gave Hobab the gift of understanding the wilderness and surviving in the desert. That made him a valuable guide. That may not seem like a great talent, but it was very useful. The talents God gave you may not seem as important as those your friends have, but they are the exact abilities God needs you to have to accomplish the work he's planned for you. Look for opportunities to develop and use those abilities.

Answer: c
"Please don't leave us," Moses pleaded. "You know the places in the wilderness where we should camp. Come, be our guide." Numbers 10:31
(The Whole Story: Numbers 10:29-36)

March 8

The Wrong Focus

Q: Which foods from Egypt did the complaining Israelites miss?
a. fish, cucumbers, melons
b. fish, manna, unleavened bread
c. fish, grapes, turnips

Do you like eating at a buffet restaurant? You can choose from all sorts of foods—fish, chicken, potatoes, salads, vegetables, and even desserts. Will you have the cookies or the ice cream?

The way the Israelites talked about all the food they had for free in Egypt, you might have thought they were royalty. They forgot about the long, hard hours they worked. They forgot about having to gather their own straw to make bricks all day in the hot sun. They forgot they were mistreated.

Every time things got tough, the Israelites looked back and longed for their old life, even though it was a life of slavery. They didn't look ahead to the land God had promised them. They didn't celebrate being free and becoming a new nation. They didn't marvel at God's previous miracles and confidently face problems knowing God would work again.

When the Israelites focused only on the day's difficulties and forgot the blessings, life looked bleak. But the problem was with their focus, not their situation. We have the same problem today. Perhaps things are going really well. You have good grades on your report card, you've made new friends, and you have been strong and healthy. But then something bad happens and you forget all the good things and focus on that one failed math test or that one friend who talked behind your back. Try to see that problem as only a small piece of your life and keep your focus on the blessings.

For You

Difficult circumstances can make life look bleak. Maybe there's too much homework, a best friend let you down, or there are problems at home. Those things are tough, but try taking your eyes off the problems and focus instead on Jesus and the blessings in your life.

Answer: a
[The Israelites said,] "We remember the fish we used to eat for free in Egypt. And we had all the cucumbers, melons, leeks, onions, and garlic we wanted."
Numbers 11:5
(The Whole Story: Numbers 11:1-15)

Miriam Is Punished

Q: When Miriam complained against Moses, she
a. was struck with blindness.
b. became paralyzed.
c. was stricken with leprosy.

Moses, Aaron, and Miriam were godly siblings, but they were also human. Miriam and Aaron became jealous of Moses. They questioned his leadership. "Has the LORD spoken only through Moses? Hasn't he spoken through us, too?"

God called the three of them into the Tabernacle. He told them his relationship with Moses was special because he spoke directly to Moses, not in dreams or in visions like he'd done with other prophets. God was angry with Moses' siblings for questioning Moses' authority, and Miriam was struck with leprosy.

Why wasn't Aaron struck with the same disease? It could have been because Miriam started the complaining, or it might have been because Aaron was the high priest. If he had leprosy, he'd have been considered unclean and would have had to live separately from everyone else. He wouldn't have been able to perform the duties of the high priest.

Aaron pleaded with Moses for Miriam not to be punished in that way. Moses cried out to the Lord on his sister's behalf. God listened to Moses and said Miriam must live outside the camp for seven days. Then she would be considered clean according to Jewish law and could return to the camp.

For those seven days, the people camped and waited. Then they resumed their journey.

While sibling squabbles are normal, questioning the people God puts in authority isn't acceptable to the Lord. God wants you to accept the authority he places over you and experience his blessings.

For You

You may not agree with everything your parents do, but they are the ones God has appointed to raise you. God knows they aren't perfect, and they'll make mistakes, but his command to honor your father and mother still stands.

Answer: c
As the cloud moved from above the Tabernacle, there stood Miriam, her skin as white as snow from leprosy. Numbers 12:10
(The Whole Story: Numbers 12)

March 10

Scouting the Land

Q: Which fruit did the scouts bring back from Jericho?
a. oranges
b. grapes
c. apples

Have you ever looked at the "fresh produce" at the grocery store while shopping with a parent? Sometimes the grapes or apples don't look very fresh at all. This was not the case with the fruit the scouts brought back from the Promised Land.

The Israelites had reached Kadesh-barnea, bordering the Promised Land. It was decided that one man from each tribe would go into the land on a scouting mission. The scouts were to find out if the land was good or bad, if the people were strong or weak, and if they lived in camps or walled towns. Moses wanted to know what his people were facing.

The scouts explored for 40 days. When they returned, they had a cluster of grapes so large two men had to carry it on a pole between them! Canaan was a land of plenty, and it was the land God wanted the Israelites to have. Unfortunately, as you'll read about in the next two devotionals, 10 of the 12 spies said there were too many people and the Canaanites were too strong to defeat.

The 10 scouts focused on their fears, not God's strength. They convinced the Israelites there was no way they could defeat the enemies and take the land for themselves. They viewed the situation without faith and refused to take what God wanted to give them.

For You

The 10 scouts' fear and lack of faith spread to the other people. They gave up without even talking to God. Hadn't he already miraculously parted the Red Sea and drowned all the Egyptian enemies? If there's something you feel you should do but you are letting your own fears stop you, look to God for his strength. You don't have to act alone. You can do whatever it is by claiming his power.

Answer: b
When they came to the valley of Eshcol, they cut down a branch with a single cluster of grapes so large that it took two of them to carry it on a pole between them! They also brought back samples of the pomegranates and figs.
Numbers 13:23
(The Whole Story: Numbers 13:1-24)

The Promised Land

Q: The scouts described the Promised Land as a land
a. filled with righteous people.
b. flowing with milk and honey.
c. that was cold and barren.

The Israelites were camped on the doorstep of the land God had promised them. It was a plentiful land full of food. In fact, the scouts agreed it was a land flowing with milk and honey. What does that mean? Some believe it was an old expression for fertile land, so the scouts may have meant that an abundance of fruit and fruit trees grew there. Or *milk* may have referred to the milk given by goats, and that goats were plentiful. *Honey* may have referred to the syrup from grapes and dates.

Either way, the land had a lot of fruit and was a good place to grow things. The scouts proved that when they brought back the grapes. But only Joshua and Caleb were willing to take the land. The other scouts were too afraid of fighting the giants they also discovered there.

Joshua and Caleb were the only scouts with faith in God. They told the people, "The land we traveled through and explored is a wonderful land! And if the LORD is pleased with us, he will bring us safely into that land and give it to us. It is a rich land flowing with milk and honey. Do not rebel against the LORD, and don't be afraid of the people of the land. They are only helpless prey to us! They have no protection, but the LORD is with us! Don't be afraid of them!" (Numbers 14:7-9).

God had great things planned for his people, but only Joshua and Caleb trusted God enough to be willing to follow the Lord and accept the land he wanted to give them.

For You

God has an amazing plan for you. Don't let your fears of facing a new situation keep you from it. Trust God.

Answer: b
This was their report to Moses: "We entered the land you sent us to explore, and it is indeed a bountiful country—a land flowing with milk and honey. Here is the kind of fruit it produces." Numbers 13:27
(The Whole Story: Numbers 13:25-33)

March 12

Lack of Faith

Q: What punishment was given to the Israelites for their wickedness and complaints?
a. They would wander in the wilderness for 40 years.
b. They would be slaves in Canaan.
c. Everyone over 20 years old would be killed in battle.

Kaylee Ann walked to the entrance of her new school. It was much larger than her old school. She hesitated at the entrance. She was glad her dad was with her to fill out the paperwork. Kaylee Ann wanted to seem independent, but she felt anything but grown up at the moment.

All 12 Israelite scouts saw the same thing in Canaan: plentiful food, strong people, and strong cities (see yesterday's devotion). What was the difference? Why did the 10 scouts react so differently than Joshua and Caleb? Joshua and Caleb knew the land belonged to them. The Israelites were on the doorstep of the land God had promised them, yet they wouldn't go in. But just as Kaylee Ann's father went into the new school with her, the Israelites' heavenly Father was waiting to enter the land with them.

What was their punishment for failing to trust God? They had to wander in the wilderness one year for each day the scouts were in the land. That meant they'd be wandering for 40 years. Everyone age 20 and older who had complained against the Lord would die in the wilderness. The next generation, those who were children when they left Egypt, would be the ones to enter the land.

The people missed out on God's blessings because of their lack of faith, their disobedience in not taking the land, and their complaints against God. Joshua and Caleb were the only exceptions and would enter the land at the end of the 40 years.

For You

Sometimes it seems that if the majority of people agree about something, it must be right. But that's not always true. When people disagree, don't just follow the larger group. Ask God to help you decide what is right, and then do it.

Answer: a
[The Lord said to Moses and Aaron,] "Because your men explored the land for forty days, you must wander in the wilderness for forty years—a year for each day, suffering the consequences of your sins." Numbers 14:34
(The Whole Story: Numbers 14)

Korah and His Followers

Q: What happened to the men who rebelled against Moses?
a. They were bitten by poisonous desert snakes.
b. The people stoned them.
c. The earth opened up and swallowed them.

Korah, who was an important Levite, and several other men stirred up 250 of the leaders against Moses. Korah was jealous of Moses' authority, although God had also given Korah an important job.

Moses told the rebellious men to be at the Tabernacle the next morning with their incense burners, and God would show them whom he'd chosen as leader. At the appointed time, 250 men stood with their incense burners by the Tabernacle, but now there were others who had joined the rebellion. God told Moses and Aaron to step away from these other men so he could destroy them.

What happened next sounds like something from a movie, but it really happened. Moses told the rest of the people to move away from the rebellious men and their tents. Moses said if God opened up the earth so it swallowed the men, then it would prove God had chosen him as leader. Moses had hardly finished speaking when the earth split and swallowed all the men and their belongings. Then God sent fire and burned up the 250 men holding the incense burners. Since the incense burners were holy objects, they were collected and hammered into a thin sheet of metal to lay on the altar.

Many other people died shortly after this from a plague sent by the Lord because the people accused Moses and Aaron of killing God's people. More would have died if Aaron hadn't interceded for them.

For You

Eagerly look for what God wants you to do, and give your best. Don't be jealous of others who may be called to greater things. God knows what he's doing and has good things planned just for you to do.

Answer: c
The earth opened its mouth and swallowed the men, along with their households and all their followers who were standing with them, and everything they owned.
Numbers 16:32
(The Whole Story: Numbers 16)

March 14

The Budding Staff

Q: Aaron's budding staff was made from what kind of wood?
a. almond
b. maple
c. oak

Did you watch the movie *Tangled*? In the movie, Rapunzel's hair has magical healing powers. When she sings, her hair lights up, and the powers are unleashed. This is ultimately the sign she is the lost princess. Magical things happen in fairy tales.

How about a piece of wood that buds to prove Aaron was chosen by God to be the priest? That story may be less known, but it's a true story right from the Bible. And it shows God's power, not make-believe magical power. To end the questioning of whether or not Aaron was God's chosen priest (see Numbers 16:3), the Lord instructed the people to bring 12 wooden staffs, one from each leader of the 12 tribes of Israel. A name was written on each piece of wood. Aaron's name was written on the staff representing the tribe of Levi. The staffs were placed in front of the Ark of the Covenant in the Tabernacle.

The next day Aaron's staff had budded, blossomed, and then produced fully ripe almonds! The other staffs were unchanged. This was the sign that the Levites were to be God's servants in the Tabernacle.

The budding, blossoming staff didn't just prove that Aaron was to be the priest. It was a sign of fruitfulness from something dead. The other staffs were still dead wood, but Aaron's was fruitful. When people are truly doing what God has called them to do, their lives will blossom and produce fruit just as Aaron's staff did.

For You
You can choose to walk your own way or even try to do a job that belongs to someone else like some of the Israelites did, but only when you're doing what God has planned for you will your life be fruitful. That means you will see God at work, and he will produce results.

Answer: a
When [Moses] went into the Tabernacle of the Covenant the next day, he found that Aaron's staff, representing the tribe of Levi, had sprouted, budded, blossomed, and produced ripe almonds! Numbers 17:8
(The Whole Story: Numbers 17)

Moses' Big Mistake

Q. How did Moses disobey God?
a. He did work on the Sabbath.
b. He struck the rock twice instead of speaking to it.
c. He entered the Tabernacle of God without permission.

Why didn't Moses get to enter the Promised Land? He disobeyed God. The Israelites were staying in an area that had no water. The people were thirsty. They started blaming Moses for their troubles. So Moses asked God for help. God told Moses to speak to a rock to get water from it, but Moses hit the rock twice with his staff instead.

There are several theories on why this was a serious matter to God. One is that the rock symbolized Christ: "They drank from the spiritual rock that traveled with them, and that rock was Christ" (1 Corinthians 10:4). The rock was acting as a symbol of Christ, so God only wanted Moses to speak to the rock.

Another theory is that Moses and Aaron were trying to claim the miracle as their own. Moses had shouted to the people, "Listen, you rebels! Must we bring you water from this rock?" It wasn't Moses and Aaron that brought the water from the rock. Without God's power they could have talked to or hit the rock all day, and nothing would have happened. God deserved credit for the miracle.

The reason why Moses' disobedience was serious to God isn't as important as knowing that it's necessary to obey God in both the little and big things, and this is what Moses forgot.

For You

You may not understand why God has the rules he does, but that doesn't matter. Do your best to follow them even if you don't understand. God doesn't bless those who aren't willing to do things his way. After all, his way is the best way.

Answer: b
Moses raised his hand and struck the rock twice with the staff, and water gushed out. So the entire community and their livestock drank their fill. But the LORD said to Moses and Aaron, "Because you did not trust me enough to demonstrate my holiness to the people of Israel, you will not lead them into the land I am giving them!" Numbers 20:11-12
(The Whole Story: Numbers 20:1-13)

March 16

Follow the Cloud

Q: When the king of Edom refused to let the Israelites pass through his land, they went through it anyway.
True
False

Do you remember Jacob and Esau, the twin sons of Isaac and Rebekah? Jacob's descendants became the nation of Israel, and Esau's descendants became the nation of Edom. The Israelites were approaching Edom on their way to the Promised Land. A well-traveled trade route went through the country, and Moses asked permission to use it to pass through the land. Moses promised that his people wouldn't eat the food, drink the water, or harm the land in any way.

The king of Edom said no. He may have been afraid the Israelites would take his nation's crops. Or maybe he thought the Israelites would attack his country. Either way, he refused to let them pass through, and Moses turned back.

Did God direct Moses to turn back to avoid conflict, or did Moses turn back without consulting God? We don't know. Remember, the cloud was leading the Israelites on their journey. If the cloud went ahead, then Moses should have also. If the cloud led them around Edom, then that was the right thing to do.

There will be obstacles on your journey through life. Sometimes God may remove an obstacle, and other times he might lead you through it. Sometimes, he may lead you around it. It's important to pay attention to God's guidance so you know where he's taking you.

For You

Sometimes it's hard to know what God wants you to do. It might be easier if you had a cloud to guide you like Moses did. Even though you don't have that, you do have God's Word—the Bible—and Christian leaders to help you find the way. Stay focused so you'll know which way to go.

Answer: False
Because Edom refused to allow Israel to pass through their country, Israel was forced to turn around. Numbers 20:21
(The Whole Story: Numbers 20:14-21)

March 17

A Cure for Snakebites

Q: What did the Israelites have to do to be cured from the snakebites they received for complaining against God and Moses yet again?
a. drink bitter water
b. look at a bronze snake Moses made
c. cut the bite and suck out the poison

Movie hero Indiana Jones is known for his bullwhip, fedora hat, and leather jacket. He's also known for his phobia of snakes. Of course, Indiana Jones is able to succeed in his missions despite snake encounters.

The Israelites had a different snake problem. The people were complaining again, and God sent poisonous snakes that bit them. God told Moses to make a replica of the snake and attach it to a pole. Anyone who looked at it would live.

The bronze snake was important for more than just curing the deadly snakebites. It was a symbol of Jesus. John 3:14-15 says, "As Moses lifted up the bronze snake on a pole in the wilderness, so the Son of Man must be lifted up, so that everyone who believes in him will have eternal life." Think about this:

- Jesus was lifted up on the cross just as the bronze snake was lifted up on the pole.
- We look to Jesus for salvation just as the Israelites looked to the snake for salvation from death.
- There is no way to be saved other than through Jesus alone, and there was no other way for the Israelites to be saved from death except by the bronze snake.

Unfortunately many years later the people made the snake an idol, so King Hezekiah destroyed it (see 2 Kings 18:4). It's okay to worship Jesus, but it wasn't okay to worship the bronze snake. The snake alone had no power. The power belonged to God.

For You
Jesus has the power to forgive sins and heal broken lives. Put your trust in him, not in possessions or other people.

Answer: b
Moses made a snake out of bronze and attached it to a pole. Then anyone who was bitten by a snake could look at the bronze snake and be healed!
Numbers 21:9
(The Whole Story: Numbers 21:4-9)

March 18

Talking Animals

Q: What animal spoke to its master?
a. a donkey
b. a parrot
c. a snake

If you're familiar with the *Shrek* movies, you know about Shrek's friend, Donkey. In the first *Shrek*, a loyal, though annoying, friend, Donkey, accompanies Shrek on his mission to free Fiona. Donkey is a fictional talking donkey, but in the Bible, God used a talking donkey to get Balaam's attention.

King Balak of Moab was afraid the Israelites were going to defeat his country. He sent for Balaam, a greedy sorcerer, and asked him to curse the Israelites. Balaam knew who God was, but he wasn't a follower of God. He loved his money too much (see 2 Peter 2:15-16).

Balaam got on his donkey and set out, but the donkey saw an angel of the Lord in the road holding a sword. The donkey went off the path, and Balaam beat the animal.

Balaam and the donkey set out again, but the angel blocked the path again. This time when the donkey went off the road, it crushed Balaam's foot against a wall. Balaam struck the donkey again.

The third time, the angel blocked the path completely, so the donkey laid down. Balaam beat it again. But this time God let the donkey speak to Balaam: "What have I done to you that deserves your beating me three times?"

Instead of being shocked at his talking animal, Balaam answered it and said the donkey had made him look foolish. God let Balaam see the angel then and said the donkey had saved his life. God told Balaam he could continue, but he could only speak the words God let him speak. Instead of cursing the Israelites, Balaam blessed them. This didn't make King Balak happy at all.

For You

Sometimes people have their own ideas about how God should work. But in this case, God chose to use a talking donkey and an unbelieving sorcerer. God's work will get accomplished. It's not our job to worry about how that will happen, but to be careful to do the part he asks us to do.

Answer: a
Then the LORD gave the donkey the ability to speak. "What have I done to you that deserves your beating me three times?" it asked Balaam. Numbers 22:28
(The Whole Story: Numbers 22–24)

March 19

Facing Your Giants

Q: How big was King Og's bed?
a. 4 feet by 2 feet
b. 9 feet by 4 feet
c. 13 feet by 6 feet

The Israelites faced a big problem: King Og and his well-trained army. King Og was a giant, and the Israelites weren't sure they were up for the task of conquering his army and his 60 towns, which had high walls and gates.

The Israelites had the advantage, though—God was on their side. God told them, "Do not be afraid of him, for I have given you victory over Og and his entire army."

The Israelites probably didn't stand a chance on their own, but God handed the king and his army over to them. Not one enemy remained, and all the towns were conquered. This is just one example of a time when God stepped in and gave his people the victory.

God still does that today. There may be giants in your life that seem unconquerable—a PE teacher who is determined to make your life miserable, math story problems that don't make sense to you, or a group of kids who've chosen to shun you. On your own these problems are too big, but with God you can handle them.

You may not be able to fix every problem, but God can help you have peace and strength during these situations. God can also give you the wisdom to know how to get help.

Don't let the giants in your life defeat you. God can give you the victory just as he did for the Israelites when they faced King Og and his tough army.

For You

If you have a problem that feels as unconquerable as a giant in your life, ask God to show you what to do. Ask God to give you the victory over the problem and take the steps you need to in order to defeat it.

Answer: c
King Og of Bashan was the last survivor of the giant Rephaites. His bed was made of iron and was more than thirteen feet long and six feet wide. It can still be seen in the Ammonite city of Rabbah. Deuteronomy 3:11
(The Whole Story: Deuteronomy 3:1-11)

Moses' Instructions

Q: What does Moses instruct the people to do in the beginning of Deuteronomy?
a. set a guard over the things in their tents
b. pass the stories of the things God has done on to their children
c. offer a sin offering weekly

Can you think of an event in your dad's life when he was growing up? Can you retell a story about your mom's youth? If your family is like most, there are stories that are told over and over. You probably have a few stories of your own about how you won a contest or blew up your science fair project.

The book of Deuteronomy begins with Moses reminding the people of all God had done for them. He instructed parents to pass the stories on to their children. Moses set the example by retelling the story of their wandering through the wilderness.

Unfortunately, there came a time when no one was left who knew the stories of how God had brought the Israelites from Egypt to the Promised Land. The people did not follow Moses' instructions to pass along the stories of God.

Referring to the time after Joshua had died, Judges 2:10 says, "After that generation died, another generation grew up who did not acknowledge the LORD or remember the mighty things he had done for Israel." That led to a hard time for the Israelites. And it could have been avoided if the people had been careful to do what Moses said.

For You

If you've gone to church all your life, you've probably learned quite a few Bible stories, and that's a good thing. Never get tired of hearing the same stories over and over again. But now that you're older, don't stop at that. Read the stories in the Bible for yourself so you will never be guilty of forgetting about God or the stories in the Bible.

Answer: b
Watch out! Be careful never to forget what you yourself have seen. Do not let these memories escape from your mind as long as you live! And be sure to pass them on to your children and grandchildren. Deuteronomy 4:9
(The Whole Story: Deuteronomy 4:1-14)

March 21

A Rebellious Son

Q: The punishment for a rebellious son in Old Testament times was
a. a year in jail.
b. being stoned to death by the elders.
c. extra work duty for three years.

Do you think your parents have strict rules? Maybe you lost computer privileges for forgetting to take out the trash. Or perhaps a teacher's call about missed homework lost you a trip to a friend's house or the mall. You probably felt like you had the strictest parents to be found.

You might want to check out some of the Old Testament laws. Your punishment was nothing compared to the Old Testament. The punishment for a rebellious son in the Bible? Death. Now, this isn't talking about the son who forgot to stomp the mud off his shoes outside or who argued about his bedtime. This was the son who had turned from God and his parents' ways. It went beyond a few occasions of disobedience to the point where the son was not willing to turn from his wickedness.

First the son would be taken to the city elders at the town gate. The elders had the authority, and they discussed and decided problems at the town gate. If the town elders felt the son would not obey his parents, they may have figured he wasn't going to obey God or the town laws either. In that case, the elders killed the son by throwing rocks at him.

That isn't done today, of course, but that's not because God has changed his mind about rebellion. We still shouldn't rebel, but we can be forgiven and given grace because Jesus died on the cross and rose again. Even though rebellious sons aren't stoned today, it's still better to be obedient and reap God's blessings.

For You
In Matthew 19:19, Jesus said, "Honor your father and mother. Love your neighbor as yourself." God still wants you to follow those rules today.

Answer: b
The parents must say to the elders, "This son of ours is stubborn and rebellious and refuses to obey. He is a glutton and a drunkard." Then all the men of his town must stone him to death. In this way, you will purge this evil from among you, and all Israel will hear about it and be afraid. Deuteronomy 21:20-21
(The Whole Story: Deuteronomy 21:18-21)

The Next Leader

Q: Who succeeded Moses as leader after his death?
a. David
b. Aaron
c. Joshua

Moses was standing on the brink of the Promised Land, but he wasn't allowed to cross the Jordan River and enter it. He was 120 years old, and he knew he was about to die. Moses told Joshua, his successor, "Be strong and courageous! For you will lead these people into the land that the LORD swore to their ancestors he would give them. You are the one who will divide it among them as their grants of land. Do not be afraid or discouraged, for the LORD will personally go ahead of you. He will be with you; he will neither fail you nor abandon you."

Moses spoke those words, but it was really God who commissioned Joshua. Deuteronomy 31:23 says, "Then the LORD commissioned Joshua son of Nun with these words: 'Be strong and courageous, for you must bring the people of Israel into the land I swore to give them. I will be with you.'"

Both Moses and God told Joshua to be strong and courageous because the Lord was with him. In his own strength, he might have failed at the difficult task of getting millions of Israelites settled in their new home. But with God, he could do it.

For the second time, the Israelites were standing at the doorway of their new home. For the second time they had to decide whether to trust God and take the land, or refuse like they had the first time (see the March 12 devotion). Of all the adults who had made the journey from Egypt, only Joshua and Caleb would enter the Promised Land.

This time the people chose to trust God, but there were still battles ahead.

For You

Joshua had a big job ahead, but God had called him to it and would be with him every step of the way. When God gives you a job to do, he'll be with you, giving you the strength and wisdom to complete it.

Answer: c
[Moses said to Joshua,] "Be strong and courageous! For you will lead these people into the land that the LORD swore to their ancestors he would give them. You are the one who will divide it among them as their grants of land."
Deuteronomy 31:7
(The Whole Story: Deuteronomy 31:1-8, 23)

Books of History

Saving the Spies

Q: Where did Rahab hide the spies?
a. in her basement
b. under the bed
c. on the roof of her house

The Israelites were on the doorstep of the Promised Land just as they'd been 40 years earlier. This time they were eager to claim their land and settle into permanent homes.

Joshua sent two spies to cross the Jordan River and enter Jericho, the first major city the Israelites would have to defeat. The spies entered Jericho and went to the home of Rahab, who lived in a house on the wide wall surrounding the city. It would give them a chance to look over the city and decide the best way to defeat it.

The men were noticed, and the king was informed they were there. The king sent his men after the spies, but Rahab hid the men under flax stored in a pile on her roof. She told the king's men, "Yes, the men were here earlier, but I didn't know where they were from. They left the town at dusk, as the gates were about to close. I don't know where they went. If you hurry, you can probably catch up with them."

Rahab lied, but it saved the men's lives. Some people wonder why God blessed Rahab even though she lied. But in the danger of the moment, who knows what a person might say to save someone's life? People often lie to enemies during wartime. Rahab also didn't know God's laws about lying, and in her society, lying happened. It doesn't make it right, but it might explain why God didn't judge her for it.

Because Rahab protected the men, they agreed to keep her safe when they overthrew the city.

For You
God used Rahab in spite of her lie. That just goes to show that God is bigger than our sin, and when we mess up, he can make something good out of the mess.

Answer: c
Rahab had hidden the two men. . . . Actually, she had taken them up to the roof and hidden them beneath bundles of flax she had laid out. Joshua 2:4, 6
(The Whole Story: Joshua 2)

March 24

Saving Rahab

Q: The spies told Rahab she would be safe when the Israelites defeated Jericho if she
a. left the city.
b. hung a scarlet cord out her window.
c. waited for them at the city gate.

Even though Rahab didn't know God, word of the Israelites had reached Jericho. Rahab knew God was going to give them the land, and she requested safety. She told the spies, "Now swear to me by the LORD that you will be kind to me and my family since I have helped you. Give me some guarantee that when Jericho is conquered, you will let me live, along with my father and mother, my brothers and sisters, and all their families."

The spies agreed. They told her, "When we come into the land, you must leave this scarlet rope hanging from the window through which you let us down. And all your family members—your father, mother, brothers, and all your relatives— must be here inside the house."

The spies escaped down the rope and to safety, and Rahab left the rope in her window. She gathered her family so they would be safe also.

Rahab was a Canaanite who worshiped false gods, yet when she heard about the true God, she believed he was real. Her faith in a God she didn't know much about kept her safe.

Rahab had more faith than some of the Israelites who knew God and had seen his miracles. She recognized his power while some of God's own people doubted.

For You

Rahab knew God was going to destroy the city and made plans to be spared. Is your faith in God strong enough to cause you to take action?

Answer: b
[The men told Rahab,] "When we come into the land, you must leave this scarlet rope hanging from the window through which you let us down. And all your family members—your father, mother, brothers, and all your relatives—must be here inside the house." Joshua 2:18
(The Whole Story: Joshua 2)

March 25

A Step of Faith

Q: Which river stopped flowing when the priests' feet touched the water's edge?
a. Red River
b. Euphrates River
c. Jordan River

Before the Israelites could defeat Jericho, they had to cross a river. The priest carrying the Ark of the Covenant would go first. The Ark was a visible reminder that God was with the Israelites. The Jordan River was overflowing its banks when the Israelites had to cross, so they had to take a big step of faith. If they stepped in, and God didn't keep his word to keep them dry, they would be in over their heads!

But God always keeps his word. The river stopped flowing when the priests' feet touched the edge of the water. The journey out of Egypt started with the parting of the Red Sea and now ended with the parting of the Jordan River.

The Israelites faced the crossing with great excitement, and perhaps some anxiety. They were ready to take the land, and some had waited a long time. Yet there must have been concern about crossing a swollen river. But the priests stepped out in faith, a dry path was formed, and all the Israelites crossed safely.

For You

Sometimes excitement and anxiety go hand in hand. Maybe you'll move up to middle school next year. You're excited about the different classes, sports, and clubs you'll have. At the same time you worry you won't be able to remember your locker combination or will get lost going to class. That's normal, and it's a reminder to look to God for strength and comfort. What situations in your life are causing you both excitement and anxiety?

Answer: c
It was the harvest season, and the Jordan was overflowing its banks. But as soon as the feet of the priests who were carrying the Ark touched the water at the river's edge, the water above that point began backing up a great distance away at a town called Adam, which is near Zarethan. And the water below that point flowed on to the Dead Sea until the riverbed was dry. Then all the people crossed over near the town of Jericho. Joshua 3:15-16
(The Whole Story: Joshua 3)

March 26

A Reminder of God's Work

Q: What did God have the people do as a reminder of what he'd done for them?
a. set up 12 stones as a memorial
b. put up a sign by the river
c. write the miracles on tablets and put the tablets in the Ark of the Covenant

The people had safely crossed the Jordan River. You might think they'd rush to capture Jericho while the Canaanites were still in awe of how God had parted the river.

That's not what they did, though. God had them set up a memorial before they proceeded. Joshua told them, "We will use these stones to build a memorial. In the future your children will ask you, 'What do these stones mean?' Then you can tell them, 'They remind us that the Jordan River stopped flowing when the Ark of the LORD's Covenant went across.' These stones will stand as a memorial among the people of Israel forever."

How do you remember special times? Maybe you have a photo album or scrapbook to remind you of family vacations or holidays or a trophy from the time your team took first place. Do you also have reminders of spiritual milestones and events? If you were dedicated as a baby, your parents may have received a certificate. You might have received a Bible after taking part in believer's baptism. These, like the stones the Israelites set up, remind you of how God has worked in your life.

For You

The Israelites used standing stones or pillars as memorials so people would ask what God had done there. Did you know you can be a standing stone? Your life is a reminder God is doing something special in you. When people look at you and what you are allowing God to do through you, you are a living testimony of his work.

Answer: a
When all the people had crossed the Jordan, the LORD said to Joshua, "Now choose twelve men, one from each tribe. Tell them, 'Take twelve stones from the very place where the priests are standing in the middle of the Jordan. Carry them out and pile them up at the place where you will camp tonight.'"
Joshua 4:1-3
(The Whole Story: Joshua 4)

March 27

Unusual Plan of Attack

Q: How many times total did the Israelites walk around the city of Jericho?
a. 6
b. 13
c. 20

The tall, strong walls of the city of Jericho loomed in front of the Israelites. The gates were tightly shut. Jericho was prepared for an attack, but not for what God had planned.

God told Joshua the people would walk around Jericho one time each day for six days. On the seventh day, they'd march around it seven times. The priests would blow their horns, and when Joshua gave the command, everyone would shout.

Joshua was a military leader, but this was not a strategy he'd used before. Nor would it work apart from God's power. Joshua didn't question God's plan, he just put it into action. The people in Jericho must have wondered what was going on. They were prepared for a battle, yet their enemy just walked around the walls each day.

That changed on the seventh day. The people marched around Jericho in silence until the horns blew. Then they shouted, and the walls fell down. Did the walls fall because of a defect? No. Did they fall because of vibrations from the horns? No. Did the Israelites destroy the walls? No. Hebrews 11:30 says, "It was by faith that the people of Israel marched around Jericho for seven days, and the walls came crashing down."

God saw the Israelites' faith, and he alone sent the walls crashing down. The Israelites took the city, sparing only Rahab and the family members in her house. They were given a home near the Israelite camp.

For You

Proverbs 3:5-6 says, "Trust in the LORD with all your heart; do not depend on your own understanding. Seek his will in all you do, and he will show you which path to take." That's what Joshua did, and it led to success. The same is still true for you today.

Answer: b
[The Lord said to Joshua,] "You and your fighting men should march around the town once a day for six days. Seven priests will walk ahead of the Ark, each carrying a ram's horn. On the seventh day you are to march around the town seven times, with the priests blowing the horns." Joshua 6:3-4
(The Whole Story: Joshua 6)

March 28

Sin Has Consequences

Q: The sin of which person caused the Israelites to be defeated at Ai?
a. Moses
b. Aaron
c. Achan

The Israelites defeated Jericho because God was with them (see yesterday's devotional). The next battle looked to be an easy one. Joshua's scouts said to send only 2,000 to 3,000 soldiers and let the rest stay back. They either had a lot of faith in their army, or they'd finally learned to have faith in God.

Unfortunately, it wouldn't have mattered if the Israelites had sent 100 men or 10,000. The real strength was God's, but God wasn't with them during this battle. That's why the inhabitants of the little town of Ai killed 36 Israelites and forced the rest to retreat.

Joshua and the Israelites were stunned. Why had God helped them defeat their enemies in Canaan but then allowed them to be defeated by the people of Ai? Joshua feared the enemies would think the Israelites' God had failed.

God told Joshua someone had sinned by taking things set apart for God. Those items were meant to be consecrated to the Lord either by destroying them or by giving them as an offering.

God told Joshua to have people come forward, and he would show Joshua who had sinned. Achan was singled out, and he confessed to taking a beautiful robe as well as silver and gold and hiding them in his tent.

Achan, his wife, their children, and their animals were stoned. Their bodies were burned. This may seem like a harsh punishment, but it shows that God is very serious about sin. Achan's sin not only affected him, but it also cost the lives of 36 men in battle and the lives of his family.

For You
Your choices, good and bad, affect those around you. Stop and think about possible outcomes before making a decision.

Answer: c
Achan replied, "It is true! I have sinned against the LORD, the God of Israel. Among the plunder I saw a beautiful robe from Babylon, 200 silver coins, and a bar of gold weighing more than a pound. I wanted them so much that I took them. They are hidden in the ground beneath my tent, with the silver buried deeper than the rest." Joshua 7:20-21
(The Whole Story: Joshua 7)

March 29

Acting without Talking to God First

Q: How did the Gibeonites fool Joshua?
a. They pretended there were more of them than there really were.
b. They put on old clothes and pretended they had traveled far.
c. They hid their possessions and pretended they were poor.

The Israelites had conquered Jericho, and after a setback, they'd conquered Ai (see Joshua 6–8). Now they were going to move on to conquer more enemies and rid the land of idol worshipers.

The Gibeonites lived nearby, and they were afraid they might be next. They wanted to enter into a peace treaty with Joshua. The problem was Joshua wasn't allowed to enter into a peace treaty with a nearby nation.

The Gibeonites tricked Joshua. Some men dressed in old clothes and patched shoes. They had weathered saddlebags and moldy bread. They told Joshua, "This bread was hot from the ovens when we left our homes. But now, as you can see, it is dry and moldy. These wineskins were new when we filled them, but now they are old and split open. And our clothing and sandals are worn out from our very long journey."

Joshua entered into a binding peace treaty with the Gibeonites without talking to God about it first. Three days later Joshua found out he'd been tricked. He honored the agreement he'd made with them, but he made the Gibeonites woodcutters and water carriers for the Israelites.

Joshua didn't ask God for direction, and he was fooled by a nation that didn't believe in God. If he'd taken the time to pray, God would have shown him the truth.

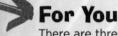

For You

There are three lessons that can be learned from the three cities you've read about in your devotions the last three days. Jericho shows us we are victorious when we trust God. Ai shows us sin has consequences. And Gibeon shows us it's important to pray about decisions. Which of these lessons can you apply today?

Answer: b
They put on worn-out, patched sandals and ragged clothes. . . . They told Joshua and the men of Israel, "We have come from a distant land to ask you to make a peace treaty with us." Joshua 9:5-6
(The Whole Story: Joshua 9)

March 30

Enemies Are Destroyed

Q: What killed more of the five kings' armies than the Israelites did?
a. hail
b. fire
c. lightning

Do you think five against two is a very fair fight? No, it's not really. But when God is part of the fight, numbers don't matter. After hearing about the Israelites' victories and how Gibeon had entered into a treaty with the Israelites, five kings joined their forces together—forming the Amorite army—to fight against the Gibeonites. They were angry Gibeon had made a treaty with Joshua.

The Gibeonites turned to Joshua for help fighting the Amorite army. Since Joshua was a man of integrity, he helped them even though he'd been tricked into entering into the treaty with them.

Joshua and his soldiers marched all night and caught the enemy troops by surprise. Even though the Israelites were doing a good job of defeating the enemy, God stepped in and threw hailstones at the enemy. God's ice cubes killed more men than Joshua's army did.

Even though Joshua was already fighting with God's strength, God stepped in and did a miracle by sending hail. Perhaps this was to make sure the idol-worshiping kings and armies knew God was responsible for the victory. And it was just one more way God showed the Israelites he was with them.

For You

Sometimes God may ask you to wait and let him work. Other times he gives you the common sense to solve your own problems. And once in a while he may make his help known in a miraculous way. That's what happened with the Israelites. Watch for God's hand in your life too.

Answer: a

As the Amorites retreated down the road from Beth-horon, the LORD destroyed them with a terrible hailstorm from heaven that continued until they reached Azekah. The hail killed more of the enemy than the Israelites killed with the sword.
Joshua 10:11
(The Whole Story: Joshua 10:1-15)

March 31

God Aids the Israelites

Q: What stood still until the Israelites had defeated their enemies?
a. the horses and chariots
b. the soldiers
c. the sun

God stepped in and performed many miracles for the Israelites. He did four just to help them take the Promised Land. First, God parted the Jordan River so the Israelites could cross on dry land (see Joshua 3). Second, God made the walls of Jericho tumble to the ground (see Joshua 6). Third, God threw hail at the enemies of Israel and killed more of them than the Israelite warriors did. Fourth, God had the sun stay in the sky until a battle was over so the Israelites could fight in sunlight, not the dark.

You can find all kinds of scientific "proof" about why the sun stayed still or why this couldn't have happened. You can read books that point out it's the earth's rotation that makes the sun appear to rise and set, so the sun doesn't really move at all. It is debated whether or not God caused the earth to actually stop rotating.

But all that isn't really important. God created the earth and the sun. If he wants the sun to shine all night, then it will happen. There doesn't have to be any more explanation than God made it so.

God created everything. He set it all in motion. He can control stars, planets, weather, or anything else he chooses. He granted Joshua's request by making the sun stay in the sky until the battle was won. This was just one more piece of evidence that he was with his people.

For You
God is in control of all things. He may not do the same miracles he did in Old Testament times, but he will still work on your behalf if you ask him to. What do you need God's help with today?

Answer: c
The sun stood still and the moon stayed in place until the nation of Israel had defeated its enemies.   Joshua 10:13
(The Whole Story: Joshua 10:1-15)

April 1

You Can Run, But You Can't Hide

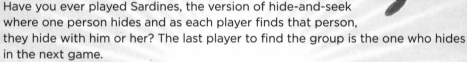

Q: Where did the five enemy kings hide from Joshua?
a. in a tree
b. in a cave
c. in a fort

Have you ever played Sardines, the version of hide-and-seek where one person hides and as each player finds that person, they hide with him or her? The last player to find the group is the one who hides in the next game.

Five enemy kings had their own version of this game. While the battle between the Israelites and the armies of the five enemy kings was in progress, the kings sneaked away and hid in a cave together. They were seen, but no one joined them like in the game Sardines. When Joshua was told where they were, he had his men block the cave entrance with large stones and then guard it so the kings couldn't escape.

After the battle was over and the Israelites—with God's help—were the victors, Joshua went to the cave. He had the five kings brought out. Joshua told his commanders, "Come and put your feet on the kings' necks." This was a well-known sign of victory at that time.

Then Joshua killed the five kings. He reminded the people, "Be strong and courageous, for the LORD is going to do this to all of your enemies."

Many times in the Old Testament books of Law and History (Genesis through Esther), people were told not to be discouraged or afraid. Why? Because God was with them. He gave them a reason to be strong and courageous.

For You

Are you feeling discouraged? Maybe your goal seems out of reach. But when you are striving for God's goals using his strength, you can always be strong and courageous.

Answer: b
During the battle the five kings escaped and hid in a cave at Makkedah.
Joshua 10:16
(The Whole Story: Joshua 10:16-27)

April 2

Settling In

Q: What was being divided in the second half of the book of Joshua?
a. land
b. the Red Sea
c. money

If you've ever moved to a new house, you probably walked through the house to see how big it was. Your family decided what would go in each room, and you may have gotten to choose which bedroom would be yours. Once you moved your things into the room, it started to feel like home.

When the Israelites reached their destination, the tribes each received a piece of land to make their homes. Joshua had the job of assigning land to the tribes, except to the Levites, who lived among the other tribes and served as priests. God chose where each tribe would live, and then Joshua told the people.

God told the Israelites to drive out all the enemies still living in the land because those people worshiped idols. God didn't want his people to be tempted to worship idols too. Unfortunately, the Israelites failed to rid their new home of the enemies, and this caused a lot of problems, which you'll read about later.

Just as God wanted his people to drive out idol worshipers from the land, he wants us to rid our lives of any sin. When we fail to do this, it causes problems for us, just as the enemies caused problems for the Israelites.

For You
Ask God to search your heart and help you get rid of any sin you find. Then you can be victorious in your Christian life.

Answer: a
Joshua took control of the entire land, just as the LORD had instructed Moses. He gave it to the people of Israel as their special possession, dividing the land among the tribes. So the land finally had rest from war. Joshua 11:23
(The Whole Story: Joshua 13–22 talks about the division of the land.)

April 3

A Place to Run To

Q: If someone accidentally killed another person, he could flee to
a. a city of refuge.
b. the Tabernacle.
c. the Levites.

In Old Testament times there were certain cities that were designated as cities of refuge, which were located on high land so they could be seen. The gates were always open. People could go to these cities to be safe.

If someone accidentally killed another person, he could flee to a city of refuge to escape revenge from the deceased's family or friends. The person who fled there was only safe within the city, and he had to stay in the city until the high priest died. Then he could leave the city, and no one could harm him to avenge the death.

The death of the high priest symbolized someone dying in place of the one who had killed another. The death of the high priest set anyone living in a city of refuge free. That might mean a person could be there many years, or only a few, depending on when the high priest died.

Jesus is like the high priest of the Old Testament, but he's better because he never dies. Hebrews 7:23-25 says, "There were many priests under the old system, for death prevented them from remaining in office. But because Jesus lives forever, his priesthood lasts forever. Therefore he is able, once and forever, to save those who come to God through him. He lives forever to intercede with God on their behalf."

Everyone is born with a sin nature, so everyone is in need of a Savior. The cities of refuge were for those who had accidentally committed a murder, but God's salvation through Jesus is for everyone.

For You
The salvation Jesus offers to sinners is forever. Have you accepted his salvation?

Answer: a
The LORD said to Joshua, "Now tell the Israelites to designate the cities of refuge, as I instructed Moses. Anyone who kills another person accidentally and unintentionally can run to one of these cities; they will be places of refuge from relatives seeking revenge for the person who was killed." Joshua 20:1-3
(The Whole Story: Joshua 20)

Cycles of Sin

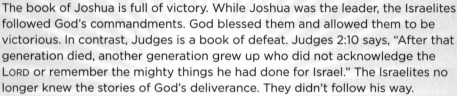

Q: After the death of Joshua, the Israelites turned from God, and God let them be oppressed by their enemies. The Israelites called on God, and he sent a deliverer, which turned into a succession of deliverers. What were the deliverers called?
a. rescuers
b. commanders
c. judges

The book of Joshua is full of victory. While Joshua was the leader, the Israelites followed God's commandments. God blessed them and allowed them to be victorious. In contrast, Judges is a book of defeat. Judges 2:10 says, "After that generation died, another generation grew up who did not acknowledge the LORD or remember the mighty things he had done for Israel." The Israelites no longer knew the stories of God's deliverance. They didn't follow his way.

God told the 12 tribes that claimed the Promised Land to rid the land of enemies. They were to destroy the idols and tear down the altars. But through the years, they failed to do this. Instead, they made agreements with the enemy and even began worshiping some of their idols.

Because of the Israelites' disobedience, God would let their enemies defeat them and rule over them. After the oppression went on for a while, the people would call out to God. God would choose a man—or in one case a woman—to be a spiritual leader for the Israelites. This person was called a judge. When the Israelites turned back to God, God would give them the victory. The land would have peace for a while. Then the Israelites would turn away from God again, and the cycle would start over. This happened over and over in the book of Judges.

You might think God used powerful, godly men to deliver the people, but God used unlikely people to be judges. That way, God would get the glory for the victory. You'll read about a few of them in upcoming devotions.

For You
Does God have your attention? If not, what would it take for you to listen to God?

Answer: c
Every time Israel went out to battle, the LORD fought against them, causing them to be defeated, just as he had warned. And the people were in great distress. Then the LORD raised up judges to rescue the Israelites from their attackers.
Judges 2:15-16
(The Whole Story: the book of Judges)

Lefty

**Q. Why didn't Ehud get his dagger back
after stabbing King Eglon?**
a. Eglon's fat closed around it.
b. It broke in two.
c. He dropped it out the window.

The Israelites turned from God, so God allowed them
to be under King Eglon's rule for 18 years. When they
finally cried out to the Lord for help, God sent a man
named Ehud to deliver his people from their enemies.

Each year money had to be paid to the ruling power,
and that meant the Israelites had to pay tribute to King
Eglon. The Israelites sent Ehud to deliver the money, so Ehud
showed up at King Eglon's palace with the tribute—and a nice,
sharp dagger.

How did Ehud get a dagger past the guards? Easy. A right-handed person
would have the dagger strapped to his left side in order to pull it out quickly,
but Ehud was left handed. His dagger was strapped to the right side and hidden
under his clothing. No one checked there.

When Ehud arrived at King Eglon's palace, he told the king he had a secret
message for him. King Eglon sent everyone out of the room. Then Ehud said,
"I have a message from God for you!" He plunged his dagger into King Eglon's
stomach. The king was so fat that when Ehud plunged the dagger into his
stomach, the fat closed over the dagger. Ehud escaped out the back way,
leaving the dagger behind.

Ehud rounded up the Israelites to go back and attack Moab now that the king
was dead. God gave the Israelites the victory, and there was peace in the land
once again.

For You

Ehud was able to succeed in winning freedom for the Israelites partly because
of being left handed. It was unusual, and the guards didn't think about it. Sometimes God uses things about a person that are considered "different" to his
advantage.

Answer: a
*The dagger went so deep that the handle disappeared beneath the king's fat. So
Ehud did not pull out the dagger, and the king's bowels emptied.* Judges 3:22
(The Whole Story: Judges 3:12-30)

Ordinary People

Q: What did Shamgar use to kill 600 Philistines?
a. a sword
b. a catapult
c. an ox goad

Do you ever feel you need a lot of talent to serve God? Maybe you sit in church and listen as the guitarist or pianist plays the special music. You know you can't do those things. You can't really carry a tune, either, so you won't be up front singing a solo anytime soon. You aren't athletic. You can't draw, and you're horrible at any kind of crafts. How can you serve God when it seems he hasn't given you any talent?

Remember from yesterday's devotion how God used Ehud, the left-handed judge, to kill King Eglon and to deliver the Israelites? Ehud was just an ordinary guy. Shamgar was another ordinary guy. He didn't have any great talent. He just knew how to use an ox goad, a common farm tool. And he used it to kill 600 Philistines!

Shamgar was willing to be used by God, and the Lord had Shamgar use a tool he was familiar with to accomplish God's purpose. The thing about God is, he doesn't choose only the supertalented, rich, or famous to do his work. He chooses ordinary people. You just have to read the book of Judges to see that.

The Bible says, "Remember, dear brothers and sisters, that few of you were wise in the world's eyes or powerful or wealthy when God called you. Instead, God chose things the world considers foolish in order to shame those who think they are wise. And he chose things that are powerless to shame those who are powerful" (1 Corinthians 1:26-27). A rich or powerful person might claim credit for himself or herself, but by using ordinary people, God gets the credit.

For You

Ehud used a dagger, and Shamgar used an ox goad. What tool do you have that you can use for God? A pen? You can write a poem that praises God or write an encouraging letter or note to share his love with a friend. A baseball bat? You can give God glory for a home run batted in. Look around you and see what you can use for God today.

Answer: c
After Ehud, Shamgar son of Anath rescued Israel. He once killed 600 Philistines with an ox goad. Judges 3:31
(The Whole Story: Judges 3:31)

April 7

God Uses a Woman

Q: Who was the only woman judge?
a. Rebekah
b. Esther
c. Deborah

In the Disney movie *Mulan*, the main character, Mulan, disguises herself as a young man in order to take her father's place in battle. Mulan is discovered to be female and is sent home in disgrace. But in the end, she saves her country. Unlike Mulan, Deborah, a female judge, was asked to go to war.

The Israelites had been in captivity to the Canaanites for 20 years. Jabin, the Canaanite king, had a commander in chief named Sisera. His army had 900 chariots of iron. The Israelites were afraid to go against him in battle.

During that time, a wise woman named Deborah often gave advice. One day Deborah sent for Barak, a military leader. She told him God wanted him to lead the battle against the Canaanites. What did Barak do? Did he courageously lead the fight? No. Barak said he'd only go into battle if Deborah went with him.

If Deborah went with Barak, that would mean she would be right in the middle of battle along with the soldiers. But Deborah wasn't afraid. She knew that with God the victory belonged to the Israelites. She said, "Get ready! This is the day the LORD will give you victory over Sisera, for the LORD is marching ahead of you."

Barak, with Deborah, led ten thousand men into battle. God threw the Canaanites into a panic. Sisera, their leader, fled on foot. Barak chased the other Canaanite warriors and killed them all.

God gave the Israelites the victory, just as Deborah knew he would.

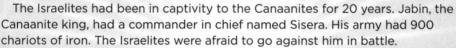

For You

Sometimes when you're trying to live for God, you may be outnumbered, but that's not what really matters. Even if you stand alone, God is standing with you. Be sure to spend plenty of time reading his Word and talking to him so you're ready when those times come.

Answer: c
Deborah, the wife of Lappidoth, was a prophet who was judging Israel at that time. She would sit under the Palm of Deborah, between Ramah and Bethel in the hill country of Ephraim, and the Israelites would go to her for judgment.
Judges 4:4-5
(The Whole Story: Judges 4:1-16)

April 8

Sisera Is Killed

Q: How did Sisera, Jabin's commander in chief, die?
a. A tent peg was driven through his head.
b. A dagger was run through him.
c. A chariot ran him over.

If anyone tries to tell you that following God makes you weak, you might suggest they read the books of Joshua and Judges. These books are filled with battles and victories. And sometimes things got a little gruesome—like with Sisera.

When Sisera fled from the battle against the Israelites, he went to the tent of a man named Heber, because he thought he'd be safe there. Jael, Heber's wife, saw Sisera coming and stepped out of her tent to greet him. "Come into my tent, sir. Come in. Don't be afraid."

Jael gave Sisera a drink and covered him with a blanket. Sisera told her, "Stand at the door of the tent. If anybody comes and asks you if there is anyone here, say no." Then he fell asleep.

Then there was a surprising turn of events. Jael quietly crept up to the sleeping Sisera with a hammer and tent peg in her hand. She drove the tent peg right through Sisera's temple and into the ground. That might seem like a strange thing for a woman to do, but she'd probably pounded tent pegs into the ground before. When Barak arrived looking for his enemy, Jael showed him what she'd done.

Sometimes God chooses to work in unusual ways. Deborah, from yesterday's devotion, and Jael demonstrate that. Never assume that God will use the person or the method you think he will to get things done.

For You

We can't go around driving tent pegs into our enemies' heads, but God still works in surprising ways at times. Be open to his leading. He may have a whole different plan in mind than you do.

Answer: a
When Sisera fell asleep from exhaustion, Jael quietly crept up to him with a hammer and tent peg in her hand. Then she drove the tent peg through his temple and into the ground, and so he died. Judges 4:21
(The Whole Story: Judges 4:17-23)

A New Judge

Q: Who was hiding in the winepress when God called him to be a judge?
a. Joshua
b. Gideon
c. Samson

Many times throughout the book of Judges, the Israelites turned from God and returned back to him. Once again they had turned from him, and God allowed the Midianites to oppress them. The Midianites took all the Israelites' sheep, goats, cattle, and donkeys. They also took or destroyed all the crops. The Israelites had little to eat, so they finally called out to God, and he sent them Gideon to be the deliverer.

When God sent an angel to talk to him, Gideon was hiding at the bottom of a winepress secretly threshing wheat so the Midianites wouldn't take it. The angel said to Gideon, "Mighty hero, the LORD is with you!"

Gideon was sure the angel had the wrong man. "How can I rescue Israel?" he asked. "My clan is the weakest in the whole tribe of Manasseh, and I am the least in my entire family!" Gideon wanted a sign that the message was really from God. He cooked a young goat and made bread without yeast and brought it, along with broth, to the angel as a sacrifice. The angel touched it with a staff, and fire consumed the sacrifice.

God told Gideon to destroy his father's altar to Baal and his father's Asherah pole and to build an altar to God instead. Gideon obeyed, but he did it at night so he wouldn't be seen.

The next morning the people found out Gideon had destroyed the idols, and they wanted to kill him. Joash, Gideon's father, told them, "Why are you defending Baal? . . . Let him defend himself and destroy the one who broke down his altar!"

Gideon was going about his everyday work when God called him to a new job. And God had lots more for him to do.

For You

Is there something new that God wants you to do? If there isn't, don't wait around to see what God has for you to do. Do your everyday work to glorify God, and know that he will lead you in the way you should go.

Answer: b
The angel of the LORD came and sat beneath the great tree at Ophrah. . . . Gideon son of Joash was threshing wheat at the bottom of a winepress to hide the grain from the Midianites. Judges 6:11
(The Whole Story: Judges 6:1-32)

April 10

Asking for Signs

Q: What object did Gideon use to have God give him a special sign?
a. wool fleece
b. dice
c. cards

The Midianites, Amalekites, and the people of the east formed an alliance against Israel. Together, they had a huge combined army. God had told Gideon that Gideon would lead an army against them (see Judges 6:14-16). But Gideon was unsure. He wanted to be absolutely certain that God was really asking him to do this. So he requested a sign.

Gideon said to God, "I will put a wool fleece on the threshing floor tonight. If the fleece is wet with dew in the morning but the ground is dry, then I will know that you are going to help me rescue Israel as you promised."

Gideon put the fleece out, and the next morning the fleece was wet, but the ground around it was dry. Gideon still wasn't convinced, so he asked for the opposite to be true. He said to God, "Please don't be angry with me, but let me make one more request. Let me use the fleece for one more test. This time let the fleece remain dry while the ground around it is wet with dew." It happened just as Gideon requested.

Now Gideon was convinced, so he gathered up his army. There were 32,000 men ready to go to war. But God had other plans to show that God, not the Israelites, would defeat the Midianite army. (You'll read about it in tomorrow's devotion.)

God called Gideon, but Gideon was afraid and unsure of himself. Once he was convinced that God really had chosen him, he moved forward in faith.

For You

Gideon's fear made him hesitate to do what God asked him to do. Don't let your fears make you slow to obey God. Today God guides his people through the Bible, so when you need proof, you don't have to ask for signs. Instead, study the Word and listen for God to speak to you.

Answer: a
That night God did as Gideon asked. The fleece was dry in the morning, but the ground was covered with dew. Judges 6:40
(The Whole Story: Judges 6:33-40)

April 11

Doing Battle God's Way

Q: Gideon's army was cut from 32,000 to _____ men.
a. 30,000
b. 3,000
c. 300

It was time to go to battle, so Gideon rounded up his 32,000 soldiers. Then God said to him, "You have too many warriors with you. If I let all of you fight the Midianites, the Israelites will boast to me that they saved themselves by their own strength." God told Gideon to have everyone who was afraid leave and go back home. How many do you think left? 22,000!

Now there were 10,000 soldiers left to fight with Gideon. God told Gideon to take them to the spring for a test. Gideon must have wondered what God was up to, but he obeyed. God told Gideon to divide the men into groups based on whether they cupped water in their hands to drink or leaned down to drink from the spring.

Only 300 of the men cupped the water in their hands to drink, and it was those men God chose for battle. God cut the army of 32,000 down to 300! Gideon then divided the men into three groups. Each man received a ram's horn and a clay jar with a torch in it.

Just after midnight, the soldiers reached the edge of the enemy camp. They blew their horns, broke the clay jars, held the torches high, and yelled, "A sword for the LORD and for Gideon!"

The enemy army panicked. They became confused and started fighting each other. The enemy army was defeated not by the Israelites' strength but by Gideon's obedience to God.

For You

God doesn't want you to act in your own strength, but in his. The Israelites won the battle not because of power but because of obedience to God. Your obedience and commitment to God—not your talents or popularity or possessions—are your strength as you journey through life following the Lord.

Answer: c
Only 300 of the men drank from their hands. All the others got down on their knees and drank with their mouths in the stream. The LORD told Gideon, "With these 300 men I will rescue you and give you victory over the Midianites. Send all the others home." Judges 7:6-7
(The Whole Story: Judges 7)

April 12

God's Revenge

Q: Who killed all but one of his 70 brothers in order to be in power?
a. Jotham
b. Abimelech
c. Saul

In the movie *The Lion King*, Scar kills his brother, Mufasa, and scares away Mufasa's son and heir, Simba, in order to become king. Things don't go well under Scar's rule, and eventually Simba returns to take his rightful throne.

Gideon, who led 300 men against the Midianites, had 71 sons by many wives. One son, Abimelech, was born to Gideon's servant woman. Abimelech was a lot like Scar. He was ambitious but wicked. The people of Shechem agreed he could be their leader, but he killed 69 of his 70 brothers in order to take charge. Only Jotham escaped.

Abimelech's desire for power made him a ruthless leader. He not only killed his brothers, but he also destroyed whole cities that refused his leadership. He set the tower of Shechem on fire, and a thousand people who had gathered there died. He went to Thebez to capture it next. All the people there fled to the city tower. When Abimelech went to set it on fire, a woman standing on the tower roof dropped a millstone on his head and cracked his skull.

Abimelech knew he was dying. He asked his armor bearer to kill him with a sword so no one could say a woman killed him. The armor bearer did what Abimelech asked.

Abimelech coveted power, and it took control of him. He caused a lot of harm and was only stopped by death.

For You

It's okay to have goals and strive to reach them, but it's not okay to hurt others to achieve those goals. Surrender your goals to God, and he will help you reach them if they are part of what he wants for your life.

Answer: b

One day Gideon's son Abimelech . . . [hired] some reckless troublemakers who agreed to follow him. He went to his father's home at Ophrah, and there, on one stone, they killed all seventy of his half brothers, the sons of Gideon. But the youngest brother, Jotham, escaped and hid. Judges 9:1, 4-5
(The Whole Story: Judges 9)

April 13

A Foolish Promise

Q: Which judge's foolish promise cost him his daughter?
a. Samson
b. Jephthah
c. Samuel

Have you ever made a promise but not been able to keep it? Perhaps you promised that if God would help you pass your test, you'd study every night so you'd be ready next time. Or maybe you promised a friend you'd do something for him or her in exchange for a favor. Even though you meant well, you didn't follow through.

Jephthah promised that if God gave him victory over his enemies, he'd sacrifice the first thing that ran out his door to meet him when he got home. He may have been expecting the family pet, but unfortunately his daughter was the one who ran out to greet him.

There is a lot of debate over how Jephthah kept his promise. Did he sacrifice his daughter as a burnt offering? Or did he sacrifice her to the Lord's work, where she would serve in the Tabernacle the rest of her life instead of getting married? Most scholars believe Jephthah's daughter was given to serve in the Tabernacle because God forbids human sacrifice.

The sad thing is that Jephthah didn't need to make the promise in the first place. God chose him to be the deliverer, so the victory was already Jephthah's as long as he obeyed God. He just had to claim the victory.

For You

God will help you when you ask him. You don't have to promise him anything. God won't be swayed by promises, anyway. All he asks for is a heart that loves him.

Answer: b

When Jephthah returned home to Mizpah, his daughter came out to meet him, playing on a tambourine and dancing for joy. She was his one and only child; he had no other sons or daughters. When he saw her, he tore his clothes in anguish. "Oh, my daughter!" he cried out. "You have completely destroyed me! You've brought disaster on me! For I have made a vow to the LORD, and I cannot take it back." Judges 11:34-35
(The Whole Story: Judges 11:29-40)

April 14

Samson's Secret

Q: Delilah asked Samson the secret of his strength. He gave her four answers. Three were wrong. Samson said, "I would become as weak as anyone else if _____." Which answer was the truth?

a. I were tied up with seven new bowstrings that have not yet been dried

b. I were tied up with brand-new ropes that had never been used

c. my head were shaved

d. you were to weave the seven braids of my hair into the fabric on your loom and tighten it with the loom shuttle

In the Disney movie *Hercules*, Hades, the Lord of the Underworld, sends beautiful Meg to find Hercules's weakness. But Meg herself is Hercules's weakness. Later, Hercules, thinking Meg is in trouble, trades his strength for her freedom only to find out she is working for the enemy. Hercules isn't the only strong man who was fooled by a beautiful woman.

Samson made poor choices when it came to women. The Philistine rulers offered Delilah, Samson's girlfriend, 1,100 pieces of silver each to find out the secret of his strength. Three times Samson gave Delilah wrong answers when she asked the secret of his strength, and three times she tried to take his strength.

Finally Samson told her if his hair were cut, he'd lose his strength. The long hair was a sign of his Nazirite vow to God. Delilah waited until Samson was asleep, and then she had a man shave his head. Samson's strength was gone. The Philistines captured him and gouged out his eyes.

The story didn't end there, but things were never the same for Samson. If he'd fully committed himself to God's laws, he might have lived a life of triumph and victory. But he let his own desires get in the way, and that brought him down.

For You

It's easy to let your selfish desires determine your choices. But that won't lead to the amazing life God wants for you. Surrender your desires to him, because he has a better plan for you.

Answer: c

Finally, Samson shared his secret with her. "My hair has never been cut," he confessed. . . . "If my head were shaved, my strength would leave me, and I would become as weak as anyone else." Judges 16:17

(The Whole Story: Judges 16:4-22)

April 15

Final Revenge

Q: What god did the Philistines praise for delivering Samson to them?
a. Baal
b. Dagon
c. Sorek

The Philistines, with Delilah's help, captured the mighty Samson. They took Samson to Gaza. During his captivity, Samson was chained to a grinding mill, where he ground grain by hand. This was usually the work of female slaves.

Being a prisoner under these circumstances gave Samson time to think about his life. It's possible he even repented of the sins that led to his downfall. One of the last things Samson did was make a request of God.

The people were gathered to offer a sacrifice to their god Dagon, whom they said had allowed them to capture Samson. They had Samson brought out so they could make fun of him. But time had passed, and Samson's hair had grown. No one realized that might mean the return of his power. His strength was really from God, but his hair was the sign of his Nazirite vow and that God was with him, giving him strength.

Samson asked to be led to the pillars of the Philistine temple so he could lean against them. Then Samson asked God for strength to destroy the Philistines, even though it meant that he would die too. He pushed against the pillars, and the building collapsed, killing everyone in it.

Perhaps God didn't like the false god Dagon getting credit for capturing Samson. Or maybe Samson had a changed heart, and God honored it. Whatever the reason for God's help, Samson killed several thousand people that day, both in the building and on the roof. In this way he killed more in his death than in his life.

For You

Live in a way that honors God during your lifetime. Don't let wrong choices keep you from all God has planned for you. Seek his will for your life, and he will use you to accomplish good things.

Answer: b
The Philistine rulers held a great festival, offering sacrifices and praising their god, Dagon. They said, "Our god has given us victory over our enemy Samson!"
Judges 16:23
(The Whole Story: Judges 16:19-31)

Leaving Bethlehem

Q: Why did Elimelech move his family to Moab?
a. There was a flood in his hometown.
b. There was a famine in his hometown.
c. There was violence in his hometown.

The book of Ruth takes place during the time of the judges. These were dark days because the people did whatever they wanted rather than follow God's laws. But during this time there were a few who were loyal to God. Naomi and Ruth were two of them.

The story begins with Elimelech, Naomi's husband, moving his family from Bethlehem to Moab due to a severe famine in the land. Moab was one of the nations that oppressed the Israelites during the time of the judges. They were a pagan nation, and although the Moabites lived near the Promised Land, the Israelites were discouraged from being friendly with them.

Not only was Moab a pagan nation, but the Moabites were not even allowed to worship at the Tabernacle, because they had refused to let the Israelites pass through their land on the way to the Promised Land.

We don't know why Elimelech chose to move to Moab to escape the famine. Perhaps Elimelech felt his family stood a better chance of surviving there than in their homeland. Sadly Elimelech died in Moab. His two sons married Moabite women, and then the sons died also. So Elimelech's move to Moab to save his family failed. Naomi was left in a foreign land with two foreign daughters-in-law.

Elimelech's family suffered hardship and tragedy, but God chose to work through this to accomplish his will. You can see the plan unfold as you read the book of Ruth.

For You

Sometimes it's our own choices that bring us hardship, but God can work even through these circumstances. Try to follow God's leading, but if you mess up, don't worry. Your mistakes don't catch God by surprise. He can use even the tough times for his good.

Answer: b
In the days when the judges ruled in Israel, a severe famine came upon the land. So a man from Bethlehem in Judah left his home and went to live in the country of Moab, taking his wife and two sons with him. Ruth 1:1
(The Whole Story: Ruth 1:1-5)

Naomi's Daughters-in-Law

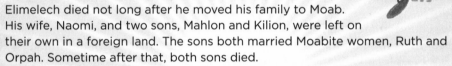

Q: What two women married Naomi and Elimelech's sons?
a. Mary and Elizabeth
b. Ruth and Deborah
c. Ruth and Orpah

Elimelech died not long after he moved his family to Moab. His wife, Naomi, and two sons, Mahlon and Kilion, were left on their own in a foreign land. The sons both married Moabite women, Ruth and Orpah. Sometime after that, both sons died.

When a woman was widowed in Old Testament times, her husband's closest relative would take care of the woman, or her husband's brother would marry the woman. But Elimelech and both of his sons were dead. Naomi didn't know if any of her relatives were still alive in her hometown, Bethlehem.

Naomi decided it was time to return to Bethlehem. She had heard things had gotten better there, and she didn't have a reason to stay in Moab alone.

Naomi told Ruth and Orpah to return to their families so they might have a chance to marry again. Orpah went home, but Ruth decided to stay with Naomi. This meant leaving her own land, Moab, and going to Bethlehem with Naomi. This was unusual because Ruth was a Gentile (a person who isn't a Jew), and the Moabites weren't welcome in Israel. Ruth didn't share a common faith or background with Naomi either. But they were both alone, and Ruth told Naomi, "Don't ask me to leave you and turn back. Wherever you go, I will go; wherever you live, I will live. Your people will be my people, and your God will be my God."

Ruth chose to go with Naomi and to worship God rather than the idols she'd grown up worshiping. Because of this, although she was a Gentile, she played an important part in Jewish history.

For You

God didn't let Ruth's background keep him from using her. God can use you no matter what kind of family you are from or whatever circumstances you may face. He looks at your heart, not your background or family history.

Answer: c
The two sons married Moabite women. One married a woman named Orpah, and the other a woman named Ruth. Ruth 1:4
(The Whole Story: Ruth 1)

April 18

Working for Food

Q: In whose field did Ruth gather left-over grain?
a. Boaz's
b. Samuel's
c. Gideon's

Have you seen people standing by the road holding signs that say, "Will Work for Food"? While some of them may be willing to work for food, many are hoping people will just give them money. Ruth was not like that. She was a willing worker.

It was harvesttime when Ruth and Naomi arrived in Naomi's hometown (see yesterday's devotion). During the harvest, reapers would cut down the wheat and barley stalks and tie them into bundles. The grain that was dropped was then left on the ground for the poor to gather. This was called gleaning.

In order to support herself and Naomi, Ruth went to glean grain. She wasn't reluctant to work in order to have food. Ruth went to a field owned by Boaz, a relative of Elimelech, her deceased husband's father.

When Boaz saw Ruth's good attitude and hard work, he told her not to go to any other field, but to glean only in his field. He promised she'd be safe, and he shared his food and water with her.

Boaz was drawn to Ruth's positive attitude and strong work ethic. Ruth noticed the good reputation Boaz had with his workers. His good character was evident in the way he treated others. Ruth and Boaz were married, and their descendants are well known in the Bible. You'll read more about them in the next devotion.

Ruth was willing to work for what she needed, and she did it with a positive attitude. Others noticed, and she had a good reputation because of it.

For You

Be willing to work for what you want without complaining, and others will notice your hard work, just as Boaz noticed Ruth's. It's much better to have a reputation as an energetic worker than as a whiner or complainer.

Answer: a
Ruth went out to gather grain behind the harvesters. And as it happened, she found herself working in a field that belonged to Boaz, the relative of her father-in-law, Elimelech. Ruth 2:3
(The Whole Story: Ruth 2)

April 19

Family Ties

Q: What king was the great-grandson of Boaz and Ruth?
a. Solomon
b. Josiah
c. David

The book of Ruth may seem like a nice love story between two people who followed God, but it was more than that. God orchestrated the events to bring about the birth of Ruth and Boaz's son Obed:

> the famine that took Elimelech's family to Moab
> Ruth meeting Naomi
> Ruth gleaning in Boaz's field
> the marriage between Ruth and Boaz

Obed was Jesse's father. And Jesse was the father of David, a well-known king and an important link in Jesus' family tree.

God didn't let the fact that Ruth was a Moabite keep her from playing a part in Jesus' earthly family tree. Her love for God was real, and that mattered more than her background.

Ruth didn't know that God was using all the events in her life as stepping-stones to the future, when a Savior would be born to take away the sin of the world. In the same way, we don't know the impact our lives will make after we're gone. That's why it's important to make each decision a good one.

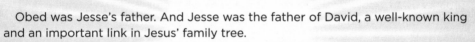

For You

It was because of her faithful obedience that Ruth left the legacy she did, even though she didn't have any idea at the time. It's through faithful obedience that God will make your life count for things that will last long after you go to live with him in heaven.

Answer: c
Salmon was the father of Boaz. Boaz was the father of Obed. Obed was the father of Jesse. Jesse was the father of David.   Ruth 4:21-22
(The Whole Story: Ruth 4:13-22)

April 20

Hannah's Prayer

Q: When Eli saw Hannah praying in the Tabernacle, he thought
a. she was happy to be there.
b. she was tired from walking so far.
c. she had drunk too much wine.

Hannah lived during the time of the judges. She was married to Elkanah, who had another wife named Peninnah. Peninnah had children, but Hannah didn't have any. However, Elkanah loved Hannah more than Peninnah. Peninnah knew it and reacted by taunting Hannah because Hannah was childless.

Every year Elkanah traveled to the Tabernacle at Shiloh to take part in religious feasts. One year Hannah went to the Tabernacle to ask God to give her a son. She promised she would dedicate him to the Lord. Eli the priest saw Hannah's mouth moving but didn't hear any words. He said, "Must you come here drunk? Throw away your wine!"

Hannah assured him that she was okay and that she was pouring out her heart to the Lord. Once Eli understood, he told her, "Go in peace! May the God of Israel grant the request you have asked of him."

Hannah went home and soon was pregnant. She delivered a son she named Samuel. Just as Hannah promised, she took him to the Tabernacle to serve as soon as he was old enough to be away from her.

Hannah kept her promise to God and dedicated Samuel to the Lord's work. All of us should be dedicated to God's work, but Samuel lived and worked full time in the Tabernacle. God has different plans for everyone, but he expects each person to serve wherever he or she is.

For You

God has a plan for you. He may call you to be a pastor or a missionary, or he may plan for you to serve as a teacher, doctor, lawyer, janitor, or plumber. God needs dedicated Christians to reach people in all areas of life.

Answer: c
As she was praying to the LORD, Eli watched her. Seeing her lips moving but hearing no sound, he thought she had been drinking. 1 Samuel 1:12-13
(The Whole Story: 1 Samuel 1)

April 21

God Calls Samuel

Q: How many times after calling did God have to wait for Samuel to answer?
a. Three. Samuel answered the fourth time.
b. None. Samuel answered the first time.
c. One. Samuel answered the second time.

Once Samuel was old enough to be away from his mom, Hannah took her son to the Tabernacle to serve God, just as she'd promised (see yesterday's devotion). Samuel served under Eli. Eli's sons served in the Tabernacle, too, but they were wicked. They didn't follow the rules for sacrifices, and they cheated the people who came to offer sacrifices. The sons knew what was right, but they chose not to do it. Eli did not punish them for their wickedness.

One night Samuel was lying on his bed when he heard a voice call his name. He thought it was Eli, so he went to him. Eli said he hadn't called, and he sent Samuel back to bed. This happened three times. On the third time, Eli realized it must be God calling Samuel. He told Samuel to say, "Speak, LORD, your servant is listening."

God called Samuel's name again, and Samuel said what Eli had told him to say. God had a message for Samuel. God said since Eli had not disciplined his sons, he would judge them for their wickedness. Their sins were so awful they could not be forgiven by offering sacrifices.

The next day Samuel was reluctant to face Eli. He didn't want to tell him what God had said. But Eli insisted on knowing. Samuel gave him the Lord's message. Samuel was righteous and obeyed God, and the Lord spoke to him many more times while Samuel served in the Tabernacle.

For You

Eli's sons couldn't be used for the Lord's work because of their wickedness, but Samuel became an important judge and priest. The difference was that Samuel did everything God told him to do. You may not always want to do the right thing, but it's what God asks of you. When you do that, he can use you as he used Samuel.

Answer: a
The LORD called a third time, and once more Samuel got up and went to Eli. "Here I am. Did you call me?" Then Eli realized it was the LORD who was calling the boy. 1 Samuel 3:8
(The Whole Story: 1 Samuel 2:12-17; 3)

April 22

Bad News for Eli

Q: What happened when Eli received the news that his two sons had died in battle and the Ark of the Covenant had been captured?
a. He fell over and died.
b. He sent a rescue party for the Ark.
c. He offered a sacrifice to God.

The Israelites and the Philistines were at war. The Philistines attacked Israel and killed four thousand men. The Israelite army retreated and wondered what had gone wrong. They decided to take the Ark of the Covenant into the next battle, so they had it brought from Shiloh for that purpose.

The Ark of the Covenant had always been a sign that God was with his people, but it wasn't a good luck charm. The Ark was kept in the holiest place of the Tabernacle—the Holy of Holies. Only the high priest could enter that room one time each year, but Eli's sons entered the room and took the Ark. The Ark didn't give them the protection they wanted in battle. Instead, the Israelites were defeated, and more than thirty thousand men were killed. Among them were Eli's two sons. Besides that, the Ark was captured. A messenger ran to Shiloh with the news.

Eli, elderly and overweight, fell backward off his chair upon hearing the news. He broke his neck and died. That was tragic enough, but Eli's daughter-in-law was near the time her baby would be born. When she heard the news of her husband's death, she went into labor and delivered a son, but she died in the process.

Several tragic events happened because of wrong choices. It was a sad day for Israel, but it wasn't the end of the story. God raised up Samuel as a judge and spiritual leader to get the people back on track.

For You

Bad choices and sin have consequences. Ask God to show you any sin in your life that needs to be dealt with. Things go better for everyone when you're living God's way.

Answer: a
When the messenger mentioned what had happened to the Ark of God, Eli fell backward from his seat beside the gate. He broke his neck and died, for he was old and overweight. He had been Israel's judge for forty years. 1 Samuel 4:18
(The Whole Story: 1 Samuel 4)

April 23

Returning the Ark

Q: After the Philistines captured the Ark of the Covenant, what happened to them?
a. They suffered a plague of tumors.
b. They were successful in all their battles.
c. They became followers of God.

The Philistines' chief god was Dagon, whom they believed sent rain and a good harvest. They had other gods, too, because they thought more gods meant more protection. That may be why they wanted the Ark of the Covenant. To them it was one more assurance of success and well-being.

The Philistines placed the Ark in the temple of Dagon next to an idol of Dagon. The next morning the people found Dagon face down on the ground in front of the Ark. They put him back in his place. The next morning Dagon was on the ground again, and this time his arms and legs were broken off.

This wasn't the only thing that happened. Everyone in and near Ashdod, where the Ark was, was struck with a plague of tumors. The Philistines moved the Ark to two more towns, but the same thing happened.

The Philistines decided to send the Ark back to Israel, hoping they would be healed. They put the Ark on a new cart and hitched it to two cows that had recently given birth. They used this as a test. If the cows followed their natural instincts and returned to their calves, the Philistines would know it was a coincidence they had the plague. But if the cows headed toward Israel with the Ark, they'd know the plague was from God. The cows headed straight to Israel to return the Ark of the Covenant to the Israelites.

Both the Philistines and the Israelites thought of the Ark as a trophy or good luck charm, not a sign of God's presence. His desire was for the people to acknowledge him as God and to follow his rules, but they missed the point many times.

For You

God has given you a sign of his presence because he's given you his Holy Spirit. The Holy Spirit can help guide you on the right path if you allow him to. Just listen for his leading as he speaks to you through the Word or your conscience.

Answer: a
The LORD's heavy hand struck the people of Ashdod and the nearby villages with a plague of tumors. When the people realized what was happening, they cried out, "We can't keep the Ark of the God of Israel here any longer! He is against us! We will all be destroyed along with Dagon, our god." 1 Samuel 5:6-7
(The Whole Story: 1 Samuel 5:1–7:1)

April 24

God's People Want a King

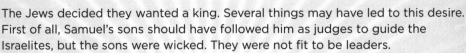

Q: When the Jews (Israelites) asked for a king, they were rejecting _____.
a. God
b. Samuel
c. David

The Jews decided they wanted a king. Several things may have led to this desire. First of all, Samuel's sons should have followed him as judges to guide the Israelites, but the sons were wicked. They were not fit to be leaders.

Another reason they might have wanted a king was that each tribe had its own land and its own leader. It was hard for the tribes to work together. A king would provide unity for the tribes.

One other reason the Israelites might have wanted a king was because the nations around them all had kings. They wanted to be like their neighbors.

God didn't want them to have a king, though. He wanted to be their leader, and he knew having an earthly king would make them forget that he was in charge. The people thought a king would solve their problems, but their real problem was disobedience to God. So unless the king pointed the Jews back to God, having a king wouldn't solve their problems.

Samuel was unhappy about the Israelites' request for a king, but God told him the Israelites were rejecting the Lord, not Samuel. He told Samuel to listen to the people and to warn them of the bad points of having a king, but the people wouldn't listen. They were determined to have a king, and God let them go ahead with their plans.

For You

Sometimes God allows people to go their own way and experience the consequences of their poor decisions. It's important not to blame God when bad things happen due to our own choices. Only by following God's plan can we avoid making mistakes that will result in unpleasant consequences.

Answer: a

Samuel was displeased with their request and went to the LORD for guidance. "Do everything they say to you," the LORD replied, "for they are rejecting me, not you. They don't want me to be their king any longer." 1 Samuel 8:6-7
(The Whole Story: 1 Samuel 8)

Saul Is Anointed King

Q: What was Saul looking for when he met Samuel?
a. his lost donkeys
b. a well to draw water
c. a place to stay

There was a rich and influential man named Kish who was from the tribe of Benjamin. He had a son named Saul, who was the tallest and most handsome man in the land. This is who God had chosen to become king. In fact, God told Samuel that Saul would show up at Samuel's house the next day.

Donkeys were all-purpose animals in Bible times. They were used for transportation and farming. Even the poor owned a donkey. Since Saul's father was wealthy, he owned many donkeys, but they were missing.

Saul and a servant were looking for the donkeys in the hill country. They couldn't find them. The servant had heard that Samuel was a man of God and that the things he said always came true. Saul and the servant went to look for Samuel to see if he could help them locate the lost donkeys.

When Saul and the servant met Samuel, God told Samuel that Saul was to be anointed king. Samuel did this, and then he told Saul to go home because the donkeys had been found.

Later Samuel called all the people together to tell them Saul would be king. But Samuel couldn't find Saul. Where was he? He was hiding among baggage! Saul wasn't sure he should be king, but God worked in his heart. At first Saul obeyed God and was a successful king, but later things changed.

For You

When Saul obeyed God, things went well. When God calls you to do something, he will give you the wisdom and strength to do it. But if you don't listen to him, he won't work through you to accomplish his plans. Be determined to listen to God and follow him.

Answer: a
[Samuel said to Saul,] "Don't worry about those donkeys that were lost three days ago, for they have been found. And I am here to tell you that you and your family are the focus of all Israel's hopes." 1 Samuel 9:20
(The Whole Story: 1 Samuel 9–10)

April 26

Saul's Oath

Q: What did Jonathan do that broke Saul's oath?
a. ate a little honey
b. killed a man in battle
c. stayed home from battle

One day King Saul's son, Jonathan, and Jonathan's armor bearer sneaked away from the Israelite camp and went to the Philistine camp to attack the enemy. Jonathan knew that if God was with them, it wouldn't matter if there were only two soldiers. The victory would be theirs.

Jonathan's attack threw the Philistine army into confusion. When Saul realized what was going on, he rushed to prepare his men for battle. He made an oath: "Let a curse fall on anyone who eats before evening—before I have full revenge on my enemies."

God hadn't asked for an oath in exchange for victory, and Saul's oath caused the men to be weak with hunger because they couldn't eat even the honeycomb they found on the ground. Jonathan wasn't present when Saul made the oath, though, and he ate a piece of the honeycomb.

Some of the men told Jonathan about his father's oath. Jonathan thought the oath was a bad choice. He said the soldiers would have done better if they'd had something to eat.

When Saul found out that Jonathan had eaten before the enemies were all killed, he planned to kill him. The other soldiers stopped him and saved Jonathan from dying as a consequence of Saul's rash vow.

While Saul made oaths to try and gain God's favor, Jonathan stepped out in faith and took action. He knew that he and his armor bearer alone were enough to defeat the Philistines if God willed it.

For You
If you know God wants you to do something, do it even if you have to step out in faith with only God at your side. You and God are the majority.

Answer: a
"I tasted a little honey," Jonathan admitted. "It was only a little bit on the end of my stick. Does that deserve death?" 1 Samuel 14:43
(The Whole Story: 1 Samuel 14)

April 27

God Chooses a New King

Q: People judge by outward appearance, but the LORD looks at the ____.
a. family
b. intelligence
c. heart

In the legend of King Arthur, only the rightful heir to the throne would be able to remove a sword that had been set in stone. When looking for a sword to use in a tournament, Arthur pulled the sword from the stone, much to the surprise of the onlookers. It proved he was the rightful heir to the throne, although he was an unlikely choice. God didn't use a sword and a stone to let everyone know who the next king after Saul would be, but he did choose an unlikely candidate.

Saul had started out listening to God, but he stopped consulting God about decisions and about following his rules. So God rejected Saul as king.

Samuel went to Jesse's home, where God said he'd find the next king. God told Samuel, "Don't judge by his appearance or height. The LORD doesn't see things the way you see them. People judge by outward appearance, but the LORD looks at the heart." God didn't choose one of Jesse's older sons who were tall and strong. He chose the youngest, David, who was only a shepherd boy at the time.

People sometimes quote "People judge by outward appearance, but the LORD looks at the heart" to say it doesn't matter what you wear or what kind of hairstyle you have, but that's not exactly what this verse is about. God told Samuel not to look at a person's size or age when choosing a king. Even though David was the youngest and smallest, he had a heart for God and was the chosen one.

For You

You don't have to be tall, strong, handsome, or beautiful to be used by God. He looks at what's in your heart. What does God see when he searches your heart?

Answer: c
The LORD said to Samuel, "Don't judge by his appearance or height, for I have rejected him. The LORD doesn't see things the way you see them. People judge by outward appearance, but the LORD looks at the heart." 1 Samuel 16:7
(The Whole Story: 1 Samuel 15:1–16:13)

April 28

David's Music Soothes Saul

Q: What instrument did David play?
a. flute
b. harp
c. horn

Have you ever heard the expression "Music soothes the savage beast"? That is actually a misquote from a play written in the 1600s, but the misquote is what is most well known. The saying means that music can soothe a person's emotions or soul, and that is something King Saul badly needed.

Today, if you accept Jesus as your Savior, his Spirit is always with you. This wasn't true in Old Testament times. In those times, the Spirit of God would come upon someone, but it would also leave when he stopped following God. When the Lord rejected Saul as king, his Spirit left Saul, and Saul became very troubled.

Harps were popular musical instruments in Saul's time. Not only was David a brave and wise shepherd, but he was also a musician. Others knew of David's talent, and messengers were sent to bring him to Saul. David had already been appointed king in Saul's place, but Saul didn't know that yet. Being invited to the palace to play music for Saul gave David a chance to watch life in the palace firsthand. David's music soothed Saul's troubled spirit, so David returned to the palace many times to play his harp for Saul.

God was orchestrating events in David's life to prepare him to be a wise and godly king. God's Spirit was on David, unlike Saul, preparing him to be used in a mighty way.

For You

David would one day be king. In the meantime God was preparing him through everyday circumstances. Look around you and ask God what he wants you to learn today that will help you in the future.

Answer: b
One of the servants said to Saul, "One of Jesse's sons from Bethlehem is a talented harp player. Not only that—he is a brave warrior, a man of war, and has good judgment. He is also a fine-looking young man, and the LORD is with him." So Saul sent messengers to Jesse to say, "Send me your son David, the shepherd." 1 Samuel 16:18-19
(The Whole Story: 1 Samuel 16:14-23)

April 29

David Defeats Goliath

Q: How many smooth stones did David gather before he faced Goliath?
a. 1
b. 3
c. 5

The Israelites and the Philistines were in a standoff at opposite sides of a valley with steep walls. Neither army was willing to rush down the wall, across the valley, and up the steep wall on the other side to attack because they would be at a big disadvantage. The armies had each held their ground for 40 days, waiting for the other to attack first.

Every morning a nine-foot-tall giant named Goliath would shout a challenge. "I am the Philistine champion, but you are only the servants of Saul. Choose one man to come down here and fight me! If he kills me, then we will be your slaves. But if I kill him, you will be our slaves! I defy the armies of Israel today! Send me a man who will fight me!" This challenge filled the Israelites with fear.

Then David arrived on the scene with food for his older brothers who were in Saul's army and camped by the valley. Despite his brothers' protests, David convinced Saul to let him fight the giant. Refusing the offer of Saul's extra-large armor, David picked up five smooth stones and put them in his shepherd's bag.

Goliath jeered at David. "Am I a dog that you come at me with a stick? Come over here, and I'll give your flesh to the birds and wild animals!"

David responded, "You come to me with sword, spear, and javelin, but I come to you in the name of the LORD of Heaven's Armies." David, armed with his slingshot, sent a stone flying and brought the mighty giant down.

Humanly speaking, the odds were against David—a boy armed with a slingshot against a mighty giant. But God was with David, and that's all he needed to slay the giant.

For You
When the odds seem to be against you, think of David with a bag full of stones and a heart full of faith in God. You might feel alone facing the giants in your life, but you can have God's strength if your trust is in him.

Answer: c
[David] picked up five smooth stones from a stream and put them into his shepherd's bag. Then, armed only with his shepherd's staff and sling, he started across the valley to fight the Philistine. 1 Samuel 17:40
(The Whole Story: 1 Samuel 17)

April 30

Signs of Friendship

Q: What signs of friendship did Saul's son Jonathan give David?
a. a gold ring, sword, and crown
b. part of his inheritance as firstborn
c. his robe, tunic, belt, sword, and bow

In Disney's *The Fox and the Hound*, Tod (the fox) and Copper (the hound) become friends. Since they are natural enemies, their friendship is complicated and challenging. Similarly, David and Jonathan were unlikely buddies with a complicated friendship.

Jonathan and David, best friends, were an unlikely pair because David would become king instead of Jonathan, the rightful heir to the throne.

At first King Saul liked David. Whatever Saul asked him to do, David did it well. Saul made David a commander in his army. One day the army returned from a battle with the Philistines, and the women of the towns came out with tambourines and cymbals and sang, "Saul has killed his thousands, and David his ten thousands!"

Saul was jealous and angry. The next day when David was playing the harp, the king hurled a spear at David, trying to pin him to the wall. From then on, Saul wanted David dead.

Meanwhile, the friendship between David and Jonathan remained strong. More than once, Jonathan warned David of King Saul's plans so David could escape. Jonathan was loyal to Saul because Saul was his father, and he was loyal to David because David was his friend. But it was Jonathan's loyalty to God above all else that allowed him to be able to treat both his father and his friend fairly.

For You

Jonathan had reason to be jealous of David, who was going to take Jonathan's rightful place as king, but he wasn't. Jonathan recognized this as God's plan. Jealousy is a friendship killer, so if you find it creeping into your life, accept that no matter what you might wish for, God's plans for you are best.

Answer: c
Jonathan made a solemn pact with David, because he loved him as he loved himself. Jonathan sealed the pact by taking off his robe and giving it to David, together with his tunic, sword, bow, and belt. 1 Samuel 18:3-4
(The Whole Story: 1 Samuel 18:1-16)

David Spares Saul

Q: What proof did David have that he could have killed Saul if he'd wanted to?
a. He had Saul's sword.
b. He had a piece of Saul's robe.
c. He had Saul's horse.

David often found himself hiding from King Saul, who wanted to kill him. One time David and his 600 men were hiding in the desert of En-gedi. It was a good place to hide because some of the caves in the area were large enough to hold thousands of people.

One day while Saul and his men were searching for David, they entered the cave where David and his men were hiding farther back. David sneaked up and cut off a piece of the king's robe. He could have easily killed Saul, but David knew it would be wrong to kill the anointed king. God would deal with Saul in his own time and in his own way.

David followed Saul out of the cave and said, "Look, my father, at what I have in my hand. It is a piece of the hem of your robe! I cut it off, but I didn't kill you. This proves that I am not trying to harm you and that I have not sinned against you, even though you have been hunting for me to kill me."

David could have dealt with King Saul in his own way, but he did what he knew was right. David trusted God to settle the score for him.

For You

It's normal to want to get back at someone who is mean to you, but that's not God's way. When you do that, you're handling things your own way, not the Lord's. Don't keep track of wrongs or retaliate. Wait on God, and do what he leads you to do.

Answer: b
[David said to Saul,] "Look, my father, at what I have in my hand. It is a piece of the hem of your robe! I cut it off, but I didn't kill you. This proves that I am not trying to harm you and that I have not sinned against you, even though you have been hunting for me to kill me." 1 Samuel 24:11
(The Whole Story: 1 Samuel 24)

May 2

Quick Thinking

Q: What woman's quick actions saved her household from David's vengeance?
a. Abigail's
b. Esther's
c. Rachel's

There was a rich but foolish man named Nabal who had large flocks of sheep and many shepherds. While they were in the field, David's men, who were still hiding from Saul, didn't raid the flocks for food like so many men did at the time. In fact, they helped protect the flocks.

During sheep-shearing time Nabal provided abundant food and drink for the shearers. David sent a messenger to Nabal asking for food for his hungry men too. But Nabal insulted David and sent the messenger away empty handed.

When the messenger told David this, David was ready to go to Nabal's house and kill him, along with all the other males in the household. Thankfully, a servant who had heard Nabal's conversation with David's messenger quickly went to find Nabal's wife, Abigail, to tell her what had happened.

Abigail got to work and prepared food for David and his 600 men. This was no easy task, but Abigail was a quick thinker and a hard worker. She and her servants met David and his men as the men were on the way to destroy Nabal. Abigail gave David the food for his men. She told him, "I know Nabal is a wicked and ill-tempered man; please don't pay any attention to him. He is a fool, just as his name suggests. But I never even saw the young men you sent."

Abigail's quick thinking saved David from acting in haste out of hurt feelings, and it saved the men in her household. She was a wise woman and a peacemaker. Abigail married David after her husband, Nabal, died.

For You
Rather than reacting to a situation, step back and look at the whole picture. What can you do to be the peacemaker or the problem solver?

Answer: a
David replied to Abigail, "Praise the LORD, the God of Israel, who has sent you to meet me today! Thank God for your good sense! Bless you for keeping me from murder and from carrying out vengeance with my own hands."
1 Samuel 25:32-33
(The Whole Story: 1 Samuel 25)

May 3

Saul and the Medium

Q: Whose spirit did Saul ask a medium to call up?
a. David's
b. Samuel's
c. Jonathan's

Saul was afraid. God wasn't giving him directions anymore because he'd ignored the Lord's commandments too many times. Samuel, who had often advised Saul, had died. The Philistines set up camp for their enormous army near the Israelites, and Saul wanted someone to tell him what to do. He told his advisers he wanted to find a medium (someone similar to a fortune-teller) for advice.

Saul dressed as a common person and went to Endor to visit the medium. Saul himself had made it illegal to consult with mediums, so when she recognized him, she was afraid. He assured her no harm would come to her. Saul asked her to call up Samuel's spirit.

Samuel was not happy Saul had done this. He told Saul that God was Saul's enemy and that the Philistines would defeat the Israelites the next day. What's more, Samuel told Saul that he and his sons would be killed.

What Samuel said came true, but Saul shouldn't have asked a medium to summon Samuel. The Bible forbids any kind of witchcraft or sorcery, including calling up the spirits of the dead. We don't know why God allowed Samuel's spirit to talk to Saul, or even if it was truly Samuel's spirit. Perhaps God chose to allow it just to deliver the message to Saul, or perhaps the medium just made up a message based on what she knew about Saul.

God doesn't want people to try to predict the future or ask others to predict what's ahead. It's okay to ask your parents and other trusted adults for advice in making choices about your future, but only God knows what the years ahead will hold for you.

For You

Ask God to help you make wise choices now and when planning for the future. He will guide you through his Spirit, his Word, and spiritually mature people.

Answer: b
Finally, the woman said, "Well, whose spirit do you want me to call up?" "Call up Samuel," Saul replied. When the woman saw Samuel, she screamed, "You've deceived me! You are Saul!" 1 Samuel 28:11-12
(The Whole Story: 1 Samuel 28)

May 4

Saul's Death

Q: How did Saul die?
a. He was killed by an enemy in battle.
b. He was killed accidentally in battle.
c. He was killed by falling on his own sword.

The Philistine army attacked Israel. Fighting was fierce, and the Israelites fled. The Philistines were closing in on Saul and his sons. They killed his three sons and wounded Saul with an arrow.

Saul didn't want the Philistines to be able to take credit for killing him. Saul told his armor bearer, "Take your sword and kill me before these pagan Philistines come to run me through and taunt and torture me."

The armor bearer wouldn't kill the king, so Saul fell on his sword and killed himself. When the armor bearer saw what Saul had done, he fell on his sword, too, and died beside his king.

Saul, his three sons, his armor bearer, and many of the troops all died together that day. God wanted Saul to be faithful to him and to follow his commands. But Saul went his own way and ignored God. As a result, the Lord didn't bless Saul with victory and success.

Proverbs 14:12 says, "There is a path before each person that seems right, but it ends in death." Saul's life demonstrated this. He did what was right in his own eyes, and it resulted in God turning from him. It also resulted in Saul's death. It's much better to live out Proverbs 3:5-6: "Trust in the LORD with all your heart; do not depend on your own understanding. Seek his will in all you do, and he will show you which path to take."

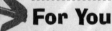

For You

Seek out what God wants for your life. His plan is better than one you might think up on your own. Each morning ask God to direct you to what he wants you to do that day.

Answer: c
Saul groaned to his armor bearer, "Take your sword and kill me before these pagan Philistines come to run me through and taunt and torture me." But his armor bearer was afraid and would not do it. So Saul took his own sword and fell on it. 1 Samuel 31:4
(The Whole Story: 1 Samuel 31:1-6)

May 5

Michal Is Filled with Contempt

Q: Michal, one of David's wives, was filled with contempt for David when she saw him
a. leaping and dancing.
b. kissing another woman.
c. murdering a man.

Michal was David's first wife. He had won the right to marry her by killing 100 Philistines (see 1 Samuel 18:26-27). That may sound unusual, but it wasn't all that uncommon back then. Michal was in a difficult situation. She was married to the person her father, King Saul, wanted to kill. Early on Michal helped David escape from her father. While David was away, Saul gave Michal to another man, but David eventually got her back.

Michal's life wasn't easy, and unlike David, she didn't have a strong faith in God to see her through. She became bitter and resented David's worship of God.

One day, after David had become king, he and several men were returning the Ark of the Covenant to its place in a special tent. As they entered the city, David and the men shouted for joy, and some blew rams' horns. David danced before the Lord.

Michal heard the joyous noise and looked out her window. When she saw David leaping and dancing, she was filled with contempt. She told him he'd looked foolish and undignified.

Michal allowed bitterness to reign in her heart because of circumstances in her life. This resulted in contempt for David's open worship and celebration of God. Rather than dealing with her feelings, Michal allowed them to ruin her relationship with David.

For You

Is there something you're bitter about? You can't control everything that happens to you, but you can control your response to it. Trust that God is still in control even when bad things happen, and ask him to help you deal with the negative feelings.

Answer: a
As the Ark of the LORD entered the City of David, Michal, the daughter of Saul, looked down from her window. When she saw King David leaping and dancing before the LORD, she was filled with contempt for him. 2 Samuel 6:16
(The Whole Story: 2 Samuel 6:16-23)

May 6

God Says No

Q: What request of David's did God deny?
a. the honor of building a temple for the Lord
b. the prestige of building a great kingdom
c. the right to become king

God has a unique plan for each person. This was true for David, and one time David found out his own desire was not part of what God had planned for him.

David loved and worshiped God, and he wanted to build a permanent temple for the Lord. David felt it was wrong that he, the king, was living in a palace, while the Ark of the Covenant was being kept in a tent rather than a permanent place.

However, God spoke to the prophet Nathan and told him David was not the one who would build a temple. David's job was to unify the people and destroy the enemies. A warrior couldn't build God's house, and David was a mighty warrior. But God promised that one of David's children would build a temple.

David's desire to construct a permanent place for God was good, but God had other things in mind for the king. Building a temple was not part of the plan God had for David, but it was part of God's plan for David's son, Solomon.

God promised to continue David's family tree, and Jesus was a descendant of David. What greater plan could God have than that for David?

For You

There may be something you want to do for God. You have good intentions, but God may have something different in mind for you. If God directs you to do something other than what you've planned, it's because he has a greater good in mind. Be open to God's leading.

Answer: a

[The Lord said to David through the prophet Nathan,] "When you die and are buried with your ancestors, I will raise up one of your descendants, your own offspring, and I will make his kingdom strong. He is the one who will build a house—a temple—for my name. And I will secure his royal throne forever."
2 Samuel 7:12-13
(The Whole Story: 2 Samuel 7:1-17)

David Shows Kindness

Q: To whom did David show kindness for Jonathan's sake?
a. Saul
b. Mephibosheth
c. Solomon

Have you seen a movie where someone living in poverty or bad circumstances suddenly becomes rich or is invited to live with someone who is rich? There's a story like that in the Bible.

Before Jonathan's death, when David and Jonathan were close friends, David made a promise to always show kindness to Jonathan's family (see 1 Samuel 20:14-17). Years passed, and David returned to Saul's house. Saul and his three sons were dead, but David remembered his promise and asked, "Is anyone in Saul's family still alive—anyone to whom I can show kindness for Jonathan's sake?"

A servant told him one of Jonathan's sons, Mephibosheth, who was crippled in both feet, was still alive. Mephibosheth was uncertain what King David wanted with him. He was fearful and felt unworthy. "Who is your servant, that you should show such kindness to a dead dog like me?" he asked.

David restored all of Saul's property and belongings to Jonathan's son, and from then on Mephibosheth dined at David's table as though he were the king's own son.

David honored a commitment he'd made long before. The agreement was between David and Jonathan, but Jonathan was dead. No one else knew or would hold David responsible to keep it. But David was an honest man and kept the vow made between him and his best friend years before.

- -

For You

It's good to honor your commitments (unless it is one that is harmful to you or others) even if no one else would know. It shows true honesty, and that is worth more than a broken commitment.

- -

Answer: b
His name was Mephibosheth; he was Jonathan's son and Saul's grandson. When he came to David, he bowed low to the ground in deep respect. David said, "Greetings, Mephibosheth." Mephibosheth replied, "I am your servant."
2 Samuel 9:6
(The Whole Story: 2 Samuel 9)

May 8

Nathan's Story

Q: In the story Nathan told David, what was the only thing the poor man had?
a. his home and children
b. two donkeys
c. one little lamb

David is described in the Bible as a man after God's own heart, but that doesn't mean he never sinned. David tried to follow God's ways, but he messed up at times. One of those times was with Bathsheba.

Even though Bathsheba was married to someone else, she became pregnant with David's child. David tried covering it up by having Bathsheba's husband, Uriah, moved to the front battle lines where the fighting was most fierce so he'd be killed. After Bathsheba's time of mourning for her husband Uriah was up, she married David and gave birth to their son.

The prophet Nathan told David a story. There were two men; one was rich and one was poor. The rich man had many sheep and cattle, but the poor man had only one lamb. When a traveler visited the rich man, instead of killing one of his many sheep to feed the guest, the rich man killed the lamb belonging to the poor man.

David was angry. He demanded the rich man repay the poor man with four lambs. Then Nathan told David the rich man represented David, and the poor man represented Uriah. David was wealthy and had more than one wife, but he'd taken Uriah's wife and had Uriah killed.

David realized how wrong he'd been. He confessed his sin but still had to face the consequences. The baby born to David and Bathsheba died. It was a sad time, but it was also a reminder that although God forgave David, his sin had consequences.

For You

It's better to confess your sins and face the punishment than try to cover them up and face even worse consequences later. It may be hard to be truthful about something you've done, but confess it and move on.

Answer: c
One day a guest arrived at the home of the rich man. But instead of killing an animal from his own flock or herd, he took the poor man's lamb and killed it and prepared it for his guest. 2 Samuel 12:4
(The Whole Story: 2 Samuel 11:1–12:20)

David's Disloyal Son

Q: Which of these happened to Absalom during battle?
a. He fell off his horse and was killed.
b. He fell on his sword and killed himself to avoid capture.
c. He was killed with a dagger while hanging by his long hair from a tree.

David had sons with his many wives and concubines. This was not God's plan, and it created a lot of competition among the sons who all wanted to be king after David. Absalom, David's third son, wasn't loyal to David. He wanted to be king, but he didn't want to wait until David named a successor. He wanted to be king right then.

Absalom gained followers through scheming and deceit. He moved to Hebron and declared himself king. He was so successful that David had to flee. Then Absalom declared himself king in Jerusalem also.

Absalom and David ended up going into battle against each other. Absalom didn't fare well against his father, God's chosen king. Absalom lost twenty thousand men, and the rest fled. He then attempted to flee on a donkey but got his hair caught in a tree. While he was hanging in the tree, Joab, one of David's commanders, ran three daggers into Absalom's heart. That was the end of the rebellion against David.

Even though Absalom had not been a good son to David, the king was still sad. Absalom was dead. He grieved for his son.

For You

Absalom rebelled against David, but David still loved his son and mourned his death. In the same way God loves his children even when they walk away from him. He longs to show them mercy and welcome them back. If you are doing things that are keeping you from God, turn from them and back to God.

Answer: c

During the battle, Absalom happened to come upon some of David's men. He tried to escape on his mule, but as he rode beneath the thick branches of a great tree, his hair got caught in the tree. His mule kept going and left him dangling in the air. . . . "Enough of this nonsense," Joab said. Then he took three daggers and plunged them into Absalom's heart as he dangled, still alive, in the great tree.
2 Samuel 18:9, 14
(The Whole Story: 2 Samuel 15:1-14; 18:1-18, 33)

May 10

Standing Alone

Q: What were the names of David's mighty men?
a. Shadrach, Meshach, Abednego
b. Jashobeam, Eleazar, Shammah
c. Friar Tuck, Little John, and Will Scarlett

There are a lot of stories that involve a hero and his sidekicks. There's King Arthur and his Knights of the Round Table, and of course Robin Hood and his Merry Men. How about David and his mighty men?

The Israelites had problems with the Philistines. One of the judges, Samson, fought against the Philistines. Later, David defeated the Philistine giant Goliath. When David became king, the Israelites were still having problems with them.

David had three men, known as his "mighty men," who were strong and courageous. First was Jashobeam. He killed 800 Philistines with his spear. Second was Eleazar. He fought against the Philistines until he could no longer raise his sword.

And there was Shammah, a farmer. That might not seem like an exciting or daring job, but every year the Philistines took his crops. One day Shammah and the Israelite soldiers were in the field when Philistine soldiers mounted a surprise attack! Israel's troops fled. Shammah found himself standing alone as the Philistine army charged at him. He beat back the enemy, but the Bible doesn't tell us how he did it. He may have used a sword or a spear or even a piece of farm equipment like Shamgar (see Judges 3:31).

Shammah showed great courage facing the enemy by himself, but the victory wasn't his. God chose to use Shammah to bring about the victory because he was the only one who stood strong against the enemy.

For You

You may not physically have to defeat an enemy, but sometimes standing up to peers can be just as scary. Ask God to give you the victory just as he did for Shammah, because you are being courageous in standing up for what's right.

Answer: b
These are the names of David's mightiest warriors. The first was Jashobeam. . . . He once used his spear to kill 800 enemy warriors in a single battle. . . . Once Eleazar and David stood together against the Philistines when the entire Israelite army had fled. . . . One time the Philistines gathered at Lehi and attacked. . . . The Israelite army fled, but Shammah held his ground in the middle of the field and beat back the Philistines. 2 Samuel 23:8-12
(The Whole Story: 2 Samuel 23:8-17)

A New King Is Named

Q: What son became the true successor to David?
a. Adonijah
b. Solomon
c. Josiah

David's son Absalom tried to take the throne from David and died as a result (see May 9 devotion). Time passed, and Adonijah, the next oldest son after Absalom, appointed himself king.

Nathan, the prophet, knew Adonijah wasn't supposed to be king. He told Bathsheba to go to David and say, "My lord the king, didn't you make a vow and say to me, 'Your son Solomon will surely be the next king and will sit on my throne'? Why then has Adonijah become king?"

David listened to Bathsheba and declared Solomon his successor. Nathan and Zadok, the priest, led Solomon on a donkey to Gihon Spring, where he was anointed with oil and declared king.

About that time, Adonijah was having a celebration feast after declaring himself king. He heard trumpets and found out it was a royal procession announcing Solomon as king. Adonijah's guests fled, and he ran to the sacred tent and grabbed hold of the horns of the altar. This was a sign that he was putting himself under the grace and protection of God. Solomon promised to spare Adonijah if he would be loyal and not cause any trouble.

David had learned a lot about being a king. Before he died, David gave Solomon these instructions: "Take courage and be a man. Observe the requirements of the LORD your God, and follow all his ways. Keep the decrees, commands, regulations, and laws written in the Law of Moses so that you will be successful in all you do and wherever you go."

For You

David told Solomon he'd be successful as long as he followed God's commands and ways. The same is true for you today. Doing what you know is right will help you be successful in God's eyes, and that's the most important kind of success.

Answer: b
The king repeated his vow [to Bathsheba]: "As surely as the LORD lives, who has rescued me from every danger, your son Solomon will be the next king and will sit on my throne this very day, just as I vowed to you before the LORD, the God of Israel." 1 Kings 1:29-30
(The Whole Story: 1 Kings 1:5–2:3)

May 12

Solomon's Request

Q: When God told Solomon he could ask for anything, what did Solomon ask for?
a. a bigger kingdom
b. a wise heart to rule the people
c. peace in the country

In the movie *Aladdin*, a genie appears and gives Aladdin three wishes. Aladdin wishes to become a prince, and his wish is granted. All does not go well in Aladdin's new life as a prince, but of course the movie has a happy ending. *Aladdin* is only a movie, but in the Bible, God told King Solomon he could ask for anything and his request would be granted.

Solomon, David's son, became king after David. He was a good king who loved God and followed his commands. He also offered burnt offerings to the Lord. God was pleased with Solomon and appeared to him in a dream. He said to Solomon, "What do you want? Ask, and I will give it to you!"

There were lots of things King Solomon could have asked for—money, power, more land, a bigger kingdom, or greater fame. But Solomon asked for a wise heart to be able to rule the people well.

God was pleased with Solomon's answer, so he not only gave him wisdom, but he also promised him riches and fame. Solomon became well known throughout the land for both his wisdom and his riches. He shared some of his wisdom in the book of Proverbs, a practical book that can help guide your life.

For You

The book of Proverbs has 31 chapters. Some people read the whole book of Proverbs each month by reading one chapter a day (Proverbs 1 on the first day of the month, Proverbs 2 on the second day, and so on). Why not try reading it through? You can start now and read a chapter a day or wait and start on the first day of next month. Pick a key verse from each chapter that you are going to apply to your life that day.

Answer: b
Give me an understanding heart so that I can govern your people well and know the difference between right and wrong. For who by himself is able to govern this great people of yours? 1 Kings 3:9
(The Whole Story: 1 Kings 3:1-15)

May 13

A Tricky Situation

Q: One of the first disputes Solomon had to settle as a new king was
a. which woman a baby belonged to.
b. which piece of land belonged to a farmer.
c. how much to tax the people.

Solomon's wisdom was put to the test in a tricky situation. Two women lived in the same house. They both gave birth to baby boys just days apart. One baby died during the night, and the mother of the child who'd died switched her baby with the living one.

When the second mother saw the dead infant beside her, she realized it wasn't her son. But the other mother claimed it was. The mothers went to Solomon to have him decide what to do.

Solomon didn't know which woman was the mother of the living child, so he gave them a test. He said they should cut the baby in half and give half of the baby to each mother. Of course Solomon wouldn't have done that. He just wanted to see their reactions.

The real mother of the child said, "Oh no, my lord! Give her the child—please do not kill him!"

The other woman said, "All right, he will be neither yours nor mine; divide him between us!"

Solomon knew the real mother was the one who wanted the child to live even if it meant giving him to the other lady.

That was a tricky situation for Solomon since he didn't know whom the baby really belonged to. But he knew that a mother would protect her child, so he tested them to see which woman was the baby's mother.

For You

God gave Solomon discernment (another word for wisdom), but it was up to Solomon to use it. It's important not to just ask God for wisdom, but to be willing to apply it to all areas of your life.

Answer: a
The king said, "Let's get the facts straight. Both of you claim the living child is yours, and each says that the dead one belongs to the other. . . ." Then the king said, "Do not kill the child, but give him to the woman who wants him to live, for she is his mother!" 1 Kings 3:23, 27
(The Whole Story: 1 Kings 3:16-28)

May 14

Solomon Builds the Temple

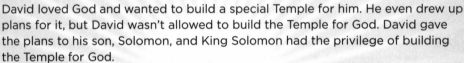

Q: What did Solomon get from the Lebanon mountains to build the Temple?
a. goats
b. timber
c. gold

David loved God and wanted to build a special Temple for him. He even drew up plans for it, but David wasn't allowed to build the Temple for God. David gave the plans to his son, Solomon, and King Solomon had the privilege of building the Temple for God.

Hiram of Tyre, one of David's loyal friends, heard that Solomon was now king and sent ambassadors to congratulate him. Solomon told the ambassadors about his plans to build the Temple. This was an important project, so Solomon wanted the best wood and stone and the best craftsmen. Solomon wanted Hiram to supply cedar and cypress timber and workers to cut down the trees. Hiram told Solomon that the timber would come from the Lebanon mountains and be floated along the coast to him.

The Temple was rectangular and had three areas. First there was an area like a grand porch. Then there was an area where the people worshiped God. Last there was a place called the Holy of Holies. The Temple was built of wood and stone with lots of gold overlaid inside. You can read more about it in 1 Kings 5–7 or 2 Chronicles 2–4.

Building the magnificent Temple was a lot of work. It took seven years to complete it, but Solomon made sure it was completed before he built his own palace. The king knew it was important to finish a project, especially one done for the Lord.

For You

Do you finish what you start, or do you give up and leave projects half done? It's important to be realistic about what you can do, and then do it to the best of your ability. This is especially important when you're doing something for the Lord.

Answer: b
My servants will bring the logs from the Lebanon mountains to the Mediterranean Sea and make them into rafts and float them along the coast to whatever place you choose. 1 Kings 5:9
(The Whole Story: 1 Kings 5)

May 15

Solomon's Visitor

Q: Who came to visit Solomon to see if all the stories about him were true?
a. the queen of Sheba
b. the king of Egypt
c. the magi from the East

Have you ever gone on a trip that seemed endless? Perhaps you went to visit a relative or went on a vacation in another state. What if you had to travel by camel? A single-rider camel might cover 70 miles in a day, but a loaded-down camel caravan would probably only cover around 20 miles a day. You might find yourself asking, "Are we there yet?" for weeks before you reached your destination.

News about Solomon's wisdom and wealth traveled by word of mouth. People far away heard stories about the rich and wise king. One person to hear about him was the queen of Sheba, but she didn't believe the stories.

The queen of Sheba decided to see for herself if the stories about King Solomon were true. So she traveled about 1,200 miles in a caravan with camels, servants, supplies, and gifts of spices, gold, and precious jewels to visit him. It took months to make the journey, but the queen's curiosity was great enough that she was willing to make the trip. Once there, the queen asked Solomon questions to test his wisdom. She was amazed at his answers and finally agreed that the things she'd heard about him were true. She presented him with expensive gifts.

The queen of Sheba was from a pagan land, but after meeting Solomon, she said, "Praise the LORD your God, who delights in you and has placed you on the throne of Israel. Because of the LORD's eternal love for Israel, he has made you king so you can rule with justice and righteousness."

For You

Does your curiosity cause you to check things out? Does your longing to know more about God cause you to dig deeper into your Bible? Think of one question you have about God and then search for the answer in your Bible.

Answer: a
When the queen of Sheba heard of Solomon's fame, which brought honor to the name of the LORD, she came to test him with hard questions. 1 Kings 10:1
(The Whole Story: 1 Kings 10:1-13)

May 16

Solomon's Wives

Q: How many wives did Solomon have?
a. 10 wives of royal birth and 10 concubines
b. 100 wives of royal birth and 2 concubines
c. 700 wives of royal birth and 300 concubines

Solomon started out as a king who loved God and followed his commands. But then he began making poor choices. He married 700 wives and had 300 concubines. (Concubines were women who lived with Solomon but weren't married to him.) King Solomon's wives and concubines worshiped idols, and they turned his heart away from God.

How did Solomon end up with so many wives and concubines? Some Bible scholars suggest it was because Solomon was aggressive in foreign policy. It was the custom at the time for the lesser king to give the greater king a daughter in marriage when a treaty was signed as a gesture of goodwill. So this may be how Solomon ended up with so many wives.

Whether that is true or not doesn't change the fact that in Genesis 2 God said one woman and one man should leave their parents, marry, and begin life together. God also forbade marriage to women from countries that did not worship God. He knew the women could turn their husbands from the Lord. Solomon not only had 700 wives and 300 concubines, but these wives and concubines were idol worshipers. Solomon began worshiping the idols his wives and concubines brought from their cultures.

Because of Solomon's disobedience, God said he would take the kingdom from Solomon's son and give it to the king's servant. Solomon's son would only rule a small part of the kingdom, and the servant would rule the rest.

For You

God commanded his people not to marry idol worshipers because they'd turn his people's hearts from him. That is exactly what happened to Solomon. It's important not to become friends with people who will cause you to act against your beliefs and God's Word. If someone is encouraging you to do wrong, he or she is not someone who should remain your friend.

Answer: c
[Solomon] had 700 wives of royal birth and 300 concubines. And in fact, they did turn his heart away from the LORD. 1 Kings 11:3
(The Whole Story: 1 Kings 11:1-13)

The Divided Kingdom

Q: Just as God told Solomon, after Solomon's death, his kingdom was divided into two separate kingdoms. They were called
a. the Eastern Kingdom and the Western Kingdom.
b. Israel and Judah.
c. Jerusalem and Babylon.

Solomon's many foreign wives turned his heart from God (see yesterday's devotion). Solomon not only allowed their idol worship, but he also took part in it. Because of this, God said the kingdom would be taken from Solomon's son. The kingdom divided a few years after Solomon's death.

Rehoboam, Solomon's son, became king after him. The people asked Rehoboam to lighten the load Solomon had put on them and lower their taxes. Rehoboam asked some older, wise counselors who had served Solomon what to do. They told him to do as the people asked. If he did this, the people would be loyal to him. Rehoboam asked some younger counselors the same question. They told him to be tough on the people and to increase their burdens. So that's what Rehoboam chose to do.

The 10 northern tribes revolted and formed their own kingdom. They became known as Israel (or the northern kingdom). Jeroboam, one of King Solomon's officials, became their king. The two southern tribes that stayed loyal to Rehoboam became known as Judah (or the southern kingdom).

If Rehoboam had listened to the wise counsel of his father's advisers instead of the young men he'd grown up with, things might have turned out differently.

For You

People gain experience as they live, as they encounter problems and solve them. The advisers who had served Solomon had more experience and wisdom than the younger counselors. But Rehoboam chose to listen to the younger ones because they told him what he wanted to hear. Listen to the advice of trusted adults when you need to make a decision. They are speaking to you with wisdom gained by experience.

Answer: b
Rehoboam continued to rule over the Israelites who lived in the towns of Judah. . . . When the people of Israel learned of Jeroboam's return from Egypt, they called an assembly and made him king over all Israel. 1 Kings 12:17, 20
(The Whole Story: 1 Kings 12:1-20)

May 18

Punished

Q: The prophet God sent to rebuke Jeroboam disobeyed. What was the result?
a. His hand was paralyzed.
b. A lion killed him.
c. God struck him dead.

Growing up, Samantha shared a room with her older sister, Emily. During a dispute, Samantha drew a line down the middle of their room with a purple marker. Emily and Samantha agreed each would stay on her own side of the room. The problem was, the closet with all the clothes was on Samantha's side, and the door to the room was on Emily's side. The divided room didn't last long.

Jeroboam had a similar problem. He ruled the northern kingdom, but the Temple was in the southern kingdom. He didn't want his people going to the Temple, because they might become loyal to the southern kingdom. So Jeroboam created his own form of worship with idols, shrines, false priests, and false feast days.

God sent a messenger to speak to Jeroboam. Jeroboam asked the messenger to dine with him, but God had told the messenger not to eat or drink while there. So the messenger left without dining with Jeroboam.

There was an old prophet nearby who sent his son to find the messenger. The messenger refused to dine with him, too, but the prophet said an angel had told him the messenger was to dine with him.

The old prophet was lying, but the messenger believed him. Even though the messenger disobeyed God as a result of someone else's lie, God held him responsible. As he started out for home, a lion killed him, but it left his body by the road. The old prophet found the messenger and buried his body.

When the old prophet told the messenger that an angel said something different from what God said, the messenger should have consulted God himself. Even people who appear to be servants of God can be dishonest and lead you astray.

For You

There are many pastors and leaders who preach their own message but act as though it is from God. God's Word is the true authority, so always check the Bible when someone says something that doesn't match what you think God said.

Answer: b
The man of God started off again. But as he was traveling along, a lion came out and killed him. His body lay there on the road, with the donkey and the lion standing beside it. 1 Kings 13:24
(The Whole Story: 1 Kings 12:26–13:34)

May 19

A Godly King

Q: Whose heart remained completely faithful to the Lord throughout his life?
a. Asa's
b. Abijam's
c. Ahab's

Idol worship became a big problem in both Israel and Judah. Some of the kings took part in idol worship, some ignored it, and a few tried to get rid of it. Abijam (also known as Abijah), a grandson of Solomon, inherited the kingdom from his father, Rehoboam. The kingdom was a mess because of Rehoboam's foolish decisions. Abijam followed Rehoboam's sinful ways.

In case you are getting confused about who's who, here's the way it goes:

- Solomon reigned while everyone was part of one kingdom.
- Rehoboam, Solomon's son, didn't listen to his wise advisers and lost most of the kingdom to Solomon's servant Jeroboam, who led the northern kingdom (Israel). (See 1 Kings 12:12-20.)
- Abijam succeeded his father, Rehoboam, as king of the southern kingdom (Judah). He was equally wicked.
- Abijam's son, Asa, succeeded him as king of Judah. Asa was different. The Bible says, "Asa did what was pleasing in the LORD's sight, as his ancestor David had done."

Asa started cleansing the land of wicked practices. He got rid of the sinful people working in the Temple. He destroyed the idols. The land was rid of everything except the pagan shrines. It would have been good to destroy them, too, but Asa didn't. Despite that, Asa's heart remained true to God through his reign.

Asa was a godly king who was also successful in defending Judah against enemies. Even though he made mistakes, like not tearing down the pagan shrines, he was devoted to the Lord.

For You

Asa removed the idols and tried to turn the people to God, and God blessed him because of his godly heart. God does not expect you to be perfect. You will make mistakes, but God sees your heart and motives—that's what really matters.

Answer: a
Asa's heart remained completely faithful to the LORD throughout his life.
1 Kings 15:14
(The Whole Story: 1 Kings 15:1-24)

May 20

An Evil King

Q: What king angered God more than any king before him?
a. Ahab
b. Saul
c. Josiah

The kingdom was divided into two kingdoms, Judah and Israel. They were ruled by separate kings. While the godly King Asa was ruling in Judah, Israel had several wicked kings. Then came the king the Bible says did more to provoke the Lord's anger than any of the kings before him—King Ahab.

The problem started when King Ahab married a Baal-worshiping Phoenician princess named Jezebel. This was unacceptable to God, and together Ahab and Jezebel did great harm to Israel. Jezebel not only made Baal worship popular, but she tried to kill all the prophets of the Lord (see 1 Kings 18:4).

King Ahab could have stood up to Jezebel and turned the people's hearts back to the Lord, but he was weak and went along with all of her plans. Jezebel built temples to her false gods and had her own false prophets. Seeing all this evil, the Lord sent a prophet named Elijah to tell Ahab there would be no rain for the next few years because of his wickedness.

The lack of rain led to a drought, and no food grew. Queen Jezebel was very angry! She wanted to kill Elijah, but God wouldn't allow it. Instead, God protected Elijah and sent him back later to bring a challenge to Ahab, Jezebel, and the prophets of Baal. You can read more about this in the May 24 devotion.

For You

Ahab grew up believing in God. Even after marrying Jezebel, he still believed in God, but he allowed her false god Baal to have equal importance with God. If Ahab had married someone from Israel who believed in God, his life may have turned out very differently. Make sure the relationships you form now and in the future don't draw you away from God.

Answer: a

Ahab son of Omri did what was evil in the LORD's sight, even more than any of the kings before him. . . . Then he set up an Asherah pole. He did more to provoke the anger of the LORD, the God of Israel, than any of the other kings of Israel before him. 1 Kings 16:30, 33
(The Whole Story: 1 Kings 16:29–17:1)

Rebuilding Jericho

Q: Who tried to rebuild Jericho at the cost of his sons?
a. Absalom
b. Hiel
c. Malachi

Back in the time of Joshua, the Israelites had faced a big challenge—destroying Jericho (see Joshua 6). God gave Joshua the game plan for demolishing the city. The people would march around Jericho one time each day for six days. On the seventh day the people would march around the city seven times with priests blowing horns. At the sound of a long blast, the people were to shout, and the walls would fall. This happened exactly as God said, and Jericho was destroyed.

Once Jericho was destroyed, Joshua gave a solemn oath: "May the curse of the LORD fall on anyone who tries to rebuild the town of Jericho. At the cost of his firstborn son, he will lay its foundation. At the cost of his youngest son, he will set up its gates" (Joshua 6:26).

Around 500 years passed, but the oath Joshua gave never changed. Up until the time of Ahab, no one even attempted to rebuild Jericho. But then Hiel, a wealthy and well-known man of Bethel, wanted to rebuild Jericho. When Hiel laid Jericho's foundation, it cost him the life of his oldest son, Abiram. He completed it and set up its gates at the cost of the life of his youngest son, Segub.

This was a great loss for Hiel. Furthermore, it shows how far from God the people were at that time. If they were still following God, they would have never thought to do something that had been considered off limits for so many years.

For You

Disobedience has consequences and obedience has rewards. It's better to walk God's way and experience his blessings rather than risk the consequences of disobedience.

Answer: b

It was during [Ahab's] reign that Hiel, a man from Bethel, rebuilt Jericho. When he laid its foundations, it cost him the life of his oldest son, Abiram. And when he completed it and set up its gates, it cost him the life of his youngest son, Segub. This all happened according to the message from the LORD concerning Jericho spoken by Joshua son of Nun. 1 Kings 16:34
(The Whole Story: 1 Kings 16:34)

May 22

God Provides for Elijah

Q: What delivery system did God use for Elijah's food?
a. Manna fell from heaven.
b. A raven brought food.
c. The exact amount of food Elijah needed grew on fruit trees near him.

The northern kingdom, Israel, had a long line of wicked kings who served pagan gods. There were only a few good priests left from the tribe of Levi, because most of them had moved south to Judah. God was tired of the wickedness and sent Elijah to deliver a message to King Ahab. There would be no rain for several years. King Ahab told his wife, Jezebel. Since she worshiped Baal, who was supposed to be the god who sent rain and provided bountiful harvests, this was a blow to her and the other Baal worshipers. Jezebel, the queen of mean, wanted to kill Elijah when she heard his message.

God told Elijah to go and hide by the Kerith Brook near where it entered the Jordan River. God didn't leave Elijah to fend for himself. He sent ravens twice a day with bread and meat for Elijah.

Ravens are large black birds related to crows, but much bigger. Their wingspan is about 50 inches. Ravens are considered intelligent birds, but they are mostly known for being scavengers. They eat berries, fruit, insects, and even the flesh of dead animals. Being fed by ravens was probably not what Elijah would have chosen, but it's how God chose to supply Elijah's needs twice every day.

God could have delivered hot meals by simply having them appear in Elijah's hands, but sometimes God uses unusual ways to accomplish things. He has a purpose for what he does, although we don't always know his reasons.

For You

Don't expect God to always work the same way. God is the God of creativity. He has blessed you with the creativity to accomplish the things he asks you to do. Be willing to look for less traditional ways of solving problems or accomplishing a task.

Answer: b
The ravens brought him bread and meat each morning and evening, and he drank from the brook. 1 Kings 17:6
(The Whole Story: 1 Kings 17:1-7)

The Widow of Zarephath

Q: All the widow of Zarephath had was
a. a goat for milk.
b. kiwi and pomegranates.
c. oil and flour.

The widow of Zarephath and her son were poor. Normally she would have probably grown enough barley or olives for herself and her son to live on, but since there hadn't been any rain, nothing was growing. She had only a handful of flour and a little oil left, so she and her son were about to eat the last of the food.

God sent Elijah to the village of Zarephath and told him a widow there would feed him. The prophet journeyed to the village, where he saw a woman gathering sticks for a fire. The widow told Elijah that she and her son were about to eat their last meal before they would die of starvation. There was no extra food to feed Elijah.

Elijah asked the woman to make bread for him first and then for herself and her son. He told her not to fear because she would not run out of oil or flour until there was rain again and crops could grow.

The widow didn't know what to do. She didn't know Elijah or his God. The woman decided to believe Elijah, though. She made his food and then food for herself and her son. Everything happened just as Elijah said. She cooked for the three of them, and the food never ran out.

The widow gave Elijah what she had, believing that what he said was true. God supplied her daily needs, and he provided for Elijah at the same time.

For You

God supplied the widow's needs, but only what she needed for each day. Sometimes when we ask God to meet our needs, we are really asking him to meet our wants. God may not give you everything you want, but he will supply what you truly need.

Answer: c
[The widow] said, "I swear by the LORD your God that I don't have a single piece of bread in the house. And I have only a handful of flour left in the jar and a little cooking oil in the bottom of the jug. I was just gathering a few sticks to cook this last meal, and then my son and I will die." 1 Kings 17:12
(The Whole Story: 1 Kings 17:8-24)

May 24

The Prophets of Baal

Q: How many prophets of Baal did Elijah challenge to a contest?
a. 50
b. 300
c. 450

Jezebel, King Ahab's wife, tried to have all the prophets of the Lord killed, but Obadiah, a follower of the Lord who worked in Ahab's house, hid 100 prophets of God in caves to keep them safe from Jezebel.

Three years into the famine, Elijah returned to Ahab to challenge the 450 prophets of Baal to a contest. The prophets of Baal placed a bull on an altar and called on Baal to set fire to it, but there was no answer. They danced and called louder, but there was still no answer. They cut themselves with knives and there was still silence from Baal. The whole day passed with no fire to prove Baal's power.

Then it was Elijah's turn. He rebuilt the altar of the Lord using 12 stones to represent the 12 tribes of Israel. Elijah placed wood and a bull on the altar. Then he had 12 large jars of water poured over the sacrifice. After that was done, Elijah prayed, "O LORD, God of Abraham, Isaac, and Jacob, prove today that you are God in Israel and that I am your servant. Prove that I have done all this at your command. O LORD, answer me! Answer me so these people will know that you, O LORD, are God and that you have brought them back to yourself."

Immediately fire fell from heaven and burned up the bull, wood, stones, and even the water. God had proven himself the true God.

For You

God will help you accomplish what he wants you to accomplish. He may not flash fire from the sky as he did for Elijah, but he will give you what you need, whether it is strength, courage, faith, wisdom, or willpower. Ask God for his help with achieving the same faith Elijah displayed.

Answer: c
Elijah said to them, "I am the only prophet of the LORD who is left, but Baal has 450 prophets. . . . Then call on the name of your god, and I will call on the name of the LORD. The god who answers by setting fire to the wood is the true God!" And all the people agreed. 1 Kings 18:22, 24
(The Whole Story: 1 Kings 18)

May 25

Ahab Pouts

Q: What did Naboth have that Ahab wanted?
a. a large herd of cattle
b. a vineyard
c. a beautiful wife

Have you ever known any people who were so used to getting their own way that if they didn't, they'd pout or try to trick others into giving in to them? That's what happened in the story of Ahab and Naboth.

Ahab owned lots of land and plenty of vineyards, but Naboth owned a fruitful vineyard near Ahab's palace. Ahab decided he wanted the vineyard and told Naboth, "Since your vineyard is so convenient to my palace, I would like to buy it to use as a vegetable garden. I will give you a better vineyard in exchange, or if you prefer, I will pay you for it."

Naboth told Ahab, "The LORD forbid that I should give you the inheritance that was passed down by my ancestors."

King Ahab lay on his bed pouting and refusing to eat. Wicked Queen Jezebel, Ahab's wife, took things into her own hands. She got two men to lie and say Naboth had been heard cursing God and the king. That was a serious offense, so Naboth was stoned to death. Since Naboth was dead, Ahab was able to claim the vineyard as his own.

God sent Elijah to tell Ahab that his family members would be destroyed because of what he'd done. Ahab humbled himself before God, so God said it would not happen in Ahab's lifetime, but God would destroy the king's dynasty after his death.

Ahab did many things to anger God. If he'd made better choices, he may have been remembered for better reasons.

For You

Ahab is described as the king who did more to anger God than any king before him (see 1 Kings 16:33). That was his legacy—what people remembered about him or how he influenced them. What might people remember about you? Will they have been influenced for the better by your life?

Answer: b
One day Ahab said to Naboth, "Since your vineyard is so convenient to my palace, I would like to buy it to use as a vegetable garden. I will give you a better vineyard in exchange, or if you prefer, I will pay you for it." 1 Kings 21:2
(The Whole Story: 1 Kings 21)

May 26

Elisha's Request

Q: What did Elisha want from Elijah?
a. his cloak
b. his scroll
c. a double share of his spirit

Elisha, a younger prophet, traveled with Elijah. As it
grew nearer to the time God would take Elijah to heaven, Elisha refused to leave
Elijah's side. On the final day, Elijah said to Elisha, "Tell me what I can do for you
before I am taken away."

Elisha replied, "Please let me inherit a double share of your spirit and become
your successor."

In Bible times, a firstborn son would always receive a double portion of the
inheritance. By asking for a double portion of Elijah's spirit, Elisha may have
been asking to be the leader of the other prophets once Elijah went to heaven.

"You have asked a difficult thing. If you see me when I am taken from you,
then you will get your request. But if not, then you won't," Elijah said.

As they were walking, a chariot of fire drawn by horses of fire appeared and
carried Elijah away. Elijah's cloak dropped to the ground, and Elisha picked it up.
He struck the river with the cloak, and the river divided just as it had done earlier
for Elijah. God had given Elisha his request.

God didn't have to grant Elisha's request. But Elisha asked for a double share
of Elijah's spirit and to become his successor in order to do more for God—not
to be thought of as greater than Elijah. So the Lord granted his request.

For You

It's okay to ask God for great things as long as your motives are pure. Don't be
afraid to ask for more courage or wisdom to do the things God wants you to do.

Answer: c
*When they came to the other side, Elijah said to Elisha, "Tell me what I can do for
you before I am taken away." And Elisha replied, "Please let me inherit a double
share of your spirit and become your successor."* 2 Kings 2:9
(The Whole Story: 2 Kings 2:1-18)

The Children Mock Elisha

Q: What pair of animals attacked the children who mocked Elisha for his baldness?
a. tigers
b. lions
c. bears

Kids can be cruel. If you've ever been the victim of a bully, you know that. Some bullies physically harm their peers. Some bullies use words to hurt people, or they get others to ignore or make fun of a peer who is different. Sometimes bullies even make fun of the elderly or those who have a disability.

Things weren't much different in Elisha's day. One day after Elisha had done his first miracle of purifying water for some people, he was walking along the road. A group of more than 40 boys started mocking him for his baldness. They chanted, "Go away, baldy!" over and over.

The boys weren't just teasing Elisha. They were showing disrespect for Elisha's message and his God. Jeering at God's messenger cost the boys their lives. Elisha cursed them in the name of the Lord, and God sent bears that mauled the boys.

God doesn't always immediately punish those who make fun of his chosen leaders, but in this case he sent a strong message that Elisha was his prophet declaring the Lord's word to others.

For You

God was angry with the boys who showed disrespect to his message and messenger. God still wants young people to respect their spiritual leaders, so if you are ever tempted to make fun of a pastor, youth leader, or Sunday school teacher, you might want to rethink that. Give them respect to honor God.

Answer: c
Elisha left Jericho and went up to Bethel. As he was walking along the road, a group of boys from the town began mocking and making fun of him. "Go away, baldy!" they chanted. "Go away, baldy!" Elisha turned around and looked at them, and he cursed them in the name of the LORD. Then two bears came out of the woods and mauled forty-two of them. 2 Kings 2:23-24
(The Whole Story: 2 Kings 2:19-25)

May 28

Elisha's Miracle

Q: What did Elisha tell the widow to borrow from her neighbors?
a. jars
b. wheat
c. money

Elisha was God's prophet, and other prophets served under him. One day a woman came to Elisha and said, "My husband who served you is dead, and you know how he feared the LORD. But now a creditor has come, threatening to take my two sons as slaves."

Elisha asked the woman what she had in her house. She told him she had only a little oil. Elisha told her, "Borrow as many empty jars as you can from your friends and neighbors. Then go into your house with your sons and shut the door behind you. Pour olive oil from your flask into the jars, setting each one aside when it is filled."

The woman did as Elisha said. Her sons handed her jar after jar, and she filled each with the little oil from her flask. Finally they ran out of jars, and the oil stopped flowing. Elisha told her to sell the oil and pay her debts. Then she could live on the leftover money.

The woman had not only lost her husband, but she was about to lose her sons, too. She may have felt abandoned by God and the other prophets. Elisha gave her a task that required her to have faith in him and God. He could have just multiplied the jars along with the oil, but he asked her to be part of her own solution.

For You

God will meet your needs, but he may want you to help. Perhaps you ask God for money to go to summer church camp. He may provide the opportunity for you to mow lawns or walk dogs rather than just prompt your parents to give the money to you. Be willing to be part of the solution.

Answer: a
Elisha said, "Borrow as many empty jars as you can from your friends and neighbors. Then go into your house with your sons and shut the door behind you. Pour olive oil from your flask into the jars, setting each one aside when it is filled." 2 Kings 4:3-4
(The Whole Story: 2 Kings 4:1-7)

Common Denominator

Q: What did the Shunemite's son have in common with Lazarus and Eutychus?
a. They were raised from the dead.
b. They had no fathers.
c. They lived in Jericho.

A rich and well-respected couple who worshiped God lived in Shunem. The woman often saw Elisha trudging down the road in front of her house. One day she invited him in for a meal. The couple then built a small room for Elisha on their roof and furnished it for him to stay in any time he was in the area.

Elisha wanted to do something for the kind couple, but they had everything they needed. They didn't have children, however, and the husband was old. Elisha told the woman that God would send her a child.

The woman had wanted a child for many years, but it seemed impossible that she would have one now. She told Elisha not to get her hopes up.

The woman did give birth to a son and was overjoyed, but the child died a few years later. The woman was upset. "Did I ask you for a son, my lord? And didn't I say, 'Don't deceive me and get my hopes up'?" She felt it was unfair that she'd finally had a child only to lose him so soon.

Elisha went to her house. He lay down on the child twice, and the child grew warm again. The boy sneezed seven times and opened his eyes. He was alive again.

God showed his power by allowing the woman to give birth to a son and by allowing Elisha to raise the child from the dead. God has power over both life and death.

For You

God is the creator of life. That's why it's important to respect life. When you make fun of how someone looks or a difference he or she has, it's not showing respect for God's creation. Seek to appreciate the unique way in which God made each of your family members and classmates.

Answer: a
When Elisha arrived, the child was indeed dead, lying there on the prophet's bed. . . . The boy sneezed seven times and opened his eyes! 2 Kings 4:32, 35
(The Whole Story: 2 Kings 4:8-37; John 11:43-44; Acts 20:9-10)

Naaman is Cured

Q: How many times did Naaman dip in the Jordan River to be cured of leprosy?
a. 1
b. 3
c. 7

Naaman, who was a commander of the Syrian army, had leprosy. Today there is a cure for leprosy, but there wasn't in Bible times.

Naaman's wife had a servant girl who'd been taken captive on one of his raids on Israel. The girl told Naaman's wife, "I wish my master would go to see the prophet in Samaria. He would heal him of his leprosy."

Naaman loaded up many expensive gifts and went to see the king of Israel. The king didn't know what to do, but the prophet Elisha heard about Naaman and sent a message to have Naaman come and see him.

Naaman went to Elisha's house. Because Naaman was commander of the army, he was used to being treated as an important man. But Elisha didn't even come out of his house to talk to Naaman personally. He sent a servant to tell him, "Go and wash yourself seven times in the Jordan River. Then your skin will be restored, and you will be healed of your leprosy."

Naaman wanted Elisha to come out and cure him instantly. He didn't want to wash in a river. Naaman's servants reasoned with him, "Sir, if the prophet had told you to do something very difficult, wouldn't you have done it? So you should certainly obey him when he says simply, 'Go and wash and be cured!'"

Naaman decided it was worth a try, so he went and dipped himself in the river seven times. Naaman was healed.

For You

When you ask God for something, he may not just give it to you. He may require you to act in faith in order to get what you want. Naaman wasn't willing to do what was asked at first, but after he did, he got the cure he wanted. The same may be true for you.

Answer: c
Naaman went down to the Jordan River and dipped himself seven times, as the man of God had instructed him. And his skin became as healthy as the skin of a young child, and he was healed! 2 Kings 5:14
(The Whole Story: 2 Kings 5:1-14)

Gehazi Is Struck with Leprosy

Q: Why did Gehazi have leprosy?
a. He lied to Elisha.
b. He caught it from Naaman.
c. He was born with it.

Naaman had taken many expensive gifts with him when he went to see Elisha. After Naaman was cured of his leprosy, he went back to Elisha to present him with the gifts. Elisha didn't want the gifts, though. He was simply doing God's work and didn't require a reward.

Gehazi, Elisha's servant, saw all the things Naaman had offered Elisha, and he wanted them. Gehazi ran after Naaman and told him that two young prophets had just arrived, and Elisha wanted 75 pounds of silver and two sets of clothes to give them. Naaman gave him twice the amount of silver along with the two sets of clothes. When Gehazi arrived back at the house, he hid them.

"Where have you been?" Elisha asked.

"I haven't been anywhere," Gehazi said.

Elisha faced him and said, "Don't you realize that I was there in spirit when Naaman stepped down from his chariot to meet you? Because you have done this, you and your descendants will suffer from Naaman's leprosy forever."

Gehazi witnessed the miracles of God and saw God's power through Elisha, yet he chose to lie to Naaman and to Elisha. The lies had the immediate consequence of leprosy, not only for Gehazi, but for his children and their children and on down the line.

For You

Gehazi had a good position as Elisha's servant, but his greed caused him to act foolishly. Focus on God and his goodness, and avoid the problems that greed can cause.

Answer: a
[Elisha said to Gehazi,] "Because you have done this, you and your descendants will suffer from Naaman's leprosy forever." When Gehazi left the room, he was covered with leprosy; his skin was white as snow. 2 Kings 5:27
(The Whole Story: 2 Kings 5)

June 1

The Lost Ax Head

Q: A man borrowed an ax to cut down trees. The ax head fell into the river. How did the man get it out?
a. He swam to the bottom of the river to get it.
b. Elisha parted the river, and the man walked in and got it.
c. Elisha threw a stick in the water, and the ax head floated so the man could grab it.

Elisha's group of prophets was growing, and they needed a larger place to meet. They decided to build a new meeting place by the Jordan River. As they were cutting down trees, one of the ax heads fell into the water. A younger prophet was upset. He'd borrowed the ax, and now part of it was at the bottom of the Jordan. The prophet went and told Elisha the problem.

"Where did it fall?" Elisha asked.

The man pointed to the spot, and Elisha cut a stick and threw it into the water at that spot. Then the ax head floated to the surface. The younger prophet reached out and grabbed it. Problem solved.

Even though the younger prophet was doing a good thing, something went wrong. He couldn't continue his work because he'd lost the ax head. Perhaps if he'd asked God directly what to do, the Lord would have given him a solution. But the man did what he thought was best and went to Elisha, a man of God he respected. The Lord gave Elisha the power to raise the ax head from the bottom of the river.

For You

Doing a task for God is no guarantee something won't go wrong, but if God wants the job done, he'll provide a solution. Don't be discouraged when it seems you're facing defeat. Ask God how he wants you to handle it. And don't be afraid to ask advice of spiritual leaders just like the man who lost the ax head did.

Answer: c
"Where did it fall?" the man of God asked. When he showed him the place, Elisha cut a stick and threw it into the water at that spot. Then the ax head floated to the surface. "Grab it," Elisha said. And the man reached out and grabbed it.
2 Kings 6:6-7
(The Whole Story: 2 Kings 6:1-7)

June 2

Jezebel's Death

Q: How did Jezebel die?
a. God struck her with leprosy.
b. She was thrown from her window.
c. She was devoured by fire.

In the northern kingdom (Israel), wicked Jezebel was influencing people to do evil. She turned them from God to idol worship, and she ruthlessly killed innocent people.

Jezebel's own death was prophesied when she had Naboth killed in order to get possession of his vineyard for her husband Ahab (see the May 25 devotion). At that time, Elijah the prophet told Ahab that dogs would lick Ahab's blood where they licked Naboth's blood, and that dogs would devour Jezebel's body in Jezreel, where the vineyard was located.

Jehu was chosen by God as king of Israel and given instructions to wipe out Ahab's family. Jehu went to Jezreel to see Jezebel, but Jezebel taunted him from her window. Jehu called, "Who is on my side? Throw her down."

Jezebel's own servants tossed her from the window, and she was trampled under Jehu's horses' hooves. When servants went to bury her later, they found only her skull, feet, and hands. Dogs had eaten most of her body, just like Elijah had prophesied.

Jezebel was wicked and had no respect for human life. She killed innocent people such as Naboth and many of God's prophets. Because of this, she had a horrible death.

In her lifetime, Jezebel had power and wealth, but at the end her prestige and worldly goods did nothing to help her. What a tragic way to live and die.

For You

Jezebel's death was the end of a wicked woman. For the Christian, death is more than the end of life on earth. It's the beginning of eternal life. Your money and the things you own will be worthless, but the good you've done for Jesus will last.

Answer: b

"Throw her down!" Jehu yelled. So they threw [Jezebel] out the window, and her blood spattered against the wall and on the horses. And Jehu trampled her body under his horses' hooves. 2 Kings 9:33

(The Whole Story: 2 Kings 9:6-7, 30-37)

June 3

Jehu Ends Baal Worship

Q: What did Jehu do with the temple of Baal after he'd killed all the Baal worshipers in the land?
a. built an altar to God
b. converted it to a public toilet
c. had it torn down

The prophet Elisha told Jehu that God had chosen Jehu to destroy Ahab's entire family (see 2 Kings 9:6-8). This was a big task because Ahab had 70 sons and many other family members.

Jehu was serious about ridding the land of evil and planned to kill all the priests and worshipers of Baal, as well as Ahab's family. Jehu spread the news around the land that he was going to present a special offering to Baal. He ordered every priest and worshiper of Baal to attend. They arrived, and he posted 80 of his men outside the temple of Baal. Jehu ordered them not to let even one person escape, or they'd pay for it with their own lives. All the Baal worshipers were slain with swords and not one escaped.

Jehu tore down the sacred pillar and wrecked the temple of Baal. What did he do then? If you guessed he did something sacred like building an altar to God, you're wrong. He converted it to a public toilet! Why did he do that? The Bible doesn't say. Maybe he thought a temple of Baal wasn't worthy of being anything other than a toilet. Perhaps he had his own reasons that aren't shared in the biblical account. But for whatever reason, Jehu thought a public toilet was the best use of the temple.

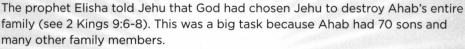

For You

God used Jehu to rid the land of false prophets. Today you would be in big trouble for slaying false teachers and prophets with a sword like Jehu did, but the Bible can be your sword for confronting false beliefs. Whenever you aren't sure if something is true or not, check it against God's Word.

Answer: b
They smashed the sacred pillar and wrecked the temple of Baal, converting it into a public toilet, as it remains to this day. 2 Kings 10:27
(The Whole Story: 2 Kings 10:18-30)

June 4

The Royal Family Killed

Q: What member of the royal family survived Athaliah's murder spree?
a. Jehoiada
b. Josiah
c. Joash

Athaliah was the daughter of King Ahab and Queen Jezebel of the northern kingdom, and she was just as wicked as her parents. She worshiped Baal, the god her mother served. A marriage was arranged between Athaliah and God-worshiping King Jehoram of the southern kingdom (Judah). Athaliah took her Baal worship with her to Judah.

Because of Athaliah's influence, Jehoram built pagan shrines and tried to lead the people away from God. Following Athaliah's wicked ways, Jehoram killed his six younger brothers and some of the leaders who still worshiped God (see 2 Chronicles 21). The Lord got fed up with Jehoram's ways and struck him with a disease. He died two years later, and his son Ahaziah took the throne.

When Ahaziah became king, Athaliah influenced him to do evil also. Her wickedness spread to all who were near her. Ahaziah hadn't been king long when Jehu, who was trying to wipe out Ahab's family line completely, killed him. Athaliah wanted to be in charge, but Ahaziah had sons who were next in line for the throne. That was no problem for Athaliah; she simply killed them all—or so she thought.

Athaliah didn't realize that Ahaziah's one-year-old son, Joash, was rescued and taken to the Temple. He lived there under the influence of godly people who taught him to honor and worship God. When he was seven, he was crowned king, and Athaliah was killed. There was a godly king once again in Judah.

- -

For You

Sometimes it seems evil people get away with wickedness, but it's only for a time. God always wins in the end. So don't be discouraged if it seems the mean kids get away with more or have more fun. Those who follow God will win in the end.

- -

Answer: c
Ahaziah's sister Jehosheba, the daughter of King Jehoram, took Ahaziah's infant son, Joash, and stole him away from among the rest of the king's children, who were about to be killed. She put Joash and his nurse in a bedroom, and they hid him from Athaliah, so the child was not murdered. 2 Kings 11:2
(The Whole Story: 2 Kings 11)

June 5

A Faithful King

Q: What Bible king was given 15 extra years of life because of his faithfulness?
a. Hezekiah
b. Jeremiah
c. Solomon

The king of Judah was sick in bed. The prophet Isaiah visited and told him, "This is what the LORD says: Set your affairs in order, for you are going to die. You will not recover from this illness."

The king cried out to the Lord, "Remember, O LORD, how I have always been faithful to you and have served you single-mindedly, always doing what pleases you." Then he broke down and wept bitterly.

That king was Hezekiah, the thirteenth king in the southern kingdom. Hezekiah was a good king who destroyed pagan altars, idols, and temples in Judah. He even destroyed the bronze snake Moses had made in order for the people to be cured from snakebites (see Numbers 21), because people had begun to worship it as an idol.

After telling Hezekiah he would die, Isaiah left the room. But before he'd gone far, God sent him back to tell Hezekiah that in three days Hezekiah would go to the Temple, and the Lord would add 15 years to his life.

Hezekiah wanted a sign that this was true. Isaiah asked Hezekiah if he wanted the shadow on a sundial to go forward or backward 10 steps.

"The shadow always moves forward," Hezekiah replied, "so that would be easy. Make it go ten steps backward instead."

Everything happened as Isaiah said, and God gave Hezekiah 15 more years to rule in Judah.

- -

For You

The Bible says of Hezekiah, "He remained faithful to the LORD in everything, and he carefully obeyed all the commands the LORD had given Moses" (2 Kings 18:6). What a great thing it would be to have God say that about you at the end of your life. Live each day with that goal in mind.

- -

Answer: a
[The Lord said to Isaiah,] "Go back to Hezekiah, the leader of my people. Tell him, 'This is what the Lord, the God of your ancestor David, says: . . . I will add fifteen years to your life, and I will rescue you and this city from the king of Assyria. I will defend this city for my own honor.'" 2 Kings 20:5-6
(The Whole Story: 2 Kings 20:1-11)

June 6

The Find

Q: What was found during the repairs to the Temple?
a. the Book of the Law
b. the gold candlesticks
c. the silver cups

King Hezekiah did his best to get rid of idol worship in Judah, but the next king, Manasseh, rebuilt the pagan shrines and even sacrificed one of his own sons (see 2 Kings 21). He practiced sorcery in the Temple and murdered some of his people. He turned the hearts of the people away from God. They lived that way many years. Then Josiah became king at the age of eight.

Josiah wanted to follow God, so he began getting rid of the idols. He tore down the shrines and altars. Then Josiah went a step further. He decided to have the Temple of God repaired. During this time, the high priest found the Book of the Law. It was read to Josiah. The king was upset because he realized the people hadn't been following God's rules. He wanted to know more about the things he'd heard.

Some of the men went to the Temple to find Huldah, a prophetess of God. She was known for speaking God's word, and the men knew she'd be able to tell Josiah what he wanted to know.

The message Huldah gave them wasn't a happy one. She told them God said that since Judah had walked away from him and served false gods, the Lord's anger would be poured out on them. But since Josiah had humbled himself before God and repented when he heard the Book of the Law, God's anger would not be poured out against Judah in Josiah's lifetime.

For You

Huldah was a woman who spoke the truth of God. Are you faithful in reading your Bible and learning more about God so you can share God's truth with others the way Huldah did? If not, start today. Read "The Whole Story" passage about Josiah and Huldah, and then share it with someone else.

Answer: a
Hilkiah the high priest said to Shaphan the court secretary, "I have found the Book of the Law in the LORD's Temple!" Then Hilkiah gave the scroll to Shaphan, and he read it. 2 Kings 22:8
(The Whole Story: 2 Kings 22)

June 7

Why It Matters

Q: First Chronicles 1–9 pertains to
a. genealogy.
b. the reign of David.
c. the reign of Solomon.

Much of what is in 1 and 2 Chronicles is the same as 2 Samuel and 1 Kings and 2 Kings. You read of David's reign, Solomon's reign, and the kingdom of Judah. However, Chronicles is written from a different point of view by Ezra, a scribe who was also in exile in Babylon. The book wasn't finished until the southern kingdom was taken captive (because of their constant idolatry and turning away from God) and then released to go back to their homeland years later.

The book of 1 Chronicles starts with nine chapters of genealogy. You might be tempted to just skip over all those names, but they were very important at the time. The list is the family records compiled after Judah was taken captive to Babylon. The people probably wondered if they'd ever return to their homeland, and they may have been fearful that family history would be lost.

The genealogy was also important to the people because they wanted to prove they were descendants of Abraham, the father of the Jewish nation. Then they could claim the blessings God promised to Abraham and his descendants. The genealogy was also important to show that Jesus was part of both Abraham and David's family line.

When you read a long list of names in the Bible, you may not give much thought to each one, but each person listed played a role in Jewish history, some more important than others. God knew each person on the list personally, and he had a plan for each one.

For You

You may feel lost in the crowd, but just like the people on the long list of names, God knows you personally. He knows your name and the number of hairs on your head.

Answer: a
So all Israel was listed in the genealogical records in The Book of the Kings of Israel. 1 Chronicles 9:1
(The Whole Story: 1 Chronicles 1–9)

June 8

The Return

Q: How long were the captives from the southern kingdom in exile before they were allowed to return to their homeland?
a. 10 years
b. 70 years
c. 110 years

God's people in both the northern and southern kingdoms turned from God to idols many times. The Lord gave them repeated chances to turn back to him. Sometimes a godly king would rid the kingdom of idols, but it wasn't long before the people would turn back to their false gods. Finally God allowed his people to be taken captive by other nations.

Around 722 BC, the northern kingdom was taken captive by Assyria. That was the end of the northern kingdom. The people never returned to their land.

Around 586 BC (remember, in BC the year numbers get smaller, not bigger, in time progression) the southern kingdom was taken captive by Babylon. King Nebuchadnezzar took all the valuable things from the Temple and the palace. His army burned down the Temple of God and tore down the city walls.

The people of the southern kingdom were in exile in Babylon for 70 years. Then the Persians conquered Babylon, and the people were allowed to return to their homeland. Many of the exiles returned home in three groups, years apart, but some never returned to their homeland. They had built homes, started families, and acquired wealth while in captivity, and they didn't want to leave. They preferred the comfort and security of their new life to the long and somewhat dangerous trip back to a homeland they'd have to rebuild.

Zerubbabel led the first group home. Ezra led the second group about 80 years later. After that, Nehemiah led a third, smaller group.

God allowed his people to be captured by enemies, but he later redeemed them and let them return home. God still wants those who are walking away from him to find salvation. He desires for those who know him but are not living right to turn back to him.

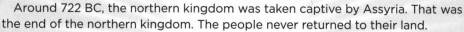

For You

If you mess up, don't worry. God gives second chances to his people. Just confess your sin to God, and continue to follow him.

Answer: b

The message of the LORD spoken through Jeremiah was fulfilled. The land finally enjoyed its Sabbath rest, lying desolate until the seventy years were fulfilled, just as the prophet had said. 2 Chronicles 36:21
(The Whole Story: 2 Chronicles 36:17-21)

June 9

Joy and Weeping

Q: What event caused people to both laugh and weep from joy?
a. seeing their homeland for the first time in 70 years
b. cleaning the rubble out of their houses and moving back in
c. seeing the foundation of the Temple being laid

The first group of captives to arrive back in their homeland after the Exile was led by Zerubbabel. They found Jerusalem in bad condition. King Nebuchadnezzar's men had burned down the Temple of God and torn down the city walls.

The first thing the people did was rebuild the altar so they could offer sacrifices to God. But they were afraid because while they were gone for 70 years, pagan people had moved into their land. The Jews were afraid of what the pagans might do when the Jews rebuilt the altar, but they did it anyway.

Then the people began the work of rebuilding the Temple. Masons and carpenters were needed for the building, and supplies had to be gathered. The workers started with the foundation. Once the foundation was laid, the priests put on their robes and blew their trumpets. Some of the people sang and praised God for the finished foundation. They shouted for joy. But many of the older men who'd seen the first Temple wept. The weeping was probably not for joy but because they longed for their old Temple, which had been more ornate and elaborate.

The people began rebuilding the Temple, which would be used for worshiping God, before they began rebuilding the wall, which would be used for protection. The people were putting God first and trusting him to protect them.

For You

The Jews had their priorities right in putting the things of God first. Are you careful to put God and what he wants for you ahead of what you want? Do you try to do what his Word says, even when it goes against what you want to do? If you do, God will be able to use you in great ways.

Answer: c
Many of the older priests, Levites, and other leaders who had seen the first Temple wept aloud when they saw the new Temple's foundation. The others, however, were shouting for joy. Ezra 3:12
(The Whole Story: Ezra 3)

The Temple Is Finished

Q: How long did it take to complete the Temple?
a. 5 years
b. 10 years
c. 20 years

Have you ever been excited about a project you were going to do? You started out strong, but your enthusiasm wore off, and you slowed down or stopped completely.

The Jews started out strong with their project of rebuilding the Temple, but they gave up on the project for many years before finally completing it. What happened?

After the Jews had been in exile for 70 years, King Cyrus allowed the people to return to Jerusalem to rebuild the Temple under the direction of Zerubbabel and Jeshua. Enemies living in the land tried to stop the work. First they volunteered to help with the rebuilding to keep an eye on how things progressed, but God wouldn't want pagans to help build God's Temple. So the Jews turned down their offer.

Next the enemies tried to discourage the people and make them afraid to continue building. Then there was a disagreement on whether or not the Jews had permission to rebuild.

The building project stopped for many years, but it was finally finished 20 years after it was first begun. You can read more about the obstacles and solutions in the book of Ezra.

For You

There will always be obstacles when you're trying to do things for the Lord. The important thing is to seek the Lord and see if he really wants you to do the project. If the answer is yes, push on and ask for God's help and the help of stronger Christians in completing the task.

Answer: c
The Temple was finally finished, as had been commanded by the God of Israel and decreed by Cyrus, Darius, and Artaxerxes, the kings of Persia. The Temple was completed on March 12, during the sixth year of King Darius's reign.
Ezra 6:14-15
(The Whole Story: Ezra 3–6)

June 11

More Rebuilding

Q: The book of Ezra tells about the rebuilding of the Temple, and the book of Nehemiah tells about the rebuilding of the
a. walls.
b. houses.
c. town center.

When the Babylonians took the people in Judah captive, they destroyed the Temple and the walls in Jerusalem. They also moved some of their own people into Judah. So when the Jews came back to Jerusalem to rebuild their Temple and walls, the Babylonians who'd lived there for 70 years caused a lot of problems (see yesterday's devotion). Yet, both the Temple and the walls were rebuilt with God's help.

Walls, such as the Great Wall of China or the Berlin Wall, are built to establish borders and to provide protection. Sometimes walls, like the Vietnam Veterans Memorial Wall, are built as a memorial or as art. The walls of Jerusalem were originally built to protect it from invasion.

The book of Nehemiah in the Bible focuses on the rebuilding of the walls around Jerusalem. Nehemiah heard that the walls of Jerusalem were in need of repair. He felt burdened to get the walls rebuilt, so he talked to the king of Persia and got permission to do so. Nehemiah left an important job serving the king of Persia to go to Jerusalem to be in charge of the wall-rebuilding project.

There were obstacles in rebuilding the wall of Jerusalem just as there were with the rebuilding of the Temple, but Nehemiah stood firm in his belief that God wanted him to rebuild the walls, and he succeeded.

For You

When you are sure God wants you to do something for him, stand firm. Don't let others talk you out of what you know God wants you to do. But do listen to your parents and spiritual leaders, because God uses them to help you know what his plan for you is.

Answer: a
I told them about how the gracious hand of God had been on me, and about my conversation with the king. They replied at once, "Yes, let's rebuild the wall!" So they began the good work. Nehemiah 2:18
(The Whole Story: Nehemiah 1–2)

June 12

The Walls Are Rebuilt

Q: How long did it take to rebuild the city walls?
a. 52 months
b. 52 weeks
c. 52 days

After the Exile, the Jews returned to Jerusalem to rebuild the Temple and the walls. It took 20 years to finish rebuilding the Temple, so just how long did it take to rebuild the walls? A lot less time than that! Nehemiah did several things that made the building project go more quickly than the rebuilding of the Temple. Here's how it happened.

Nehemiah served King Artaxerxes of Persia as the person who brought the wine to ensure no one poisoned the king. When Nehemiah heard that the walls were in bad shape and needed to be rebuilt, the king noticed that he was sad and learned it was because of the broken-down wall in Jerusalem. Nehemiah asked the king for permission to go and rebuild the wall.

Upon receiving a royal letter giving him permission to rebuild the wall, Nehemiah went to Jerusalem and organized the builders so that each had a specific place to work on the wall. Of course there were people who tried to stop the work by ridiculing, threatening, and insulting the men who were working on the wall. The workers became discouraged and fearful, but Nehemiah was a man of prayer, and that gave him the strength to push on.

Nehemiah encouraged his workers, and he also put men on guard duty. He confronted some of the troublemakers face-to-face. Nehemiah stood firm against those who tried to stop the work, and the walls were finished in only 52 days!

For You

Nehemiah was a successful worker and leader. He prayed over the task at hand, but he didn't stop there. He planned his work, and he kept working even in the face of discouragement. Prayer is the starting place, but planning and pushing on are important too. You will accomplish little of importance without perseverance.

Answer: c
On October 2 the wall was finished—just fifty-two days after we had begun. When our enemies and the surrounding nations heard about it, they were frightened and humiliated. They realized this work had been done with the help of our God. Nehemiah 6:15-16
(The Whole Story: Nehemiah 1–6)

June 13

The Queen Is Banished

Q: Who lost her position as queen because she refused to show off her beauty to her partying husband and his friends?
a. Queen Esther
b. Queen Vashti
c. Queen Elizabeth

Esther is a book full of drama and stories. Some people have even questioned whether it really belongs in the Bible, because the book never mentions God's name. But if you read the book of Esther, you can't miss seeing God working in the events that take place.

The book starts with King Xerxes, also called Ahasuerus, throwing a six-month-long feast. The king decided he wanted to show off his wife. So he called for his servants to bring Queen Vashti to the banquet hall to show off her beauty.

Queen Vashti didn't want to be shown off before a bunch of partying men, so she refused to go. The king was angry, and he asked his advisers what should be done. The advisers told the king that if Queen Vashti got away with refusing him, soon all the wives in the land would treat their husbands with disrespect. They said that Queen Vashti must be banished and never allowed back in the palace.

The king listened to his advisers and decreed that Queen Vashti would be banished from the palace. Later the king started thinking about Vashti and was sorry he'd made the decree. His men decided he needed a new queen, and they began searching for a replacement.

Vashti was a woman of honor and dignity. She knew it was wrong for her to parade her beauty among the men, and she refused, despite the personal cost. But while the king and his advisers were angry with her, it's likely that the women looked up to her for her courage.

For You

Vashti stood up for herself to preserve her honor and dignity despite the consequences. She lost her wealth and position, but she kept her dignity and the respect of others. Do you make the same kind of choices in the situations you face today?

Answer: b
When they conveyed the king's order to Queen Vashti, she refused to come. This made the king furious, and he burned with anger. Esther 1:12
(The Whole Story: Esther 1:1–2:2)

June 14

A New Queen

Q: How did the king pick a new queen?
a. by beauty
b. by royal birth
c. by godly characteristics

As we read about in yesterday's devotion, King Xerxes banished Queen Vashti from the palace forever for refusing to appear before his friends to show off her beauty. The king later regretted it, so his personal attendants decided to find a new queen for him.

How would you choose a new queen? Perhaps you'd look for someone who was kind and friendly. Or maybe you'd look for someone who was brave and strong. You might choose someone with royalty in her background. Here's how the king's personal attendants suggested the king choose his new queen: "Let us search the empire to find beautiful young virgins for the king. Hegai, the king's eunuch in charge of the harem, will see that they are all given beauty treatments. After that, the young woman who most pleases the king will be made queen instead of Vashti."

The king's men gathered the most beautiful, young, unmarried women in the land. These women received beauty treatments, and then went to show off their beauty before the king—the same king who ordered Vashti to show off her beauty for his partying friends.

Despite the king's decision to choose a queen based on beauty and appeal, God already had a plan in place to have Esther chosen as queen and for her to be in the right place at the right time to help the Jews, which you can read about in the June 17 devotion.

For You

Rather than choose a queen by her character traits or abilities, the king chose her for her beauty. The same thing happens today. You rarely see an ugly boy or girl on the cover of a magazine. But God judges the heart and motives. Be careful to respond to people based on those things, too, not only on outward appearance.

Answer: a
His personal attendants suggested, "Let us search the empire to find beautiful young virgins for the king." Esther 2:2
(The Whole Story: Esther 2:1-20)

June 15

Haman's Pride

Q: Why did Haman want revenge on Mordecai?
a. Mordecai was better looking.
b. Mordecai had more money.
c. Mordecai wouldn't bow before Haman.

The Holocaust, which took millions of Jewish lives during World War II, is an event you've probably studied in history. But this wasn't the first time someone wanted to kill Jews. The book of Esther tells the story of Haman, a man who planned to rid Persia of all the Jews.

Esther and her cousin Mordecai were both Jews. When King Xerxes met Esther, he chose her to be his queen, not knowing she was Jewish. Jews in the kingdom weren't uncommon since they'd been brought there in exile, and some families stayed even after they were free to leave.

Haman was a powerful official above all the other nobles in the kingdom. The nobles would bow to him out of respect when he passed by, just as the king had commanded. But Mordecai, an official in the kingdom, refused to bow to Haman. That made Haman angry. He found out that Mordecai was a Jew and formed a horrible plan. He wouldn't just get rid of Mordecai; he'd get rid of all the Jews. You'll read more about that in the next devotion.

Mordecai wasn't against showing respect to leaders, but he would not bow to Haman because Haman's people, the Agagites, were old enemies of the Jews. Haman hated God's people and their dedication to God. Haman considered himself better than the Jews, and that led to his downfall.

For You
There will always be people opposed to God and his followers. That doesn't catch God by surprise. In the book of Esther, he already had a Jewish queen in place to help her people before the problems began. How do you think God wants you to help others who are being persecuted?

Answer: c
[The palace officials] spoke to [Mordecai] day after day, but still he refused to comply with the order. So they spoke to Haman about this to see if he would tolerate Mordecai's conduct, since Mordecai had told them he was a Jew. When Haman saw that Mordecai would not bow down or show him respect, he was filled with rage. Esther 3:4-5
(The Whole Story: Esther 3:1-6)

Mordecai Is Honored

Q: Mordecai was honored for
a. exposing a plot to kill the king.
b. getting rid of Haman.
c. being the richest man in the land.

One day Mordecai, an official in the Persian kingdom, was sitting at the king's gate. He heard two of the king's guards angrily plotting to kill the king. Mordecai told his cousin Esther, who warned the king. The two guards were killed, but Mordecai was never rewarded.

One night the king was unable to sleep, so he decided to look back at the history of his reign. His servant read to him how Mordecai had uncovered the guards' plot to kill the king. The king found out Mordecai hadn't been rewarded. Shortly after that, Haman was on his way to ask the king for permission to kill Mordecai. The king asked Haman, "What should I do to honor a man who truly pleases me?"

Haman assumed it was himself the king wanted to honor. He told the king that the man should wear the king's robe and be led around on the king's horse with a person leading the horse and shouting, "This is what the king does for someone he wishes to honor!"

Imagine Haman's surprise when the king said, "Excellent! Quick! Take the robes and my horse, and do just as you have said for Mordecai the Jew, who sits at the gate of the palace. Leave out nothing you have suggested!"

Haman had no choice but to do what the king had said. Afterward, Mordecai went back to his position, and Haman went home totally humiliated.

For You

It's okay to be proud of your accomplishments, but it's also good to have a realistic picture of who you are. Rejoice more in who you are in the Lord—a child of the heavenly Father and a unique creation of his—rather than in what you've accomplished.

Answer: a
In those records he discovered an account of how Mordecai had exposed the plot of Bigthana and Teresh, two of the eunuchs who guarded the door to the king's private quarters. They had plotted to assassinate King Xerxes. Esther 6:2
(The Whole Story: Esther 6)

Esther's Courage

Q: Where was Haman when Esther revealed Haman's plot against the Jews?
a. hiding at home
b at a banquet given by Esther
c. at Mordecai's house

Haman, a very powerful official in Persia, had started a plan to get rid of all the Jews. He had told King Xerxes that the Jews kept themselves apart from other people and refused to follow the king's laws. He said the Jews should be killed.

The king believed Haman and decreed the Jews would be killed on a certain day. Mordecai learned of the plot against the Jews and talked to Esther. He told her she must go talk to the king even though she could be killed for approaching him without being summoned. Mordecai told her, "Who knows if perhaps you were made queen for just such a time as this?" He was telling her that maybe God's whole plan in her being queen was so that she could save her people, the Jews.

Esther went to the king, and he welcomed her and asked her what she wanted. Esther invited the king and Haman to a banquet she would prepare just for them.

The king and Haman arrived and dined. The king asked her again what she wanted, and she invited them to a second banquet. It was at that banquet that Esther told the king about Haman's plot against the Jews. Haman was killed, and although the decree to kill the Jews couldn't be taken back, the Jews were allowed to defend themselves. When the time came, the Jews were ready, and with God on their side, they were victorious over their enemies.

For You

Esther asked the Jews to fast and pray for three days before she approached the king. Although you probably don't go without food or drink when you need to make a decision, it is good to spend time in prayer when you have a choice to make. Allow God to speak to you through his Holy Spirit, his Word, and more mature Christians.

Answer: b
The king and Haman went to Queen Esther's banquet. . . . Esther [said], "This wicked Haman is our adversary and our enemy." Haman grew pale with fright before the king and queen. Esther 7:1, 6
(The Whole Story: Esther 3:8–5:8; 7)

Books of Poetry

June 18

Job Is Tested

Q: Job, a righteous man, lived in the land of
a. Uz.
b. Oz.
c. Nod.

An earthquake devastates a country. Families lose their homes after a flood. Children have nothing to eat because of a drought. Bad things happen in our world—and sometimes they don't make sense to those reading about or experiencing them. That was true for Job, an Old Testament follower of God. Job lived at the time of Abraham, even though the book of Job comes much later in the Bible.

Job was both righteous and wealthy. Satan went to God and told him Job was only faithful because God had always protected and blessed him. So God allowed Satan to test Job by taking his worldly goods—his donkeys, oxen, sheep, servants, camels, and even his children—through a series of disasters. Satan must have been very disappointed when Job said, "I came naked from my mother's womb, and I will be naked when I leave. The Lord gave me what I had, and the Lord has taken it away. Praise the name of the Lord!"

After that God allowed Satan to test Job further by afflicting him with sores from head to toe. Job was so miserable that he took a piece of pottery and scraped himself with it. He must have wondered what he'd done wrong to cause him to lose everything and be covered in sores.

Job's wife said, "Are you still trying to maintain your integrity? Curse God and die."

But Job told her, "You talk like a foolish woman. Should we accept only good things from the hand of God and never anything bad?"

Even in the face of everything that had happened, Job's faith was steadfast. Even though he didn't understand why everything was happening to him, he accepted it.

For You

An often-asked question is, "Why do bad things happen to good people?" Unfortunately, we won't have a satisfactory answer to that this side of heaven. For now we can only say, like Job, "Should we accept only good things from the hand of God and never anything bad?"

Answer: a
There once was a man named Job who lived in the land of Uz. He was blameless—a man of complete integrity. He feared God and stayed away from evil. Job 1:1
(The Whole Story: Job 1–2)

June 19

Job's Friends

Q: How many friends came to sit with Job during his suffering?
a. none
b. 3
c. 10

When you have good news, you want someone to share it with. And when you're going through tough times, you want someone to listen to your concerns.

When Job's friends heard about all that had happened to him, they came to visit. They barely recognized him because of all he'd been through. At first Job's friends sat in silence with him to show their support. But then they told Job he must be suffering because of some sin he committed. They tried to get him to repent, and their empathy turned to judgment.

Sometimes God does allow bad things to happen to get our attention. And often when we sin, we do face consequences. If you cheat on a test and get caught, you will receive a zero for that test and face punishment from your parents. If you hang out with friends who love to break rules and cause trouble, you'll find yourself facing consequences from teachers and parents.

But when something bad happens to a person, it's not always because the person has done wrong. Bad things happen to innocent people. Job's three friends were accusing him of sin, but Job was not guilty. Everything that had happened to him was because Satan was testing him. Job gave in to despair for a while and wished he'd never been born, but he never turned his back on God.

For You
Job needed someone to care about what he was going through, but his friends judged him and made him feel worse. If you have a friend who's hurting, how can you offer encouragement and support?

Answer: b
When three of Job's friends heard of the tragedy he had suffered, they got together and traveled from their homes to comfort and console him. Their names were Eliphaz the Temanite, Bildad the Shuhite, and Zophar the Naamathite.
Job 2:11
(The Whole Story: Job 2:11-13 and 4:1-7, although much of the book of Job is dialogue between Job and his friends)

June 20

Job's Wealth Restored

Q: God's voice is like _____.
a. lightning
b. wind
c. thunder

God is almighty and powerful. Perhaps Job's acknowledgement of this is why he accepted what happened to him without turning his back on God. Although Job was discouraged, his faith held strong.

No one likes to suffer, and people handle suffering differently. Suffering makes some people turn their backs on God and become bitter and withdrawn. They believe it's unfair that they're going through a difficult time when their friends or family aren't. They refuse to take a close look at their lives and ask what they can learn from the situation.

Other people draw closer to God in order to claim his strength to get through hard times. They seek out help with their problems and use the difficult time to make changes in their lives or learn something from the pain. Once they've come through the suffering, they're ready to help others.

Even though Job suffered through no fault of his own, he was in the group of people who draw closer to God during hard times. After the time of testing was over, God gave Job double the herds he'd had before and new children. They didn't lessen the pain Job felt losing his first children, but Job knew he'd see his children again in heaven one day.

Following God leads to inner joy and peace, but it's not a guarantee of an easy life. Job went through great suffering, but he came out with his faith still strong.

For You

As long as we live in this imperfect world, people will suffer. Often God uses that to accomplish good, although we may not know at the time what good might come from the suffering. If we could understand God's ways, then he wouldn't be God. It's better to accept that we don't have all the answers and continue to trust.

Answer: c
Then comes the roaring of the thunder— the tremendous voice of his majesty. He does not restrain it when he speaks.   Job 37:4
(The Whole Story: Job 37–42)

June 21

Psalms

Q: How many psalms are there in the book of Psalms?
a. 50
b. 150
c. 500

The book of Psalms was like a hymnbook to the Jews long ago. Many of the psalms were written to be sung. David wrote more than half of the 150 psalms, but there were other authors too. Psalm 90 was written by Moses. Two psalms were written by Solomon, and other psalms were written by a group known as the sons of Korah, who were in charge of the singing in Israel. Asaph and King Hezekiah also wrote psalms.

Psalms is the longest book in the Bible and was written over a time span of one thousand years. Psalms shows us the deepest emotions of the authors, from joy to sorrow, from peace to despair.

Some of the psalms are called messianic psalms. That means they have a clear prophecy about Jesus in them. One example of this is Psalm 22. It says, "My enemies surround me like a pack of dogs; an evil gang closes in on me. They have pierced my hands and feet. I can count all my bones. My enemies stare at me and gloat. They divide my garments among themselves and throw dice for my clothing." These verses describe events from the Crucifixion, yet they were written hundreds of years before Jesus was born.

It's good to read the Psalms because they teach us how to worship God, how to offer our praise, and how to express our deepest feelings. The Psalms offer comfort, strength, and encouragement.

For You

The Psalms are very beneficial to you. Why not read a psalm a day at bedtime? Keep a journal about what each psalm says to you and how it helps you.

Answer: b
Search me, O God, and know my heart; test me and know my anxious thoughts. Point out anything in me that offends you, and lead me along the path of everlasting life. Psalm 139:23-24
(The Whole Story: Psalms 1–150)

June 22

Two Paths

Q: What is the godly person compared to in Psalm 1?
a. a deer longing for water
b. a fruit-bearing tree
c. freshly fallen snow

There is a well-known poem written by Robert Frost called "The Road Not Taken." In it, the traveler sees two roads and wants to travel them both. But of course he can't. He must choose only one. At the end he says, "I took the one less traveled by, and that has made all the difference."

There are two paths in life, the path of obedience to God and the path away from God. Psalm 1:1 says, "Oh, the joys of those who do not follow the advice of the wicked, or stand around with sinners, or join in with mockers."

You may have friends who try to get you to go against what God wants you to do. They may make fun of you or tell you you're too serious about life when you try to make right choices. You may be less popular with some kids because you don't go with the flow, but instead choose to stand out as someone who follows God's way.

Even though trying to obey God may make you less popular or less cool in some groups, you may find other friends who are serious about following God. And obeying God will give you inner joy and peace.

How can you know what God wants you to do? Stay in God's Word. Read it. Think about it. Live it. There are two paths—the one toward God and the one leading away from God. The one toward God is the only right choice.

For You

Do your closest friends encourage you to walk with God or go the wrong direction? Your real friends should build you up in your faith, not hinder you. And you can do the same for them.

Answer: b
They are like trees planted along the riverbank, bearing fruit each season. Their leaves never wither, and they prosper in all they do. Psalm 1:3
(The Whole Story: Psalm 1)

June 23

Displays of God's Greatness

Q: What does Psalm 19 say displays God's craftsmanship?
a. sun
b. stars
c. skies

Everywhere you look you see displays of God's greatness—
the ocean with its waves and tides; the sky with its sun, stars,
and moon; the earth with its mountains, valleys, rivers, and plains. All of these
things point to a wonderful creator who planned things far beyond our ability to
understand.

Nature proclaims God's existence. It would be silly to think everything happened
by chance. Do the planets just happen to stay in orbit without crashing into each
other? Does the earth just happen to be the right distance from the sun to make it
possible to live here? Not likely.

The skies display God's craftsmanship. If you've ever stood outside and looked
at the sky filled with stars, you may have felt pretty small in comparison. That's
because God, who is far greater than we can imagine, hung the stars in place.
That might be how the psalmist was feeling when he penned Psalm 8, which
says, "When I look at the night sky and see the work of your fingers—the moon
and the stars you set in place—what are mere mortals that you should think
about them, human beings that you should care for them?"

Yet God does care about human beings. He knows each one of us personally,
and he cares about each trial or joy we have. It's amazing to think that the same
God who hung the sun, moon, and stars cares about our daily lives.

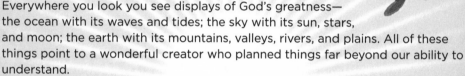

For You
If you have a chance, sit outside under the stars and read Psalms 8 and 19 (you
may need a flashlight). Consider the ways that God's power is displayed in
nature.

Answer: c
The heavens proclaim the glory of God. The skies display his craftsmanship.
Psalm 19:1
(The Whole Story: Psalm 19)

June 24

The Shepherd's Psalm

Q: In Psalm 23 the Lord is compared to a shepherd. Where does the shepherd lead us?
a. through mountains
b. beside peaceful streams
c. in the desert

David spent many years caring for sheep when he was growing up. He may have used this time to play his harp while keeping watch over his flock. Perhaps he composed some of the psalms as he spent hours alone with the sheep. The time alone gave him a chance to think about God, pray, and sing. Out of that background, he wrote Psalm 23, also known as the Shepherd's Psalm.

Jesus is called both the good shepherd and the great shepherd in the New Testament. Sheep need a shepherd. They depend on him to take them where there is food, as well as to guide and protect them. They follow the shepherd wherever he leads them because they trust him. In Psalm 23 David says that with God as his shepherd, he has everything he needs. The Lord leads him to where there are green pastures and calm waters.

God knows what we need and where to find it. He knows the path we should take to be safe and protected. When we listen to his voice and follow him, he'll guide us safely along the path.

For You

Are you following the Good Shepherd's leading? When you allow him to guide you, you'll find fulfillment and safety along life's journey.

Answer: b
He lets me rest in green meadows; he leads me beside peaceful streams.
Psalm 23:2
(The Whole Story: Psalm 23)

June 25

Confession

Q: David prayed that God would make him whiter than what?
a. snow
b. cotton
c. milk

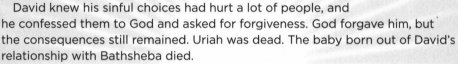

Psalm 51 is David's confession and plea for forgiveness. He had taken Bathsheba, who was already married, as his own. (You can read more about this story in 2 Samuel 11–12.) And then David had put her husband, Uriah, on the front line in battle so he'd be killed. David had committed two serious sins, and he was sorry he'd done them.

David knew his sinful choices had hurt a lot of people, and he confessed them to God and asked for forgiveness. God forgave him, but the consequences still remained. Uriah was dead. The baby born out of David's relationship with Bathsheba died.

It took a lot of courage and humility for David to confess his sins rather than make excuses for them or pretend it was okay for him to do those things because he was king. Sometimes we justify our sins rather than confess them. The problem with that is that sin results in guilt and in feeling far from God. The joy is gone. When David asked God to forgive his sins, he also asked him to "restore to me the joy of your salvation."

God wants you to feel close to him and experience his peace and joy. But if you continue in sin, that won't happen. When you turn from sin and confess it to him, he will restore the joy of your salvation just as he did for David.

For You
Read Psalm 51:7-10 aloud, and make it your prayer too.

Answer: a
Purify me from my sins, and I will be clean; wash me, and I will be whiter than snow. Oh, give me back my joy again; you have broken me—now let me rejoice. Don't keep looking at my sins. Remove the stain of my guilt. Create in me a clean heart, O God. Renew a loyal spirit within me. Psalm 51:7-10
(The Whole Story: Psalm 51)

June 26

From Fear to Faith

Q: Which psalm says God hides us under his wings?
a. Psalm 23
b. Psalm 91
c. Psalm 100

The Psalms give us a glimpse into the thoughts and feelings of their authors. We experience their joy in psalms such as Psalm 145 which begins, "I will exalt you, my God and King, and praise your name forever and ever. I will praise you every day; yes, I will praise you forever. Great is the LORD! He is most worthy of praise! No one can measure his greatness."

We experience the author's repentance in psalms such as Psalm 32 where David rejoices that God has forgiven his sins: "Finally, I confessed all my sins to you and stopped trying to hide my guilt. I said to myself, 'I will confess my rebellion to the LORD.' And you forgave me! All my guilt is gone."

We feel David's despair in psalms such as Psalm 13: "O LORD, how long will you forget me? Forever? How long will you look the other way? How long must I struggle with anguish in my soul, with sorrow in my heart every day? How long will my enemy have the upper hand?"

In Psalm 91, written by an unknown author, we share the author's feelings of protection and victory found in God: "The LORD says, "I will rescue those who love me. I will protect those who trust in my name. When they call on me, I will answer; I will be with them in trouble. I will rescue and honor them. I will reward them with a long life and give them my salvation."

The book of Psalms is filled with a variety of thoughts, emotions, and even history and prophecy. It chronicles the psalmists' journeys from fear and despair to faith and victory. The book of Psalms is a good place to turn when you need encouragement, courage, advice, or peace.

For You

The psalmists wrote what was in their hearts. Take a few minutes and write your own psalm expressing how you are feeling about life right now.

Answer: b
He will cover you with his feathers. He will shelter you with his wings. His faithful promises are your armor and protection. Psalm 91:4
(The Whole Story: Psalm 91)

June 27

A Psalm of Thanksgiving

Q: Fill in the missing words: "Enter his gates with _____; go into his courts with _____. Give _____to him and praise his name."
a. offerings, sacrifices, tribute
b. thanksgiving, praise, thanks
c. praise, joy, thanks

What gets you really excited? Is it watching a good football game on television with your dad? Is it scoring a goal for your team in your Saturday morning soccer game? Is it getting a perfect test score in math? Different things cause different people to become excited.

Psalm 100 calls us to have the same kind of excitement and enthusiasm in worshiping God. That doesn't mean standing up and cheering for God during a church service like you would cheer for a home run during a baseball game, although that would certainly show enthusiasm. It means being excited about the chance to worship the very God who created you and everything around you.

Psalm 100:1-2 says, "Shout with joy to the LORD, all the earth! Worship the LORD with gladness. Come before him, singing with joy." God wants us to be joyful about spending time with him. He wants us to "enter his gates with thanksgiving; go into his courts with praise. Give thanks to him and praise his name." How can you do that? By making time each day to spend with him. By singing and praying enthusiastically. And by attending Sunday school and church willingly and cheerfully rather than grumbling about how early you have to get up or what you have to wear.

Psalm 100 is a short psalm having only five verses, but those verses have a lot to say about joyfully worshiping God.

For You

Why should you worship God joyfully? (Hint: Today's verse has the answer.)

Answer: b
For the LORD is good. His unfailing love continues forever, and his faithfulness continues to each generation. Psalm 100:5
(The Whole Story: Psalm 100)

June 28

Memorizing Scripture

Q: Complete the verse: "I have hidden your word in my heart _____."
a. so I will not forget it
b. so I can praise your name
c. that I might not sin against you

In the movie *Akeelah and the Bee*, 11-year-old Akeelah overcomes many obstacles as she advances to the National Spelling Bee. Along the way, Akeelah, who has to learn to spell thousands of difficult words, finds that she can learn them best when she jumps rope while spelling them.

Akeelah's technique in the movie works for her because she learns by using her body and movement. Some people learn by hearing and repeating things aloud, and others learn by seeing them.

Scripture memory is very important. When you memorize Scripture and think about what the verses say, they help you overcome temptation, guide you in sharing your faith with others, encourage you during difficult times, and allow you to learn more about God. Having Scripture in your heart and mind helps you focus on God and become more like Jesus.

Perhaps memorizing Scripture is hard for you. If that's true, find a way to memorize that works for you. You might find that Akeelah's trick of jumping rope helps you. Say a word each time you jump over the rope. Or bounce a basketball and say one word per bounce. Maybe singing the words or rapping them is what will work for you. Or try writing out the verse. Erase a word and say the verse. Erase a second word and say it again. Repeat this until all the words are erased and you have the verse memorized.

For You
Pick three verses from the Psalms to memorize. Try a different way of memorizing each verse and find out which works best for you. If you aren't sure what to memorize, try three of these: Psalm 19:14; Psalm 119:9; Psalm 119:105; Psalm 139:14; or Psalm 139:23-24.

Answer: c
I have hidden your word in my heart, that I might not sin against you.   Psalm 119:11
(The Whole Story: Psalm 119:1-16)

June 29

Proverbs

Q: One of the purposes of the book of Proverbs is
a. to help the readers do what is right, just, and fair.
b. to help the readers become rich and successful.
c. to help the readers become teachers.

When you buy something new, you normally get a user's or owner's manual. Buy an electronic game system, and you get a book that shows you how to hook up the system so you can see the games on screen. It shows you how to load the games. Each individual game comes with a manual too.

Did you ever wish there was a manual for life? It could tell you how to make right choices; get correct answers; deal with parents, siblings, and friends; pass math; avoid trouble; and succeed in life. God has actually given you a manual like that. It's the book of Proverbs, and it's your guide for successful living.

If you've read the May 12 devotion, you might remember when God asked Solomon, David's son and the third king of the nation of Israel, what he wanted. Solomon said he wanted an understanding heart to rule the people well and to tell right from wrong (see 1 Kings 3:9). God granted him that, and Solomon passed on some of his wisdom in the book of Proverbs. It's a book of practical advice for successful living.

The book of Proverbs begins by giving the purpose: "to teach people wisdom and discipline, to help them understand the insights of the wise. Their purpose is to teach people to live disciplined and successful lives, to help them do what is right, just, and fair. These proverbs will give insight to the simple, knowledge and discernment to the young." The book of Proverbs is a book worth reading.

For You
If you've never read the book of Proverbs, consider reading at least two or three verses a day. Some may not apply to you, but many will.

Answer: a
These are the proverbs. . . . Their purpose is to teach people to live disciplined and successful lives, to help them do what is right, just, and fair. Proverbs 1:1, 3
(The Whole Story: Proverbs 1:1-7)

June 30

Seeking God

Q: When you seek God's will in all you do, he will
a. grant you success.
b. answer your prayers.
c. show you which path to take.

Have you ever had to trust someone? A school class did a project where one student was blindfolded and a partner wasn't. The partner who could see was responsible to lead the blindfolded partner around the school. This was to teach what it felt like to be blind. But it also taught trust. The sightless partner had to trust the other partner to get him or her safely from room to room.

Proverbs 3:5 says to "trust in the LORD with all your heart." If you know God well, you'll feel confident trusting God in all areas of life because you'll feel his presence and know he's looking out for you. When you trust him, you learn that God is better able to lead you than you are when you choose your own way.

That doesn't mean God didn't give you the ability to reason and make decisions, but that he wants you to talk to him about these decisions and to use the Bible as your guide.

What happens when you trust God and seek his will in all you do? He'll show you which path to take. Just as we need a map to guide us down unfamiliar roads, we need God's guidance and his Word to guide us through life.

For You

Try playing the blindfold game. Blindfold yourself and have someone lead you around your house and your neighborhood. Then decide, did you trust your partner? How did your trust or lack of trust of your partner affect your willingness to be guided by him or her? Remember that you can always trust God to lead you down the right path.

Answer: c
Seek [the Lord's] will in all you do, and he will show you which path to take.
Proverbs 3:6
(The Whole Story: Proverbs 3)

The Wellspring of Life

Q: What determines the course of your life?
a. your choices
b. your knowledge
c. your heart

Imagine this. You live in a village in a poor country where you must get water from a stream for cooking and drinking. The water flows down to your village, but by the time it gets there, it's muddy and polluted. You try to strain the water or boil it to make it usable, but it's not much use. The water is too contaminated.

Finally one day you decide to walk upstream to find out why the water is so dirty. You journey until you reach a natural well that is the source of the water. You find that the well is full of trash because people are throwing their garbage into the water.

It's a lot of work, but you clean out the well. Then you have to decide how to keep it from becoming impure again. Will you build a fence around it? Station a guard nearby? You know if you don't protect the well, trash will be thrown into the stream and pollute the water you and your village depend on.

The Bible says, "Above all else, guard your heart, for it is the wellspring of life" (Proverbs 4:23, NIV). What you feed your heart determines what your life is like. If you feed it bad words, disrespectful talk, or bad pictures, those will take over your mind and your actions. Your life will become polluted. The only way to prevent that from happening is to carefully guard what you see and what you hear.

What should you fill your heart with? Philippians 4:8 says, "And now, dear brothers and sisters, one final thing. Fix your thoughts on what is true, and honorable, and right, and pure, and lovely, and admirable. Think about things that are excellent and worthy of praise."

- -

For You

What are you filling your heart with? If you fill it with good things, those things will help direct you down the right path, and your life will be pollution free.

- -

Answer: c
Guard your heart above all else, for it determines the course of your life.
Proverbs 4:23
(The Whole Story: Proverbs 4)

July 2

Learn from It

Q: What animal should the lazy person learn from?
a. an ant
b. a sparrow
c. a lion

God has created many amazing animals that we can learn from. One of the smallest creatures teaches us many lessons. That animal is the ant.

Did you know these fun facts about ants?

- The ant can lift at least 20 times its own weight.
- Ants live in colonies.
- Each ant has a specific purpose or job.
- Ants work together and may even train others to do their job.
- When an ant finds a food source, it leaves a scent trail so other ants can find it.
- The average life span of an ant is 45 to 60 days.
- When ants fight, they fight to the death.

So what can you learn from the ant?

Each of us has a job, and we all need to do our job in order to keep things running smoothly. If you neglect doing your chores at home or you don't do your part of the group project at school, you might run into trouble.

Working together gets things done more efficiently. Everyone has different strengths, so working together just makes sense.

Being a good example for others is a beneficial use of your time. You might be just the encourager and motivator someone else needs to start moving the right direction.

It's wise to pass on useful information. That keeps others from making unnecessary mistakes or doing unneeded work.

Life is short—make it count. What's done for Jesus is what really matters.

Choose your battles carefully. Is it really worth fighting over? Your faith and values are worth defending, but it's sometimes best to just let the little stuff go.

For You

What lesson from ants could help improve your life? Put one into action today.

Answer: a

Take a lesson from the ants, you lazybones. Learn from their ways and become wise! Proverbs 6:6

(The Whole Story: Proverbs 6)

July 3

Walk with Integrity

Q: Complete the proverb: "People with integrity walk safely, but those who follow crooked paths _____."
a. will be defeated
b. will slip and fall
c. will be harmed

Jasmine's school gives out awards each quarter. Each letter in her school's motto, Bobcat Pride, stands for a character trait students should have. Jasmine won the "I for Integrity" award. But she was confused. She didn't know what integrity was, so she had no idea why she'd won the award. When Jasmine looked up the word in the dictionary, she read that *integrity* is "complete honesty, following a strict moral code."

Jasmine learned that integrity means always doing the right thing even if no one else is watching. Jasmine's teacher said she appreciated Jasmine's honesty and knew she could trust Jasmine even if she, the teacher, stepped out of the classroom for a minute.

The book of Proverbs talks about integrity too. People of integrity walk boldly because they know they're doing the right thing. They have God's blessing and protection. This doesn't mean that nothing bad will ever happen to honest people. As can be seen in the book of Job, bad things do happen to good people. But people with integrity will miss out on the trouble that's caused by being dishonest or deceitful. They stand firm against temptation to do wrong.

People who lack integrity walk their own paths, following their own desires and rules. Proverbs says they will slip and fall. How much better it is to walk in safety!

For You

You might be honest when people are watching you, but what about when they aren't? Be a person of integrity and do the honest and right thing even if no one else would know the difference. God and you always know.

Answer: b
People with integrity walk safely, but those who follow crooked paths will slip and fall. Proverbs 10:9
(The Whole Story: Proverbs 10)

July 4

Getting Ahead in Life

Q: According to Proverbs, who has plenty of food?
a. a hard worker
b. a thief
c. a rich man

Mark is a high school student who says he wants to get a job and save for college. Really, he'd rather have his parents pay his way, but they insist he earn at least half of the money himself. Mark complains he can't find a part-time job. But when people tell him about one, he complains that he has too much homework or the boss is too hard to work for. Sometimes he just doesn't show up for work. Mark hopes his parents will give in and pay his way.

Today's verse from Proverbs says a person should have a good job working diligently day after day to earn a living. This is written to adults, but the verse also has meaning for you now. Your work is to get the best education you can. God wants you to listen in class, write your papers, study for tests, and learn all you can. But there are ways to be lazy. You could cut and paste information from the Internet for your report rather than writing it yourself. You could talk people into giving you the answer to the math assignment by making them feel sorry for you. You could let others do all the work on group projects. But none of these things would lead to success. None of them would give you joy or allow you to be proud of what you've accomplished. Do your best at all you do, and you will be successful in God's eyes.

For You

If you've gotten into the habit of being lazy in your work, stop now. When the new school year begins, do the best you can on every assignment no matter how small, and hard work will soon become a habit. The reward will be knowing you did your best—and a report card to be proud of.

Answer: a
A hard worker has plenty of food, but a person who chases fantasies has no sense. Proverbs 12:11
(The Whole Story: Proverbs 12)

July 5

Think First

Q: According to Proverbs 13, what can ruin everything?
a. cheating to get ahead
b. opening your mouth
c. stealing from a neighbor

Have you ever been told to think before you speak? If you have, it was probably because you had said something that wasn't entirely appropriate or useful. Thinking before you speak is a good habit to learn.

When you stop and think before saying something, ask yourself if what you're about to say will build another person up or tear the person down. Will it encourage or discourage? Does it show love and kindness to the other person?

Here are some of the things that should be eliminated:

- Gossiping—spreading rumors or negative information only hurts others.
- Cutting down—making fun of someone or tearing someone down with words causes deep wounds.
- Name-calling—calling others names never helps a situation. It only leads to hurt feelings.
- Lying—being dishonest to cover up a mistake or avoid punishment is always wrong.

What are some good uses of words?

- Explaining something to someone who doesn't understand
- Encouraging someone who is feeling down
- Cheering on a teammate, friend, or even someone you don't like very well
- Praising someone for a good deed or job well done
- Praying for a friend or family member
- Praising God for who he is
- Thanking someone for what he or she did for you

There are both good and bad ways to use words. Choose the good today.

For You

How do you use your words? Take time today to think about how you can use your words for good.

Answer: b
Those who control their tongue will have a long life; opening your mouth can ruin everything. Proverbs 13:3
(The Whole Story: Proverbs 13)

July 6

Foolishness

Q: According to the proverb, who does foolish things?
a. a child
b. a dreamer
c. a short-tempered person

Sean is a good basketball player, but no one wants to play with him. Why not? His anger flares quickly, and no one is safe from his temper. If he's fouled, he'll charge the offending player or yell at him. If Sean fouls someone else, his temper flares at the player for being in the way.

Even though Sean is a talented player, the coach dismissed him from the team. In fits of rage, Sean had thrown the ball into the bleachers, thrown his water bottle at another player, and cursed at and even pushed another player to the ground and kicked him. His temper cost the team the game more than once.

According to Proverbs, a short-tempered person does foolish things. That's easy to see. Many people are harmed physically or emotionally because of someone's temper. But James 1:19 says, "Understand this, my dear brothers and sisters: You must all be quick to listen, slow to speak, and slow to get angry."

Anger *reacts*. But wisdom *acts*. Foolish people let their tempers flare and do things they will be ashamed of later. Godly people are slow to get angry. They look at the situation, think it through, and then do the right thing.

For You

Are you the foolish person who acts in anger or the wise one who thinks things through and then acts? If anger is a problem for you, talk to a trusted adult about how to get it under control.

Answer: c
Short-tempered people do foolish things, and schemers are hated. Proverbs 14:17
(The Whole Story: Proverbs 14)

July 7

Defusing Anger

Q: What turns away anger?
a. a gentle answer
b. a man with many friends
c. doing good

Have you ever tried to argue in a pleasant tone of voice? Probably not. When you argue, you use a harsh or loud voice. There is usually a lot of anger. For example, imagine you get home and find your bicycle knocked over in the driveway when you know you left it propped up. Your brother is nearby.

"You knocked my bike over. Pick it up."

"You pick it up. You left it right in my way."

"You always leave your junk lying around. Pick my bike up or I'll . . ."

The situation quickly turns into a fight. Voices are raised. Threats and put-downs are made.

Want to know the best way to ruin an argument? Give a pleasant answer, or as the Bible says, "a gentle answer." Occasionally you will run into someone who is so determined to fight that nothing helps, but with most of your friends, you'll find it works. Next time someone speaks to you in an angry voice, try it. Instead of yelling back or making a threat or accusation, respond in a calm voice with a comment:

- "How can I help you with this?"
- "What do you need me to do?"
- "It sounds like you've had a bad day."
- "Let's talk about it."

You may not feel like giving a pleasant answer, but someone has to be the peacemaker. Let it be you.

For You

Use kind words to defuse anger. When you do that, you are modeling Jesus' love for others.

Answer: a
A gentle answer deflects anger, but harsh words make tempers flare.
Proverbs 15:1
(The Whole Story: Proverbs 15)

July 8

Examination

Q: Complete the proverb: "People may be pure in their own eyes, but the LORD examines their _____."
a. hearts
b. thoughts
c. motives

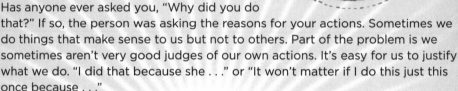

Has anyone ever asked you, "Why did you do that?" If so, the person was asking the reasons for your actions. Sometimes we do things that make sense to us but not to others. Part of the problem is we sometimes aren't very good judges of our own actions. It's easy for us to justify what we do. "I did that because she . . ." or "It won't matter if I do this just this once because . . ."

Today's proverb says people might think they are right, but God examines their motives. A motive is your reason for doing something. In fact, you can do something good but do it for all the wrong reasons. This happens a lot at church. You might memorize Bible verses, which is a good thing. But you might only do it to win a prize your Sunday school teacher offered for learning those verses. Or you might help clean up a mess in the youth room, which is a good thing. But you only do it so others will notice how helpful you are. You may befriend the new girl, which is a good thing. But you only do it because you know the youth pastor is watching and will say good things about you to your parents.

What should your motive be? There are two verses that answer that question. Colossians 3:23 says, "Work willingly at whatever you do, as though you were working for the Lord rather than for people." Do everything you do for God, not for attention or because you have to.

The Bible also says, "Whether you eat or drink, or whatever you do, do it all for the glory of God" (1 Corinthians 10:31). Make sure that you seek to glorify God in all you do.

If you keep these two verses in mind, then you can always have the right motive.

For You

Before you act, stop and examine your motives. Are you doing it for the Lord? Are you doing it to glorify God? It's easy to justify the things you do, but God knows the reason behind your actions.

Answer: c
People may be pure in their own eyes, but the LORD examines their motives.
Proverbs 16:2
(The Whole Story: Proverbs 16)

July 9

A True Friend

Q: Which describes a real friend?
a. someone who can bear a crushed spirit
b. someone who is the first to speak up
c. someone who sticks closer than a brother

In the movie *The Voyage of the Dawn Treader*, based on one of the books in the Chronicles of Narnia series, Edmund and Lucy are transported to the Narnian ship the *Dawn Treader* through a painting of the ship. Along with them is their annoying cousin Eustace, who doesn't believe in Narnia or magic.

Eustace sulks over his fate, causing the crew to ignore or dislike him. Eustace takes an instant dislike to Reepicheep, a large talking mouse. However, when Eustace is turned into a dragon, it is Reepicheep who stays with him night and day, encouraging him. Through his interactions with Reepicheep, Eustace becomes a much more likable person. The two remain friends once Eustace is human again, and there is sadness as they part at the end of the movie.

Reepicheep demonstrates the traits of a true friend. He remains loyal during hard and trying times. He is an encourager, and he spurs Eustace to greater heights. Reepicheep sees the good in Eustace and believes in him.

Since you can't have a talking mouse as your best friend, you'll have to find a human who, like Reepicheep, is loyal, is an encourager, and believes the best of you. And even more importantly, you can be that kind of friend to someone else.

For You

Human friends will fail you, but Jesus never will. Make him your best friend, because he loves you more than anyone on earth is capable of loving you. You can talk to him and share your good times and bad just as you would with any friend.

Answer: c
There are "friends" who destroy each other, but a real friend sticks closer than a brother. Proverbs 18:24
(The Whole Story: Proverbs 18)

July 10

Lending to the Lord

Q: Fill in the blanks: "If you ____ ____ ____, you are lending to the LORD—and he will repay you."
a. give your tithe
b. give your offering
c. help the poor

Have you ever loaned something to someone and not gotten it back? Maybe you let your friend borrow your baseball mitt, and he lost it. Or you lent your sister two dollars when she forgot her lunch, and she never paid you back. Thankfully God is much better at paying back what you loan him.

Today's verse says if you help the poor, you are lending to the Lord. It's just as if you were doing it for the Lord himself. And he will repay you. Here's what Jesus said: "I was hungry, and you fed me. I was thirsty, and you gave me a drink. I was a stranger, and you invited me into your home. I was naked, and you gave me clothing. I was sick, and you cared for me. I was in prison, and you visited me. . . . I tell you the truth, when you did it to one of the least of these my brothers and sisters, you were doing it to me!" (Matthew 25:35-36, 40).

Sometimes it's easy to look down on the poor, and that was true in Bible times, too. Jesus told the people that when they did these acts of mercy and kindness unselfishly for the poor or sick, it was as though they did it for him.

For You

You can do simple acts of kindness and mercy for the poor around you. But if these things are done with wrong motives, they don't count. What is the right motive for helping others? Read 1 Corinthians 13 to find out. Then talk to your parents about one thing you can do to help the poor in your town.

Answer: c
If you help the poor, you are lending to the LORD—and he will repay you!
Proverbs 19:17
(The Whole Story: Proverbs 19)

Beauty Is More Than Skin Deep

Q: What makes a person attractive?
a. loyalty
b. beauty
c. charm

If you go shopping with your mom or dad, you might notice the magazines in the rack near the checkout line. Some feature news about television and movie stars. Others have outrageous claims such as alien babies being born. A few magazines are about sports, and some magazines are for women or teenage girls, with models on the cover.

What makes people choose a certain model to put on the cover of a magazine? They choose a person whose looks will catch people's attention and cause them to notice the magazine and buy it.

What makes a person attractive according to today's proverb? It's not blue or brown eyes, shiny hair, or a pretty face. It's not a muscular build. It's loyalty.

What are you loyal to? You might be loyal to a certain sports team or player. You may be loyal to your school or church. You might be loyal to your best friend. These are okay as long as they build you up and help you seek to be a better person. But most of all, your loyalty should be with Jesus and your faith. When it is, people will see Jesus shining through you, and that will make you attractive.

For You

People often judge you by your physical appearance. Those with "perfect" teeth, hair, skin, face, and figure are noticed. But that's not how God judges you. Proverbs says loyalty makes a person attractive. In what ways do you show your loyalty to Jesus and your faith? How can you improve?

Answer: a
Loyalty makes a person attractive. It is better to be poor than dishonest.
Proverbs 19:22
(The Whole Story: Proverbs 19)

July 12

Honor

Q: What is a mark of honor?
a. avoiding a fight
b. ending a fight
c. being right

There is always someone looking for a fight. Every school has bullies who physically hurt others and people who want to fight just to fight. They feel they have something to prove. But a confident person doesn't feel the need to prove himself or herself to others by displaying physical strength or power.

Today's proverb says that avoiding a fight is a mark of honor. Winning a fight might prove you are tougher than the other person, but avoiding the fight makes you someone to look up to and worthy of respect.

It's not always easy to avoid either a verbal or physical fight. So how can you do it?

• Avoid known troublemakers. You don't have to fear them, but you can steer clear of the places they hang out.
• Stay calm and try to talk things out. If the bully is shouting and you are answering calmly and quietly, he or she is going to look silly.
• Walk away. Some people may take it as weakness, but others will recognize the strength in refusing to get pulled into a fight.
• Act with honor. Remind yourself of today's proverb. Be above engaging in a fight. Be the one other students can look up to for refusing to take part in fights and drama.

The second half of today's proverb says, "Only fools insist on quarreling." You can't change other people's behaviors, but you can control your reactions to them.

For You

Walk away from verbal or physical fights. Refuse to take part. If this is difficult, find a friend to stand with you, or talk to a trusted adult about the situation.

Answer: a
Avoiding a fight is a mark of honor; only fools insist on quarreling. Proverbs 20:3
(The Whole Story: Proverbs 20)

More Important Than Riches

Q: What should you choose over great riches?
a. a good education
b. a healthy body
c. a good reputation

Forbes magazine, a business magazine for adults, publishes a list of the 400 richest people in America. Each of those have a net worth in the billions, with Bill Gates topping the list at $66 billion. That means all his money, property, and investments added together, minus any debts, are in the billions.

The Bible says there is something you should want more than money and wealth. What is it? A good reputation. While your true character is who you really are, your reputation is how others see you or judge you based on what they see in your life.

The best thing is for people's true character and their reputation to match, but this isn't always the case. Sometimes people can appear to be honest, dependable, and caring, but it's all a show. Inside they are deceitful and selfish.

As a Christian, you should have both godly character and a good reputation. God is the true judge of your character, and he knows what you really are in your heart. But how others see you makes a difference too. If you tell others you are a Christian but have a reputation of being deceitful or of having a bad temper, people will not take your faith very seriously. Ask God to help you be a person of godly character and to let it shine through for others to see.

For You

Does your character as well as your reputation please God? If not, what changes do you need to make?

Answer: c
Choose a good reputation over great riches; being held in high esteem is better than silver or gold. Proverbs 22:1
(The Whole Story: Proverbs 22)

July 14

How Brave Are You?

Q: The godly are as bold as what?
a. a mighty soldier
b. a lion
c. a ruling king

Who is "king of the beasts"? The lion is, of course.
Lions are strong and courageous, with the exception of the lion in *The Wizard of Oz*, who goes to the Emerald City to ask the wizard for courage.

How do the godly become bold? By having confidence in God. "God has not given us a spirit of fear and timidity, but of power, love, and self-discipline" (2 Timothy 1:7).

In the New Testament, the apostle Paul was known for his boldness. First he was bold for wrong reasons, and he persecuted Christians. That was a wrong use of courage. The righteous are bold in the way they live because of God's strength and because they are doing the Lord's work.

After Jesus spoke to Paul on the road to Damascus, Paul was changed, and he became courageous in his witness for Christ even though he was beaten, stoned, chased out of cities, and arrested. Peter and John were bold witnesses too. Acts 4:13 says, "The members of the council were amazed when they saw the boldness of Peter and John, for they could see that they were ordinary men with no special training in the Scriptures. They also recognized them as men who had been with Jesus." They were bold because they had absolute confidence that what they were doing was right.

Are you courageous like Paul, Peter, and John were? God has given you that boldness. It's up to you to put it into practice.

For You

As a child of God, you can have courage instead of fear when facing new situations, unexpected circumstances, or the class bully. God's boldness doesn't make you act foolishly but gives you confidence as you grow in your faith day by day.

Answer: b
The wicked run away when no one is chasing them, but the godly are as bold as lions. Proverbs 28:1
(The Whole Story: Proverbs 28)

July 15

Small but Wise

Q: What four things does Proverbs 30 say are small but wise?
a. ants, bees, tadpoles, garter snakes
b. ants, wasps, locusts, hummingbirds
c. ants, hyraxes, locusts, lizards

The world is filled with amazing animals that showcase God's creativity. Proverbs 30 talks about four of them.

Ants. The ant, a hardworking creature, carries many times its own weight. It has an outer shell that protects it against the environment. As a Christian, you have protection against the environment too. God has given you spiritual armor. You can read about it in Ephesians 6.

Hyraxes. Also called rock rabbits, they inhabit the rocky terrain in Africa and the Middle East. They know the rocks will provide security for them. Psalm 18:2 says, "The LORD is my rock, my fortress, and my savior; my God is my rock, in whom I find protection." God is our rock and place of safety.

Locusts. By themselves, locusts are pretty insignificant, but together they make a big difference. God used locusts as one of the 10 plagues to convince Pharaoh to let the Israelites leave Egypt. Working together, the locusts were destructive. But when Christians work together, they can accomplish a lot of good for God.

Lizards. Lizards are persistent. It's important to stay persistent when doing God's work. We can find encouragement in these words in 1 Corinthians 15:58: "My dear brothers and sisters, be strong and immovable. Always work enthusiastically for the Lord, for you know that nothing you do for the Lord is ever useless."

There's a lot to learn from God's creation, and these four animals each teach an important lesson.

For You
Can you think of another animal that teaches a lesson? What is the animal, and what's the lesson?

Answer: c
There are four things on earth that are small but unusually wise: Ants—they aren't strong, but they store up food all summer. Hyraxes—they aren't powerful, but they make their homes among the rocks. Locusts—they have no king, but they march in formation. Lizards—they are easy to catch, but they are found even in kings' palaces. Proverbs 30:24-28
(The Whole Story: Proverbs 30)

July 16

What Matters Most?

Q: What does not last?
a. wisdom
b. beauty
c. love

Every year there are many beauty pageants. There's Miss America and Miss Universe as well as local and state beauty contests. Some of the pageants include displays of talent or questions for the contestants to answer, but without outward beauty, the contestants wouldn't be there.

What do you think the winners will look like 10, 20, or 30 years down the road? Chances are, their bodies won't be as firm, and their faces won't be wrinkle free. Physical beauty changes with the years. The young beauty is replaced by a more mature look—or else a lot of money is spent for procedures and products to keep the appearance of youth.

The good thing is that real beauty—inner beauty—doesn't fade. In fact, it becomes stronger. The things that happen in life shape who you are on the inside. The trials of life—money issues, the death of family members or friends, problems at school and work, health problems, challenges of moving—make some people bitter, but they cause others to draw closer to the Lord. People who allow God's Spirit to work in them during times of testing will grow in their faith and relationship to the Lord, and that is evident by a godly attitude and outlook on life. They develop inner beauty that shines through.

If you think you're off the hook because you're a boy reading this devotional, you're not. Men care about their looks, too, and they fight to look as muscular and fit as they did in their younger years. They see the passing of time in weathered skin and thinning hair. But just as with women, it's the inner character that counts.

For You

Good looks are temporary. Make sure you spend more time developing godly character through Bible reading, prayer, and serving God than you do on your outward appearance.

Answer: b
Charm is deceptive, and beauty does not last; but a woman who fears the Lord will be greatly praised. Proverbs 31:30
(The Whole Story: Proverbs 31)

July 17

Reruns

Q: What does the book of Ecclesiastes say repeats itself?
a. history
b. prophecy
c. a teacher

There are many quotes about history repeating itself, but the original one is found in Ecclesiastes. Solomon writes, "History merely repeats itself. It has all been done before. Nothing under the sun is truly new."

This verse isn't talking about the new technology that people invent, although those things were known all along to God. It's referring to life and the things in nature that repeat. The sun rises and sets just as it has done for thousands of years. The seasons repeat—winter, spring, summer, fall—year after year. Planets orbit, and the earth rotates. People are born, they live, and they die. But thank God, that's not the end. For Christians, death is the beginning of life in heaven.

There is also no new source of satisfaction in life. It's impossible to find happiness and fulfillment in different forms of pleasure. Solomon says, "I observed everything going on under the sun, and really, it is all meaningless—like chasing the wind." Buying more things, going more places, and trying new things are empty without God.

The one thing that gives meaning to life is a relationship with God. Video game systems and games, DVDs, televisions, smartphones, and other things only provide temporary happiness. They can be broken or stolen. The fun wears off. Friends may make you happy, but they can fail you. They may drop you for a new friend or hurt you. Jesus is the one you can count on to be with you all the time and to never change. That doesn't mean it's wrong to have fun things and friends to share them with. That's just not the true source of happiness. Look to God first, and the rest will fall into place.

For You

If you're feeling unhappy, make sure you are taking time to work on your personal relationship with God. It might be that other things have gotten in the way of that relationship.

Answer: a
History merely repeats itself. It has all been done before. Nothing under the sun is truly new. Ecclesiastes 1:9
(The Whole Story: Ecclesiastes 1)

July 18

The Right Time

Q: Fill in the blanks: "For everything there is a _____, a _____ for every activity under _____."
a. time, place, the sun
b. reason, meaning, God
c. season, time, heaven

God gave you a very special gift: time. You have 24 hours a day to use well. Some things happen at certain times—the sun rises in the morning and sets at night. The tide comes in and goes out according to schedule. The seasons change in a predictable way.

There are other things that you—or your parents—control, such as when you get up and when you go to bed, when you eat, when you watch television, when you do homework, when you use the computer, when you go to church, and so on.

Do you make the best use of your time? It's good to have some kind of plan for how you will spend your day or else you may find yourself spending too much of it playing video or computer games or just hanging out with friends talking.

There are lots of good things to do with those free minutes you have. You can surprise your parents or a neighbor by doing a job without being asked. You can start a new hobby such as model building, knitting, or drawing. You can practice your music or sports skills. You could read all the books written by your favorite author. Set aside time to read your Bible and a devotion book and to pray and journal about what God is showing you through his Word.

There are lots of good things to do with the gift of time God has given you. Plan how to use it well this week.

For You

While you're deciding how to use your time, try to spend at least fifteen minutes reading the Bible or listening to an audio version of it. Set aside time to help others and build relationships too. These things have more lasting value than time spent just having fun.

Answer: c
For everything there is a season, a time for every activity under heaven.
Ecclesiastes 3:1
(The Whole Story: Ecclesiastes 3:1-15)

July 19

Tough Stuff

Q: What is not easily broken?
a. a triple-braided cord
b. a new rope
c. iron

There is a fable about an old man who is ready to die. He calls his three sons together to give them some final advice. The sons often quarrel and can't seem to get along. The man knows that if the sons can't get along, they'll soon lose all the property and goods he'd worked hard to get.

The old man has his servant bring a bundle of sticks bound together. The old man gives each of his sons a chance to break the bundle of sticks, but none of them can do it. Then the man tells his sons to untie the bundle and each take a stick and break it. They easily break the sticks.

The man explains to his sons that if they stay united like the bundle of sticks, they will prosper and do well. But if they don't work together, they'll soon be in poverty.

What the man told his sons is what Solomon said thousands of years ago in the book of Ecclesiastes: "A person standing alone can be attacked and defeated, but two can stand back-to-back and conquer. Three are even better, for a triple-braided cord is not easily broken."

By yourself, it's easy to give in to temptation or go along with the crowd, but with other Christians surrounding you, you have more strength. Even better, with Jesus as part of your braided cord, you have the strength you need to stand up for those things that are right.

For You

If you feel like you're standing alone, look for others around you who share your faith, and be sure to ask God to help you stand for what's right every day.

Answer: a
A person standing alone can be attacked and defeated, but two can stand back-to-back and conquer. Three are even better, for a triple-braided cord is not easily broken. Ecclesiastes 4:12
(The Whole Story: Ecclesiastes 4:7-12)

July 20

Hair like What?

Q: To what is the woman's hair compared in the book of Song of Songs?
a. a swarm of bees
b. a school of fish
c. a flock of goats

Has anyone ever given you a compliment? Maybe he or she said you had beautiful eyes or good coordination. Perhaps the person said you had good handwriting or a talent for singing. Perhaps the person said your hair was shiny, or maybe that it was like a flock of goats. Wait! Would you consider that a compliment?

It would be a compliment if you lived at the time the book of Song of Songs was written. Hair was important, and it wasn't uncommon to compare hair to the fleece of a fine flock of goats. These weren't goats like in the petting area at the zoo. The goats from Mount Gilead were well-fed goats with long, smooth, glistening hair.

Even though hair like a flock of goats was a sincere and appreciated compliment in the days of Solomon (the author of Song of Songs), it wouldn't be taken that way today. But an honest compliment is one way to make someone's day. It shows a person you are aware of him or her and care about that person's feelings.

If you aren't used to complimenting others, it may feel awkward at first, but it doesn't have to. A simple "Nice outfit" or "Good job on your math test" is all that's needed.

It's important to graciously accept compliments too. Perhaps someone says she likes your jacket, but it's an old one that you don't like that well. Don't downplay the compliment by saying, "I hate this old thing." A simple "thank you" is all that's needed.

Want to make someone's day? Pay that person an honest compliment. See how he or she responds.

For You

Look for someone who's having a rough day and give that person a word of encouragement or a compliment. Kind words are free, and they make a difference.

Answer: c
You are beautiful, my darling, beautiful beyond words. Your eyes are like doves behind your veil. Your hair falls in waves, like a flock of goats winding down the slopes of Gilead. Song of Songs 4:1
(The Whole Story: Song of Songs 4:1-15)

Major Prophets

July 21

Know Your Master

Q: Fill in the blanks: "Even an ____ knows its owner, and a ____ recognizes its master's care—but ____ doesn't know its master."
a. alpaca, horse, a king
b. ox, donkey, Israel
c. opossum, horse, a mule

Jessica got a 10-month-old puppy from the animal shelter and named him Caspian after Prince Caspian from the Chronicles of Narnia series. This was a new name for the puppy, but he quickly learned to recognize his name and his new owner. He liked the rest of the family, but when Jessica arrived home from somewhere, he raced in circles and jumped up and down in excitement. He knew his owner, and there was a special place in his heart just for her.

Today's question comes from the book of Isaiah. The books of prophecy take place at the same time as the events in 1 and 2 Samuel, 1 and 2 Kings, and 1 and 2 Chronicles. God sent these prophets to the kings with messages and warnings. This passage in Isaiah talks about the southern kingdom, Judah. God made a deal with his people, the Jews, that he would take care of them and bless them if they would follow him. But they turned away from him and served other gods. They didn't listen to or follow God's laws. Isaiah points out that even an animal recognizes its owner, but God's own people no longer listened to his voice.

God wants us to listen to and obey him just as he desired that the Jews obey him. Children listen to their earthly father and trust him to provide for them and guide them; in the same way, we should listen to God, our heavenly Father, and trust him to know what's best for us.

For You
Do you have a pet dog or cat? If so, they probably respond quickly to your voice. Try to respond to God with that same enthusiasm and devotion.

Answer: b
Even an ox knows its owner, and a donkey recognizes its master's care—but Israel doesn't know its master. My people don't recognize my care for them.
Isaiah 1:3
(The Whole Story: Isaiah 1:1-20)

July 22

Be Gone!

Q: What did God promise to do about the people's sins?
a. accept a burnt offering for forgiveness
b. make them white as wool
c. erase them

Adam grabbed his dirty soccer uniform from the floor of his room. He could hear the washer running and needed his uniform washed right away. It was bright red and had never been washed before. Adam opened the washer lid and added the uniform to the load of clothes. Later when Adam's mom went to put the clothes into the dryer, she was shocked to see her load of whites was now pink! Those whites could be made white again by using bleach, but the same is not true of the scarlet, or crimson, mentioned in Isaiah.

The book of Isaiah says, "Though your sins are like scarlet, I will make them as white as snow. Though they are red like crimson, I will make them as white as wool." Scarlet, or crimson, was the color of a dark red dye, and it was permanent. That's how sin is. When we do anything against God's law, it leaves a stain in our lives we can't remove. Only God can remove the stain of sin.

God was talking to the southern kingdom, assuring the few who still remembered him that he would remove their sins. He promises us the same thing. His Word says, "If we confess our sins to him, he is faithful and just to forgive us our sins and to cleanse us from all wickedness" (1 John 1:9).

Sin leaves a stain in your life, but God promises to make your heart clean again.

For You
Search your heart and life for sin, and ask God to give you a clean heart.

Answer: b
"Come now, let's settle this," says the LORD. "Though your sins are like scarlet, I will make them as white as snow. Though they are red like crimson, I will make them as white as wool." Isaiah 1:18
(The Whole Story: Isaiah 1:1-20)

July 23

Your Guilt Is Removed

Q: What did the seraphim (angel) touch to Isaiah's lips?
a. a burning coal
b. water
c. a rag dipped in ointment

Isaiah was a great Old Testament prophet who prophesied during the reign of four different kings of Judah. Isaiah wasn't born a prophet; God called him to it. But first God had to get Isaiah's attention, and he did that with a vision.

Isaiah saw a vision of the Temple. God was sitting on a majestic throne, with angels calling out, "Holy, holy, holy is the LORD of Heaven's Armies! The whole earth is filled with his glory!" God's glory filled the Temple.

Instead of being comforted by the vision of God's greatness, Isaiah realized how sinful he was compared to God's holiness. He said, "It's all over! I am doomed, for I am a sinful man. I have filthy lips, and I live among a people with filthy lips. Yet I have seen the King, the LORD of Heaven's Armies."

An angel took a burning coal from the altar, carried it using tongs, and touched it to Isaiah's lips. The angel said, "See, this coal has touched your lips. Now your guilt is removed, and your sins are forgiven." The angel didn't mean that the coal had the power to forgive sins but that it was a symbol that God had forgiven Isaiah's sins.

Sometimes preachers focus only on God being our friend or our Father, and we forget how majestic and holy God really is. He is far beyond anything we can imagine. He is powerful and mighty, yet in his love for us he calls us his friends because of our relationship with his Son, Jesus (see Romans 5:11).

For You

God is a powerful and majestic king over all, yet he desires to be your friend if you have Jesus as your Savior. If you've never accepted Jesus into your life, talk to someone today about how to do that.

Answer: a
One of the seraphim flew to me with a burning coal he had taken from the altar with a pair of tongs. He touched my lips with it and said, "See, this coal has touched your lips. Now your guilt is removed, and your sins are forgiven."
Isaiah 6:6-7
(The Whole Story: Isaiah 6)

July 24

Who Will Go?

Q: How did Isaiah answer the questions "Whom should I send as a messenger to this people? Who will go for us?"
a. "Here I am. Send me."
b. "There are many faithful prophets."
c. "The harvest is great, but the laborers are few."

Jessica and Jasmine went on a summer mission trip. Both went through several days of training before the team left for their mission field. The team members learned simple construction techniques, practiced painting, and mastered a tough obstacle course that taught teamwork. On the final night before the trip, there was a commissioning service. All the lights were turned off, and a single candle was lit. That candle was used to light another, and the flame was passed until all the candles were glowing in order to symbolize taking the light of Jesus into a dark world. By lighting the candle, each team member was showing his or her willingness to be a witness for Jesus.

Isaiah didn't run an obstacle course each day at 5:30 a.m. or learn to pour concrete or even light a candle, but he was called to be a light for God in a dark world. After Isaiah realized his own sinfulness and was cleansed by God, he heard the Lord saying, "Whom should I send as a messenger to this people? Who will go for us?"

Isaiah immediately responded, "Here I am. Send me." Isaiah eagerly volunteered to do God's work without even knowing what it would be.

God is still asking, "Whom shall I send?" How will you answer?

- -

For You
When God calls, are you willing to say, "Here I am. Send me"? God will never ask you to do something that is unsafe or too difficult for you to do. He will give you the wisdom and ability to do the job he calls you to do.

- -

Answer: a
I heard the Lord asking, "Whom should I send as a messenger to this people? Who will go for us?" I said, "Here I am. Send me." Isaiah 6:8
(The Whole Story: Isaiah 6)

July 25

God with Us

Q: Which of these words means "God with us"?
a. *Jehovah*
b. *Immanuel*
c. *Jesus*

Long before Jesus was born, the prophet Isaiah foretold his coming. This baby wouldn't be just any child. He would be the Son of God. Jesus would live on earth and be totally human yet still totally God. That's a hard thing to understand, even for Bible scholars.

Isaiah said this baby would be called Immanuel, which means "God with us." In some ways God had always been with people. He was with them through his creation, and he made a covenant with his chosen people to be with them and protect them. But they had turned from him. Their sins had caused a separation between them and God. Isaiah 59:1-2 says, "Listen! The LORD's arm is not too weak to save you, nor is his ear too deaf to hear you call. It's your sins that have cut you off from God. Because of your sins, he has turned away and will not listen anymore."

When Jesus was born in Bethlehem, he walked physically with people on earth. He also provided salvation and forgiveness of sins so we could have God's Spirit with us all the time. Anyone who receives Jesus becomes a child of God (see John 1:12), and God is with him or her in a new way.

Saint Augustine said, "You have made us for yourself, O Lord, and our hearts are restless until they rest in you." God made us in his image for the purpose of knowing and worshiping him. Your life is not complete until Jesus is a part of it.

For You
God created each person and desires for each of us to have a relationship with him. You begin that relationship when you accept his Son, Jesus, as your Savior. Share that good news with a friend or classmate today, or invite him or her to church to hear the Good News.

Answer: b
The Lord himself will give you the sign. Look! The virgin will conceive a child! She will give birth to a son and will call him Immanuel (which means "God is with us").
Isaiah 7:14
(The Whole Story: Isaiah 7:10-16)

July 26

A Child Is Born

Q: Fill in the blanks: "For a child is born to us, a son is given to us. The government will rest on his shoulders. And he will be called: _____, _____, _____, _____."

a. Heavenly Father, Good Shepherd, Wonderful Counselor, Prince of Peace
b. Wonderful Counselor, Mighty God, Everlasting Father, Prince of Peace
c. Everlasting Father, King of Kings, Good Shepherd, Prince of Peace

Have you ever been in a situation where you didn't know what to do? Maybe a friend was angry with you, and you didn't know how to fix the problem. Perhaps you had to choose between two activities and didn't know which was the best choice. There are all kinds of situations where you might need some advice.

When you need answers, you usually turn to someone you can trust. Today's verse calls Jesus "Wonderful Counselor." Why is Jesus the best one to talk to about your problems?

Jesus created you, so he is the one who knows you best. He knows why you feel the way you do and what it will take to fix your problems.

Jesus loved you enough to die for you. He wants you to have a relationship with him. He cares about you more than anyone else does.

Jesus has the answers. He reveals them to you through the Bible, your parents, your Sunday school teacher, and your pastor. He has also gifted some Christians to be counselors who are able to help you sort through your problems. But you can always ask Jesus for the answers.

For You

Sometimes life can be tough, and you aren't sure where to go for answers. Start by asking Jesus, and then your parents, so they can help you find the solutions you need.

Answer: b
A child is born to us, a son is given to us. The government will rest on his shoulders. And he will be called: Wonderful Counselor, Mighty God, Everlasting Father, Prince of Peace. Isaiah 9:6
(The Whole Story: Isaiah 9:1-7)

Jesus Our Savior

Q: To what is Jesus compared in Isaiah 53?
a. a priest
b. a lamb
c. a servant

In C. S. Lewis's book *The Lion, the Witch and the Wardrobe*, Edmund meets the evil White Witch, who has a profound effect on him. She tricks Edmund into betraying his brother and sisters, along with the talking beavers they are visiting.

The White Witch confronts the great lion, Aslan, son of the Emperor who created Narnia: "You know that every traitor belongs to me as my lawful prey and that for every treachery I have a right to a kill."

After Edmund realizes what he's done, the White Witch says Edmund must die for his betrayal. But Aslan steps in and is killed on the Stone Table in Edmund's place. However, that's not the end of the story. When Edmund's sisters, Lucy and Susan, go to the table the next morning, they find it broken in two and Aslan standing before them. Aslan sacrificed himself for Edmund's treachery and then overcame death. A battle between the good and evil occupants of Narnia follows, and the good side wins.

According to Old Testament law, blood had to be shed for the forgiveness of sin. God sent Jesus to die as the perfect sacrifice for sins. Now we don't have to offer an animal sacrifice for sins because Jesus' death was the final sacrifice. John the Baptist said of Jesus, "Look! The Lamb of God who takes away the sin of the world!" (John 1:29). We can be forgiven of sin because of Jesus' sacrifice for us.

For You

You can have forgiveness of sin just by asking. It's free to you, but it wasn't free for Jesus. He paid the penalty for sin in order to offer salvation freely to us. Be sure to thank him for that today.

Answer: b
He was oppressed and treated harshly, yet he never said a word. He was led like a lamb to the slaughter. And as a sheep is silent before the shearers, he did not open his mouth.   Isaiah 53:7
(The Whole Story: Isaiah 53)

July 28

Called by God

Q. Fill in the blanks: "I _____ you before I formed you in your mother's womb. Before you were born I set you _____ and appointed you as my _____ to the nations."
a. called, aside, teacher
b. saw, out, leader
c. knew, apart, prophet

Before Jeremiah was even born, God already had a plan for him in place. Jeremiah didn't wander aimlessly through life wondering what to do, because he had purpose. God had chosen him to be a prophet.

For 40 years Jeremiah spoke to the people of Judah on God's behalf, but no one listened. Jeremiah didn't give up because he knew this was the job he was called to do. He stood firm and declared God's message to the people over and over.

Knowing God had a purpose for his life got Jeremiah through some tough times. Jeremiah was thrown in prison and at another time thrown into a well where he sank into the mud at the bottom. He was forced to go to Egypt, and he was rejected by his family, neighbors, friends, and kings. Often Jeremiah stood alone for what was right.

By the world's standards, Jeremiah was a total failure. But he was successful in God's eyes because he knew his calling, and he lived with purpose.

God has a plan for your life too. When you're older he may call you to be a teacher, doctor, athlete, musician, or electrician. He will bring you in contact with the people he wants you to reach. You don't have to wait until you're older to have purpose, though. You can live with purpose today by doing the best you can at your schoolwork, chores, and relationships while keeping your eyes open for the opportunities God brings your way.

For You

Be faithful in the things God has for you today. Schoolwork and chores may not seem that important, but they are your training ground for the things God has for you later.

Answer: c
"I knew you before I formed you in your mother's womb. Before you were born I set you apart and appointed you as my prophet to the nations." Jeremiah 1:5
(The Whole Story: Jeremiah 1)

July 29

A Faithful Friend

Q: Who wrote down the prophecies Jeremiah spoke to him?
a. Daniel
b. Baruch
c. Ezra

The book of Jeremiah tells about the ministry of Jeremiah the prophet. Jeremiah reveals more about his life and his struggles than any of the other prophets. He was from the Hilkiah family of priests. God instructed Jeremiah not to marry and have children because of the coming judgment on God's people in Judah.

Because of his messages of doom and judgment, Jeremiah wasn't popular. He had few friends. His closest companion was his secretary, Baruch, who faithfully wrote down Jeremiah's words. Baruch stayed with Jeremiah on the road to exile in Egypt. He was also probably responsible for putting the book of Jeremiah together.

Baruch isn't as well known as Jeremiah, but he had abilities and knowledge that were important for assisting the prophet. Baruch not only wrote down Jeremiah's words, he delivered the message to the Temple and to kings. He was with Jeremiah every step of the way.

Even though Baruch was a behind-the-scenes kind of guy, God cared about him as much as he cared about Jeremiah. Baruch handwrote each word out of Jeremiah's mouth. If you look at the book of Jeremiah, you'll see there are a lot of words. Yet when Baruch delivered the message God gave Jeremiah to King Jehoiakim, the king threw it into the fire on his hearth. Baruch's work literally went up in flames.

Jeremiah 45 is God's message to Baruch himself. Baruch is told to take his eyes off himself and look to God. Even though Baruch worked behind the scenes, he was as valuable in the Lord's eyes as Jeremiah was.

For You

Whether you are the one up front or the behind-the-scenes person, you are valuable to God. He will use you to do the job he's planned for you.

Answer: b
Jeremiah sent for Baruch son of Neriah, and as Jeremiah dictated all the prophecies that the LORD had given him, Baruch wrote them on a scroll.
Jeremiah 36:4
(The Whole Story: Jeremiah 36)

July 30

New Every Morning

Q: What does the book of Lamentations say is new every morning?
a. God's love
b. God's mercy
c. God's wisdom

Jeremiah wrote the book of Lamentations after God allowed his people to be taken captive because of their sins. Jeremiah was deeply distressed and said, "I have cried until the tears no longer come; my heart is broken. My spirit is poured out in agony as I see the desperate plight of my people" (Lamentations 2:11). Jeremiah was known as the "weeping prophet" because he was constantly in tears over the people's sin and the consequences of that sin.

The book of Lamentations isn't totally full of despair, though. During the time of trouble, there was hope—not because of the people, but because of God's compassion and mercy. If you've sung the hymn "Great Is Thy Faithfulness," then you've sung the words of hope from Lamentations 3:22-23 (today's Scripture).

There was hope for the people because the Lord is faithful and merciful. God wanted his people to repent and worship him and follow his ways.

God is still faithful and merciful today. Things around us change. Political leaders come and go, countries change their names and boundaries, friends grow apart or move away, teachers retire and new ones arrive, we grow older and circumstances change. But God does not change. He is always ready to forgive sins and have a relationship with the people he created.

For You

Things in your life constantly change, but God remains the same. He is as faithful and full of mercy now as he was in Jeremiah's time. He is ready to listen to you and help you with anything you need. Just ask and seek his answer.

Answer: b
The faithful love of the LORD never ends! His mercies never cease. Great is his faithfulness; his mercies begin afresh each morning. Lamentations 3:22-23
(The Whole Story: Lamentations 3)

July 31

Thrown in the Street

Q: What does Ezekiel say people will throw in the streets?
a. money
b. trash
c. food

Ezekiel was a prophet to the Jews who had been taken captive to Babylon. He lived among them in exile. Just as with Jeremiah, God called Ezekiel to be a prophet. Before being called, Ezekiel was training to be a priest in God's Temple.

Ezekiel had many visions that he describes in the book that shares his name. He saw visions of beasts, wheels, fire, and more. Ezekiel prophesied the total destruction of Israel. He said the Israelites would end up throwing their money in the street like trash.

The people had allowed their money to lead them into sin. They used their money for their own pleasures, and they became proud. God gave them silver and gold, but they used it to make idols. Those idols couldn't deliver them from the trouble they were in.

God has blessed us with money, homes, clothes, and other good things. He wants us to use what we have for him and to share it with the poor. Yet many times it's the things people own that keep them from God.

The things God gives us are best used to accomplish his plans, not our own selfish desires. If you have game systems and games, share them with a friend who is discouraged or lonely, or use them to entertain younger siblings to give your mom a break. If you have a bike, ask your parents' permission to run errands nearby. If you have an allowance, put part of it in the offering to help support your church and missionaries. Share what you have with others, and it will mean more than just having things for your own pleasure.

For You

Be careful to never let your possessions become more important than God or seeking his will. Be a good guardian of all he's given you by using it well and sharing it with others.

Answer: a
They will throw their money in the streets, tossing it out like worthless trash. Their silver and gold won't save them on that day of the Lord's anger. It will neither satisfy nor feed them, for their greed can only trip them up. Ezekiel 7:19
(The Whole Story: Ezekiel 7:14-27)

Far from Home

Q: Another name Daniel was called was
a. Nebuchadnezzar.
b. Belteshazzar.
c. Meshach.

When Nebuchadnezzar became king of Babylon, he seized Jerusalem and took captives back to Babylon, including Daniel. Once in Babylon, Daniel was soon noticed for his intelligence and wisdom. He and three friends were chosen to serve in the palace, so they were trained and educated for three years.

The young men were in privileged positions and even allowed to eat the king's food. Daniel, given the Babylonian name Belteshazzar, and his friends didn't want to eat the food. It may have been considered unclean by Jewish law or offered to pagan idols. Or maybe the young men didn't want to depend on the king for food. Daniel asked that he and his friends be allowed to have only vegetables and water instead. The official agreed to a 10-day trial period.

At the end of the 10 days, Daniel and his friends were healthier and stronger than the young men who ate the king's food. And at the end of the three years of education and training, Daniel and his friends were found to be 10 times wiser than all the others.

Daniel was far from home, but he determined to do what was right and to honor God in his choices. In return, God blessed him and made him successful. This gave Daniel a chance to make a difference for God.

For You

Daniel purposed in his heart to do what was right even though many times no one would know the difference. Because of Daniel's determination to serve God, the Lord was able to use him to be an example to others and to accomplish good things. Do you determine to do right even if no one else would know? If not, choose to be like Daniel today, and serve God in everything you do.

Answer: b
The chief of staff renamed them with these Babylonian names: Daniel was called Belteshazzar. Hananiah was called Shadrach. Mishael was called Meshach. Azariah was called Abednego. Daniel 1:7
(The Whole Story: Daniel 1)

August 2

A Fiery Furnace

Q: What three young men were thrown into the fiery furnace?
a. Hosea, Joel, Amos
b. Jashobeam, Eleazar, Shammah
c. Shadrach, Meshach, Abednego

King Nebuchadnezzar made a statue of himself that was 9 feet wide and 90 feet tall! In Babylon, statues were often worshiped, and Nebuchadnezzar made sure his big statue couldn't be missed.

The king called everyone together for the dedication of the statue. Daniel, a Jewish exile serving the Babylonian king, wasn't there at the time, but his three friends, Shadrach, Meshach, and Abednego, were.

King Nebuchadnezzar instructed that when the musicians played, the people were to bow before the statue or else they would be thrown into a huge furnace with flames leaping out the top opening.

The musicians played, but Shadrach, Meshach, and Abednego stood firm. The king had the musicians play again, but the three young men still stood. The king, filled with rage, ordered the furnace heated seven times hotter and had the three friends thrown in. The flames were so hot they killed the guards who threw the three men into the furnace.

When the king looked at the furnace, he saw not three but four men walking around in it unharmed. The king called for the three young men to come out, and they walked out without even a singed hair or the smell of smoke on them!

The king said, "Praise to the God of Shadrach, Meshach, and Abednego! He sent his angel to rescue his servants who trusted in him."

The three young men could have pretended to bow to fool the king or justified bowing down because this was a command from the king. Yet they chose to stand firm for God despite the consequences.

For You
You may be surrounded by people who want you to join them in making bad choices or compromising your faith. Remind yourself that if the three men could risk being burned alive in the furnace, you can stand firm for God too.

Answer: c
Nebuchadnezzar was so furious with Shadrach, Meshach, and Abednego that his face became distorted with rage. He commanded that the furnace be heated seven times hotter than usual.   Daniel 3:19
(The Whole Story: Daniel 3)

August 3

Daniel's Gift

Q: God blessed Daniel with the ability to
a. interpret dreams.
b. speak foreign languages.
c. make many friends.

Have you ever had a crazy dream and wondered what it meant? It may not have meant anything. But back in Daniel's day, before people had the entire Bible to guide them, God often used dreams and visions to speak to people.

One night King Nebuchadnezzar had a dream. He called for his magicians, enchanters, sorcerers, and astrologers to tell him both what the dream was and what it meant. The king's men couldn't do it, but Daniel was able to describe and interpret the dream because God revealed it to him. The king had dreamed of a large statue. This statue represented four kingdoms that would become four world powers. But all of these kingdoms would be brought to an end by the Kingdom of God, which will last forever.

Daniel later interpreted another dream for the king. The king would live like an animal for a period of time. Once he acknowledged God, he would be restored. God gave Nebuchadnezzar a year to change, but the king would not acknowledge God. The king was driven away from the people and ate grass like a cow.

Finally Nebuchadnezzar realized he was wrong. He said, "After this time had passed, I, Nebuchadnezzar, looked up to heaven. My sanity returned, and I praised and worshiped the Most High and honored the one who lives forever."

God gave Daniel the gift of interpreting dreams and put him in the palace where he was able to tell the king what his dreams meant. God used Daniel to serve him in the palace of a pagan nation.

For You

Daniel lived out his faith among people who didn't believe in God. Instead of avoiding people who don't share your faith, reach out to them and pass on the gospel message.

Answer: a

[Daniel said,] "There is a God in heaven who reveals secrets, and he has shown King Nebuchadnezzar what will happen in the future. Now I will tell you your dream and the visions you saw as you lay on your bed." Daniel 2:28
(The Whole Story: Daniel 2, 4)

Another King Needs Daniel's Help

Q: What happened during King Belshazzar's banquet?
a. The sky went dark.
b. A hand wrote on the wall.
c. The wine turned to water.

King Belshazzar held a feast for one thousand of his nobles. He called for someone to bring the gold and silver goblets Nebuchadnezzar had taken from God's Temple. The people drank from those goblets while they praised their idols. This was a bad choice.

The people saw a hand writing on the wall of the room. The king called for his astrologers and fortune tellers, and he promised royal robes, a gold chain, and a position of third highest in the kingdom to whoever could tell him the significance of the writing. But no one could.

The queen mother knew about Daniel, a Jewish exile, who was in service to the king and had a gift for interpreting things, and she had him brought in. The king offered him the same reward he'd offered the others, but Daniel didn't want rewards. He said he'd interpret the words without being paid.

The writing on the wall read, "*Mene, Mene, Tekel, Parsin.*" These words meant God had numbered the days of Belshazzar's reign and that it would soon end. God had found him corrupt and would divide his kingdom between the Medes and the Persians. Belshazzar was killed that very night.

Daniel interpreted the words, but he wasn't motivated by fancy things or an important job. Daniel had served God all his life, and doing what God wanted was his motivation for giving God's message to Belshazzar.

For You

It's important to do God's work because it's what God has called you to do, not for any reward. When you do things for God and others, let love for God and obedience to him be your motivation.

Answer: b
Suddenly, they saw the fingers of a human hand writing on the plaster wall of the king's palace, near the lampstand. The king himself saw the hand as it wrote.
Daniel 5:5
(The Whole Story: Daniel 5)

August 5

Dare to Be a Daniel

Q: Daniel was thrown into the lions' den for doing which of these things?
a. fighting
b. praying
c. prophesying

Have you ever known someone who was so jealous of another person that he or she tried to hurt that person or damage his or her reputation? The rulers who served with Daniel were like that.

Daniel, 80 years old now, was one of the top three administrators in the kingdom of the Medes and Persians. The other officials were jealous, but they couldn't find anything wrong to criticize Daniel about. So they tricked King Darius into making a law. The law said that it was illegal to pray to anyone other than King Darius for the next 30 days. Offenders would be thrown into the lions' den. The law couldn't be changed by anyone, not even the king.

As was his custom, Daniel continued to pray to God three times a day in his upstairs room with his window open. Daniel's enemies took him to the king. King Darius was unhappy because he liked Daniel. But there was nothing the king could do.

Daniel was thrown into the lions' den, but God protected him. The next morning King Darius hurried to the den and called, "Daniel, servant of the living God! Was your God, whom you serve so faithfully, able to rescue you from the lions?"

"Long live the king! My God sent his angel to shut the lions' mouths so that they would not hurt me, for I have been found innocent in his sight," Daniel answered.

Daniel was released, and the men who had been responsible for putting him in the den were thrown to the lions.

Despite the new law, Daniel stood firm in his faith and prayed the way he'd always done. God honored that and protected Daniel.

For You

Daniel remained strong in his faith his entire life. Never once did he compromise his faith or worship God in secret. Do you have the courage to live your faith out loud and up front like Daniel?

Answer: b
They told the king, "That man Daniel, one of the captives from Judah, is ignoring you and your law. He still prays to his God three times a day." Daniel 6:13
(The Whole Story: Daniel 6)

Minor Prophets

August 6

Hosea's Unfaithful Wife

Q: What was the name of Hosea's unfaithful wife?
a. Gomer
b. Mary
c. Jezebel

Hosea was a prophet to the northern kingdom, Israel, during the time they turned from God to idols. God told Hosea to marry a woman named Gomer. Gomer was unfaithful to Hosea, and she left him for other men. Although Hosea was heartbroken, he loved his wife and went after her to win her back.

Hosea and Gomer are a picture of God and his people. The people in the northern kingdom ignored God and no longer worshiped him. They turned to other gods and to their own pleasures and desires. Even in the midst of their wickedness, God offered forgiveness and hope. He wanted them to repent of their sins and return to him, but they didn't.

God calls us to be his children and to be faithful to him. When you turn from God's standards and choose ungodly standards as your own, you are unfaithful to him just as Israel was. Walking away from God is often a gradual thing. You listen to music with bad words and attitudes, or use bad words you hear others use. You spend less time reading your Bible and more time hanging out with friends who don't share your faith. As time passes, you give more time to the wrong things, and less time and commitment to God. It's easy to find yourself far from God. If this is true for you, God is calling you back to himself. Just as Hosea went to bring his unfaithful wife back home, God wants to bring you back to relationship with him.

For You
Each time you compromise your values and principles, you take a step away from God. It can be so gradual that you don't notice at first. Examine your life today and see if you are still strong in your commitment to God or if there are areas of your life you need to turn over to him.

Answer: a
Hosea married Gomer, the daughter of Diblaim.   Hosea 1:3
(The Whole Story: Hosea 1, 3)

August 7

God's Desire

Q: According to Hosea, God wanted his people to know him more than he wanted what?
a. gold
b. burnt offerings
c. worship

The book of Hosea shows God's consistent love for his people. Even though they weren't worshiping him as they should, he still gave them the chance to turn from their wicked ways.

Sometimes people go through rituals that make them look spiritual, but their actions are empty. Through Hosea, God told the people that he wanted them to show love more than offer sacrifices, and he wanted them to know him more than offer burnt offerings.

We don't offer sacrifices today, but there are still times when people go through the motions of a Christian life without having the right heart attitude toward God. You can put money in the offering plate, sing praise and worship songs with hands raised, and even take Communion or be baptized but not love God. God would rather you know him personally than do all the right things without any meaning.

You get to know people by spending time with them and finding out all about them. The same is true of God. The Bible is your main source for learning about him. Listening in Sunday school and church are good ways to learn about God. Reading a daily devotional book like this one or a version of the Bible you can understand is also a good way to become better acquainted with God.

If you truly desire to know God, he will help you understand the things you read and hear. God desires a relationship with you.

For You
Make getting to know God a priority. What things are you already doing to know God better? What new things can you try?

Answer: b
[The Lord says,] "I want you to show love, not offer sacrifices. I want you to know me more than I want burnt offerings." Hosea 6:6
(The Whole Story: Hosea 6)

August 8

A Terrible Army

Q: The prophet Joel said an army of what had invaded the land?
a. Philistines
b. Amorites
c. locusts

In the movie *The Land Before Time 5: The Mysterious Island*, a cloud of swarming leaf gobblers (locusts) eat all the green plants in the Great Valley. Because the dinosaurs depend on plants for food, they go on a search for a place with food where they can live. As they journey, they find the leaf gobblers have left a lot of devastation, and not many green plants, throughout the land. The dinosaurs have many adventures before finding a place to stay until the green plants of the Great Valley grow again.

In the Bible, Joel, a prophet to the southern kingdom, describes a plague of locusts. Locusts are one of the worst things that can happen to farmers who depend on their plants for a living. Locusts can cover miles of land at a time, stripping it of everything green. Once they pass through, all the plants are gone, and the trees are stripped of their bark and leaves. The land is desolate.

Joel told the people in Judah that the devastation the locusts caused was nothing compared to what would happen to them when God's judgment came on them. Joel told the people to turn from their sins and return to worshiping God while there was still time.

Today, God wants people to turn back to him. If they repent of their sins (which means they turn away from their sins) and seek God's forgiveness, he offers them an eternal home in heaven.

For You

God still calls people to himself. He promises to be with them while they are here on earth and to provide an eternal home in heaven. Take time to read about it in John 14 and Revelation 21.

Answer: c

A vast army of locusts has invaded [the Lord's] land, a terrible army too numerous to count. Its teeth are like lions' teeth, its fangs like those of a lioness. Joel 1:6
(The Whole Story: Joel 1–2)

August 9

Amos's Occupation

Q: What was Amos's job?
a. doctor
b. fisherman
c. shepherd

Amos wasn't specially trained to be a prophet. He wasn't the son of a prophet or a priest. In fact, he was a shepherd. And he grew figs. By human standards, he may not have been a likely candidate to be a prophet, but he was listening to God and willing to be used. Amos wrote the book of the Bible that shares his name.

Amos wasn't the only person God used who didn't have special training. Moses, Hosea, and Amos were shepherds, although for a while Moses was also a prince in Egypt. David was also a shepherd before he became king. Andrew, Peter, James, and John were fishermen. Paul was a tentmaker. Matthew was a tax collector. Joshua was a military leader, and Nehemiah was cupbearer to the king. God called people in many positions to help do his work, whether it was preaching, prophesying, or writing a book of the Bible.

God chooses people who are willing to serve him. They may be plumbers, cashiers, teachers, nurses, garbage collectors, electricians, and even students still in school. He puts them in the right place at the right time to do a job for him. God doesn't look at their credentials, only their hearts. When God looks at your heart, does he find you willing and ready to serve?

For You

God doesn't look at your math grade or your singing ability to decide if you can serve him. He doesn't look at test scores and IQs to find the best person for a job. He looks at your obedience to him and your desire to serve. If you are willing and ready, God will use you. Look around for the opportunities he sends your way today.

Answer: c
This message was given to Amos, a shepherd from the town of Tekoa in Judah. He received this message in visions two years before the earthquake, when Uzziah was king of Judah and Jeroboam II, the son of Jehoash, was king of Israel.
Amos 1:1
(The Whole Story: Amos 1:1-2)

August 10

Caring for the Poor

Q: What were Israel's women compared to in the book of Amos?
a. fat cows
b. colorful birds
c. sleek cats

In the Disney movie *The Emperor's New Groove*, Kuzco is a vain and selfish emperor. He's planning to build a water park for himself for his birthday. However, this means destroying a village to make room for his new park. Kuzco thinks nothing of destroying the homes in order to provide entertainment for himself. When Kuzco is accidentally turned into a llama, though, one of the villagers, Pacha, comes to his rescue.

The wealthy women in the northern kingdom of Israel were worse than Kuzco. Like the cattle who grazed in the lush pastures of their area, they were pampered and well fed. But instead of sharing what they had with others, they oppressed the poor in order to maintain their lifestyles.

Several times in the Bible the Lord says those who help the poor will be blessed.

- "Give generously to the poor, not grudgingly, for the LORD your God will bless you in everything you do." (Deuteronomy 15:10)
- "Blessed are those who help the poor." (Proverbs 14:21)
- "Blessed are those who are generous, because they feed the poor." (Proverbs 22:9)
- "They share freely and give generously to the poor. Their good deeds will be remembered forever." (2 Corinthians 9:9)

God makes it clear that we are to help those in need and share what we have. The women of Israel failed to do that, and this was just one of the many sins God judged them for.

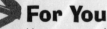

For You

How can you help the poor? Luke 3:11 gives advice on how to start: "If you have two shirts, give one to the poor. If you have food, share it with those who are hungry." God looks at your attitude about giving, not the amount you give. You will be blessed for the things you do for him.

Answer: a
Listen to me, you fat cows living in Samaria, you women who oppress the poor and crush the needy, and who are always calling to your husbands, "Bring us another drink!" Amos 4:1
(The Whole Story: Amos 4)

August 11

Judah's Neighbors

Q: The Edomites were proud because they
a. lived in a rock fortress high on the mountain.
b. had superior technology.
c. were scholars.

Edom was Judah's neighbor to the south. But the people of Edom and Judah weren't friendly with each other. The Edomites were descendants of Esau, and the Jews were descendants of his trickster brother, Jacob. Just as those brothers didn't always get along (see Genesis 27), neither did the Edomites and the Jews.

When the Babylonians came to attack Judah (the southern kingdom), the Edomites stood by and watched without helping. Obadiah, the shortest book in the Old Testament, is God's message to the Edomites because they didn't help the Jews—in fact, they gloated when Judah was taken captive, and they looted Judah's goods.

The Edomites felt safe from harm because they lived in the mountains where they thought no one could attack them in their rock fortress with cities cut into rock cliffs. They were proud and overly confident, but God humbled them and wiped out their nation.

The Edomites trusted in their surroundings to keep them safe. They were also fierce warriors and didn't think they'd ever be defeated. But trusting in power or location isn't wise.

People today trust in the wrong things too—popularity, money, intelligence, and position. It's okay to be proud of the talents and abilities God gave you, but don't trust in them. Trust in God alone.

For You

God gave you talents and abilities in order to complete the work he has for you. Don't put your trust in your own talents or possessions, but put your trust in the one who gave them to you.

Answer: a
You have been deceived by your own pride because you live in a rock fortress and make your home high in the mountains. "Who can ever reach us way up here?" you ask boastfully. Obadiah 1:3
(The Whole Story: Obadiah 1)

August 12

Saying Yes to God

Q: A great fish swallowed Jonah because
a. he refused to go to Tarshish.
b. he refused to go to Jerusalem.
c. he refused to go to Nineveh.

It's never a good idea to say no to God. Just look at Jonah. God told Jonah, "Get up and go to the great city of Nineveh." But Jonah went the opposite way. You can't flee from God, though, because the Lord sees and knows everything. God saw Jonah headed the wrong way and sent a storm that tossed the ship around so much the sailors feared for their lives. They threw the cargo overboard to lighten the load, but that didn't help.

The sailors cast lots to see who had offended the gods, and they identified Jonah. Jonah told them if they cast him into the sea, the storm would stop. The sailors tried to row to shore instead, but that didn't work, so they finally threw Jonah overboard. The storm stopped immediately.

God sent a big fish to swallow Jonah. Three days later the fish spit him up on dry land. Jonah had lots of time to think about his wrong choice while he was inside the fish.

God used extreme measures to get Jonah's attention. It would have been much better if Jonah had chosen to obey God in the first place.

For You

God still asks his people to do his work, and people still say no to him. He may not use a real storm or send a fish to swallow them to get their attention, but he still uses situations, or allows things to happen, to get people's attention. Learn from Jonah, and say yes the first time God asks you to do something.

Answer: c
But Jonah got up and went in the opposite direction to get away from the LORD. He went down to the port of Joppa, where he found a ship leaving for Tarshish. He bought a ticket and went on board, hoping to escape from the LORD by sailing to Tarshish. Jonah 1:3
(The Whole Story: Jonah 1–2)

August 13

A Savior Is Born

Q: Which minor prophet prophesied Jesus would be born in Bethlehem?
a. Micah
b. Obadiah
c. Malachi

The Old Testament contains many prophecies about Jesus' birth. One prophecy tells exactly where Jesus would be born—Bethlehem, a small village just south of Jerusalem. This prophecy came true since Matthew and Luke both name Bethlehem as the place the Savior was born. Matthew 2:5-6 even refers to the Old Testament prophecy: "This is what the prophet wrote: 'And you, O Bethlehem in the land of Judah, are not least among the ruling cities of Judah, for a ruler will come from you who will be the shepherd for my people Israel'" (Matthew 2:5-6).

God gave information to the Old Testament prophets (and even before) about the coming Savior. All of the prophecies came true. Here are a few of them:

Jesus would be from the line of David.　　　　Isaiah 7:13-14; Jeremiah 23:1-7
(Fulfilled: Matthew 1:1-6; Luke 1:27; Revelation 5:5)

Jesus would be born in the town of Bethlehem.　　Micah 5:2-4
(Fulfilled: Matthew 2:1; Luke 2:4-6)

Kings would bring him gifts.　　　　　　　　　Psalm 72
(Fulfilled: Matthew 2:1-11)

These prophecies show that God had a plan in place from the very beginning to provide a Savior to take away the sins of the world. These clues would help people recognize the Messiah when he came. Yet many still didn't accept Jesus.

For You

Sometimes prophecy is overlooked because it seems difficult to understand. Take time to read the verses that give the prophecies about Jesus, and then read the verses that show they were fulfilled. Why are these prophecies important?

Answer: a
You, O Bethlehem Ephrathah, are only a small village among all the people of Judah. Yet a ruler of Israel, whose origins are in the distant past, will come from you on my behalf. Micah 5:2
(The Whole Story: Micah 5:2-5)

August 14

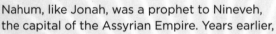

Obedience

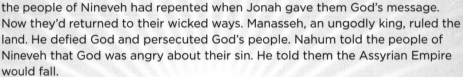

Q: The Lord is a _____ God according to Nahum 1:2.
a. worthy
b. mighty
c. jealous

Nahum, like Jonah, was a prophet to Nineveh, the capital of the Assyrian Empire. Years earlier, the people of Nineveh had repented when Jonah gave them God's message. Now they'd returned to their wicked ways. Manasseh, an ungodly king, ruled the land. He defied God and persecuted God's people. Nahum told the people of Nineveh that God was angry about their sin. He told them the Assyrian Empire would fall.

Nahum 1:2 says, "The LORD is a jealous God, filled with vengeance and rage. He takes revenge on all who oppose him and continues to rage against his enemies!" God's jealousy isn't a selfish jealousy like ours is. He has the right to ask for allegiance from his people. He punishes those who continue in wickedness so they will turn back to him.

On the other hand, God's mercy and love are a refuge to those who follow him. Nahum 1:7 says, "The LORD is good, a strong refuge when trouble comes. He is close to those who trust in him."

God is a loving God, but he's also a just God. Much like an earthly father, he expects obedience. He blesses and rewards those who follow him and punishes those who don't. That may make God sound harsh and uncaring, but he's not. He gives people second and third chances (and even more after that).

If you disobey your earthly father or another authority figure, you probably face a consequence. If you are obedient, you may earn extra privileges. In the same way, if you obey your heavenly Father, you will be blessed, although it doesn't guarantee a problem-free life. But he will help you make sense of the tough times. Obedience is always better.

For You

God wants the best for you. The Bible says Jesus came to give us a rich and satisfying life (see John 10:10). If you aren't experiencing that, look for things in your life that might be keeping God from blessing you.

Answer: c
The LORD is a jealous God, filled with vengeance and rage. He takes revenge on all who oppose him and continues to rage against his enemies! Nahum 1:2
(The Whole Story: Nahum 1)

August 15

Surefooted

Q: Fill in the blank: "The Sovereign LORD is my strength! He makes me as sure-footed as a ____, able to tread upon the heights."
a. mountain goat
b. mountain lion
c. deer

Habakkuk lived in dark times. The last kings of Judah were wicked men who rejected God and made life hard for the people. It was a time of fear, oppression, and godlessness. What Habakkuk saw troubled him. Because of that, he often asked God difficult questions: "Why is there evil in the world?" "Why do the wicked seem to win?" "Why don't you listen when I cry for help?" "Why do you tolerate wrong?" Habakkuk couldn't understand why God didn't do something about the people's wickedness.

God told Habakkuk he would use Babylon, a nation even more wicked than Judah, to punish Judah. Then Babylon would later be punished too. Habakkuk didn't understand why God was doing these things, but he had to realize God would work everything out in his own time and trust him.

Habakkuk ended his book with a prayer of praise to God. He said, "The Sovereign LORD is my strength! He makes me as surefooted as a deer, able to tread upon the heights." Habakkuk knew even in difficult times when God's people were living as pagans, God would give him confidence to run like a deer. God looks out for those who are living for him and gives them his strength to endure. God gives his followers the confidence and surefootedness of a deer to navigate in this world.

- -

For You
God offers you his strength and confidence to endure just as he provided it for Habakkuk. Habakkuk pictured himself as a surefooted deer when he was follow-ing God, and you can too.

- -

Answer: c
The Sovereign LORD is my strength! He makes me as surefooted as a deer, able to tread upon the heights. Habakkuk 3:19
(The Whole Story: Habakkuk 3)

August 16

A Good Leader

Q: Zephaniah said Jerusalem's leaders were like
a. roaring lions.
b. soaring eagles.
c. the raging sea.

Who are the leaders in your life? Your parents or guardians, teachers, principal, pastor, and youth group leader or Sunday school teacher may fill that role. And there are probably students who are club or sports team leaders. You expect leaders to be good examples and demonstrate responsibility and integrity, but that's not always the case.

One of the problems in Zephaniah's time was that the leaders of Jerusalem were wicked. The officials, rulers, prophets, and priests who should have been leading others in worshiping God and obeying his laws were as bad as the pagans in neighboring countries. They were not good leaders.

What makes a good leader? We just have to look to Jesus for an example of that.

Jesus was truthful. He never tried to say things to make himself popular, but rather he spoke the truth. Good leaders don't hide their beliefs to fit in with others or compromise what they believe in order to be popular.

Jesus treated everyone fairly. His message was the same for all people. Good leaders respect everyone, no matter their race, social standing, or income.

Jesus was committed to his purpose. He knew his task on earth, and he fulfilled it. Good leaders know what they need to do. They are enthusiastic about their cause, and they work with passion and vision.

Jesus was a servant. Instead of demanding special treatment, he washed his disciples' feet. Good leaders don't leave the hard work to others. They lead the way in getting the job done.

The leaders in Zephaniah's time fell short, but Jesus was the perfect leader.

For You

Take a look at the leaders in your life. Are they more like Jesus or like the leaders in Zephaniah's time? Determine that if you are ever in a leadership position, you will be a leader like Jesus.

Answer: a
[Jerusalem's] leaders are like roaring lions hunting for their victims. Its judges are like ravenous wolves at evening time, who by dawn have left no trace of their prey. Zephaniah 3:3
(The Whole Story: Zephaniah 3:1-7)

August 17

Priorities

Q: God sent Haggai to tell the people to do what?
a. rebuild their homes
b. rebuild the Temple
c. tear down the idols

Do you know what the word *priority* means? Something that is a priority to you is more important or of more value to you than other things. It's usually what you spend your time, energy, and sometimes even money on. If football is a priority, you may spend hours practicing or watching games. You might buy football cards and spend time talking to other football fanatics about the different players. Lots of things can be a priority—homework, your school sports team, a club, a hobby, or even a friend.

When the people of the southern kingdom were taken captive, they were away from their homeland for 70 years. During that time the Temple was ruined. When the Jews returned to their land, they rebuilt the foundation of the Temple. But they stopped work, and 15 years passed without their completing the Temple. God sent Haggai to tell the Jews to finish the construction project.

The Jews had wrong priorities. They built homes for themselves, but they hadn't finished God's Temple. They were neglecting spiritual things and focusing on their own comforts.

God wants first place in our lives. He wants us to use our talents, money, time, and energy to do his work. It's okay to do things that aren't specifically spiritual, but doing what God wants is the top priority.

For You

It's easy to tell what people's priorities are by how they use their time and what they talk about the most. What might others think your priorities are by how you spend your time and energy?

Answer: b
The LORD sent this message through the prophet Haggai: "Why are you living in luxurious houses while my house lies in ruins?" Haggai 1:3-4
(The Whole Story: Haggai 1:1-11)

August 18

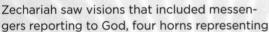

Today

Q: What did Zechariah see flying through the air?
a. a scroll
b. horses
c. an angel

Zechariah saw visions that included messengers reporting to God, four horns representing four world powers, a man measuring Jerusalem, dirty clothes being exchanged for clean ones, a lamp stand continually burning, a flying scroll representing God's curse, a woman named Wickedness being sent away in a basket, and four horses and chariots representing God's judgment. You can read about these visions in the book of Zechariah in the Bible. God used the visions to show Zechariah what was coming. God allowed Zechariah a glimpse of the future.

Sometimes people want to know what's ahead for them. They may consult horoscopes or astrologers to get answers, but those are not real answers. God is the only one who knows what the future holds. He revealed pieces of the future to Zechariah through visions. He reveals some of the future to us through the Bible.

God doesn't want us to be so focused on the future that we neglect to follow his plan for today. Matthew 6:33-34 says, "Seek the Kingdom of God above all else, and live righteously, and he will give you everything you need. So don't worry about tomorrow, for tomorrow will bring its own worries. Today's trouble is enough for today." What is God's advice about the future? According to these verses in Matthew 6 it's the following:

Seek God's will for your life.
Put God first every day.
Live a godly life.
Trust God for tomorrow's needs.

For You

God is in control of your future. When you get up each morning, commit your day to him, and look for the things he has planned for you. Live each day for God, and the future will fall into place day by day.

Answer: a
I looked up again and saw a scroll flying through the air. "What do you see?" the angel asked. "I see a flying scroll," I replied. "It appears to be about 30 feet long and 15 feet wide." Zechariah 5:1-2
(The Whole Story: Zechariah 5:1-4)

Pour Out a Blessing

Q: God promised to open the windows of heaven and pour out a blessing if the people would do what?
a. finish rebuilding the Temple
b. bring their tithes to him
c. observe the reading of Scripture

The people in Malachi's day didn't pay much attention to God. And they didn't give him part of their money and goods like they were supposed to do. Tithing, or giving part of one's money or crops, began during Moses' time. The Levites, who were the priests, didn't own their own land or have their own crops, so they received some of the tithes for food. When the people during Malachi's time didn't give their tithes, the Levites had to work to support themselves and weren't able to do their duties at the Temple.

The people forgot that all their money, crops, cattle, and other goods came from God and really belonged to the Lord, not to them. People today, too, sometimes fail to acknowledge that what they have is from God. The talents they have that allow them to earn money are from God. The intelligence or strength they have to work comes from God. He only asks for a small part in return.

God promised in Malachi that he'd pour out blessings if the people would give, and he promises the same today. Luke 6:38 says, "Give, and you will receive. Your gift will return to you in full—pressed down, shaken together to make room for more, running over, and poured into your lap. The amount you give will determine the amount you get back."

For You

You may not have much money to give to God, but you can give him your talents and time, as well as part of your allowance or other money you receive.

Answer: b
"Bring all the tithes into the storehouse so there will be enough food in my Temple. If you do," says the LORD of Heaven's Armies, "I will open the windows of heaven for you. I will pour out a blessing so great you won't have enough room to take it in! Try it! Put me to the test!" Malachi 3:10
(The Whole Story: Malachi 3:6-15)

New Testament: Gospels

August 20

Zechariah's News

Q: When Zechariah came out of the Temple after being told he and his wife would have a son, he couldn't
a. walk.
b. talk.
c. eat.

Zechariah was a godly man from a family of priests. His wife, Elizabeth, was also born into a family of priests. Zechariah and Elizabeth were old, and they had never been able to have a child. One day Zechariah was in the Holy Place in the Temple burning incense. A crowd was gathered outside to pray.

Even though Zechariah was chosen to burn the incense by casting lots, it was no accident he was chosen. God wanted to give him a message. God sent an angel to tell Zechariah that he and his wife would have a son who would prepare the way for the Lord.

Instead of being overjoyed, Zechariah was doubtful. It wasn't that he doubted God's ability, but he knew it was humanly impossible for him and Elizabeth to have a child. Because of his doubts, the angel said Zechariah wouldn't be able to speak again until his son was born.

Zechariah had been in the Temple a long time, and the people outside wondered why he hadn't come back out. When he exited the Temple, he was unable to speak, and the people knew he must have seen a vision.

Elizabeth became pregnant just as the angel had said, and she rejoiced because God had blessed her. God had chosen to do the impossible in order for John to be born and prepare the way for Jesus' work on earth.

For You
Often God works through ordinary situations, but sometimes he chooses to do what seems impossible to us. Be open to what God wants to do in and through you.

Answer: b
[The angel said,] "But now, since you didn't believe what I said, you will be silent and unable to speak until the child is born. For my words will certainly be fulfilled at the proper time." Luke 1:20
(The Whole Story: Luke 1:5-25)

August 21

God's Plan Set in Motion

Q: What angel announced both John's and Jesus' births?
a. Michael
b. Gideon
c. Gabriel

When God sent an angel to tell Zechariah he'd have a son (see yesterday's devotion), the Lord was setting his plan of salvation in motion. Zechariah and Elizabeth's son, John, was born for a specific purpose—to announce the coming of the Messiah.

The next step was for the Savior to be born. God sent the same angel, Gabriel, to tell a young, unmarried woman by the name of Mary that she'd have a baby and that she should name him Jesus because he would be the Savior of the world.

Mary was an unlikely candidate to be Jesus' mother. She was young, poor, and probably uneducated. By the world's standards, she didn't have much to offer. God could have found someone from a rich family, where Jesus would have received the best food, clothing, education, and worldly possessions. But this wasn't God's plan. Jesus was born to a humble and obedient young woman who had a strong faith in God. He was born in a lowly stable surrounded by animals.

God chose the people who would be part of the salvation story—Zechariah and Elizabeth, Joseph and Mary, John and Jesus—and he gave them a mission and purpose. When things got difficult, they remembered it was God who called them to the task. When people ridiculed them, they knew it was okay because they were living out God's purpose for their lives.

For You

God has a special purpose for your life too. He won't show you the whole plan at once, but he will lead you in it day by day. Each day ask God to direct you, and he will show you the things he wants you to do.

Answer: c
Gabriel appeared to her and said, "Greetings, favored woman! The Lord is with you!" Confused and disturbed, Mary tried to think what the angel could mean. "Don't be afraid, Mary," the angel told her, "for you have found favor with God! You will conceive and give birth to a son, and you will name him Jesus."
Luke 1:28-31
(The Whole Story: Luke 1:26-38)

August 22

A Long Journey

Q: Why did Mary and Joseph go to Bethlehem?
a. to visit a relative
b. to have a better place to give birth
c. to be counted in a census

At the time Jesus was born, Rome ruled Palestine where Joseph and Mary lived. Emperor Caesar Augustus called for a census to find out how many people there were to serve in the army and to pay taxes. The Jews didn't have to serve in the Roman army, but they did have to pay the taxes.

Caesar Augustus's decision to count the people fit into God's timing for Jesus' birth. Joseph had to travel a long way to Bethlehem, his hometown, to pay his taxes. Mary made the journey with him. She was very close to giving birth to Jesus at this time.

When Joseph and Mary arrived in Bethlehem, it was crowded, and there was nowhere for them to stay other than in a stable. And that's where Jesus was born.

God brought together all the pieces of the plan in order for the prophecies about Jesus to be fulfilled. Jesus was to be born into the family line of David, and both Mary and Joseph were descendants of David. It was prophesied that Jesus would be born in Bethlehem, and that happened because of the census.

God uses circumstances to work out his will. Nothing catches him unaware, because he already knows what is going to happen before it happens.

For You

When it seems like everything is going wrong—or at least not the way you planned it—be patient and watch for God to work. He may orchestrate those very circumstances to work out his will.

Answer: c
All returned to their own ancestral towns to register for this census. And because Joseph was a descendant of King David, he had to go to Bethlehem in Judea, David's ancient home. He traveled there from the village of Nazareth in Galilee.
Luke 2:3-4
(The Whole Story: Luke 2:1-7)

Jesus' Birth Is Announced

Q: What did the shepherds see that terrified them?
a. angels
b. a bright star
c. a cloud of fire

When a baby is born, usually some sort of birth announcement is sent out, from a simple written card to a more elaborate photo announcement. Since God's Son was born in a lowly stable with little celebration, you might think there was no birth announcement, but God outdid everyone in that area.

At the time Jesus was born, there were shepherds in a field watching over flocks of sheep. God announced his Son's birth to these shepherds. And what an announcement! One moment the sky was filled with stars or perhaps clouds. Suddenly an angel appeared, and it was light all around. The shepherds were frightened. Nothing like this had happened to them before. The angel said to them, "Don't be afraid! I bring you good news that will bring great joy to all people. The Savior—yes, the Messiah, the Lord—has been born today in Bethlehem, the city of David! And you will recognize him by this sign: You will find a baby wrapped snugly in strips of cloth, lying in a manger."

The angel was joined by many more angels saying, "Glory to God in highest heaven, and peace on earth to those with whom God is pleased."

The angels left, and all was dark and quiet again. The shepherds hurried to find Mary, Joseph, and baby Jesus. After they'd seen him, they told everyone what had happened. Then they returned to their lives as shepherds, but they never forgot the angel's announcement or meeting the newborn Savior.

For You

The shepherds' lives were changed by the newborn Savior. Our lives are changed by Jesus too. Jesus offers hope, peace, and a reason for living. Who can you tell about the change Jesus makes in people's lives? Someone needs to hear that message today.

Answer: a
Suddenly, the angel was joined by a vast host of others—the armies of heaven—praising God and saying, "Glory to God in highest heaven, and peace on earth to those with whom God is pleased." Luke 2:13-14
(The Whole Story: Luke 2:8-20)

August 24

Worth the Wait

Q: What two people were in the Temple when Jesus was brought there at eight days old?
a. Zechariah and Elizabeth
b. Simeon and Anna
c. Elkanah and Hannah

Youth is valued in our society. Many times people believe that if you are young and strong, you are worth more than people who are old and weak. But in Jesus' time, the elders were respected and listened to. This was true of Simeon and Anna, very old people who served in the Temple.

At one time Anna had been married, but her husband died, and she spent the rest of her years serving God in the Temple. Simeon also served in the Temple, and God had let him know he wouldn't die until he'd seen the promised Messiah.

Anna and Simeon never lost hope that the Messiah would come. When Mary and Joseph took baby Jesus to the Temple in Jerusalem to be consecrated to God, Anna and Simeon both recognized him as the Savior. Simeon took baby Jesus in his arms and said, "Sovereign Lord, now let your servant die in peace, as you have promised. I have seen your salvation, which you have prepared for all people. He is a light to reveal God to the nations, and he is the glory of your people Israel!"

Some people thought the Messiah was coming to bring salvation only to the Jews, but Simeon declared that Jesus would be a light to reveal God and bring salvation to all the nations.

Jesus died on the cross for the sins of the whole world. Anyone who accepts him as Savior can be forgiven of his or her sins and have eternal life in heaven.

For You
Jesus' death on the cross was for you, your family, your friends, and even your enemies. Invite someone to your church today.

Answer: b
Simeon . . . was righteous and devout and was eagerly waiting for the Messiah to come. . . . Anna, a prophet, was also there in the Temple . . . and she was very old. . . . She never left the Temple but stayed there day and night, worshiping God with fasting and prayer. Luke 2:25, 36-37
(The Whole Story: Luke 2:21-40)

The Magi

Q: What three gifts did the wise men give baby Jesus?
a. gold, frankincense, and myrrh
b. gold, silver, and frankincense
c. gold, myrrh, and sapphires

Do you set out a nativity scene in your house at Christmas? Mary, Joseph, and baby Jesus are the central figures. The nativity also probably has one or two shepherds and three magi, or wise men. People traditionally talk about three wise men because the Bible tells us about the three gifts they gave Jesus—gold, frankincense and myrrh. But there may have been more than three magi.

The wise men, following a star to find Jesus, stopped to ask King Herod where they could find the newborn king. Herod thought the Messiah would be a great military or political leader and wanted to kill him, so he asked the wise men to return after they found the baby, claiming he wanted to worship the baby too.

The wise men found Jesus, presented their gifts, and worshiped him. They were warned in a dream not to go back to Herod to tell him they'd found Jesus, and Joseph was told to escape to Egypt with Mary and their baby.

When Herod realized the magi were not going to return, he ordered all the baby boys age two and under to be killed, in hopes of killing the new king. Herod didn't understand who Jesus really was or that he'd come to earth to be a Savior, not an earthly king.

Some people today don't understand that the Son of God came to earth to forgive sins and change lives. Just as the shepherds (see the August 23 devotion) and the magi were changed by their encounters with Jesus, people today are still transformed by meeting him.

For You

If you know Jesus, your life is forever changed. If you don't notice much difference, your Christian walk may need some help. Spend time reading the Bible, praying, and sharing what you learn with someone else. That will help you grow in your faith.

Answer: a
[The wise men] entered the house and saw the child with his mother, Mary, and they bowed down and worshiped him. Then they opened their treasure chests and gave him gifts of gold, frankincense, and myrrh. Matthew 2:11
(The Whole Story: Matthew 2:1-16)

August 26

Growing

Q: How old was Jesus when he amazed the men at the Temple with his knowledge?
a. 12
b. 16
c. 18

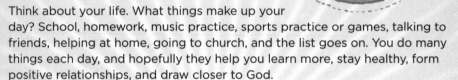

Think about your life. What things make up your day? School, homework, music practice, sports practice or games, talking to friends, helping at home, going to church, and the list goes on. You do many things each day, and hopefully they help you learn more, stay healthy, form positive relationships, and draw closer to God.

We don't know much about Jesus' early years, but Luke 2:52 says, "Jesus grew in wisdom and in stature and in favor with God and all the people." That means he grew in all areas of his life—intellectually, relationally, physically, and spiritually.

Jesus visited the Temple when he was 12 years old. The spiritual leaders were amazed at all he knew. Jesus asked and answered questions with understanding and wisdom.

Can you imagine what it would be like to have Jesus in your Sunday school class or Bible club? He'd be the one ignoring the whispering and the goofing around, and he'd be focusing on the teacher's words instead. He'd be the one asking questions to make sure he understood the lesson. He may even be asking questions the teachers would have to research. How about you? Would you be listening with him, or would you be more focused on what your friends were doing?

For You

Jesus grew in all areas of his life. Ask yourself, *Do the activities I take part in each day help me to grow physically? Intellectually? Spiritually? Relationally?* If not, it might be time to look for some new activities.

Answer: a
Every year Jesus' parents went to Jerusalem for the Passover festival. When Jesus was twelve years old, they attended the festival as usual. . . . All who heard him were amazed at his understanding and his answers. Luke 2:41-42, 47
(The Whole Story: Luke 2:41-52)

August 27

John the Baptist

Q: Which of these do we associate with John the Baptist?
a. cotton clothes, goat's milk, and honey for food
b. camel hair clothes, a leather belt, locusts and honey for food
c. denim clothes and a leather belt, wine, and bread for food

John the Baptist was a man with an important job. He was the forerunner of Jesus. That means he started his ministry before Jesus did, and he told people that the Messiah would be coming. He got them ready for the Savior.

John was different from the other religious leaders of that time. Most of them were more interested in looking and acting important than in really knowing God or preparing for the coming Messiah.

John the Baptist was different in other ways too. He wore camel hair clothes and a leather belt. He ate locusts and honey. John was the first real prophet in around 400 years. He courageously proclaimed the truth and spoke out against sin. This didn't make him very popular with some people, but other people heard his message and believed.

John stood out as different both in his lifestyle and in his message. While the religious leaders of the day were interested in impressing people, John was only concerned with impressing God. It was obvious to those around him that John lived what he believed. His faith was for real.

When you have a real faith in God, it shows in the way you live each day. It shows in how you dress and how you act. It shows in the decisions you make and the people you choose to spend time with. What does your life say about your faith?

For You

John was a light in a world that had been dark for a long time. God used him to prepare hearts for the coming Messiah, Jesus. Do you live in a way that will draw others to the Savior? If not, what changes do you need to make?

Answer: b
John's clothes were woven from coarse camel hair, and he wore a leather belt around his waist. For food he ate locusts and wild honey. Matthew 3:4
(The Whole Story: Matthew 3:1-12; Mark 1:1-8; Luke 3:2-18; John 1:19-28)

August 28

Jesus' Baptism

Q: At Jesus' baptism, the Holy Spirit appeared as a
a. parrot.
b. dove.
c. raven.

During John the Baptist's time, people were baptized to show their repentance. They were baptized in the Jordan River, the same river God's chosen people had had to cross hundreds of years earlier in order to enter the Promised Land under Joshua's leadership.

Jesus went to John to be baptized, but not because he had any sin to repent of. The Savior was perfect and without sin. Jesus was baptized to mark the beginning of his ministry and to show others that he was set apart for a special purpose. At Jesus' baptism, the Holy Spirit came to Jesus like a dove, and a voice from heaven said, "You are my dearly loved Son, and you bring me great joy."

Jesus' baptism also set an example for others. Before Jesus went back to heaven after his resurrection, he told his disciples, "Go and make disciples of all the nations, baptizing them in the name of the Father and the Son and the Holy Spirit" (Matthew 28:19). Baptism doesn't forgive sins, because only Jesus' death and resurrection can do that. We are forgiven when we confess our sins and ask God to forgive us. Baptism is a sign of our obedience to God and willingness to let others know that we believe in God.

For You

Some churches have age requirements for baptism or require people to take a class first to make sure they understand baptism. Other churches will immediately baptize anyone who confesses Jesus as his or her Savior. Which does your church do? Have you already been baptized? If not, talk to your parents and then your pastor about it.

Answer: b

As Jesus came up out of the water, he saw the heavens splitting apart and the Holy Spirit descending on him like a dove. Mark 1:10
(The Whole Story: Matthew 3:13-17; Mark 1:9-11; Luke 3:21-22; John 1:29-34)

August 29

Jesus' Temptation

Q: Satan told Jesus to change stones into what?
a. water
b. doves
c. bread

After Jesus was baptized, he went to the desert, where he spent 40 days with no food to eat. Jesus had a physical body, so he was hungry just as we would be. Satan knew Jesus was hungry and tried to get him to prove that he was God by changing stones into bread. Satan also asked Jesus to throw himself off the top of the Temple to prove the angels would protect him. Then Satan told Jesus that if Jesus worshiped him, he would give Jesus all the kingdoms of the world.

Satan didn't tempt Jesus at his baptism when he had the support of John the Baptist. He waited until Jesus was alone, tired, and hungry. It's easy to give in to temptation when you aren't well rested and fed. It's easy to rationalize things when you are alone. Yet Jesus resisted. How? He quoted Scripture to Satan. But just knowing Scripture isn't enough, because Satan quoted Scripture to Jesus, too.

Scripture is our weapon for spiritual battle. The Bible says, "Put on salvation as your helmet, and take the sword of the Spirit, which is the word of God" (Ephesians 6:17). It's important to both know and obey Scripture. If you are willing to do both, Scripture is a powerful weapon against temptation.

For You

Fill your heart and mind with Scripture for the times you are tempted. It will also help you when you are afraid, lonely, or discouraged. Use a concordance (there may be one in the back of your Bible) and look for a word such as *anger, love, patience, holy,* or *trust.* Look up all the Bible references listed for that word and memorize one.

Answer: c
The devil said to him, "If you are the Son of God, tell this stone to become a loaf of bread." But Jesus told him, "No! The Scriptures say, 'People do not live by bread alone.'" Luke 4:3-4
(The Whole Story: Matthew 4:1-11; Mark 1:12-13; Luke 4:1-13)

August 30

Fishermen

Q: Fill in the blank: "Jesus called out to them, 'Come, follow me, and I will show you how to fish for _____!'"
a. trout
b. people
c. perch

Some of Jesus' disciples were fishermen. Jesus met them by the Sea of Galilee, a large lake with about 30 fishing towns around it. Jesus called Peter and Andrew to leave their fishing business and follow him. He wanted them to be fishers of men. He planned for them to tell others about salvation and pull people to the Good News just as a fisherman pulls in fish with a net. Jesus also called James and John, who were fishermen too.

When Jesus began looking for men to follow him, he didn't go into the Temple or court. He didn't go to the schools. He walked along the Sea of Galilee among the fishermen. He didn't look for the richest or most intelligent men. They may have had pride in themselves and claimed some part of Jesus' power. Jesus called Peter, Andrew, James, and John, who left their work to follow Jesus without looking back or making elaborate plans.

Don't fear that God won't call you to do something special for him because you aren't good at science or aren't one of the better athletes. Don't expect him to overlook you because you don't have many friends and you sit alone at lunch. That's not how God works. He chooses people who are willing and who will give him the praise for accomplishments.

For You

The fishermen immediately left their jobs to follow Jesus. That doesn't mean Jesus expects you to leave school or your chores, but he wants you to do things for him now, not wait until you are an adult. God has certain things only you can accomplish, so be open to God's prompting, and he will show you what to do.

Answer: b

Jesus called out to them, "Come, follow me, and I will show you how to fish for people!" And they left their nets at once and followed him. Matthew 4:19-20
(The Whole Story: Matthew 4:18-22; Mark 1:16-20; Luke 5:1-11)

Jesus' First Miracle

Q: Where did Jesus' first miracle take place?
a. in the Temple
b. at a wedding
c. on Mount Moriah

One day Jesus was at a wedding along with his mother and his disciples. During the celebration, the wine ran out. (This was not like our wine today. It was more like grape juice.) Wedding celebrations often lasted a week, and everyone was invited to come and take part. To run out of wine would have been an embarrassing situation.

Mary realized the wine was gone and told Jesus about the problem. She may not have been asking him to do a miracle, but just for a solution. Jesus had not yet performed any miracles, but he chose to do one at the wedding.

Jesus ordered the men to fill six large pots with water. Then he told them to dip some out and take it to the chief steward. The chief steward tasted it and declared it to be much better than the previous wine.

By doing this miracle, Jesus met the need at hand—in this case, the need for wine for a celebration. That may not seem like a big deal. It's not like healing someone, calming a storm, or raising someone from the dead. But it made a difference to those hosting the celebration and to those attending the festivities.

Jesus still meets needs. He may not be here to do a miracle in person, but he answers prayers, gives us wisdom to make good decisions, and orchestrates events. He changes hearts, and he changes lives.

For You

What difference do you think Jesus' first miracle made for the disciples? His mother? Those hosting the celebration? What has Jesus done in your life lately?

Answer: b
The next day there was a wedding celebration in the village of Cana in Galilee. Jesus' mother was there, and Jesus and his disciples were also invited to the celebration. The wine supply ran out during the festivities, so Jesus' mother told him, "They have no more wine." John 2:1-3
(The Whole Story: John 2:1-12)

September 1

A Nighttime Visitor

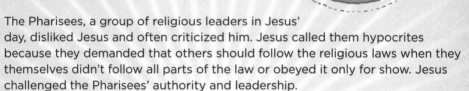

Q: Who came to see Jesus at night?
a. Zacchaeus
b. Nicodemus
c. John the Baptist

The Pharisees, a group of religious leaders in Jesus' day, disliked Jesus and often criticized him. Jesus called them hypocrites because they demanded that others should follow the religious laws when they themselves didn't follow all parts of the law or obeyed it only for show. Jesus challenged the Pharisees' authority and leadership.

Nicodemus was a Pharisee searching for answers. Since the Pharisees opposed Jesus, Nicodemus went to see Jesus at night so no one would see him. Nicodemus wanted to know for himself who Jesus was and what he taught, not what the other Pharisees said about him.

Jesus told Nicodemus he must be born again. Jesus meant that just as Nicodemus had been born physically, he must be born spiritually. Jesus told him, "I assure you, no one can enter the Kingdom of God without being born of water and the Spirit. This is how God loved the world: He gave his one and only Son, so that everyone who believes in him will not perish but have eternal life."

We don't know more about Nicodemus other than he was a changed person because of his meeting with Jesus. After Jesus was crucified, Nicodemus went with Joseph of Arimathea to ask for Jesus' body in order to bury it (see John 19:38-39). This was a bold move for the man who originally met with Jesus in secret.

Nicodemus was changed because he met Jesus. Countless people over the years have had that same experience. Once you meet Jesus, your life is never the same.

For You

Nicodemus went to talk to Jesus to find out for himself who Jesus was. If you, like Nicodemus, want to know more about Jesus, take time each day to read from the Gospels in the Bible (Matthew, Mark, Luke, and John).

Answer: b

There was a man named Nicodemus, a Jewish religious leader who was a Pharisee. After dark one evening, he came to speak with Jesus. "Rabbi," he said, "we all know that God has sent you to teach us. Your miraculous signs are evidence that God is with you." Jesus replied, "I tell you the truth, unless you are born again, you cannot see the Kingdom of God." John 3:1-3
(The Whole Story: John 3:1-21)

September 2

The Woman at the Well

Q: What did Jesus offer the Samaritan woman?
a. fish and bread
b. coins
c. living water

Samaria was the capital of the northern kingdom. When the northern kingdom was taken captive, foreigners moved into Samaria and lived among the remaining Jews. Some of the Jews married the foreigners, and their children were known as Samaritans. The Samaritans were looked down on and avoided by Jews because they were a mixed race.

Jesus didn't care about race. He came to save everyone, including the Samaritans. While other Jews would travel extra miles to avoid Samaria, Jesus traveled through it.

One day Jesus stopped in Samaria at a well. Women came to draw water from the well in the morning and at night. But one woman came at noon. She was a woman known for her sinful lifestyle and was probably trying to avoid the other women who might have said mean things about her.

When the sinful woman came to the well, Jesus asked her for a drink. Then he told her, "Anyone who drinks this water will soon become thirsty again. But those who drink the water I give will never be thirsty again. It becomes a fresh, bubbling spring within them, giving them eternal life."

Jesus went on to tell her all about her life. The woman thought Jesus was a prophet because he knew things about her that he'd never been told. The woman went and told her friends to come and meet Jesus. Many Samaritans believed in Jesus that day because of Jesus' encounter with the woman at the well.

For You

After the Samaritan woman met Jesus at the well, she immediately shared her experience with others. They came and believed too. Sometimes our enthusiasm for telling others about Jesus wears off, but it shouldn't. If you aren't sharing Jesus with your friends and classmates, ask God to make you not only willing to share your faith but eager to do it.

Answer: c
Jesus replied, "If you only knew the gift God has for you and who you are speaking to, you would ask me, and I would give you living water." John 4:10
(The Whole Story: John 4:1-42)

September 3

Early in the Morning

Q: What did Jesus get up before day-break to do?
a. go fishing
b. eat
c. pray

Are you a morning person? Do you hop right out of bed when your alarm goes off, or does one of your parents have to drag you out of bed?

The Bible tells us that Jesus got up very early in the morning, went outside by himself, and prayed. Even though Jesus was the Son of God, he found it important to rise early and find a place alone to talk to God. If it was important for Jesus to do that, it's important for us to do that too.

Jesus may have picked early morning because the busyness of the day hadn't started yet. He wanted to spend the first minutes with his heavenly Father before he spent time with the disciples, taught the crowds, or healed the sick.

Starting the day with God is a good idea. When you wake up, you are fresh for the day. You haven't faced home, school, or friendship issues yet.

Jesus also went to a place where he was totally alone. It's important for you to find a place with no cell phone, iPod, or computer for distractions and where you don't hear your siblings arguing about who gets the bathroom first or who finished off the cereal.

Try to follow Jesus' example and start each day alone with God this week.

For You

Your parents may not want you to get up at daybreak like Jesus, but perhaps you could get up 10 minutes early and go outside and sit on your trampoline or lawn chair to pray. If you aren't sure what to say, just share your hopes for the day with God. Be sure to listen to what he has to say to you, too.

Answer: c
Before daybreak the next morning, Jesus got up and went out to an isolated place to pray. Mark 1:35
(The Whole Story: Mark 1:35-39; Luke 4:42-44)

September 4

Where There's a Will, There's a Way

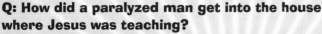

Q: How did a paralyzed man get into the house where Jesus was teaching?
a. His friends carried him through the front door.
b. His friends lifted him through a window.
c. His friends lowered him through the roof.

Have you heard the saying, "Where there's a will, there's a way"? That means if you really want to do something, you'll find a way. And that was true for a paralyzed man and his friends.

The paralyzed man wanted to walk. The man's friends knew Jesus could heal him, so they took him to a house where Jesus was teaching. When they got there, the house was so crowded that they couldn't get inside.

The men weren't willing to give up. They came up with a plan. Back then most houses had flat roofs, and often there were steps leading to the roof from the outside. The friends carried the man to the rooftop. Then they cut a hole through the roof, which was probably made of hardened clay tiles, and lowered the man on a mat down right in front of Jesus. Jesus healed him.

The paralyzed man was blessed to have good friends who knew Jesus was the answer. Their faith gave them the motive to get their friend face-to-face with Jesus. When one thing didn't work, they tried another. As a result, the paralyzed man was healed.

For You

The paralyzed man's friends didn't give up when they couldn't get their friend to Jesus. They tried something else. When you face a problem with schoolwork, a friend, or a family member, ask Jesus to help you, and find good Christian friends to talk to. You may discover a different solution to your problem.

Answer: c
They couldn't bring him to Jesus because of the crowd, so they dug a hole through the roof above his head. Then they lowered the man on his mat, right down in front of Jesus. Mark 2:4
(The Whole Story: Matthew 9:1-8; Mark 2:1-12; Luke 5:17-26)

September 5

The Tax Man

Q: What other name was Matthew known by?
a. Levi
b. Simon
c. Thaddaeus

In Jesus' time, there was a man named Matthew, also known as Levi, who was a Jew paid to collect taxes for Rome. The tax collectors were despised and were called sinners. But when Jesus walked by Matthew's collection booth, he said, "Follow me and be my disciple."

Matthew got up and immediately followed Jesus. Perhaps he'd heard others talk about Jesus or had heard Jesus teach. Or maybe it was the way Jesus seemed to look right into Matthew's heart and know he needed a change in his life. Whatever the reason was, Matthew went with Jesus.

Later Matthew invited Jesus and Jesus' disciples to dinner at his home with some other tax collectors. The Pharisees, who were very strict about keeping the religious laws, were disgusted that Jesus would dine with known sinners. They asked Jesus' disciples, "Why does your teacher eat with such scum?"

Jesus heard and answered them, "Healthy people don't need a doctor—sick people do. I have come to call not those who think they are righteous, but those who know they are sinners."

People assumed Jesus came to save those who didn't follow the religious laws, but he came to save all sinners. Often the righteous people didn't think they needed a Savior because they followed all the religious rules. They thought they were good enough.

Even today it may not be the "good enough" people who come to Jesus, but those who realize they are sinful and need a Savior.

For You

Don't assume the "bad kids" at school or in your neighborhood won't listen when you talk about Jesus. Everyone needs to hear the Good News. Although some people may not listen at first, you are planting the seed of the gospel in their lives. That's exactly what Jesus asks you to do.

Answer: a

Then Jesus went out to the lakeshore again and taught the crowds that were coming to him. As he walked along, he saw Levi son of Alphaeus sitting at his tax collector's booth. "Follow me and be my disciple," Jesus said to him. So Levi got up and followed him.   Mark 2:13-14

(The Whole Story: Matthew 9:9-13; Mark 2:13-17; Luke 5:27-32)

Missing the Miracle

Q: Why were the Pharisees angry that a crippled man had been healed?
a. They wanted to be healed first.
b. Jesus healed on the Sabbath.
c. The crippled man was a sinner.

Tyrone, a middle school basketball player, was tripped during a game and broke his leg. He had to be in a cast for several weeks. Once the cast was off, Tyrone did hours of physical therapy in order to be able to use his leg again. The months of wearing a cast and going to physical therapy were tough, and Tyrone thought he'd never get back to the basketball court.

In Jesus' time there was a man who couldn't walk, not just for a few weeks or months, but for 38 years. Jesus saw the man's need and told him, "Stand up, pick up your mat, and walk!"

The man was instantly healed. He rolled up his mat and walked away carrying it. Instead of being joyful about the miracle, the Pharisees were angry because the man was healed on the Sabbath. They told the man it was against the law to work on the Sabbath and that carrying his mat was considered work.

Carrying the mat did not break a law, but it broke the Pharisees' interpretation of the law. They believed that "remember the Sabbath day and keep it holy" meant the man could not carry his mat. The Pharisees were so busy enforcing their own interpretation of the law that they missed the greater thing—a man had been miraculously healed by Jesus.

Sometimes in trying to live by the strictest interpretation of rules or Scripture, people miss out on seeing or receiving God's blessings.

For You

God wants us to follow his rules, but sometimes people try to live by rules meant for the people who lived in Old Testament times. Jesus' death changed many of those laws. The important thing is to try to live like Jesus wants you to. Ask him to show you if you are doing things he doesn't want you to do. You have the Holy Spirit and the Bible to guide you and point out what's wrong in your life.

Answer: b

Instantly, the man was healed! He rolled up his sleeping mat and began walking! But this miracle happened on the Sabbath, so the Jewish leaders objected. They said to the man who was cured, "You can't work on the Sabbath! The law doesn't allow you to carry that sleeping mat!" John 5:9-10
(The Whole Story: John 5:1-16)

September 7

Jesus' Teachings

Q: Where was Jesus when he gave the Beatitudes?
a. on a mountainside
b. on the Sea of Galilee
c. in the desert

Some of Jesus' most famous teachings are part of what is known as the "Sermon on the Mount" because they were given on a mountainside near Capernaum. Jesus' teachings went on for many days as he talked about the law, authority, money, anger, making a difference, and more. The most familiar part of that sermon is probably the Beatitudes.

The Beatitudes tell us how to be blessed by God. They are keys to happiness (see Matthew 5:4-10, ICB):

Those who are sad now are happy. God will comfort them.
Those who are humble are happy. The earth will belong to them.
Those who want to do right more than anything else are happy. God will fully satisfy them.
Those who give mercy to others are happy. Mercy will be given to them.
Those who are pure in their thinking are happy. They will be with God.
Those who work to bring peace are happy. God will call them his sons.
Those who are treated badly for doing good are happy. The kingdom of heaven belongs to them. (Matthew 5:4-10, ICB)

During Jesus' time, the Pharisees lived by strict religious laws, but following the laws didn't help them have a relationship with God. When Jesus spoke the Beatitudes, they were different from how the Pharisees lived and believed. The Beatitudes are good attitudes all Christians should have. God will bless those who live for him.

For You

Do you see the attitudes taught in the Beatitudes lived out around you? In your own life? Which ones do you need to work on today?

Answer: a
One day as he saw the crowds gathering, Jesus went up on the mountainside and sat down. His disciples gathered around him, and he began to teach them.
Matthew 5:1-2
(The Whole Story: Matthew 5:1-12; Luke 6:17-26)

September 8

The Way to Live

Q: In the Sermon on the Mount, what two things does Jesus tell the people they should be like?
a. light and darkness
b. sheep and goats
c. light and salt

Jesus' teachings on the mountainside were about how people should behave and think. He challenged many of the popular attitudes and beliefs. His words weren't just for Bible times; they are good standards to live by today.

Jesus told the people they should be like salt. Some foods are bland without seasoning. Salt adds flavor. When we allow love, kindness, compassion, patience, and joy to radiate from our lives, we add seasoning to those around us. They will be drawn to us because they desire what we have.

Jesus also told the people they were the light of the world, a city on top of a hill whose light could be seen from far away. Sometimes it's easy to hide our light, like when we see something that is wrong and we don't speak up. We hide our light when we see a need and ignore it because we don't want to go out of our comfort zone.

Our lights shine bright when we reach out to others, speak an encouraging word, lend a hand, stand by someone who's being bullied, tell someone about Jesus' love, or share Scripture.

We are here on the earth as salt and light, but if we are flavorless or dark, we aren't doing what Jesus intends for us to do.

For You

Do you add flavor and light to your corner of the world? Is your life making a difference? Try to do one thing each day this week that impacts someone near you.

Answer: c
[Jesus said,] "You are the salt of the earth. But what good is salt if it has lost its flavor? Can you make it salty again? It will be thrown out and trampled underfoot as worthless. You are the light of the world—like a city on a hilltop that cannot be hidden. No one lights a lamp and then puts it under a basket. Instead, a lamp is placed on a stand, where it gives light to everyone in the house. In the same way, let your good deeds shine out for all to see, so that everyone will praise your heavenly Father." Matthew 5:13-16
(The Whole Story: Matthew 5:13-16; Mark 9:50; Luke 14:34-35)

September 9

Prayer

Q: The Bible says that if we keep on _____, we will _____ what we ask for.
a. hoping, get
b. asking, receive
c. praying, see

Martin Luther, the leader of the Protestant Reformation, once said, "I have so much to do that I shall spend the first three hours in prayer." That is not the way most of us live, though.

One of the subjects of Jesus' teachings on the mountainside was prayer. He encouraged the people to continue to ask for what they needed and to seek answers. Jesus wants us not just to pray, but to seek after God and his answers for us. That requires a commitment to prayer.

Prayer is simply communicating with God. Adam and Eve talked to God while walking in the Garden of Eden, Daniel prayed in his room in front of an open window, Elijah prayed by a brook, and Jesus prayed in many places, including on the mountain and in the garden of Gethsemane.

You can pray wherever you are. In the morning while you're showering, pray for your teachers. If you ride the bus to school, spend that time praying about situations you'll face that day. On the ride home, thank God for being with you. Before bed, pray for those who are sick or facing difficulties.

Prayer is talking to the God who created the universe, but you don't have to use a certain set of words or phrases to make your prayer meaningful. Just share with God from your heart.

For You

Take five minutes each morning to commit your day to the Lord and ask for his guidance. Pray throughout the day whenever you think of it. Prayer keeps the line of communication open between you and God.

Answer: b
Keep on asking, and you will receive what you ask for. Keep on seeking, and you will find. Keep on knocking, and the door will be opened to you. For everyone who asks, receives. Everyone who seeks, finds. And to everyone who knocks, the door will be opened. Matthew 7:7-8
(The Whole Story: Matthew 7:7-11; Luke 11:9-13)

Standing Firm in the Storm

Q. Where did the foolish man build his house?
a. next door
b. on the sand
c. on the rock

Have you seen pictures of the Leaning Tower of Pisa? This tower began leaning while it was still under construction. The tower was built on sandy, marshy soil, and it had a poor foundation. After the first three stories were built, the tower started to sink. The foundation didn't support its weight, and the soil underneath wasn't firm. Foundations are important. If a building is constructed on an inferior foundation, the whole building is at risk.

Jesus told the story of the foolish man who built his house on the sand. The rain came down, the winds blew, the streams rose, and the house fell flat. The wise man built his house on a foundation of rock, and the house stood firm through storms.

Jesus used the story to help the people think about their lives. Everyone builds his life on some kind of foundation. Some people build on the weak foundations of riches, popularity, or talents. Some build on the strong foundation of Jesus Christ.

When the storms of life come—a friend moving, a family member dying, struggles in school, and other problems—it will be easy to tell what kind of foundation you have. If Jesus is your foundation, you can trust God in the hard times and ask God for strength to endure. You can look with hope to the future.

Some people build on rock, some on sand. Which foundation are you choosing?

For You

How can you build on a firm foundation? Trust Jesus as your Savior. Read your Bible and pray to God, so you can get to know him more. Ask God to help you, and seek advice from godly people when you have decisions to make. Then, when the storms in life come, you will stand strong.

Answer: b
[Jesus said,] "Anyone who hears my teaching and doesn't obey it is foolish, like a person who builds a house on sand." Matthew 7:26
(The Whole Story: Matthew 7:24-27; Luke 6:47-49)

September 11

The Faith of a Roman Officer

Q: A Roman officer asked Jesus to heal
a. his wife.
b. his daughter.
c. a young servant.

One day a centurion, a Roman army officer who had control over 100 soldiers, approached Jesus. Many Jews hated the centurions because Rome occupied the Jewish nations, and the Romans often treated the Jews unkindly. Despite this, the army officer came to see Jesus because his servant was very ill, and the centurion believed Jesus could heal him.

Jesus told the officer he would come and heal the servant. But the centurion said, "Lord, I am not worthy to have you come into my home. Just say the word from where you are, and my servant will be healed."

Jesus was amazed at the man's faith. The centurion was not even a Jew, yet he believed Jesus could heal the servant from far away just by speaking the words. Jesus told the Jews who were gathered that many of them would not be in heaven because they didn't believe in him. They trusted in their traditions and rituals, but they didn't believe Jesus was the Son of God, the promised Messiah.

Many Jewish leaders believed the Messiah was still to come and that he would provide salvation only for the Jews, but Jesus offered salvation to anyone who believed in him. The same is still true today. God's message isn't for any certain group. It's for everyone who believes in Jesus and asks him to be their Savior.

For You

Some of the Jews in Jesus' time trusted in their own laws and traditions, not in Jesus. Only faith in Jesus saves. Make sure you have accepted Jesus for yourself rather than counting on your church attendance to save you.

Answer: c
Jesus said to the Roman officer, "Go back home. Because you believed, it has happened." And the young servant was healed that same hour. Matthew 8:13
(The Whole Story: Matthew 8:5-13; Luke 7:1-10)

September 12

Jesus Is Anointed

Q: Who anointed Jesus while he was dining at a Pharisee's house?
a. the head Pharisee
b. the Samaritan woman
c. a sinful woman

Simon, a Pharisee, invited Jesus to dinner with other Pharisees, the religious elite. These men thought they were better than others because they carefully studied and followed religious laws.

While Jesus was at Simon's house, a woman who was known for her sin entered. She wasn't invited, but she knew Jesus was there and wanted to see him. The woman knelt by Jesus and cried. When her tears fell on his feet, she wiped them off with her long hair. She anointed his feet with perfume and kissed them. That would be a strange sight today, but it was a sign of respect in Jesus' time.

Simon and his religious friends were indignant. They told Jesus that if he was really a prophet, he'd know the woman was a sinner. Jesus told them a story:

"A man loaned money to two people—500 pieces of silver to one and 50 pieces to the other. But neither of them could repay him, so he kindly forgave them both, canceling their debts. Who do you suppose loved him more after that?"

Simon answered, "I suppose the one for whom he canceled the larger debt."

"That's right," Jesus said. He told them the women had shown her love for him by pouring perfume on his feet and kissing them. Jesus assured the woman that her sins were forgiven.

For You

Ephesians 2:8-9 says, "God saved you by his grace when you believed. And you can't take credit for this; it is a gift from God. Salvation is not a reward for the good things we have done, so none of us can boast about it." The woman recognized her need for a Savior, but the Pharisees were trusting in their good works for their salvation. Why can't good works save us?

Answer: c
When a certain immoral woman from that city heard he was eating there, she brought a beautiful alabaster jar filled with expensive perfume. Then she knelt behind him at his feet, weeping. Her tears fell on his feet, and she wiped them off with her hair. Then she kept kissing his feet and putting perfume on them.
Luke 7:37-38
(The Whole Story: Luke 7:36-50)

September 13

A Changed Woman

Q: How many demons did Jesus cast out of Mary Magdalene?
a. 1
b. 5
c. 7

Mary Magdalene is sometimes believed to be the sinful woman in yesterday's devotion, but she's not. We don't know that woman's name, but Mary is called by name in her story. The only thing we know about Mary is that she was from the fishing village of Magdala on the northwest shore of the Sea of Galilee. She is called Mary Magdalene because there are many other women named Mary in the Gospels.

Mary Magdalene had seven demons living in her. Demons were evil spirits that took over a person's body and caused a lot of trouble for that person. They could make a person deaf, blind, or mute. Or they could cause seizures and many other things because they took complete control of the person.

Mary Magdalene didn't want to be possessed by demons, but there wasn't much hope for her. When Jesus cast out the seven demons from Mary, she was a changed woman. Mary was no longer an outcast. She became a faithful follower of the Lord.

Mary didn't return to her home, but she traveled with Jesus along with several other women who helped support Jesus and his disciples financially. They may have helped with some of their other practical needs too. Because Mary followed Jesus, she witnessed both his death and his resurrection.

After Jesus cast out Mary's demons, her life was forever changed. She followed Jesus and never looked back.

For You
Jesus changed Mary's life completely. Can you name some ways your life is different because you know Jesus?

Answer: c
[Jesus] took his twelve disciples with him, along with some women who had been cured of evil spirits and diseases. Among them [was] Mary Magdalene, from whom he had cast out seven demons. Luke 8:1-2
(The Whole Story: Luke 8:1-3)

September 14

Jesus' Stories

Q: The stories Jesus told to help people understand his teachings are called what?
a. parables
b. allegories
c. psalms

Have you ever sat in church listening to the sermon and not understanding it? Then the pastor told a personal story in order to explain a point of the sermon. Even if you didn't understand the whole sermon, you probably understood and remembered the story that the pastor told.

Jesus would teach his followers by using stories called parables. Some people define a parable as "an earthly story with a heavenly meaning." Jesus talked about salt, seeds, light, sheep, bread, and other things from everyday life that his listeners would be familiar with. But the story was always about something more than those earthly things.

Why did Jesus speak in parables? One reason may have been because the Pharisees were always looking for ways to accuse Jesus of doing wrong. His teachings were in the form of stories that couldn't be criticized. On the surface, they were simply everyday stories.

Another reason Jesus spoke in parables was to make the message clear to those who wanted to learn from him. Some people heard the words but didn't understand the message because they were not willing to hear it. The message was clear to those willing to receive it.

The parables also caused people to make a choice. They either listened and thought about the meaning of the parables, or they closed their ears and hearts and walked away.

There are many of Jesus' parables recorded in the Gospels. Their messages are still true for us today.

For You

Take time to read through the Gospels and look for the parables. (Hint: Matthew 13 is a great place to start.) See if you can figure out what the parables mean for you.

Answer: a
Jesus always used stories and illustrations like these when speaking to the crowds. In fact, he never spoke to them without using such parables. Matthew 13:34
(The Whole Story: Matthew 13)

September 15

The Kingdom of Heaven

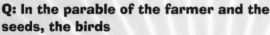

Q: In the parable of the farmer and the seeds, the birds
a. ate the insects that were damaging the crops.
b. ate the seeds.
c. took the seeds and scattered them elsewhere.

Jesus used many parables when teaching about the Kingdom of Heaven. He told stories about everyday things in order to teach spiritual truths about God's Kingdom. The people who were open to the things of God would understand, but those who rejected Jesus' teaching would only hear the earthly story, not the spiritual truth.

Matthew 13 records seven parables about the Kingdom of Heaven. According to the parables, the Kingdom of Heaven is like soil and seeds, sprouting weeds, a mustard seed, yeast, a hidden treasure, a pearl of great price, and a fishing net.

First Jesus told a parable about four kinds of soil. A farmer went out to sow his seeds. Some fell along the path and were eaten by birds. Some fell in rocky places with little soil so they sprang up quickly, but then scorched and withered because they didn't have deep roots. Some seeds fell among thorns, which grew up and choked the plants. Other seeds fell on good soil and produced an abundant crop. All of the seeds were good, but not all of them produced a crop.

When Jesus told this story, he was talking about how people receive his message. Some people are too shallow to receive the gospel, and some are too hard hearted. Some are too distracted by other things, but some are ready to hear and believe.

For You

Has God's Word taken root in your heart? Are you sowing the seeds of the gospel in your friends' lives? Some of them won't be ready to receive it, but others will be ready, and the truth will grow in their hearts.

Answer: b
[Jesus] told many stories in the form of parables, such as this one: "Listen! A farmer went out to plant some seeds. As he scattered them across his field, some seeds fell on a footpath, and the birds came and ate them."
Matthew 13:3-4
(The Whole Story: Matthew 13; Mark 4; Luke 8:1-18)

September 16

The Storm

Q: What was Jesus doing during a storm?
a. preaching
b. eating
c. sleeping

In the summer, many people like to go out on the water on Jet Skis or boats. But if it looks like a storm is moving in, they pull the watercraft out of the water and head home.

One day Jesus and his disciples were out on the Sea of Galilee when a storm moved in too quickly for them to get to shore. Even though some of the disciples were experienced fishermen, they panicked when the storm came up. The waves were breaking over the boat, and they feared for their lives.

Where was Jesus? Sound asleep in the boat. The disciples woke him. "Teacher, don't you care that we're going to drown?" they shouted.

Jesus spoke to the waves, "Silence! Be still!" The wind stopped, and the storm ended. Then Jesus turned to his disciples, "Why are you afraid? Do you still have no faith?" Jesus wanted them to have faith that they would be okay even in the midst of a storm.

The storm the disciples were in was a real storm. But Jesus knew the disciples would have other kinds of storms ahead. They would face ridicule and persecution, and some of them would even face death because of their beliefs. Jesus wanted the disciples to be strong in faith so they could face whatever was ahead.

For You

John 16:33 says, "You may have peace in me. Here on earth you will have many trials and sorrows. But take heart, because I have overcome the world." Jesus knew we'd face problems here on earth, but he's already given us his Holy Spirit, his strength, and his wisdom to handle them.

Answer: c
Jesus was sleeping at the back of the boat with his head on a cushion. The disciples woke him up, shouting, "Teacher, don't you care that we're going to drown?" When Jesus woke up, he rebuked the wind and said to the waves, "Silence! Be still!" Suddenly the wind stopped, and there was a great calm.
Mark 4:38-39
(The Whole Story: Matthew 8:23-27; Mark 4:35-41; Luke 8:22-25)

September 17

Two Men Freed

Q: When Jesus cast many demons out of two men, where did the demons ask to be sent?
a. into a herd of pigs
b. into another man
c. into heaven

Jesus and the disciples had sailed across the Sea of Galilee to the other side. When Jesus got out of the boat, two demon-possessed men came out to meet him. These men normally ran among tombs like wild animals, naked and out of control. All the people were afraid of them. It seemed there was no hope for the men.

The two men ran to Jesus and fell at his feet. The demons possessing the men recognized Jesus. They asked not to be sent into the abyss, but to be allowed to go into a herd of pigs nearby. To the Jews, pigs were unclean animals that could not be touched or eaten.

Jesus sent the demons into the pigs, and the herd plunged down the hillside into the water and drowned. When the herdsmen responsible for the pigs saw this, they ran into town telling everyone what had happened. They probably didn't want to be responsible for the loss.

The two men who were now healed from demon possession wanted to follow Jesus, but Jesus sent them back to their own homes so they could share what had happened to them with their own families and their community.

For You

Jesus delivered the two men, and they wanted to follow him. But Jesus had different plans. He sent them back to their own community as witnesses there. God needs some people to travel to foreign countries with the gospel, but he also needs people who will be witnesses right where they are. Why not make your school or your neighborhood your mission field?

Answer: a
There happened to be a large herd of pigs feeding in the distance. So the demons begged, "If you cast us out, send us into that herd of pigs."
Matthew 8:30-31
(The Whole Story: Matthew 8:28-34; Mark 5:1-20; Luke 8:26-39)

September 18

A Woman with Faith

Q: Why did a woman touch Jesus' clothing?
a. to get his attention
b. so she would be healed
c. to stop him from leaving

Have you ever attended a big sports event? If you have, you know leaving can be difficult. There are so many people you can get jostled by, tripped over, or knocked into.

The crowd that had gathered to see Jesus might have been like a sports crowd. Among the people was a woman with a medical condition that couldn't be cured. She felt hopeless until she heard about the man who could heal people.

The woman knew if she could just touch the hem of Jesus' garment, she'd be healed. She worked her way through the crowd until she was close enough, and then she reached out and touched the hem of Jesus' cloak. The woman was instantly healed.

Jesus said, "Someone deliberately touched me, for I felt healing power go out from me." Many people were touching Jesus, but only one had touched him with faith enough to be healed.

The woman fell at Jesus' feet and told him her problem. She hoped Jesus would understand and allow the healing that had taken place. Jesus told her, "Your faith has made you well. Go in peace."

Touching Jesus' garment didn't heal the woman. Her faith in Jesus did. Jesus alone holds the power to heal and do miracles. These still happen today, but only if it's in God's will and in his timing.

For You

The woman had enough faith to reach out to Jesus and be healed. Do you have faith that Jesus can help you with your problems? Then reach out to him in prayer. He may not give you an immediate answer, but he may speak to you through his Word or trusted adults in your life. He may open doors for you to find the answers and opportunities you need.

Answer: b
She thought to herself, "If I can just touch his robe, I will be healed." Immediately the bleeding stopped, and she could feel in her body that she had been healed of her terrible condition. Mark 5:28-29
(The Whole Story: Matthew 9:18-26; Mark 5:21-43; Luke 8:40-56)

September 19

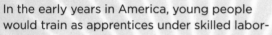

Two by Two

Q: Which person below was *not* one of Jesus' 12 disciples?
a. Philip
b. Bartholomew
c. Mark

In the early years in America, young people would train as apprentices under skilled laborers. If you wanted to be a carpenter, your parents would arrange for you to live with a carpenter's family. You'd work for free as you learned your job, but they'd feed you and give you a place to sleep.

When Jesus lived on earth, 12 men followed him as he preached to the crowds and healed the sick. These 12 men learned from Jesus and witnessed his miracles. They could never be like him because he was the Son of God, but they trained under him to do his work.

When it was time, Jesus sent his disciples out two by two. By going in pairs, they could encourage and strengthen each other. Each could be a support to the other when they faced rejection.

The disciples had God's power to work miracles and his strength to stay strong, but Jesus still had them work in pairs. It's often easier to work as a team than alone. Today when churches send out church members to visit in homes and invite others to church, they often go out in groups of two or three. It's good to have a partner to strengthen and support you.

For You

If you are trying to live God's way alone at school, on a sports team, or in your neighborhood, it's probably hard. It's easier if there's someone else to take a stand with you. Look around for another Christian who can be your partner in living for God each day.

Answer: c
At daybreak [Jesus] called together all of his disciples and chose twelve of them to be apostles. Here are their names: Simon (whom he named Peter), Andrew (Peter's brother), James, John, Philip, Bartholomew, Matthew, Thomas, James (son of Alphaeus), Simon (who was called the zealot), Judas (son of James), Judas Iscariot (who later betrayed him). Luke 6:13-16
(The Whole Story: Mark 3:13-19; 6:7-13; Luke 6:12-16)

September 20

Dealing with Sin

Q: How did John the Baptist die?
a. He drowned.
b. He was crucified.
c. He was beheaded.

John the Baptist loved God and followed his laws. Because of that, he made some enemies. One of those enemies was Herodias. Herod Antipas married Herodias, his brother's wife. John told him that was wrong. John's words made Herodias furious, but she couldn't harm John without Herod's permission.

Herod threw a big party on his birthday. All the important people were there. His daughter, also named Herodias, came in and danced for him. Herod told her she could have anything she wanted, even up to half of his kingdom.

Herodias asked her mother what she should request. What would you ask for if you were in her place? Jewels? Expensive clothing? A horse and carriage? We'll never know what Herodias may have wanted, because her mother told her to ask for John the Baptist's head on a tray.

Herod didn't want to kill John, but he didn't want to break the promise after so many people had heard him. So he had John, who was in prison as a favor to Herod's wife, beheaded, and he presented the head to his daughter.

Herod's wife, Herodias, hated John the Baptist for pointing out the sin in her life. Rather than repent, she chose to have him killed. John died for standing up for what was right.

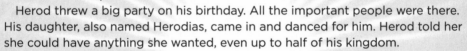

For You

God wants us to turn from sin. In Psalm 139:23-24, David prayed, "Search me, O God, and know my heart; test me and know my anxious thoughts. Point out anything in me that offends you, and lead me along the path of everlasting life." It is better to be like David and confess sin than to be like Herodias and knowingly continue in sin. Pray David's prayer as your own today.

Answer: c
The girl hurried back to the king and told him, "I want the head of John the Baptist, right now, on a tray!" Then the king deeply regretted what he had said; but because of the vows he had made in front of his guests, he couldn't refuse her. Mark 6:25-26
(The Whole Story: Matthew 14:1-12; Mark 6:14-29; Luke 9:7-9)

September 21

Feeding the Crowd

Q: What food did Jesus use to feed the five thousand?
a. bushels of manna from heaven
b. five loaves of bread and two fish
c. a net full of fish caught by Peter and John

When you plan to be gone for the day, you might pack a lunch or stop for fast food. But in Jesus' time, burgers and fries weren't an option, and on one particular day, no one had brought a sack lunch when they came to hear Jesus preach—except one boy.

Jesus taught for a long time, and everyone was hungry. There were more than five thousand people gathered, and Jesus wanted to feed all of them. It would take a lot of food to feed a crowd that size.

Andrew brought a boy to Jesus and said, "There's a young boy here with five barley loaves and two fish. But what good is that with this huge crowd?" The disciples had already forgotten Jesus turned water into wine at the wedding. They questioned what good one lunch would do.

Jesus had the people sit down. He blessed the food and then began breaking it into pieces and passing them out. There was enough food for the whole crowd! After everyone was full, Jesus had the disciples collect the leftovers. There were 12 baskets of food left over. The people were amazed at Jesus' power.

The disciples saw an impossible situation, but Jesus saw the opportunity for a miracle. The people had a need, and he did a miracle to meet that need.

For You

The boy's small lunch was enough for Jesus to use. If you feel like what you have to offer Jesus—your money, your talents, your time—isn't enough, remember he used the boy's loaves of bread and fish to feed a multitude. Jesus can multiply what you have to meet needs too.

Answer: b
[Andrew said,] "There's a young boy here with five barley loaves and two fish. But what good is that with this huge crowd?" John 6:9
(The Whole Story: Matthew 14:13-21; Mark 6:30-44; Luke 9:10-17; John 6:1-15)

Jesus Walks on Water

Q: When Jesus walked on water, his disciples thought he was a
a. mirage.
b. sea creature.
c. ghost.

Jesus' disciples were crossing a lake in a boat. A strong wind came up, and soon the waves were high and powerful. The boat was being tossed about. It was dark, and the disciples wished Jesus was with them. He'd calmed the storm with his words the last time (see the September 16 devotion).

The disciples looked out into the dark and saw a figure moving toward them. They were terrified and thought they were seeing a ghost, but it was Jesus walking on the water to join them. When Jesus climbed into the boat, the wind died down, and all was calm again.

The disciples had witnessed Jesus performing so many miracles that they should have been expecting Jesus' help and looked for him, but they didn't. The disciples were focused on the rough waves around them instead. So even when Jesus approached them walking on the water, they didn't recognize him.

Sometimes when people go through problems, they try to solve them alone. Like the disciples, they are looking only at the situation, not at what God may do. God wants his children to look to him during tough times instead of trying to get through them alone.

For You

No matter what situation you are facing—even if it's a problem you've gotten yourself into—God wants you to turn to him for strength and wisdom to deal with it. Don't panic. Don't act in a hurry. Take time to pray and wait for direction from God.

Answer: c
About three o'clock in the morning Jesus came toward them, walking on the water. When the disciples saw him walking on the water, they were terrified. In their fear, they cried out, "It's a ghost!" Matthew 14:25-26
(The Whole Story: Matthew 14:22-33; Mark 6:45-52; John 6:16-21)

September 23

A Gentile Woman

Q: Finish the quote: "Even dogs are allowed to eat _____."
a. the scraps that fall beneath their masters' table
b. the food that is discarded after a meal
c. the food they've been given

Jesus came to save the world. He went first to his own people, the Jews. But he also healed the Gentiles. One day a Canaanite woman approached Jesus. In ancient times Canaanites were enemies of the Jews, so some of the Jews watching her approach Jesus may have had bad feelings toward her.

The woman cried out to Jesus, "Have mercy on me, O Lord, Son of David! For my daughter is possessed by a demon that torments her severely."

Jesus said to her, "It isn't right to take food from the children and throw it to the dogs." The Jews often called Gentiles dogs, and Jesus used the term to show how the Jews felt. Jesus himself didn't feel that way, but he wanted his healing to stand out as opposite of how the Jews felt.

The woman answered Jesus, "That's true, Lord, but even dogs are allowed to eat the scraps that fall beneath their masters' table."

Jesus liked the woman's faith. He told her, "Your faith is great. Your request is granted." When the woman arrived home, she found her daughter healed.

Jesus used the Gentile woman's request to show he would heal anyone with faith. He healed not only their bodies, but also their hearts. Jesus' salvation was—and is—for everyone.

For You

Some Christians think certain groups of people are not good enough for salvation, but Jesus will accept anyone who truly repents and turns to him in faith. Be careful not to judge people, but try to see them the way Jesus does—as people in need of a Savior.

Answer: a
Jesus responded, "It isn't right to take food from the children and throw it to the dogs." She replied, "That's true, Lord, but even dogs are allowed to eat the scraps that fall beneath their masters' table." Matthew 15:26-27
(The Whole Story: Matthew 15:21-28; Mark 7:24-30)

The Transfiguration

Q: Who appeared with Jesus at the Transfiguration on the mountain?
a. Elijah and Elisha
b. Moses and Aaron
c. Elijah and Moses

Some movies use special effects to make the story more sensational. During the Transfiguration, God used many special effects. He didn't do it to make things more sensational, but to show who Jesus was.

One day Jesus took Peter, James, and John to the top of a mountain. While Jesus was praying, his face changed and his clothes became dazzling white. Those changes in Jesus are why this is referred to as the Transfiguration. *Transfiguration* means a change in form or appearance.

Moses and Elijah appeared on the mountaintop. Moses represented the Old Testament law, and Elijah represented prophecy. Jesus fulfilled both the law and prophecy by his coming to earth as a baby and later by his death and resurrection. God spoke from heaven, "This is my Son, my Chosen One. Listen to him." After that, Elijah and Moses were gone.

The disciples never forgot what they saw that day. Later Peter wrote, "We saw his majestic splendor with our own eyes when he received honor and glory from God the Father. The voice from the majestic glory of God said to him, 'This is my dearly loved Son, who brings me great joy'" (2 Peter 1:16-17). Because of that experience, Peter had more confidence in taking a stand for his faith in later years.

When the three disciples realized Jesus was truly the Son of God, it changed everything about their witness and their lives.

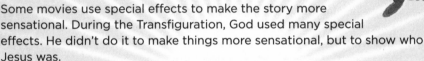

For You

We don't get to physically see Jesus, but as we draw closer to God, we can come to better understand who Jesus is. When that happens, our lives will change in incredible ways. We will become more like Jesus.

Answer: c
A cloud overshadowed them, and a voice from the cloud said, "This is my dearly loved Son. Listen to him." Suddenly, when they looked around, Moses and Elijah were gone, and they saw only Jesus with them.   Mark 9:7-8
(The Whole Story: Matthew 17:1-13; Mark 9:2-13; Luke 9:28-36)

September 25

Help Me Believe

Q: What did the demons do to the boy they possessed?
a. forced him to sing and babble
b. caused him to run away
c. threw him into fire and water

One day a father brought his demon-possessed son to the disciples to be healed. But the disciples couldn't force the demons to leave the boy. The religious leaders criticized the disciples for not having any power.

Then Jesus arrived. He rebuked the disciples for their lack of faith. The boy's father told Jesus the demons would make the boy fall into fire and water. "Have mercy on us and help us, if you can," the father said.

"What do you mean, 'If I can'?" Jesus asked. "Anything is possible if a person believes."

"I do believe, but help me overcome my unbelief!" the father said, and Jesus healed the boy.

This story shows that there are different kinds of faith. The disciples didn't claim God's power, and they tried to heal the boy on their own. Their faith was in their own abilities, and that's why they couldn't make the demons leave the boy.

The religious leaders didn't have a real faith in Jesus. They questioned his authority and doubted his power.

The father wanted to believe, but his faith wavered. He wanted to believe, but the disciples' failure had caused him to doubt.

People today are the same. Some have faith in themselves. Some question or doubt Jesus. And some have wavering faith.

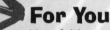

For You
Your faith may waver at times, or you may find yourself trying to do God's work without asking him for his help. Ask Jesus to give you faith, and do God's work through Jesus' strength—not your own.

Answer: c
[The boy's father said to Jesus,] "The spirit often throws him into the fire or into water, trying to kill him. Have mercy on us and help us, if you can." "What do you mean, 'If I can'?" Jesus asked. "Anything is possible if a person believes." The father instantly cried out, "I do believe, but help me overcome my unbelief!"
Mark 9:22-24
(The Whole Story: Matthew 17:14-21; Mark 9:14-29; Luke 9:37-43)

September 26

Temple Tax

Q: Where did Peter find the coin to pay the taxes?
a. on the floor
b. in a fish's mouth
c. in his pouch

Each year your parents pay taxes. This is an event not many people look forward to. Back in Jesus' time, all the males had to pay a Temple tax to help support the Temple. Tax collectors set up booths to collect these taxes.

One day tax collectors asked Peter if Jesus paid the Temple tax like everyone else. Peter went to talk to Jesus about it. Jesus told Peter that just as a king didn't pay taxes, he, the Son of God, didn't need to pay the tax either. Yet Jesus did pay so that he wouldn't offend those who didn't accept him as the Messiah. In fact, Jesus supplied the tax money for both himself and Peter. And he did it in a most unusual way.

Jesus told Peter to go down to the lake and throw in a fishing line. He told him to open the mouth of the first fish he caught. There would be a coin in it. Peter was to take that coin and pay the tax for himself and Jesus.

Even though Jesus didn't have to pay the taxes, he did. He wanted his disciples to be model citizens so people wouldn't be able to find fault with them and use that as an excuse not to believe in Jesus.

God wants you to be a model citizen too. You can be an outstanding example in your home, school, church, and community. You may not agree with every rule or decision that is made, but your job is to obey the rules to the best of your ability.

For You

You can be an example to others in the way you listen to authority and make right choices. You are Jesus' representative to those around you, and he needs you to represent him well.

Answer: b
[Jesus asked,] "Do kings tax their own people or the people they have conquered?" "They tax the people they have conquered," Peter replied. "Well, then," Jesus said, "the citizens are free! However, we don't want to offend them, so go down to the lake and throw in a line. Open the mouth of the first fish you catch, and you will find a large silver coin. Take it and pay the tax for both of us." Matthew 17:25-27
(The Whole Story: Matthew 17:24-27)

September 27

Unforgiveness

Q: How many times did Jesus tell Peter to forgive?
a. 170
b. 70 times 7
c. 700

When Peter asked how many times he should forgive someone, Jesus told him a parable. One day a king decided to collect the money people had borrowed from him. A man who owed millions of dollars and couldn't pay was brought to the king. The king declared that the man, his wife, his children, and all his belongings should be sold to pay the debt. The man begged for more time to pay the debt, and the king canceled the debt. The man didn't have to pay back the money.

The same man who had been forgiven the millions of dollars went and found a servant who owed him a few thousand dollars. He demanded the man pay him immediately. The servant begged for more time to pay, but the man had him thrown into prison.

When the king heard about this, he was angry. He'd forgiven the man millions, but the man would not forgive his servant thousands. The king had the man thrown into prison.

Jesus used this story to show Peter he must forgive others just as God had forgiven him. When Peter asked if he had to forgive someone seven times, Jesus told him to forgive 70 times 7. He wasn't telling Peter to forgive 490 times and then to stop forgiving. He was telling Peter he had to forgive over and over again in the same way God forgives.

For You

There may be someone who hurts you every chance he or she gets. God says to forgive the person each time. That doesn't mean you have to make yourself available to get hurt by that person, but that you need to let go of the anger or desire for revenge and let God deal with it.

Answer: b
Peter came to him and asked, "Lord, how often should I forgive someone who sins against me? Seven times?" "No, not seven times," Jesus replied, "but seventy times seven!" Matthew 18:21-22
(The Whole Story: Matthew 18:21-35)

September 28

The Good Samaritan

Q: In the parable of the Good Samaritan, how many people passed the wounded man without helping him?
a. 1
b. 2
c. 3

One day Jesus told the parable of the Good Samaritan. A Jew was traveling from Jerusalem to Jericho when robbers attacked him. They beat him and left him half dead. A priest came by, but instead of helping the man, he walked on the other side of the road. Next a Levite, who was a Temple assistant, came by. But he, too, passed the injured man and left him to die.

Then a Samaritan came by. The Jews despised the Samaritans because they were a mixed race, and the Jews prided themselves on being a pure race. Yet it was the Samaritan who stopped and helped the injured man.

The Samaritan bandaged the man's wounds, put him on the Samaritan's own donkey, and took him to the local inn. He even paid for the man's room.

Jesus was showing that our neighbor is anyone who needs our help. Jesus wants people to help each other without worrying about what race or color someone is. He loves everyone, and we should love everyone too.

For You

Take time to go out of your way today to help someone who needs it. Be the Good Samaritan for that person by showing love in Jesus' name.

Answer: b
By chance a priest came along. But when he saw the man lying there, he crossed to the other side of the road and passed him by. A Temple assistant walked over and looked at him lying there, but he also passed by on the other side. Then a despised Samaritan came along, and when he saw the man, he felt compassion for him. Luke 10:31-33
(The Whole Story: Luke 10:30-37)

September 29

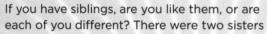

Q: Jesus was friends with sisters whose names were
a. Lydia and Dorcas.
b. Mary and Martha.
c. Rachel and Leah.

If you have siblings, are you like them, or are each of you different? There were two sisters in Jesus' time who were different from each other, and this caused problems when Jesus visited.

When Jesus traveled, he visited Mary, Martha, and their brother, Lazarus, in their home. One day when Jesus stopped by, Martha was preparing a big dinner for him while Mary sat at Jesus' feet listening to him. Martha was unhappy about getting left with all the work.

"Lord, doesn't it seem unfair to you that my sister just sits here while I do all the work? Tell her to come and help me," Martha complained.

Jesus didn't give Martha the answer she wanted to hear. "My dear Martha, you are worried and upset over all these details! There is only one thing worth being concerned about. Mary has discovered it, and it will not be taken away from her."

Jesus wasn't telling Martha that making a meal isn't important. He just knew that he wouldn't be around much longer, and he'd rather have Martha spend the time with him. In Martha's desire to serve Jesus, she neglected to spend time with him.

Collecting food for a local food bank, serving a meal at the homeless shelter, doing lawn work for the elderly, and visiting the sick are all good, but those things shouldn't take away from our time with God. Our good deeds are a result of that time with him.

For You

Mary was a worshiper. She spent time with Jesus. Martha was a doer. She kept busy working for Jesus. Both of those are good, but worship is the more important of the two. Spend time with God each day. Do good things for others, but don't let that take away from your daily time with the Lord.

Answer: b

As Jesus and the disciples continued on their way to Jerusalem, they came to a certain village where a woman named Martha welcomed him into her home. Her sister, Mary, sat at the Lord's feet, listening to what he taught. Luke 10:38-39
(The Whole Story: Luke 10:38-42)

Raised from the Dead

Q: How long had Lazarus been dead when Jesus raised him from the dead?
a. 4 hours
b. 4 days
c. 4 weeks

When Jesus lived on the earth, he experienced feelings the same as we do. He was happy, sad, and angry at different times. He had friends he loved. Mary, Martha, and Lazarus were especially close to Jesus.

Lazarus became sick, so his sisters sent a message to Jesus to come quickly. But Jesus waited before he went to see them, and in the meantime, Lazarus died. Jesus knew Lazarus would die, and that would give Jesus a chance to once again demonstrate God's power.

Martha went to meet Jesus. He told her, "I am the resurrection and the life. Anyone who believes in me will live, even after dying. Everyone who lives in me and believes in me will never ever die. Do you believe this, Martha?"

"Yes, Lord," she told him. "I have always believed you are the Messiah, the Son of God, the one who has come into the world from God."

Jesus asked her to take him to where Lazarus was buried. He had people roll the stone away, and then he prayed: "Father, thank you for hearing me. You always hear me, but I said it out loud for the sake of all these people standing here, so that they will believe you sent me." Jesus knew God understood his very thoughts, but he prayed aloud for the sake of those nearby. Then Jesus called for Lazarus to come out.

Lazarus walked out of the tomb alive again. After this, many people believed Jesus was the Son of God.

Jesus could have kept Lazarus from dying in the first place, but he wanted to do a great miracle to show the people God's power.

For You

Some people only believed after they saw Jesus' miracles, but today we believe because we have the Bible or someone has shared the Good News with us. Share with someone today how you came to believe in Jesus.

Answer: b
"Roll the stone aside," Jesus told them. But Martha . . . protested, "Lord, he has been dead for four days. The smell will be terrible." John 11:39
(The Whole Story: John 11:1-45)

October 1

The Wayward Son

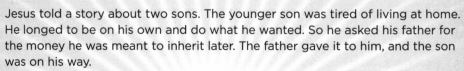

Q: What job did the Prodigal Son get when his money ran out?
a. plowing fields
b. feeding pigs
c. herding sheep

Jesus told a story about two sons. The younger son was tired of living at home. He longed to be on his own and do what he wanted. So he asked his father for the money he was meant to inherit later. The father gave it to him, and the son was on his way.

The son had a great time doing everything he wanted, but then he ran out of money. He had nowhere to live and nothing to eat. He finally got a job feeding pigs. Since the Jews consider pigs religiously unclean animals, they were not to eat or even touch pigs. But the son had sunk so low that he now took care of pigs.

Finally the son decided to return home and ask his father to hire him on as a servant. When the father saw the son coming, he ran out to welcome him home. He dressed him in fine clothes and prepared a feast.

When the older brother saw all this, he was angry. He'd been responsible and worked hard while his brother was gone. But now his brother was getting all the attention, and the father was even holding a feast for him!

Jesus told this story of the Prodigal Son to show that the Pharisees were like the older brother. They lived very righteous lives, and they were unhappy that people who were considered sinners were being welcomed into God's Kingdom. The Pharisees felt they deserved a place in God's Kingdom while those who lived sinful lives didn't.

For You

The younger brother made many mistakes and turned away from his earthly father. The older brother was bitter when the father welcomed his younger brother home. Are you like either of the brothers? If you are, ask God to help you fix what needs fixing in your life. Live for Jesus each day, and be thankful when others decide to turn to him too.

Answer: b
[The younger son] persuaded a local farmer to hire him, and the man sent him into his fields to feed the pigs. The young man became so hungry that even the pods he was feeding the pigs looked good to him. But no one gave him anything.
Luke 15:15-16
(The Whole Story: Luke 15:11-32)

October 2

Thankfulness

Q: Of the 10 men Jesus healed of leprosy, how many returned to thank him?
a. none
b. 1
c. all 10

People who had leprosy in Jesus' time had to live away from others. If they went near anyone, they were required to call out to alert people that they were lepers. If the leprosy went away, the person had to go to the priest and be declared healed so he or she could be around other people again.

As Jesus was entering a village, 10 men with leprosy called to him. Jesus told them to show themselves to the priest. This was before he'd even healed them! The lepers had to have faith that they'd be healed before they reached the priest. And they were healed by their faith as they went.

One of the men turned back and thanked Jesus. He was a Samaritan, so he was despised by the Jews for being a person of mixed race. But he was the only one who returned to show his gratitude.

It may be easy to judge the other nine lepers, but first take a look at thankfulness in your own life. When did you last thank your mom or dad for washing your clothes? For cooking a meal? When did you last thank your Sunday school teacher for taking time to prepare the lesson or your pastor for preparing the sermon? When did you last thank the school janitor for cleaning the halls and restrooms (or whoever cleans the house if you're homeschooled)? The bus driver for taking you to school or your older sibling or parent who drives you to soccer practice?

For You

You might remember to say thank you for the big things like new basketball shoes or birthday gifts, but be sure to thank others for the everyday things they do. Take time to thank at least four people today for something they do consistently.

Answer: b
One of [the ten lepers], when he saw that he was healed, came back to Jesus, shouting, "Praise God!" Luke 17:15
(The Whole Story: Luke 17:11-19)

October 3

The Rich Young Man

Q: What animal did Jesus say was more likely to go through the eye of a needle than a rich man was to get into heaven?
a. snake
b. lion
c. camel

A rich young man asked Jesus what to do to get eternal life. Jesus told him to obey the commandments. The young man replied that he'd kept the commandments. Then Jesus told him to sell all he owned, give it to the poor, and follow Jesus. At this, the young man walked away sad because he was very rich and his money was more important to him than following Jesus.

Jesus told the disciples that it is harder for a rich man to enter heaven than a camel to go through the eye of a needle. Jesus was not speaking literally, of course. He was pointing out that the man could not fulfill the first commandment, which is "You must not have any other god but me" (Exodus 20:3).

God doesn't expect Christians to give up all they own, but he wants them to be willing to do that. Christians are responsible to care for the needs of their families, and they don't have to live in poverty in order to love God. But the Lord wants first place in our lives, and he wants us to use our possessions to serve him and to share with others in need.

For You

It's okay to own things as long as they aren't more important to you than God is. The Lord, not your Xbox, smartphone, or favorite movie, is your number-one priority. Think of your possessions as being on loan to you from God to use well and to share with others.

Answer: c

Jesus said to his disciples, "I tell you the truth, it is very hard for a rich person to enter the Kingdom of Heaven. I'll say it again—it is easier for a camel to go through the eye of a needle than for a rich person to enter the Kingdom of God!" Matthew 19:23-24
(The Whole Story: Matthew 19:16-30; Mark 10:17-31; Luke 18:18-30)

A Wee Little Man

Q: Where was Zacchaeus when he first encountered Jesus?
a. at home
b. up a tree
c. by the Sea of Galilee

Zacchaeus was a well-known and important tax collector, and he'd become rich from his job. Part of his riches came from overcharging people when they paid their taxes. Zacchaeus was also short. When he heard Jesus was coming, he wanted to see him. Zacchaeus couldn't see Jesus over everyone already gathered, so he climbed up a tree for a better view.

When Jesus passed by, he looked in the tree and called Zacchaeus by name. He told him, "Quick, come down! I must be a guest in your home today."

This displeased the others in the crowd. Many of them had probably been cheated by the dishonest tax collector. Jesus told the people that salvation had come to Zacchaeus's home because he was a son of Abraham who was lost. The people didn't like to be reminded that Zacchaeus was a fellow Jew who was collecting taxes for the Romans. And they didn't like to hear that a son of Abraham could be considered lost. They were proud of their heritage.

Once Zacchaeus came face to face with Jesus, he was changed. He paid back the money he'd overcharged people along with generous interest.

God isn't concerned with who a person is by birth. Rich or poor, well known or unknown, everyone has an equal chance for salvation through Jesus.

For You

Sometimes our society shuns the poor or weak. But the rich are as lost as the poor. The do-gooder without Jesus is just as lost as a criminal. Don't hesitate to share God's love with the students around you, whether they are popular or outcast. Both groups need Jesus.

Answer: b
[Zacchaeus] ran ahead and climbed a sycamore-fig tree beside the road, for Jesus was going to pass that way. When Jesus came by, he looked up at Zacchaeus and called him by name. "Zacchaeus!" he said. "Quick, come down! I must be a guest in your home today." Luke 19:4-5
(The Whole Story: Luke 19:1-10)

October 5

The Triumphal Entry

Q: What kind of branches did the people spread on the road in front of Jesus?
a. palm
b. olive
c. green

The weeklong Passover festival was about to begin, and Jews were coming to Jerusalem from the surrounding areas to remember when the Israelites were freed from being slaves and left Egypt.

Jesus entered the city riding on a donkey's colt just as it was prophesied in Zechariah 9:9: "Look, your king is coming to you. He is righteous and victorious, yet he is humble, riding on a donkey—riding on a donkey's colt."

Word of the miracles Jesus had done and the people he'd healed had spread through the land. People lined up along the road, waving palm branches and throwing their cloaks in the road in front of him. They called out, "Praise God for the Son of David! Blessings on the one who comes in the name of the LORD! Praise God in highest heaven!"

Many of the people thought Jesus was going to set up a kingdom on earth. They didn't understand why he'd come to earth. In less than a week, many of these same people would turn on Jesus and shout, "Crucify him!" instead of the words of blessing they shouted on Palm Sunday.

For You

You may never turn on Jesus like the crowd did, but do you ever ignore him? Do you stand strong for Jesus every day at school or do your actions honor him one day and shame him the next? Make Jesus king of your heart every day.

Answer: a
The next day, the news that Jesus was on the way to Jerusalem swept through the city. A large crowd of Passover visitors took palm branches and went down the road to meet him. They shouted, "Praise God! Blessings on the one who comes in the name of the LORD! Hail to the King of Israel!" John 12:12-13
(The Whole Story: Matthew 21:1-11; Mark 11:1-11; Luke 19:28-40; John 12:12-19)

October 6

Jesus Clears the Temple

Q: Jesus said the money changers and merchants had made his house
a. a den of thieves.
b. a common marketplace.
c. an altar.

One day when Jesus went to the Temple, he saw that money changers and merchants had set up their booths in the court of the Gentiles in the Temple. They crowded out the Gentiles who'd come a long way to worship. And both the money changers and merchants were cheating the people.

The money changers were exchanging people's foreign money for Temple coins, the only acceptable currency for paying the Temple tax and merchants. But the money changers were cheating people who didn't know how much their money was worth in Temple coins. The merchants were charging too much for the animals needed for sacrifices.

Jesus was angry when he saw the money changers and merchants doing business and cheating people. He turned over their tables and ran them out of the Temple.

Jesus said, "My Temple will be called a house of prayer, but you have turned it into a den of thieves!" Jesus wanted the Temple to be a place for worship, not a place where people visiting the Temple would be cheated.

Jesus wants our churches today to be a place of worship, prayer, learning, and fellowship. Is that how you think of your church?

For You

Your attitude toward church is important to God. Do you look forward to attending church so you can learn more about God and be with other Christians? If not, what could help you look forward to church? Talk about it with your parents.

Answer: a
[Jesus] said to them, "The Scriptures declare, 'My Temple will be called a house of prayer for all nations,' but you have turned it into a den of thieves." Mark 11:17
(The Whole Story: Matthew 21:12-17; Mark 11:15-19; Luke 19:45-48)

The 10 Brides- maids

Q: The foolish bridesmaids
a. took lamps but no extra oil for the lamps.
b. arrived in the wrong clothing.
c. didn't show up.

Jesus wanted people to understand what it meant to be ready for his return, so he told the parable of the 10 bridesmaids. The bride and groom went to the wedding ceremony. Then there would be a procession and a wedding banquet. The 10 bridesmaids wanted to take part in the procession and the banquet, so they took their lamps and went out to meet the wedding party.

While the bridesmaids were waiting with lamps lit, the lamps ran out of oil. Five of the bridesmaids had brought extra oil, so they filled their lamps and were ready. But five of the bridesmaids were foolish and hadn't brought extra oil. While they were away buying oil, the procession went by. Those who were ready went on to the feast, but the others missed out.

Jesus wanted people to understand that they must be prepared for heaven. If they wait, it may be too late. Everyone is responsible for his or her own decisions, and the wise decision is to accept Jesus and be ready either for Jesus' return or to enter heaven upon death.

For You

Are you ready for heaven? How do you know? Share your answer with someone today. If you aren't sure of the answer, talk with a parent, youth pastor, or Sunday school teacher about it.

Answer: a
The Kingdom of Heaven will be like ten bridesmaids who took their lamps and went to meet the bridegroom. Five of them were foolish, and five were wise. The five who were foolish didn't take enough olive oil for their lamps, but the other five were wise enough to take along extra oil. Matthew 25:1-4
(The Whole Story: Matthew 25:1-13)

October 8

Use What You Have

Q: What did the servant with one bag of silver do with it?
a. buried it in the ground
b. invested it to make more
c. gave it to the servant with 10 bags of silver to invest for him

Jesus told a parable to help people understand what they should be doing until he returns. In the story, a man was going on a trip, so he called his three servants and entrusted them with his money. He gave five bags of silver (some translations say "talents") to one servant, two bags of silver to another servant, and one bag of silver to the third servant.

The servant with five bags of silver invested it and earned five more bags of silver. The man with two bags of silver also doubled the money. But the servant with one bag of silver buried it in the ground.

When the man returned from his trip, he called the servants together to find out what they'd done with the money. He praised the two servants who had increased the money, but he was angry with the third servant, who had buried it. He took the money from that servant and gave it to the one with the 10 bags of silver.

Jesus told this parable to show the people that God had given them abilities, money, and time to use for him until he returned or their lives were over. He told them, "To those who use well what they are given, even more will be given, and they will have an abundance. But from those who do nothing, even what little they have will be taken away." Even though Jesus told this story long ago, it's still true today. God gives us abilities and resources to use wisely to do his work.

For You
Think of one thing you can do each day this week to use your abilities, time, or money for God. Ask a friend or sibling to join you in the challenge.

Answer: a
But the servant who received the one bag of silver dug a hole in the ground and hid the master's money. Matthew 25:18
(The Whole Story: Matthew 25:14-30)

October 9

The Offering

Q: Why did Jesus say the widow had given more than all the rest of the people who gave?
a. She put a large amount of money in the offering.
b. She was more important than they were.
c. She gave all she had.

Often rich men or women will donate money to a worthy cause. They may give enough to construct a hospital wing for research or special treatment. They may donate enough money to build a library or a college dorm. Those buildings may be named after the donors. Then people will know who gave the money to fund the building.

In Jesus' time there were collection boxes in the Temple for the Temple tax and for offerings. Jesus sat by one of these boxes and watched the people drop their money in. Some rich people gave large amounts, others not as much. Then a widow entered and dropped two small coins into the box.

When Jesus saw that, he told his disciples the woman had given more than all the others. He meant that even though the rich gave a lot of money, it was still only a small part of what they owned. But the widow had given all she had.

Jesus wasn't looking at how much the money was worth but at the giver's heart. The woman gave all she had out of love for God. The rich sometimes gave a lot to appear righteous. But they didn't give generously out of love for God.

A little given joyfully counts more than a lot given grudgingly or out of duty.

For You
Be sure to give some of what you have to God. But give it because you want to, not to be noticed or to impress others.

Answer: c
"I tell you the truth," Jesus said, "this poor widow has given more than all the rest of them. For they have given a tiny part of their surplus, but she, poor as she is, has given everything she has." Luke 21:3-4
(The Whole Story: Mark 12:41-44; Luke 21:1-4)

October 10

Jesus Is Betrayed

Q: Judas agreed to betray Jesus for how much money?
a. 30 pieces of silver
b. 30 pieces of gold
c. 100 pounds of silver

Judas Iscariot was one of Jesus' 12 disciples. Even though he saw Jesus' miracles and heard Jesus' teaching, Judas didn't love Jesus the way the other disciples did. When Judas became one of the disciples, he may have thought Jesus was going to set up a kingdom on earth, and the disciples would have important jobs in that kingdom.

Judas was the treasurer for the group, and money was important to him. One day Mary of Bethany anointed Jesus with expensive perfume. Judas thought she'd wasted the perfume. It could have been sold, and the money could have been given to the poor. But Jesus praised Mary for the love she'd shown.

Judas realized that following Jesus was not going to make him rich or important. He betrayed Jesus for 30 pieces of silver and the approval of the religious leaders.

Jesus knew that Judas would betray him, yet he chose Judas as a disciple anyway. This was part of God's plan for our salvation, but in order for the plan to be fulfilled, someone had to betray Jesus to the enemies. That person was Judas.

Judas's betrayal didn't catch God by surprise. He knew everything that must happen in order for us to have salvation.

For You
Judas betrayed Jesus, but many of the other disciples died because of their belief in Jesus. Is your love for Jesus strong enough that you stand up for your beliefs at school, in your extracurricular activities, and in your community?

Answer: a
Judas Iscariot, one of the twelve disciples, went to the leading priests and asked, "How much will you pay me to betray Jesus to you?" And they gave him thirty pieces of silver. Matthew 26:14-15
(The Whole Story: Matthew 26:14-16; Mark 14:10-11; Luke 22:3-6; John 12:3-8)

October 11

Peter Denies Christ

Q: Jesus told Peter he would deny Jesus
a. twice before the sun went down.
b. once within the hour.
c. three times before the rooster crowed.

Jesus and his disciples had a last meal together the week that Jesus died. During this meal, Judas left to betray Jesus, just as Jesus knew would happen. Jesus told his disciples he would be with them only a little longer. He knew it was near the time for him to die.

Peter asked Jesus where he was going, and Jesus told him, "You can't go with me now, but you will follow me later."

Peter said, "But why can't I come now, Lord? I'm ready to die for you."

Jesus said, "Die for me? I tell you the truth, Peter—before the rooster crows tomorrow morning, you will deny three times that you even know me."

Peter had good intentions, and he wanted to be brave for Jesus. Peter thought he'd courageously face death with Jesus, but Jesus knew Peter would deny him instead. And what Jesus said came true. Peter denied knowing Jesus three times. When the rooster crowed, Peter remembered Jesus' words and was sorry he'd said he didn't know Jesus.

Peter wasn't the only one who failed Jesus. When Judas brought a group of men with swords to arrest Jesus, everyone who was with Jesus fled. This didn't change Jesus' love for them. He forgave them, and he still had work for them to do.

Our failures don't change God's plans or his love for us.

For You

There are many ways to deny Jesus without saying a word. Are there times you deny Jesus by failing to speak up for what you believe or take a stand against wrong? How can you fix that?

Answer: c
"But why can't I come now, Lord?" [Peter] asked. "I'm ready to die for you." Jesus answered, "Die for me? I tell you the truth, Peter—before the rooster crows tomorrow morning, you will deny three times that you even know me."
John 13:37-38
(The Whole Story: Luke 22:31-34, 54-62; John 13:31-38)

October 12

Judas's Money

Q: What happened to the money Judas Iscariot received for betraying Jesus?
a. Judas spent it on fancy clothes and goods.
b. Judas gave it to the Temple.
c. The religious leaders used it to buy a field to bury foreigners.

After Jesus was betrayed, he was taken before the chief priests and the elders. The men questioned Jesus and decided he should be put to death, but they didn't have the power to condemn him. They had to get the Roman government to agree.

The religious leaders had charged Jesus with blasphemy for claiming to be the Son of God, but they knew the Romans wouldn't allow Jesus to be killed for that reason. So they tried to make Jesus sound like a rebel who was claiming to be the king. They decided to take him to Pilate, the Roman governor for Samaria and Judea.

When Judas Iscariot, who had betrayed Jesus, saw the religious leaders were taking Jesus to Pilate, he was filled with regret for betraying Jesus. He tried to return the money to the priests and told them, "I have sinned for I have betrayed an innocent man."

It was the priests' job to help Judas offer a sacrifice to cover his sin. But rather than help him, they said, "What do we care? That's your problem."

Judas threw down the money, went out, and killed himself. The priests couldn't put the money in the treasury because it was given to betray Jesus. So they used it to buy a field to bury foreigners.

Judas made a very bad decision to let money be his god. He spent time with Jesus, but he never accepted Jesus as the Savior. People today still allow popularity, money, or success to be their gods rather than making Jesus their Lord.

- -

For You

How sad it was for Judas to be part of Jesus' inner circle but never accepting Jesus as his Savior. Ask God to show you anything in your life that is more important to you than Jesus.

- -

Answer: c
After some discussion [the leading priests] finally decided to buy the potter's field, and they made it into a cemetery for foreigners. Matthew 27:7
(The Whole Story: Matthew 26:59-66; 27:3-10)

October 13

Pilate

Q: Who did the crowd want released instead of Jesus?
a. Judas
b. Barabbas
c. Matthias

After Judas Iscariot betrayed Jesus, Jesus was questioned many times. First he went before Annas, then Caiaphas, and lastly the Sanhedrin. These were religious leaders who should have been looking for the Messiah, but they were interested in their own plans.

The religious leaders took Jesus to Pilate. The governor saw at once that Jesus was innocent, but he was afraid the religious leaders would cause problems for him. So Pilate sent Jesus to Herod, the ruler of Galilee, who was in Jerusalem for the Passover celebration. When Jesus refused to defend himself, Herod sent him back to Pilate.

Pilate didn't want to condemn Jesus to death, but he knew the religious leaders could make trouble for him and cost him his job if he saved Jesus' life. It was the custom to release one prisoner during Passover, and Pilate tried to get the people to release Jesus. But they chose to release Barabbas, a man who'd rebelled against Rome and committed murder. Most of the Jews didn't care about his crimes, because they hated paying taxes to Rome and being governed by the Romans.

Pilate had Jesus beaten as a compromise, but that didn't satisfy the Jews. Pilate knew Jesus wasn't guilty of any crime, but he gave in to the pressure and turned Jesus over to be crucified. He was afraid if he didn't, there would be a rebellion and it would cost him his life. Pilate knew the right thing to do, but he chose not to do it.

For You

You will never have to make the choice Pilate made, but you do make choices every day about whether you will follow Jesus and do what's right, or take the easy road. Ask God to help you when you are tempted to take the easy way out.

Answer: b
[Pilate said,] "You have a custom of asking me to release one prisoner each year at Passover. Would you like me to release this 'King of the Jews'?" But they shouted back, "No! Not this man. We want Barabbas!" (Barabbas was a revolutionary.) John 18:39-40
(The Whole Story: Matthew 27:15-31; Mark 15:6-15; Luke 23:1-25; John 18:28–19:16)

October 14

Carrying the Cross

Q: Who carried Jesus' cross for part of the journey to Golgotha?
a. Simon Peter
b. Simon the Cyrene
c. Thomas

In New Testament times, prisoners who were condemned to be crucified were often made to carry their own crosses. The whole cross would weigh 300 pounds. Prisoners were only required to carry the crossbeam, which was 75–125 pounds. That was not an easy thing to do, especially for Jesus, who'd faced many horrible things in the hours leading up to the time he was ordered to carry the cross.

Before Jesus was forced to carry the cross, he'd spent time praying in agony in the garden of Gethsemane, he'd been betrayed, and he had walked from place to place to be questioned. Then he was beaten, which left him weak and bleeding. A crown of thorns was forced onto his head. Tired, hungry, and suffering from the beating, Jesus was unable to carry the cross.

Since Jesus was not able to carry the cross, a man nearby, named Simon, was chosen to carry it for him. Simon was from Cyrene in northern Africa, and he was probably part of a Jewish colony who had traveled to Jerusalem for the Passover. That was a very long journey, and Simon never imagined that he would carry Jesus' cross to the place of crucifixion. Carrying the cross made Simon ceremonially unclean, but God had a greater purpose for him—carrying a burden for Jesus.

When Simon made the long journey for the Passover, he had no idea things would turn out the way they did. Sometimes we have our own plans, but God may need us to do something different, just as he did with Simon.

For You

You may have good plans, but God may call you to do something other than what you have in mind. Be open to his leading so you don't miss out on the chance to accomplish something great.

Answer: b

As they led Jesus away, a man named Simon, who was from Cyrene, happened to be coming in from the countryside. The soldiers seized him and put the cross on him and made him carry it behind Jesus. Luke 23:26
(The Whole Story: Matthew 27:32; Mark 15:21; Luke 23:26)

October 15

The Crucifixion

Q: Who was crucified at the same time as Jesus?
a. a murderer
b. two thieves
c. no one

Jesus was taken to a place outside the city gate known as Golgotha, or Calvary, to be crucified. Jesus was not alone on Calvary the day of his crucifixion. There were two criminals, one on each side of Jesus, being crucified also.

The two criminals responded differently to Jesus. One of them mocked Jesus, saying, "So you're the Messiah, are you? Prove it by saving yourself—and us, too, while you're at it!" The man didn't believe that Jesus was the Son of God who chose to die to save people from their sins even though he had power to save himself.

The other criminal understood who Jesus was and rebuked the first criminal: "Don't you fear God even when you have been sentenced to die? We deserve to die for our crimes, but this man hasn't done anything wrong." He turned to Jesus and said, "Jesus, remember me when you come into your Kingdom."

Jesus saw that the man believed and told him, "I assure you, today you will be with me in paradise."

One criminal believed, and one didn't. One was promised eternal life in heaven, and the other wasn't. Everyone still faces the same choice today—believe in Jesus and receive eternal life, or reject him. It's sad that many refuse to see that Jesus is the Savior and never turn to him for salvation.

For You

If you've already made the choice to accept Jesus as your Savior, share that decision with someone who needs to hear about it. If you haven't accepted Jesus as your Savior, talk to your parents or pastor about it today. Don't put it off.

Answer: b
Two others, both criminals, were led out to be executed with [Jesus]. When they came to a place called The Skull, they nailed him to the cross. And the criminals were also crucified—one on his right and one on his left. Luke 23:32-33
(The Whole Story: Matthew 27:33-38; Mark 15:22-27; Luke 23:32-43; John 19:17-18)

October 16

When Jesus Died

Q: Which of these things happened when Jesus died?
a. A strong wind blew, and the Temple crumbled.
b. Lightning split the sky and rocks.
c. The Temple veil ripped, and the earth shook.

Many people had been crucified at Golgotha before Jesus, but his crucifixion was different. Many things happened to let people know this was no ordinary death.

While Jesus was dying on the cross, there was darkness over the land. This darkness was caused by God and wasn't some act of nature. Perhaps God caused the darkness as a sign of the spiritual darkness that caused Jesus' death.

At the moment Jesus died, the curtain in the Temple separating the Holy Place (where only priests could enter) from the Most Holy Place (where the priest could only enter once a year) was torn in two. God was showing that the barrier between God and people had been removed. Because of Jesus' death, people could ask for forgiveness themselves rather than having a priest offer a sacrifice for sins.

This wasn't all that happened. When Jesus died, the earth shook, rocks split apart, the tombs broke open, and many holy people were brought back to life. These resurrected people went into the city, where the crowds saw them.

God wanted to make sure everyone knew this was no ordinary man who died, so he caused many miraculous things to happen.

For You

Jesus was no ordinary man. He was the Son of God dying not for his own sins, but for ours. Be sure to thank Jesus for the forgiveness he provides for us.

Answer: c
At that moment the curtain in the sanctuary of the Temple was torn in two, from top to bottom. The earth shook, rocks split apart, and tombs opened. The bodies of many godly men and women who had died were raised from the dead.
Matthew 27:51-52
(The Whole Story: Matthew 27:45-56; Mark 15:33-41; Luke 23:44-49; John 19:28-37)

October 17

Jesus' Burial

Q: Where was Jesus buried?
a. in the tomb of Joseph of Arimathea
b. in the garden of Gethsemane
c. near Judas Iscariot

A lot of people were present at Jesus' crucifixion. There were his disciples, the women who followed him in his ministry, his enemies, curious bystanders, and men who followed Jesus in secret.

Joseph of Arimathea, a rich and important member of the Sanhedrin—the Jewish council—was a secret follower of Jesus. After Jesus died, Joseph came forward and asked for Jesus' body in order to bury it. Nicodemus, who'd talked to Jesus in secret by night, was with Joseph.

Joseph owned a tomb cut into a hillside in the area. Joseph and Nicodemus wrapped Jesus' body, placed it in the tomb, and rolled a heavy stone across the entrance. The religious leaders watched to see where Jesus was buried. They sealed the stone and placed guards nearby so no one could steal Jesus' body and then claim he'd risen from the dead.

Joseph of Arimathea and Nicodemus were both secret followers of Jesus because of their important positions in the Jewish community, yet when the time came, they stepped forward and claimed Jesus' body. They knew this could jeopardize their standing in the Jewish council, but they knew it was time to come out of hiding and let others know they were followers of Jesus.

For You

Do you hide your faith from those around you like Joseph and Nicodemus did? Or do you let your light shine for Jesus? If you hide your faith, is it time for you to step out and take a stand?

Answer: a

Joseph, a rich man from Arimathea who had become a follower of Jesus . . . took the body and wrapped it in a long sheet of clean linen cloth. He placed it in his own new tomb, which had been carved out of the rock. Then he rolled a great stone across the entrance and left. Matthew 27:57, 59-60
(The Whole Story: Matthew 27:57-61; Mark 15:42-47; Luke 23:50-56; John 19:38-42)

October 18

Jesus Is Risen

Q: Who discovered Jesus' empty tomb?
a. the women who followed Jesus
b. Peter and John
c. all the disciples together

When Joseph of Arimathea and Nicodemus buried Jesus' body, the religious leaders remembered that Jesus had said he would rise again, so they placed guards to watch the tomb and make sure no one would steal Jesus' body (see Matthew 27:62-66). But this did no good. Jesus was the Son of God, and nothing humans did would keep him from rising again as God planned.

On the first day of the week, an angel rolled back the stone from the tomb. This wasn't so Jesus could get out. He didn't need the stone moved for that. The angel moved the stone so the women who came to the tomb could see that Jesus was gone.

The women were afraid, but the angel spoke to them: "Don't be afraid! I know you are looking for Jesus, who was crucified. He isn't here! He is risen from the dead, just as he said would happen. Come, see where his body was lying. And now, go quickly and tell his disciples that he has risen from the dead." The women were filled with joy, and they ran to tell the disciples that Jesus had risen as he said.

Jesus' death and resurrection is the key to our salvation. His death was to pay the penalty for our sins. Because he became the sacrifice for sin, we can be forgiven and have eternal life. We can be filled with joy at Jesus' resurrection, just as the women at the empty tomb were.

For You

Rejoice in Jesus' resurrection not just once a year at Easter but always, because his resurrection gives us hope. We can have a new beginning and the promise of eternal life.

Answer: a
Early on Sunday morning, as the new day was dawning, Mary Magdalene and the other Mary went out to visit the tomb. Matthew 28:1
(The Whole Story: Matthew 27:62–28:7; Mark 16:1-8; Luke 24:1-10; John 20:1-18)

October 19

Making Sure

Q: Which disciple doubted because he wasn't with the others when Jesus appeared to them?
a. Peter
b. Thomas
c. Matthew

When Jesus appeared to the disciples after his resurrection, one disciple wasn't there. When he was told about Jesus' visit by the other disciples, he was reluctant to believe. He wanted to see for himself. This has led to his being labeled Doubting Thomas. However, the fact he doubted isn't as important as the fact that Thomas was seeking the truth.

Doubting isn't always a bad thing. It makes you think more about something. You try to get the facts so you can decide for yourself. Doubt can lead you on a journey to truth.

Thomas didn't stay a doubter. When Thomas saw Jesus, he believed. Some people think they would believe on Jesus if they could see him. But Jesus told Thomas, "You believe because you have seen me. Blessed are those who believe without seeing me."

We can't physically see the Lord, but we can see his creation around us in nature and sense his work in our lives. We know he is real, because we have his Holy Spirit guiding us and speaking to us through our consciences when we're wrong.

It's okay to want to be sure that Jesus is real. John 20:30-31 says, "The disciples saw Jesus do many other miraculous signs in addition to the ones recorded in this book. But these are written so that you may continue to believe that Jesus is the Messiah, the Son of God, and that by believing in him you will have life by the power of his name."

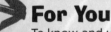

For You
To know and understand Jesus more, you just have to read the Gospels. If you have doubts like Thomas did, ask God to give you the answers you need to strengthen your belief.

Answer: b
[Jesus] said to Thomas, "Put your finger here, and look at my hands. Put your hand into the wound in my side. Don't be faithless any longer. Believe!"
John 20:27
(The Whole Story: John 20:24-29)

October 20

Breakfast with Jesus

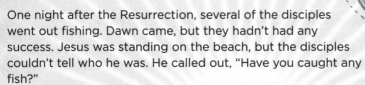

Q: What did Jesus serve the disciples for breakfast?
a. fruit and cereal
b. fish and bread
c. manna and quail

One night after the Resurrection, several of the disciples went out fishing. Dawn came, but they hadn't had any success. Jesus was standing on the beach, but the disciples couldn't tell who he was. He called out, "Have you caught any fish?"

When the disciples said they hadn't caught anything, Jesus told them to cast their net on the other side. The disciples did, and they caught so many fish that they couldn't pull the net in! Then the disciples realized it was Jesus on the shore. When they got to shore with their overloaded net, Jesus had already cooked them fish. He served it to them with bread.

Why did Jesus cook breakfast for the disciples? Jesus cared about his disciples. He fed them spiritually during his ministry on earth, and now he was feeding them physically. Jesus wanted to spend some special time with the disciples before he went back to heaven. Daybreak on the beach may have been the best time to be together.

For You

Jesus wanted to spend time with his disciples. God wants to spend time with you. Why not set aside extra time this week? Read one story about Jesus from the Gospels to review something you've learned. If you aren't sure where to read, try Matthew 8:28-34 or Mark 5:21-43.

Answer: b
When [the disciples] got there, they found breakfast waiting for them—fish cooking over a charcoal fire, and some bread. John 21:9
(The Whole Story: John 21:1-14)

October 21

The Great Commission

Q: Which of these is the first line of the Great Commission?
a. "Our father, which art in heaven . . ."
b. "Ask and it will be given unto you, seek and you will find."
c. "Therefore, go and make disciples of all the nations."

When Jesus was getting ready to leave his disciples for the final time, he had some last words for them. Jesus told them to go to all nations, preach the gospel, and make more disciples so the Good News could spread farther.

God calls all believers to be his followers and to spread the gospel. He wants you to share the gospel where you are right now. How can you do that while you're still a kid?

Ask a friend to join you for church. Offer to give your friend a ride with your family. He or she may be more likely to come.

If you can't get a classmate or neighbor to join you for Sunday church, invite him or her for a fun church activity such as a game night or fall festival.

If you have to give an oral book report at school, read and report on a Christian suspense or mystery book that others in your class might find interesting.

If you have to write a report about someone in history, pick a famous missionary or preacher.

Look for a way to include creation in your science fair project.

Talk to your parents about other ways to share your faith in your classroom or community.

For You
Look for one way to share your faith in your classroom this week. If you are homeschooled, look for a way to share the gospel with a neighbor.

Answer: c
[Jesus said,] "Therefore, go and make disciples of all the nations, baptizing them in the name of the Father and the Son and the Holy Spirit. Teach these new disciples to obey all the commands I have given you. And be sure of this: I am with you always, even to the end of the age." Matthew 28:19-20
(The Whole Story: Matthew 28:16-20; Mark 16:15-18)

Book of History

October 22

The Book of Acts

Q: The book of Acts is a "sequel" (continuation) of which Gospel?
a. Matthew
b. Mark
c. Luke

The book of Acts continues where the Gospels left off. Luke, a doctor, addressed his Gospel, Luke, and this book of history, Acts, to a man named Theophilus. Luke's Gospel covers Jesus' time on earth. The book of Acts covers the first 30 years after Jesus went back to heaven. After Jesus' resurrection, he spent 40 days on earth teaching his disciples. He was preparing them to take the gospel into all the world.

The book of Acts covers the exciting time when the church began and the early believers banded together into a community. Life wasn't easy for these early believers. They were imprisoned, beaten, stoned, and ridiculed. This opposition forced some of them to move away, and that resulted in the gospel being taken to new places too.

The important thing to remember is that the amazing courage of the early Christians and the growth of the church was through the Holy Spirit's power, not the work of individual Christians. Men such as Peter, John, James, Stephen, Philip, Paul, Barnabas, Silas, Timothy, and Ananias of Damascus allowed God's spirit to work in them and through them in order to fan the spark of Christianity into a flame that spread throughout what is now Africa, Asia, and Europe.

Although times have changed, God is still looking for believers who will allow his Spirit to work through them in amazing ways in order to get the gospel to those who need to hear it.

For You

Take time to read from the book of Acts a little each day. Ask God to work in you as he worked in the early believers so that you, too, can be a powerful witness for Jesus.

Answer: c
In my first book I told you, Theophilus, about everything Jesus began to do and teach until the day he was taken up to heaven after giving his chosen apostles further instructions through the Holy Spirit. Acts 1:1-2
(The Whole Story: Acts 1:1-11)

October 23

A New Member

Q: Who was chosen to replace Judas Iscariot as a disciple/apostle?
a. Justus
b. Demetrius
c. Matthias

After Jesus went back to heaven, the 11 remaining disciples were called apostles. A disciple is a learner, and that's what the 12 men were when Jesus was on earth teaching them. But once Jesus went back to heaven, they became apostles, which are messengers of the good news of salvation.

The early church began to grow. There were about 120 believers who had joined together. The apostles needed to choose someone to replace Judas. There were many men who'd followed Jesus during his ministry, but the apostles were the inner circle of 12, who were specifically chosen by Jesus. They now had to choose a man with God's guidance.

The apostles narrowed the choice down to two men, Joseph (also called Barsabbas or Justus) and Matthias. The apostles prayed over the men, "O Lord, you know every heart. Show us which of these men you have chosen as an apostle to replace Judas in this ministry." Then they cast lots, and the lot fell to Matthias.

Matthias became an apostle in a very exciting time as the early church was being formed. The news about Jesus' resurrection was spreading, and people were believing in Jesus and being added to God's family every day. But there were also people who hated Jesus' followers, so there were hard times and persecution, too.

For You

You live in a time and place where there are churches, and people are free to worship as they please. But there are people today who hate Jesus' followers, just as there were in the apostles' time. Be active in your local church, and join together with those who love God so you'll be strengthened for when you run into those who don't.

Answer: c
Then they cast lots, and Matthias was selected to become an apostle with the other eleven. Acts 1:26
(The Whole Story: Acts 1:12-26)

October 24

The Holy Spirit Comes

Q: What ability did the Holy Spirit give those gathered together in the early days of the church?
a. speaking other languages
b. reading minds
c. walking on water

Ten days after Jesus ascended into heaven, the believers were gathered together. Suddenly the sound of rushing wind filled the house, and they saw tongues of fire that separated and rested on each of them. The believers were filled with the Holy Spirit and could speak languages they'd never learned.

There were people in Jerusalem from many countries for the Feast of Weeks. These people were amazed when they heard the believers speaking the different languages. They could hear the gospel in their own languages.

Some people said the believers must be drunk to be speaking these languages, but Peter told them they were wrong. He boldly preached to them about Jesus. He said they needed to repent and be baptized. Over three thousand people believed in Jesus and were added to God's family that day.

The Holy Spirit was with the believers from then on, empowering them to carry the gospel nearby and far away. God still gives his Holy Spirit to believers in order to do his work.

For You

The Holy Spirit is with you each day, guiding you and helping you make the right choices. If you ask him to lead you, you'll know what God wants you to do each day.

Answer: a
Everyone present was filled with the Holy Spirit and began speaking in other languages, as the Holy Spirit gave them this ability. Acts 2:4
(The Whole Story: Acts 2:1-41)

Peter at the Temple

Q: What miracle did Peter perform outside the Temple?
a. changed water to wine
b. healed a lame man
c. gave a blind man sight

One afternoon Peter and John were on their way to the Temple for prayer. A lame man stayed by the Temple gate so he could beg from the people going to the Temple. The man asked Peter and John to give him money.

Peter said, "I don't have any silver or gold for you. But I'll give you what I have. In the name of Jesus Christ the Nazarene, get up and walk!" Peter took the man by the hand and helped him stand to his feet for the first time in his life. The man began walking and leaping. All his life he'd watched others walk and run, and now he could do it himself. The man praised God.

When the people saw the lame beggar running about praising God, they were amazed. Peter took the opportunity to tell the crowd about salvation through Jesus. This made the religious leaders so angry they put Peter and John in prison, but others heard the message and believed. Many more people were added to God's family that day.

Peter took every opportunity to tell people about Jesus. He shared the gospel with the crowd and even with the religious leaders who didn't want to hear it. God wants us, too, to use the chances we are given to share the good news of the gospel.

For You

There are chances to tell others about Jesus every day if you keep your eyes open for the opportunities. Sometimes you might just share a Bible verse with someone, and another time you might tell someone how you came to accept Jesus as your Savior. When you do this, you are planting the seeds of the gospel that may grow in someone's heart and eventually lead them to Christ.

Answer: b
Peter said, "I don't have any silver or gold for you. But I'll give you what I have. In the name of Jesus Christ the Nazarene, get up and walk!" Acts 3:6
(The Whole Story: Acts 3:1–4:4)

October 26

Lying to God

Q: What husband and wife pair both died after lying?
a. Aquila and Priscilla
b. Ananias and Sapphira
c. Ahab and Jezebel

The early believers shared all they had. Many people sold houses or land and brought the money to the apostles to be used by anyone who needed it. No one was required to sell their property. The early believers wanted to share, and they did it out of love for God.

Ananias and Sapphira wanted to be thought of as generous givers. They sold their land, but they agreed to keep part of the money for themselves. Keeping some money for themselves was okay. But what wasn't okay was that Ananias brought the money to the apostles and said it was the whole amount they had received.

Peter said, "Ananias, why have you let Satan fill your heart? You lied to the Holy Spirit, and you kept some of the money for yourself. The property was yours to sell or not sell, as you wished. And after selling it, the money was also yours to give away. How could you do a thing like this? You weren't lying to us but to God!" After Peter spoke, Ananias fell to the floor dead.

Three hours later Sapphira arrived and didn't know what had happened to her husband. Peter told her the amount her husband said they'd gotten for the land and asked her if that was the correct amount. Sapphira, too, lied and then died. Everyone who heard about this was filled with fear because they realized how serious God is about sin.

For You

Ananias and Sapphira lied to look more generous and important than they were. God wants us to be honest and real. He doesn't want us to give only to look important, but to give out of love.

Answer: b

There was a certain man named Ananias who, with his wife, Sapphira, sold some property. He brought part of the money to the apostles, claiming it was the full amount. With his wife's consent, he kept the rest. Acts 5:1-2
(The Whole Story: Acts 5:1-11)

The First Martyr

Q: Who was stoned to death for his faith?
a. Peter
b. John
c. Stephen

Many times the Jews who believed Jesus was the promised Messiah were shunned by family and friends who didn't believe. The early Christians needed to band together to help each other. Some of the people who were shunned by their families had no money, homes, or food. But the other believers shared with them.

Because the early church was growing so fast, it was important to organize how things were shared so no one was left out. Stephen was one of the men in charge of making sure everyone who needed food received it.

Stephen was courageous in his faith. He spoke out about his beliefs. Some people didn't like Stephen, so they made up lies about him. He was taken before the Sanhedrin and asked if the lies were true. Stephen took that opportunity to speak to the Jewish leaders about God. He started by reviewing Jewish history. He showed how the Jews had continually rejected God and how they'd rejected the Messiah.

The religious leaders and some of the people were so angry with Stephen that they dragged him out of the city and threw stones at him until he died. As he died, Stephen prayed for forgiveness for those who hated him. Stephen was the first Christian martyr (a person who dies for his or her beliefs). More persecution of believers followed, but at the same time the gospel spread to new countries.

For You

Stephen was full of compassion and wisdom. He was always ready to help those in need and to share his faith. He is a good example for you to follow as you live out your faith in your school and community.

Answer: c
As they stoned him, Stephen prayed, "Lord Jesus, receive my spirit." He fell to his knees, shouting, "Lord, don't charge them with this sin!" And with that, he died.
Acts 7:59-60
(The Whole Story: Acts 6–7)

October 28

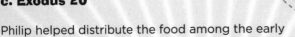

Philip

Q: What passage of Scripture was an Ethiopian man reading when Philip met him in the desert?
a. Isaiah 53
b. Matthew 1
c. Exodus 20

Philip helped distribute the food among the early Christians. But then he left Jerusalem to take the gospel to other places. Philip shared the Good News with everyone he met, but unlike many others, he took the gospel to the Samaritans, the people many Jews were prejudiced against. Philip knew that they needed to know Jesus as their Savior too.

One day God sent Philip out into the desert. Philip met an Ethiopian traveling in a chariot. The Ethiopian invited Philip to join him. The man was reading from Isaiah 53, but he didn't understand what he read, so he asked Philip to explain it. The Ethiopian believed what Philip told him about Jesus. As the chariot passed by some water, the man asked Philip to baptize him.

God was able to use Philip to reach many people because Philip was willing to share the gospel with anyone he met. He didn't just tell other Jews about Jesus; he took the message to foreigners. He reached out to people despised by other Jews, because he knew God's salvation was for anyone who believed.

For You

Do you take the first step in sharing the gospel? If you wait for someone to ask you about Jesus, you may not have many opportunities to share your faith. Look around you for one person who needs to hear about Jesus. Ask God to prepare that person's heart for the gospel and to help you look for an opportunity to talk to him or her.

Answer: a
The passage of Scripture he had been reading was this: "He was led like a sheep to the slaughter. And as a lamb is silent before the shearers, he did not open his mouth. He was humiliated and received no justice. Who can speak of his descendants? For his life was taken from the earth." Acts 8:32-33
(The Whole Story: Acts 8:4-8, 26-40)

Paul Meets Jesus

Q: After Paul's encounter with Jesus on the road to Damascus, he was
a. speechless.
b. blind.
c. crippled.

Paul was one of the most courageous and well-traveled missionaries of all time. His preaching and teaching resulted in thousands of people hearing about Jesus. He started new churches and trained people to pastor them. Although Paul was stoned, beaten, jailed, and run out of cities, he never stopped sharing the gospel. But before Paul met Jesus, he was an enemy of Christians.

Paul was very religious. He had been trained under one of the finest teachers and was a Pharisee. Paul thought the Christians were wrong in believing Jesus was the Messiah. He was determined to stop them from spreading what he thought were lies.

Paul was traveling to Damascus to bring believers back to Jerusalem as prisoners. But God had other plans. Near Damascus, a bright light shone from heaven. Paul fell to the ground. A voice said, "Saul! Saul! Why are you persecuting me?" (Paul was known as Saul then.)

Jesus told Paul to go to a house on Straight Street. When Paul stood, he was blind and stayed that way for three days. God sent a man named Ananias to talk to Paul and restore his sight. Ananias was reluctant because he'd heard how Paul had persecuted Christians, but God told Ananias that Paul was chosen to carry the gospel to the Gentiles.

Paul stayed for a few days with other believers and then began preaching the gospel. The people were surprised to hear the man who had previously persecuted Christians was now proclaiming Jesus as Savior.

For You

Ananias didn't want to talk to Paul, but he did it because God asked him to. Later he was glad he'd obeyed. God may ask you to do something hard, too, but he will be with you as you do it. He will give you the wisdom and strength for the task.

Answer: b
Saul picked himself up off the ground, but when he opened his eyes he was blind. So his companions led him by the hand to Damascus. Acts 9:8
(The Whole Story: Acts 9:1-21)

A Woman Named Dorcas

Q: What was Dorcas (Tabitha) known for?
a. baking cookies for the disciples
b. leading a Bible study
c. doing kind things for others and helping the poor

Can you think of a person in your church or community who reaches out to others in little ways that make a big difference? Dorcas, one of the early Christians who lived in Joppa, was known for her good deeds. Dorcas cared about the poor and the widows. Sometimes these people had no one to take care of them, so they lived in poverty. Dorcas sewed clothing and coats for them.

Dorcas became sick and died, and the poor and the widows mourned for her. The believers heard Peter was nearby and sent for him. When Peter arrived in the upstairs room where Dorcas was, the people showed him the clothing she'd made for them and told him about her good deeds.

Peter sent everyone out of the room, and then he knelt and prayed. Peter turned to Dorcas and told her to get up. He took her by the hand and helped her to her feet. All the people gathered there were happy to see Dorcas alive and well. Many people came to believe in Jesus after seeing Peter's miracle.

Dorcas made a difference to those around her by using her talent of sewing to help people in need. She was known for doing good. You don't have to have a lot of money or impressive abilities to help others. You just need to meet the needs around you.

For You

What things can you do to help others? It may be as simple as tutoring someone in reading or raking leaves or shoveling snow for someone who can't do it himself or herself. Take time this week to do something for someone else without accepting anything in return, so you, too, will become known for doing good deeds in Jesus' name.

Answer: c

There was a believer in Joppa named Tabitha (which in Greek is Dorcas). She was always doing kind things for others and helping the poor. Acts 9:36
(The Whole Story: Acts 9:32-43)

October 31

Peter Takes the Gospel to the Gentiles

Q: An angel told what Roman army officer to send for Peter?
a. Cornelius
b. Barnabas
c. Silas

There was a Roman army officer who lived in Caesarea, a seaport about 30 miles north of Joppa, where Peter was staying. The officer was a centurion, which meant he was a commander of 100 soldiers. This man, Cornelius, loved God and prayed daily. One day an angel appeared to him and told him to send men to Joppa to find Peter and bring him to Caesarea. So Cornelius sent two servants on the mission.

God prepared Peter for the men's request by showing him a vision that meant it was okay for him to take the gospel to the Gentiles, people who weren't Jews. Peter was uncomfortable because the Gentiles didn't live by the same religious laws as the Jews. There were things Jews were not allowed to touch or eat, but the Gentiles didn't follow those rules. Still, Peter obeyed God and went to Cornelius's home.

Cornelius gathered his friends and relatives to hear Peter. Cornelius and those in the house believed what Peter was saying, and God sent his Holy Spirit to come into them. When Peter and other Jews who were with him saw the Gentiles had the Holy Spirit, they baptized them as a sign of their salvation.

Cornelius was a wealthy military man and a Gentile. Peter was a poor Jewish fisherman who was now a preacher. The two men were very different, but God had a special plan for each of them to accomplish his work in the early church.

For You

God uses all different kinds of people to do his work. He has given you the talents and abilities you need to do what he's called you to do. Never feel you aren't good enough or talented enough to accomplish something great for God. He created you with a plan in mind.

Answer: a
There lived a Roman army officer named Cornelius, who was a captain of the Italian Regiment. He was a devout, God-fearing man, as was everyone in his household. He gave generously to the poor and prayed regularly. Acts 10:1-2
(The Whole Story: Acts 10)

November 1

The Herods

Q: How was James killed?
a. by being beheaded
b. by fire
c. by a sword

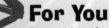

Some families are known through the years for the good they do. Other families are known for the evil passed down from generation to generation. The Bible mentions four generations of the Herod family—and they were all wicked.

You might remember Herod the Great (see the August 25 devotion). He was sure the newborn king of the Jews would replace him, so he wanted to kill baby Jesus. He killed all the baby boys in and around Bethlehem in order to accomplish that, but because God had told Joseph to flee with Mary and Jesus, Herod did not succeed.

Herod Antipas married his brother's wife, Herodias. After his daughter danced for him at a party, he told her she could have whatever she wanted. Herodias told their daughter to ask for the head of John the Baptist, and Herod Antipas granted that request (see Matthew 14:1-12).

Herod Agrippa I wanted to be liked by the Jews. He knew many of them didn't like the early Christians, especially now that the early church was growing. So he began persecuting the believers to gain favor with the Jews. Herod Agrippa I had the apostle James killed.

In the fourth generation of Herods, Herod Agrippa II played a part in the apostle Paul's story. You'll learn more about Herod Agrippa II in coming devotions.

The Herod family was bad news for many people who loved God. There are wicked families today, but there are also families with generations of preachers and missionaries. Even though there are godly families, each person must decide whether or not to follow Jesus.

For You

Determine that you will follow Jesus even if you have to stand alone. Leave a legacy of faith for future generations.

Answer: c
[King Herod Agrippa] had the apostle James (John's brother) killed with a sword. Acts 12:2
(The Whole Story: Acts 12:1-4)

Peter Is Freed

Q: How did Peter get out of prison?
a. He escaped through a window.
b. An angel released him from prison.
c. The other disciples broke Peter out of prison.

Herod Agrippa I had Peter imprisoned for preaching about Jesus. He planned to put Peter on trial and kill him after the Passover celebration in an attempt to win favor with the Jews by attempting to stamp out Christianity.

The church began to pray for Peter's release, and God sent an angel to answer their prayers. Peter was bound with chains and well guarded, but when an angel appeared and told Peter to hurry and get up, the chains fell away. Peter followed the angel out of the prison.

Peter went to the house where people had gathered to pray for him and knocked on the door. Rhoda, the servant girl, realized it was Peter, but she left him standing there while she ran to tell the others! Even though they were praying for his release, the men and women did not believe Rhoda's report.

Peter kept knocking. Finally they opened the door and were surprised to see him. The next morning the prison guards searched for Peter, but he couldn't be found.

The believers were gathered to pray for Peter's release, yet they didn't believe when it happened. God wants his people to pray with faith and to be thankful, not surprised, when the answers come.

For You

The early believers prayed, but when the answer showed up on their doorstep, they didn't believe. Pray with faith that your prayer will be answered, and expect the answer. It may not happen as quickly as it did for Peter's friends, but if it's in God's plan for you, it will happen.

Answer: b
Suddenly, there was a bright light in the cell, and an angel of the Lord stood before Peter. The angel struck him on the side to awaken him and said, "Quick! Get up!" And the chains fell off his wrists. Acts 12:7
(The Whole Story: Acts 12:3-19)

November 3

Elymas the Sorceror

Q: Why did Paul, through God's power, make Elymas (also called Bar-Jesus) blind?
a. He was keeping a Roman official from hearing Paul's message.
b. He attacked Barnabas.
c. He wouldn't stop following Paul around.

Paul, who once hurt Christians, was now a Christian himself. God told the early believers that he was calling Paul and a man named Barnabas to take the gospel to other countries. So the church prayed over Paul and Barnabas and sent them on their way.

On their journey, Paul and Barnabas traveled through the island of Cyprus and told people the good news of Jesus. When they reached the city of Paphos, an important Roman official called for the missionaries because he wanted to hear their message. Elymas, a sorcerer, didn't want the official to hear Paul's message. If the official believed, Elymas would lose his job because a believer would not need a sorcerer. Elymas did everything he could to distract the Roman official.

Paul turned to Elymas and said, "You son of the devil, full of every sort of deceit and fraud, and enemy of all that is good! Will you never stop perverting the true ways of the Lord? Watch now, for the Lord has laid his hand of punishment upon you, and you will be struck blind. You will not see the sunlight for some time."

The sorcerer was immediately blinded. When the Roman official saw what happened, he believed Paul's message and became a follower of Jesus.

The sorcerer tried to distract the Roman official from hearing about God. There are many things and people today that distract others from hearing the message of Jesus. Can you name some of them?

For You
You have already heard the gospel message, but are there things that distract you from spending time with the Lord each day? What can you do about them?

Answer: a
But Elymas, the sorcerer (as his name means in Greek), interfered and urged the governor to pay no attention to what Barnabas and Saul said. He was trying to keep the governor from believing. Acts 13:8
(The Whole Story: Acts 13:4-12)

Barnabas

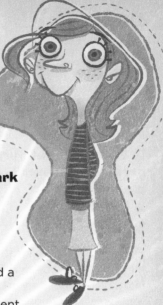

Q: Why did Paul and Barnabas part ways?
a. Barnabas wanted to go home and visit family.
b. Paul thought he'd travel faster alone.
c. They disagreed over whether or not John Mark should go with them.

Have you ever argued with a close friend and walked away to join another friend? That happens a lot when you're growing up. It can even happen when you're an adult. Paul and Barnabas, two strong Christian men, had a disagreement and parted ways.

Paul and Barnabas were chosen as missionaries and sent out on their first journey. Other believers went with them, including John Mark, a relative of Barnabas, who was their assistant. But partway through the journey, he left them and went home. We don't know if he was tired of the journey or afraid of what they'd encounter. We know only that he left (see Acts 13:13).

Later when Paul suggested revisiting the churches to see how the new believers were doing, Barnabas wanted to take John Mark with them. Paul was against it since John Mark had left them once before. Paul wasn't ready to give John Mark another chance. Paul and Barnabas disagreed so strongly that they parted ways. Barnabas took John Mark on his journey, and Paul chose Silas for his.

Even though it's sad that Paul and Barnabas couldn't work out their differences about John Mark, it did result in two missionary teams going out instead of one.

For You

Barnabas's original name was Joseph, but he was renamed Barnabas, which means encourager, because he made it a point to encourage others through his words and actions, as he did with John Mark. Are you an encourager? Do you urge others not to give up? Do you speak a kind word when someone is down? Look for ways to encourage others today.

Answer: c

Barnabas . . . wanted to take along John Mark. But Paul disagreed strongly, since John Mark had deserted them in Pamphylia and had not continued with them in their work. Their disagreement was so sharp that they separated. Barnabas took John Mark with him and sailed for Cyprus. Acts 15:37-39
(The Whole Story: Acts 15:36-41)

November 5

The Women by the River

Q: What seller of purple cloth became a believer?
a. Mary
b. Phoebe
c. Lydia

Paul and Silas traveled to the city of Philippi. On the Sabbath they went outside the city gate to the river because they thought they might find a group gathered for prayer. When they arrived they found a group of women. One of the women was Lydia, an influential merchant who sold purple cloth. Lydia was probably wealthy, because the cloth was valuable and was often worn as a sign of nobility. Lydia believed in God, but she didn't know about Jesus. After Paul told the group about Jesus' death and resurrection, Lydia became a Christian.

Lydia went back to her home and shared the news with her family. She invited Paul, Silas, and the others with them to stay with her. Lydia also offered her home as a place for other Christians to gather.

When Lydia became a believer, she didn't stop being a merchant, but she started using her money and her home to serve God. God doesn't expect every believer to be a full-time missionary or pastor, but he wants them to be like Lydia in sharing the gospel where they are and in using what they have for God.

For You

God wants you to be a witness for him in your classroom, homeschool group, art club, soccer team, karate class, or wherever you are. He needs Christians to take the light to places nearby as well as places far away. Be a light to those around you today no matter where you are.

Answer: c
One of them was Lydia from Thyatira, a merchant of expensive purple cloth, who worshiped God. As she listened to us, the Lord opened her heart, and she accepted what Paul was saying. Acts 16:14
(The Whole Story: Acts 16:11-15)

The Slave Girl

Q: Before Paul cast the demon out of the slave girl, how did she earn money for her masters?
a. fortune-telling
b. begging
c. wrestling

When Paul and Silas were in Philippi, they met a servant girl with an evil spirit in her that allowed her to tell the future. The girl's masters used her to make money. People paid to have the girl interpret signs and predict the future.

Every day the girl followed Paul and Silas and called, "These men are servants of the Most High God, and they have come to tell you how to be saved." What the girl said was true, but Paul didn't like that a demon caused the girl to yell.

Paul turned to the girl and spoke to the demon: "I command you in the name of Jesus Christ to come out of her." The evil spirit immediately left. The girl's masters were furious. How would they make money when she couldn't predict the future or read signs? To cause trouble the men said the missionaries were teaching customs that were illegal for the Romans to practice. Paul and Silas were beaten and thrown in prison.

Paul and Silas could have been upset, but instead they prayed and sang praises to God while in prison, which you will read more about in tomorrow's devotion.

For You

Paul and Silas were beaten and imprisoned, yet they praised God because they knew God would take care of them. It's hard to remember that God is with us during the hard times, but we can trust him to take care of us, just as the early missionaries trusted in him.

Answer: a
One day as we were going down to the place of prayer, we met a slave girl who had a spirit that enabled her to tell the future. She earned a lot of money for her masters by telling fortunes. . . . Paul got so exasperated that he turned and said to the demon within her, "I command you in the name of Jesus Christ to come out of her." And instantly it left her. Acts 16:16, 18
(The Whole Story: Acts 16:16-25)

November 7

The Missionaries in Prison

Q: What happened while Paul and Silas were singing and praying in prison?
a. The jailer was blinded by a bright light.
b. An earthquake freed them.
c. An angel appeared to them.

Have you ever gotten into trouble for something you didn't do? Maybe someone else was talking in class, but you got blamed. Or something got broken, and you were accused. Yesterday, you read that Paul and Silas were thrown into prison because they cast a demon out of a servant girl and she could no longer tell fortunes. Her masters could no longer make money from her, so they told lies about Paul and Silas and got everyone angry at the two missionaries. Paul and Silas were beaten and put into prison.

Paul and Silas were singing and praising God in their cell around midnight when suddenly an earthquake shook the prison. The chains fell off the prisoners, and the doors opened. When the guard woke up and saw this, he wanted to kill himself because he'd be in trouble for letting the prisoners escape. But Paul shouted, "Stop! Don't kill yourself! We are all here!"

The jailer asked Paul how to be saved. He wanted to be a believer too. Paul told him, "Believe in the Lord Jesus and you will be saved."

The jailer became a believer. He took Paul and Silas home with him so the rest of his family could hear the gospel from the missionaries. His family became believers too.

Paul and Silas openly praised God even after being beaten and while wrongly imprisoned. Their praise was a witness to those around them, and the jailer and his whole family became believers because of it.

For You

God wants you to praise him even in hard times. Others may be watching you and come to know Jesus because of your actions and attitude.

Answer: b

Around midnight Paul and Silas were praying and singing hymns to God, and the other prisoners were listening. Suddenly, there was a massive earthquake, and the prison was shaken to its foundations. All the doors immediately flew open, and the chains of every prisoner fell off! Acts 16:25-26

(The Whole Story: Acts 16:16-40)

November 8

Paul's Occupation

Q: Paul, Aquila, and Priscilla all had the same occupation. What was it?
a. doctor
b. fisherman
c. tentmaker

When Paul grew up, all the young Jewish boys were taught a trade, and Paul learned to make tents. Paul learned how to cut and sew rough goat hair cloth, other cloth, or leather into tents. Because Paul was a tentmaker, he could take his supplies with him and work wherever he went on his missionary journeys. When Paul visited Corinth, he stayed with Aquila and Priscilla, who were also tentmakers. Because of their skill, they could support themselves while they did God's work.

Paul, Aquila, and Priscilla didn't want to burden others with their needs while they served the Lord, so they continued their trade of tent making. They worked hard and were proud of their tents. It was an honorable way to support themselves instead of expecting the new churches they founded to support them.

There is nothing wrong with getting church support for missionary work, but Paul didn't want to depend on it. In his letter to the Thessalonians Paul said, "We never accepted food from anyone without paying for it. We worked hard day and night so we would not be a burden to any of you" (2 Thessalonians 3:8). He was setting an example of hard work for other believers in supporting himself and in taking the gospel to other countries.

For You

In Romans 12:11 Paul wrote, "Never be lazy, but work hard and serve the Lord enthusiastically." What do you need to work hard at today? School assignments or projects? Chores? Practicing a sports skill or music piece? Follow Paul's advice and be a hard worker.

Answer: c
Paul lived and worked with [Aquila and Priscilla], for they were tentmakers just as he was. Acts 18:3
(The Whole Story: Acts 18:1-3)

November 9

A Willing Learner

Q: What Jew really wanted to preach about the Lord but didn't know Jesus was the Messiah?
a. Apollos
b. Agabus
c. Timothy

Have you ever heard someone speak or preach a sermon, but you didn't get anything out of it? Then another person spoke on the same subject, and it was interesting and held your attention. You left with new knowledge or were inspired to do something or learn more.

Apollos was the second kind of speaker. He was an enthusiastic speaker who taught about Jesus. People enjoyed listening to him because he spoke in a way that kept their attention. But Apollos didn't know the whole story of Jesus yet. He may have still been teaching the people to watch for the coming Messiah. Aquila and Priscilla realized he needed to hear about the risen Savior. They shared the whole story of Jesus with Apollos so he'd be able to give people the whole gospel message.

Apollos didn't get defensive when Aquila and Priscilla told him there was more he needed to learn. He accepted their teaching eagerly, and then he went out and passed it on to others.

There is never a point when we've heard the same Bible stories too many times or heard too many sermons on the same subject. There's never a time when we know all there is to know about God or Jesus. There's never a time when it's okay to stop reading the Bible. As Christians, we are students until we graduate to heaven. Even there we will continue learning.

For You
Never stop learning. If you feel like you're hearing the same Bible stories over and over, ask questions and learn more about them. Research why a story is important and how the culture and lifestyle during the time it was written impacted the story. Look beyond the surface story to the significance of it both during Bible times and in your own life.

Answer: a
Meanwhile, a Jew named Apollos, an eloquent speaker who knew the Scriptures well, had arrived in Ephesus from Alexandria in Egypt. . . . However, he knew only about John's baptism. Acts 18:24-25
(The Whole Story: Acts 18:24-28)

November 10

Demetrius

Q: Who was Demetrius?
a. a silversmith who made idols
b. a temple priest in Ephesus
c. a follower of Paul

Paul and his traveling companions weren't welcomed everywhere they went. While some people willingly received the gospel message, others didn't. For some, changing the way they lived when they became Christians meant a loss of business. Here's what was happening in Ephesus.

Demetrius was a silversmith in Ephesus who made silver idols of the Greek goddess Artemis, a false god, and sold them. Other workmen also made money from things related to Artemis. There was even a festival to celebrate her. Demetrius called all the workers together and warned them that if people believed Paul's message about Jesus, they'd stop buying the idols and celebrating Artemis.

Demetrius got the people stirred up and angry. They gathered in a building and took Paul's traveling companions with them. The people shouted, "Great is Artemis of the Ephesians!" for two hours. They only stopped when the mayor addressed them and tried to calm them down. The mayor told the people that Paul and his friends hadn't done anything against them, but if they had, they would be tried in court. The riot showed Paul and his traveling companions that it was time to move on to a new city.

For You

Although you won't face what the early missionaries did, you will meet people who are closed to the gospel because they don't want to change their lifestyles. But don't let that keep you from sharing the gospel anyway. You never know the impact it'll have.

Answer: a
Demetrius [was] a silversmith who had a large business manufacturing silver shrines of the Greek goddess Artemis. Acts 19:24
(The Whole Story: Acts 19:23-41)

November 11

Don't Fall Asleep in Church

Q: What young man fell asleep in church and plunged to his death?
a. Barnabas
b. Eutychus
c. Timothy

Have you ever dozed off during a church service? If you have, probably the worst thing that happened was your parents gave you an earlier bedtime or took away a privilege. But for one young man who fell asleep during Paul's sermon, the consequences were much worse.

On Paul's last day in Troas, everyone gathered in an upper room to hear him speak. It got late, but Paul kept speaking. There were many candles burning and a large number of people gathered, which made the room overly warm. The late hour and the warmth were too much for Eutychus, who was sitting in an open window. The young man fell asleep and tumbled from the window three stories to his death.

Paul lifted Eutychus and brought life back to him through God's power. The people all went back upstairs to have a meal and continue listening to Paul until dawn.

Some Bible scholars judge Eutychus harshly for falling asleep while the Word of God was being taught, but the young man meant no disrespect to God, the Scripture, or Paul. It was the middle of the night, and he'd probably been up since early morning. He was just too drowsy to stay awake any longer. If he had planned to fall asleep while listening to Paul, he would certainly have picked a safer seat.

For You

You may find it hard to pay attention in church at times, but if you focus, you can learn something useful for your life. Try jotting down the pastor's sermon points and Scripture references in a notebook. Write down one way the Scripture applies to you and try to put it in practice during the week.

Answer: b
As Paul spoke on and on, a young man named Eutychus, sitting on the windowsill, became very drowsy. Finally, he fell sound asleep and dropped three stories to his death below. Acts 20:9
(The Whole Story: Acts 20:7-12)

The Plot against Paul

Q: Who learned of the plot to kill Paul and warned him?
a. Barnabas
b. the high priest
c. Paul's nephew

Some people wanted Paul dead. They didn't like his message about Jesus. Forty men actually promised that they would not eat or drink anything until they had killed this zealous new missionary. They planned to ask to have Paul brought before the high council. Then they would hide along the way and kill him.

Paul's nephew, his sister's son, overheard the plot. He went to where Paul was being held in prison and asked to talk to him. The nephew told Paul what he'd heard. Then Paul had a soldier take his nephew to the commander, who listened to the plot to kill the missionary.

The commander moved Paul to another city during the night, where his case would be heard by Governor Felix. Thanks to Paul's nephew, the Jews who wanted to kill Paul were outsmarted, and Paul went on to share the gospel with others, even those who held him prisoner.

We don't really know much about Paul's nephew other than he must have felt loyal to Paul in order to risk visiting him and telling him about the plan against him. Perhaps Paul's nephew shared some of Paul's boldness and his desire to spread the gospel no matter the cost.

For You

Paul shared the gospel wherever he went, even though it meant being imprisoned at times. During those times he also shared the story of salvation with those holding him captive. God gave Paul the courage to live out his faith no matter the consequences, and God will do the same for you.

Answer: c
Paul's nephew—his sister's son—heard of their plan and went to the fortress and told Paul. Acts 23:16
(The Whole Story: Acts 23:12-35)

November 13

Paul Sails for Rome

Q: What happened on the trip to Rome?
a. Paul's boat was shipwrecked.
b. Paul was thrown overboard to calm the storm.
c. Paul escaped overboard.

Paul had been arrested again for sharing the gospel. He asked to go to Rome to have his case heard. Before going, he testified to Herod Agrippa II, who found Paul innocent (see Acts 26). But because Paul had requested to go to Rome to be tried, he still had to make that trip.

Paul, along with other prisoners, was sent to Rome by boat. Luke, his doctor friend, and Aristarchus went with him.

After battling winds and making slow progress, the ship stopped in Crete. Paul urged the sailors to stay at that port for the winter, but they wanted to push on farther before taking a break in their travels.

Before they'd gone far, gale-force winds beat against the ship, tossing it in the waves. For days everyone feared they'd die. But God sent an angel to tell Paul he'd make it to Rome and not one life would be lost, although they'd be shipwrecked.

Paul urged everyone to eat, and then they threw what they didn't need overboard to lighten the load. The sailors tried to steer the ship toward a sandy shore they spotted. They hit a sandbar, and the ship ran aground and was stuck. The force of the waves began to break the ship apart. The passengers jumped into the water and made it to shore by either swimming or holding on to boards. No one was lost.

God didn't stop the storm, but he took Paul and his companions safely through it. God may not stop trouble from coming, but he will be with us as we face it.

For You

You will face trouble and storms in life. God may not stop them all, because he knows they will help you grow and learn to trust him. He also won't leave you to weather the storms alone; he'll be there to guide you through.

Answer: a
They hit a shoal and ran the ship aground too soon. The bow of the ship stuck fast, while the stern was repeatedly smashed by the force of the waves and began to break apart. Acts 27:41
(The Whole Story: Acts 26–27)

November 14

On the Island of Malta

Q: What happened to Paul on the island of Malta?
a. He was tried before Caesar.
b. He was bitten by a snake.
c. He became too ill to travel farther.

After the ship Paul was on broke apart (see yesterday's devotion), all the passengers swam or floated on boards to the shore of an island named Malta. The people there welcomed them and built a fire so they'd warm up and dry out. Paul wanted to help, so he gathered more sticks for the fire.

As Paul laid the sticks on the fire, a poisonous snake bit him on the hand. The people thought the gods had sent the snake to kill Paul because he was wicked. They expected Paul's arm to swell from the poison, but nothing happened. Paul just shook the snake into the fire.

When Publius, the island's ruler, heard about Paul, he invited the missionary and his friends to his house. Paul saw that Publius's father was very ill, so he healed him through God's power. Then others came to Paul to be healed, and Paul was able to heal them and share the gospel with many people.

Paul and his companions stayed on the island for three months. When it was time for Paul and his friends to continue their journey to Rome, the people gave them supplies for their trip.

God could have spared Paul from the shipwreck, but then Paul would have missed the chance to share the gospel with the people on Malta. The Lord used the shipwreck to land Paul where he wanted him.

For You

God plans the events in your life to put you where he wants you. When something unplanned happens, look for ways God might want to work through it.

Answer: b
As Paul gathered an armful of sticks and was laying them on the fire, a poisonous snake, driven out by the heat, bit him on the hand. . . . But Paul shook off the snake into the fire and was unharmed. Acts 28:3, 5
(The Whole Story: Acts 28:1-10)

Paul in Rome

Q: What did Paul do while he was under house arrest in Rome?
a. tried to escape
b. wrote a lot of letters
c. begged God to free him

Three months after the shipwreck, Paul and his companions boarded another ship to complete the trip to Rome. The believers in Rome were excited that Paul was coming and gathered to meet him. Paul was allowed to have his own house, but a soldier guarded him.

Paul had wanted to preach in Rome, but this probably wasn't what he envisioned—being sent to Rome as a prisoner, being shipwrecked, getting bitten by a snake, and finally arriving in Rome months after his journey began (see Acts 27:1–28:11). Despite all that, Paul was able to minister to both believers and unbelievers in Rome.

While Paul was under house arrest, he not only preached to Jews and Gentiles, but he wrote letters to the Ephesians, Philippians, and Colossians. He also wrote a letter to Philemon. These are called epistles, and they are now part of the New Testament.

It's believed that Paul was released after two years and did more traveling but was again imprisoned for preaching. Paul, once a persecutor of believers before he met Jesus, was often persecuted himself. But it didn't stop him from spreading the gospel message whenever and wherever he could. Paul viewed his trials and hardships as opportunities to minister for Jesus.

For You

Paul had wanted to preach in Rome, but writing letters to believers as a prisoner was probably not what he had planned. Sometimes our plans don't work out, but God knows the whole course of our lives. Nothing catches him by surprise. He will open the doors for you to be able to accomplish what he needs you to do.

Answer: b
For the next two years, Paul lived in Rome at his own expense. He welcomed all who visited him, boldly proclaiming the Kingdom of God and teaching about the Lord Jesus Christ. And no one tried to stop him. Acts 28:30-31
(The Whole Story: Acts 28:17-31)

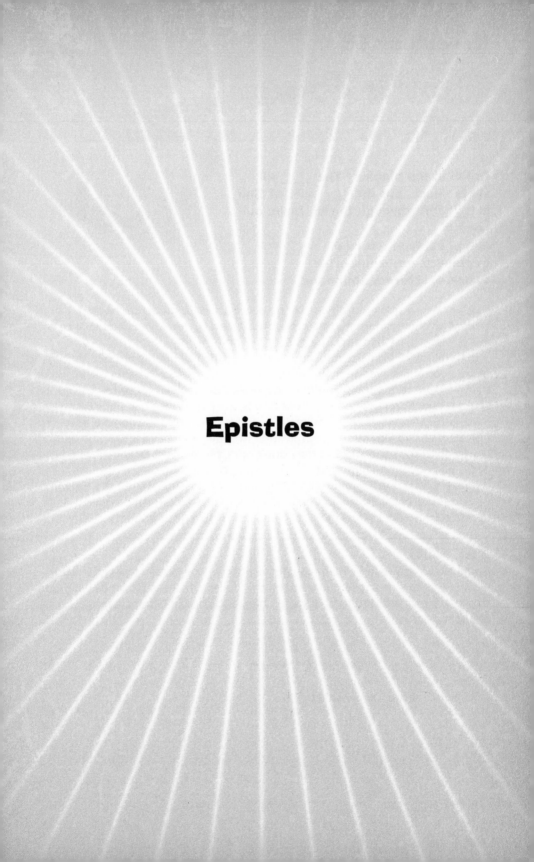

Epistles

November 16

God's Free Gift

Q: Fill in the blanks: "The _____ of sin is death, but the _____ gift of God is _____ life through Christ Jesus our Lord."
a. wages, free, eternal
b. penalty, amazing, after
c. price, offered, abundant

Paul wrote the book of Romans to the believers in Rome before he ever visited there. The church in Rome was probably started by Jews who were in Jerusalem at Pentecost and then took the gospel to Rome.

In the book of Romans, Paul explains the gospel: all people are sinners in need of a Savior, and salvation is available only by grace. Grace is being given something we have not earned and don't deserve. God showed grace to us when he sent his own Son to die on the cross to pay the penalty for our sin.

We are saved when we completely trust Jesus for our salvation because of his death and resurrection. This salvation isn't deserved, and it can't be earned. Doing good things is fine, but they don't get us to heaven. Only believing in Jesus and accepting him as Savior gets us into heaven.

Paul explains it in Romans 6:23: "The wages of sin is death, but the free gift of God is eternal life through Christ Jesus our Lord." A gift isn't earned; it is accepted. And God offers eternal life in heaven as a gift through Jesus.

For You

Romans 6:23 gives the whole plan of salvation in one verse. How would you explain this verse to someone who doesn't believe in Jesus? Practice what you would say, and ask God to give you a chance to share it with someone who needs to hear it.

Answer: a
The wages of sin is death, but the free gift of God is eternal life through Christ Jesus our Lord. Romans 6:23
(The Whole Story: Romans 6:20-23)

A Sister

Q: What woman did Paul call a sister in Christ in the last chapter of Romans?
a. Mary
b. Phoebe
c. Dorcas

While most of the book of Romans instructs the church about salvation and how to live as Christians, Paul spends the last chapter greeting many people in the church, both men and women, by name.

One of the women Paul greets is Phoebe. She lived in a seaport near the city of Corinth. Phoebe may have even delivered the letter Paul wrote to the Romans while he was in Corinth. During that time, not many people traveled, and very rarely would a woman travel alone to another country.

Phoebe was known for serving in her church and helping others. It's thought that she was wealthy and helped support Paul's ministry. Most likely she taught the women in her church and reached out to the poor and widowed. She was an involved Christian, not one who just attended church once a week and then did her own thing the rest of the week.

God needed involved Christians during the early church age, and he still needs involved believers today. Not all people have the same talents or the ability to support their church and missionaries financially, but all Christians can do something to help in their churches and reach out to others around them.

For You
God needs modern-day Pauls and Phoebes to serve in churches, share the gospel, and reach out to those around them. How can you be an involved believer this week?

Answer: b
I commend to you our sister Phoebe, who is a deacon in the church in Cenchrea. Welcome her in the Lord as one who is worthy of honor among God's people. Help her in whatever she needs, for she has been helpful to many, and especially to me. Romans 16:1-2
(The Whole Story: Romans 16:1-2)

The Temple of the Holy Spirit

Q: What does Paul say is the temple of the Holy Spirit?
a. the church
b. your body
c. heaven

If you want to rent a house or apartment, you sign an agreement with the owner. There are rules the owner will ask you to follow. The owner may not want you to have a pet that might ruin the carpet or chew on things. He or she may not want you to hang things on the wall that could damage it.

Your body is the same way. God gave you your body, and when he saved you, the Holy Spirit came to live in you. Paul refers to your body as a temple of the Holy Spirit. In Bible times, temples were carefully constructed of fine material. They were well furnished, and there were strict rules about how to take care of them. It's important that you take good care of your body just as the people in Bible times were very careful to follow all the rules about the care of the Temple.

Every day you make choices about how to care for your body. You choose to eat junk food or healthy food. You choose to sit in front of a computer or television screen or to shoot baskets, ride your bike, or be part of a sports team. You can determine that you will never take illegal drugs or drink alcohol or do other things to damage your body. You honor God when you take care of the body he's given you.

For You

You have choices to make today. What choices can you make that will help you take care of your body, the temple of the Holy Spirit?

Answer: b
Don't you realize that your body is the temple of the Holy Spirit, who lives in you and was given to you by God? You do not belong to yourself, for God bought you with a high price. So you must honor God with your body.
1 Corinthians 6:19-20
(The Whole Story: 1 Corinthians 6:12-20)

November 19

A Noisy Gong

Q: According to 1 Corinthians 13, if you don't have this, you will be like a noisy gong or clanging cymbal.
a. patience
b. love
c. hope

The Bible is full of information to help us know how to live. Some passages of Scripture are more familiar than others. For example, most people have heard of the Ten Commandments in Exodus 20. Psalm 23 is known as the Shepherd's Psalm. Matthew 5–7 contains the Sermon on the Mount and the Beatitudes.

Do you know what 1 Corinthians 13 is known as? It's called the "love chapter." That's because Paul spends the whole chapter talking about the importance of love and the characteristics of true love. Many times this passage is read at church weddings.

God has given people spiritual gifts to help win others to him and to help other Christians grow, but Paul told the people at Corinth that without love those spiritual gifts are worth nothing. People might be excellent speakers, but without love they just sound like a noisy gong. The kind of love Paul was talking about was unselfish love given to others. Here's what he says about it:

Love is patient and kind.
Love is not jealous or boastful or proud or rude.
It does not demand its own way.
It is not irritable, and it keeps no record of being wronged.
It does not rejoice about injustice but rejoices whenever the truth wins out.
Love never gives up, never loses faith, is always hopeful, and endures through every circumstance.

That kind of love is only possible if Jesus is in control of your life. Without love, all your good works and all your words might as well be a noisy gong.

For You

Read through the list of what 1 Corinthians 13 says about love. Is that the kind of love you show your family and friends? If not, work on loving others in an unselfish way this week.

Answer: b
If I could speak all the languages of earth and of angels, but didn't love others, I would only be a noisy gong or a clanging cymbal. 1 Corinthians 13:1
(The Whole Story: 1 Corinthians 13)

November 20

New Life

Q: Complete this verse: "This means that anyone who _____ to _____ has become a new person. The _____ is gone; a _____ has begun!"
a. listens, God, sin nature, new nature
b. comes, God, past, new beginning
c. belongs, Christ, old life, new life

In the winter, things seem gray and dreary. It gets dark earlier in the day, snow becomes dirty and turns to slush, trees are bare, and flowers are no longer in bloom. But then in the spring, things change. There's more daylight. Flowers bud and bloom, adding dashes of color to the world. Leaves grow on the trees, adding green to the bare branches. The dreariness of winter is replaced by the new life that arrives in spring.

Our lives are like that too. Before Jesus, our lives are full of sin. But once we accept Jesus as Savior, everything is new. Our sins are forgiven, and we become the children of God. It's not just a new start. We are new creations of God on the inside. Our hearts are remade.

Why do we become new in Jesus? Paul wrote, "We are God's masterpiece. He has created us anew in Christ Jesus, so we can do the good things he planned for us long ago" (Ephesians 2:10). God has a plan for each of us, but we can't live out that plan until we have turned to Jesus and God has done his powerful work of remaking us.

For You

If you haven't let Jesus have your heart and life, talk to someone about that today. If you've become a new creation in Jesus, seek out God's plan for your life.

Answer: c
This means that anyone who belongs to Christ has become a new person. The old life is gone; a new life has begun! 2 Corinthians 5:17
(The Whole Story: 2 Corinthians 5:11-21)

Giving Your Tithes and Offerings

Q: How does God want you to give your offering money?
a. grudgingly
b. with great thought
c. cheerfully

Zachary woke up and hopped out of bed. He went to his window and looked out. It had snowed during the night! Normally Zachary wouldn't be too excited about the first snow of the season, but this year he was going to shovel to earn money toward a new game system. Zachary dressed quickly and went downstairs to remind his parents of their promise to buy him the game system if he earned half of the money himself.

Zachary started planning how many sidewalks and driveways he'd need to shovel to earn enough money.

"Don't forget about your tithe and offering," his mom reminded him.

"You're kidding, right? That's for adults," Zachary said unhappily.

Do you ever feel like Zachary? Tithes—10 percent of your income—and offerings—the extra money you give in addition to your tithe—are for adults who earn a regular paycheck, right? Wrong. They're for everyone. We give back to God because he gives us everything we have including the ability to earn money or blessing us with it in some way.

It's good that Zachary was motivated to earn money, but he was wrong in his attitude about the money and the game system he wanted to buy. God wants us to give cheerfully and willingly to his work and to help others first.

For You

Set aside a little of all the money you receive to put in the offering at church. Be willing to give back to God by supporting your church, missionaries, and those in need.

Answer: c
You must each decide in your heart how much to give. And don't give reluctantly or in response to pressure. "For God loves a person who gives cheerfully."
2 Corinthians 9:7
(The Whole Story: 2 Corinthians 9)

November 22

Fruit of the Spirit

Q: Which is a fruit of the Spirit?
a. pride
b. self-control
c. self-esteem

The Bible talks about the fruit of the Spirit, which are characteristics evident in believers' lives when they allow God's Spirit to work in them. You can't show this fruit in your own power. It comes from listening to and obeying the Spirit's voice. The results are a life filled with the following:

Love. Only with the Holy Spirit's help can you love God, yourself, your neighbors, fellow believers, and even your enemies.

Joy. Even when things go wrong, and you don't feel happy, you can still be filled with the joy of the Lord. Joy doesn't depend on what happens around you but on Jesus.

Peace. The peace the Holy Spirit gives will keep you calm on the inside no matter what's happening on the outside, because you know that God is in control.

Patience. The Holy Spirit will keep you calm in trying situations. He can help you keep your cool all the time.

Kindness. Jesus perfectly modeled being gracious and caring, and the Holy Spirit can help you do the same.

Goodness. A Christlike goodness helps Christians live right and be positive role models to others. This will draw people to you and to God.

Faithfulness. The Holy Spirit helps you be steadfast, dedicated, and dependable, just as God is.

Gentleness. This isn't weakness. Rather, it's controlled strength, which allows you to be tender.

Self-control. Being able to restrain yourself from impulsive actions or from just doing what you want is a true sign of God's Spirit working in you.

For You

Do you see these fruits in your own life? If not, listen to God's Spirit as he prompts you to obey and live for the Lord. Take time to think about how each fruit would look if it were more evident in your life.

Answer: b
The Holy Spirit produces this kind of fruit in our lives: love, joy, peace, patience, kindness, goodness, faithfulness, gentleness, and self-control. Galatians 5:22-23 (The Whole Story: Galatians 5:16-26)

November 23

Doing Good

Q: The book of Galatians says we should do good to
a. each of our neighbors.
b. everyone, especially other believers.
c. those who do good to us.

If you plant carrot seeds, you get carrots. You don't get peppers or tomatoes. That's a simple law of nature. The same is true in our lives. In the book of Galatians, Paul tells the believers they will reap what they sow. That applies to you today, too. The things you do produce results in your life.

If you make bad choices such as lying or cheating, the results may be failure and a loss of trust. If you make good choices such as helping others, being kind to everyone, and being honest, it will result in positive feelings and in others being thankful for your deeds.

Paul encourages believers to do good to everyone, especially other believers. It doesn't mean to do good just when it's easy for you, but anytime there is an opportunity—even if it seems there is no result. When you do good, you are sowing the seeds and leaving the results up to God.

There are lots of ways to do good every day. There is someone who needs an encouraging word or advice. There is someone who is lonely and needs a friend to talk to or hang out with. There is someone who needs help finishing an overwhelming task. There are always needs. And God wants you to meet the needs you are able to.

For You

What three good things can you do for someone else this week? Ask a friend or sibling to do them with you.

Answer: b
Whenever we have the opportunity, we should do good to everyone—especially to those in the family of faith. Galatians 6:10
(The Whole Story: Galatians 6:1-10)

God's Armor

Q: Which is not part of the armor of God?
a. belt of truth
b. shoes of pride
c. shield of faith

Christians are in a battle between good and evil, and God has the armor you need. Here's the armor he promises you:

Belt of truth. Jesus is truth. "Jesus [said,] 'I am the way, the truth, and the life. No one can come to the Father except through me'" (John 14:6).

Body armor of God's righteousness. You can have God's righteousness because of Jesus' death and resurrection. Romans 5:17 says, "But even greater is God's wonderful grace and his gift of righteousness, for all who receive it will live in triumph over sin and death through this one man, Jesus Christ."

Shoes of the peace that comes from the Good News. You have peace with God because of your relationship with Jesus. Jesus said, "I am leaving you with a gift—peace of mind and heart. And the peace I give is a gift the world cannot give. So don't be troubled or afraid" (John 14:27).

Shield of faith. Your trust isn't in yourself but in God's power and promises. Romans 3:22 says, "We are made right with God by placing our faith in Jesus Christ. And this is true for everyone who believes, no matter who we are."

Salvation as your helmet. Your salvation is through Jesus. Ephesians 2:8 says, "God saved you by his grace when you believed. And you can't take credit for this; it is a gift from God."

Sword of the Spirit. Every soldier needs a sword, and yours is the Bible. "Jesus [said,] 'But even more blessed are all who hear the word of God and put it into practice'" (Luke 11:28).

All these things help you as you stand strong for God.

For You

Think about each piece of God's armor. How can you use each one in your life?

Answer: b
Stand your ground, putting on the belt of truth and the body armor of God's righteousness. For shoes, put on the peace that comes from the Good News so that you will be fully prepared. . . . Hold up the shield of faith to stop the fiery arrows of the devil. Put on salvation as your helmet, and take the sword of the Spirit, which is the word of God. Ephesians 6:14-17
(The Whole Story: Ephesians 6:10-20)

November 25

Not Done Yet

Q: When will God be done perfecting us?
a. when he returns
b. after we are baptized
c. after years of Bible study

There used to be a popular bumper sticker that read "Please be patient. God isn't finished with me yet." This is the message behind Philippians 1:6. God started working in your life the day you became a believer. It's not a onetime event; it's a lifelong process. The Holy Spirit lives in you, guiding you and helping you become more like Jesus day by day.

Do you ever feel like you mess up over and over? Even when you get discouraged and feel like giving up on yourself, God doesn't. It's not okay to sin over and over and expect God to overlook it, but you are his personal project, and he doesn't leave his projects undone.

After Paul told the Philippians that God would continue a good work in them, he said, "I pray that your love will overflow more and more, and that you will keep on growing in knowledge and understanding. For I want you to understand what really matters, so that you may live pure and blameless lives until the day of Christ's return. May you always be filled with the fruit of your salvation—the righteous character produced in your life by Jesus Christ—for this will bring much glory and praise to God" (Philippians 1:9-11). Paul didn't want the believers to just sit by and watch God work. He wanted them to learn more about God so they would know what really matters and have righteous character.

God wants you to be filled with the fruit of your salvation—showing godly characteristics in your life—just as Paul encouraged the Philippian believers to be.

For You

If you are a Christian, you will continue to grow in your faith and become more like Jesus as you listen to the Holy Spirit and as you fill your heart and mind with God's Word. Take time to do that a little each day.

Answer: a
I am certain that God, who began the good work within you, will continue his work until it is finally finished on the day when Christ Jesus returns.
Philippians 1:6
(The Whole Story: Philippians 1:3-11)

November 26

Philippians

Q: In the book of Philippians, what does Paul say we should always be full of?
a. patience
b. peace
c. joy

What would make you happy? Going to an amusement park? Getting a new game system or your own cell phone? Being chosen for a special award at school? These things may make you happy, but what happens when the day at the amusement park ends, the game system or phone breaks, or someone else gets a better award? Happiness can quickly fade.

Joy is not like happiness. Joy is an inner attitude that doesn't change when the circumstances around you change. It comes from God's Spirit dwelling in you.

Paul wrote the book of Philippians while he was imprisoned in Rome, yet he mentions the words *rejoicing* and *joy* 16 times in the book. That's because Paul learned the key to joy. He didn't let his circumstances control his heart attitude. Paul said, "I have learned how to be content with whatever I have. I know how to live on almost nothing or with everything. I have learned the secret of living in every situation, whether it is with a full stomach or empty, with plenty or little. For I can do everything through Christ, who gives me strength" (Philippians 4:11-13).

Because Paul knew he was doing God's work, he accepted his circumstances whether he was in prison or free, whether he had plenty or not much at all. He knew his strength was from God, so he could do the things he needed to do through Christ's strength and with a joyful heart.

You, too, can have joy today no matter what is going on in your life, because your joy comes from Jesus.

For You

Don't let the things that happen in your life make you angry or bitter. Life may not always be fair, but God's plan for you is bigger than that. Focus on doing what God wants you to do each day, and shake off the little stuff that gets you down.

Answer: c
Always be full of joy in the Lord. I say it again—rejoice!   Philippians 4:4
(The Whole Story: Philippians 4:4-5, 10-19)

November 27

What's on Your Mind?

Q: According to Philippians 4:8, what kind of things should we think about?
a. good, noble, temporary, pure, arrogant, and true things
b. holy, proud, right, earthly, righteous, and good things
c. true, honorable, right, pure, lovely, and admirable things

Have you heard the expression "Garbage in, garbage out"? It was first used in the computer world to mean if you put wrong or invalid data in a computer, wrong or invalid answers will come out.

Do you know your mind works the same way? If you fill your mind with games, TV shows, movies, and music full of bad words and bad attitudes, those will take root in your heart. They will be what you think and talk about.

That's why it's important to guard your mind against garbage. Instead fill it with things that are true, honorable, right, pure, lovely, and admirable. That may be difficult, but you can do it. Ahead of time, find out about the movies you are going to watch, the games you will play, and the music you will listen to. That way you can make a good choice based on what you've learned rather than going with what's popular.

God isn't trying to ruin your fun with a list of things you can't watch or do. He's encouraging you to make wise choices to fill your mind with things that will help you focus on your real purpose for being here—getting to know Jesus and helping others know him too.

For You

Write the key words from Philippians 4:8 on an index card. As you watch a TV show or listen to music, use the words as a checklist to rate what you are seeing or hearing. If it falls short, look for a better choice.

Answer: c
Now, dear brothers and sisters, one final thing. Fix your thoughts on what is true, and honorable, and right, and pure, and lovely, and admirable. Think about things that are excellent and worthy of praise. Philippians 4:8
(The Whole Story: Philippians 4:6-9)

November 28

Spiritual Clothing

Q: According to Colossians 3, you should clothe yourself with
a. tenderhearted mercy, kindness, humility, gentleness, and patience.
b. good works, joy, goodness, faith, and self-control.
c. acts of kindness, mercy, faithfulness, and peace.

One of the first things you do in the morning is get dressed. You may have a routine you follow for picking out your clothes and putting them on. You might plan ahead the night before, or you might just grab the nearest thing. If you're homeschooled, you may even stay in your pajamas.

God has clothing he wants you to put on also. It's not the same as what you wear to school. These clothes are characteristics God wants you to wear. That means being covered with them just as you are covered with your jeans and shirt. Those characteristics are tenderhearted mercy, kindness, humility, gentleness, and patience.

How can you clothe yourself with those things? Each morning as you get dressed, remind yourself of the list. Make sure you understand what each characteristic means. Ask God to show you specific ways to practice these positive qualities each day at home, at school, on your sports team, during your music lesson, at church, and everywhere else you go.

Each time you are faced with a decision, ask yourself which choice will best allow you to demonstrate mercy or patience. Which option helps you be more kind or gentle? Thinking that way may not come easily at first, but if you ask God to help you do this, soon clothing yourself with these things will be as natural as putting on your school clothes each morning.

For You

Pick one characteristic from the list—tenderhearted mercy, kindness, humility, gentleness, patience—and think of two ways to practice it this week.

Answer: a
Since God chose you to be the holy people he loves, you must clothe yourselves with tenderhearted mercy, kindness, humility, gentleness, and patience.
Colossians 3:12
(The Whole Story: Colossians 3:12-17)

November 29

Paul's Advice

Q: According to Paul, when should you be thankful?
a. when God blesses you
b. when life is good
c. in all circumstances

In the United States, Thanksgiving Day has just passed. Families have their own traditions for this day, which may include anything from Scripture reading to watching football games or home movies. They gather and celebrate with a large meal and by spending time together.

God doesn't plan for his people to limit their thankfulness to one day a year, though. He says to be thankful in all circumstances. That doesn't mean you have to be thankful for the bad things that happen. No one would expect you to be thankful for them, but it's important to still be thankful for God's salvation, his work in your life, and how he might use the bad things for his own good during those times.

The apostle Paul gives three commands in 1 Thessalonians 5:16-18: Always be joyful. Never stop praying. Be thankful in all circumstances. Doing those things may not come easily. It's easy to complain about circumstances and let them get you down. You will have to remind yourself to react in a new way. If you can learn to do those three things, it will change your life.

- -

For You

Several things you should do each day are listed in 1 Thessalonians 5. Start in verse 11 with "encourage each other and build each other up" and see how many of them you can find. Try to live out two each day.

- -

Answer: c
Always be joyful. Never stop praying. Be thankful in all circumstances, for this is God's will for you who belong to Christ Jesus. 1 Thessalonians 5:16-18
(The Whole Story: 1 Thessalonians 5:11-22)

November 30

The Trio

Q: Paul wrote 2 Thessalonians to the church at Thessalonica on behalf of himself and what two other men?
a. Silas and Timothy
b. Barnabas and John Mark
c. Luke and James

On Paul's second missionary journey, he visited Thessalonica, the capital city of Macedonia, with two other men—Silas and Timothy. They started a church there, but Paul had to leave suddenly because of persecution. That's why he wrote the first letter to the Thessalonian church. There were lots of things he wanted to tell them, but he hadn't had time during his visit. The letter was full of comfort and encouragement.

Paul wrote a second letter to the Thessalonian church to clear up a misunderstanding. In the first letter, he'd told them that Jesus would come again. Some people thought he was coming right away, so they quit their jobs to wait around for him. They were using Christ's return as an excuse for laziness. Paul wrote the second letter to clear up the misunderstanding and tell them to be busy doing the Lord's work. Paul wrote both letters to the church on behalf of himself, Silas, and Timothy, since they had all started the church together.

Paul wrote to many churches, and he almost always began his letters with words of encouragement and support even when there were problems to address. He was careful to tell each church that he thanked God for them and prayed for them continuously. He reminded them that they were fellow believers and encouraged them to stand strong.

For You

Read the first few verses of the letters Paul wrote to the early churches (Romans, 1 and 2 Corinthians, Galatians, Ephesians, Philippians, Colossians, 1 and 2 Thessalonians, 1 and 2 Timothy, Titus, Philemon) and notice how he encouraged them before he gave them instructions or correction. Try to follow Paul's example when you have to confront someone about a problem. Always include encouragement and support.

Answer: a
This letter is from Paul, Silas, and Timothy. We are writing to the church in Thessalonica, to you who belong to God our Father and the Lord Jesus Christ.
2 Thessalonians 1:1
(The Whole Story: 2 Thessalonians 1)

December 1

A Son in the Faith

Q: Whom did Paul refer to as his son in the faith?
a. Silas
b. Timothy
c. Titus

Several people traveled with Paul at different times on his three missionary journeys. Timothy, a young man, joined Paul and Silas on their second missionary journey. Timothy was raised in the Jewish faith by his mother and grandmother. He had a love for God and probably became a follower of Jesus after Paul's first missionary journey to Lystra, where Timothy lived. By the time Paul visited again, Timothy had grown in his faith and was ready to join the missionary team.

Sometimes Timothy traveled with Paul. Other times Paul left Timothy to continue work in a city while he journeyed on, or he sent Timothy to take care of a need in a different city. Paul could trust Timothy to be responsible in doing God's work. Paul and Timothy always had a close relationship, and Paul loved Timothy like a son. Paul said, "I have no one else like Timothy, who genuinely cares about your welfare. All the others care only for themselves and not for what matters to Jesus Christ. But you know how Timothy has proved himself. Like a son with his father, he has served with me in preaching the Good News" (Philippians 2:20-22).

Because Paul thought of Timothy as a son, he wrote two letters to him giving him encouragement and instruction. They are the books of 1 and 2 Timothy in the New Testament.

For You

Timothy was someone who could be counted on. Paul was able to trust him to carry out God's work in places or at times that Paul couldn't. Do others think of you as dependable and responsible? If not, what can you do to change that?

Answer: b
I am writing to Timothy, my true son in the faith. May God the Father and Christ Jesus our Lord give you grace, mercy, and peace. 1 Timothy 1:2
(The Whole Story: 1 Timothy 1:1-2)

December 2

Being an Example

Q: Which of these is *not* a way Paul told Timothy to be an example?
a. strength
b. speech
c. faith

Timothy was a young pastor and missionary. Sometimes people didn't listen to him or respect him because he was younger than many of the other Christian leaders. But Timothy loved God, and he served the Lord enthusiastically.

Paul told Timothy not to let anyone look down on him because he was young. He encouraged Timothy to be an example to others in speech, actions, love, faith, and purity. If Timothy did those things, people would respect him and look up to him no matter his age or theirs.

Timothy set a good example for others in his speech. He spoke the truth of Jesus boldly to those who needed to hear it.

Timothy was an example in his actions. He didn't want anything he did to harm his Christian testimony.

Timothy was an example in his love for his fellow believers and for God. The Bible says that Christians will be known by their love, and Timothy lived that out.

Timothy's example of faith was well known. He had a background in Jewish religion, and he quickly accepted the message of Jesus and began sharing it with others. The people in his city knew him as a young man of God.

Timothy set an example of purity. He lived in a way that would honor God, not impress the people around him. Timothy lived in a way that pleased God, whether anyone was watching or not.

Even though the advice was given to Timothy, it belongs to all of God's children. God wants us all to be examples in the way we live, talk, and love.

For You

Others watch you every day. If someone decided to follow your example, would that be a good thing? Why or why not?

Answer: a
Don't let anyone think less of you because you are young. Be an example to all believers in what you say, in the way you live, in your love, your faith, and your purity. 1 Timothy 4:12
(The Whole Story: 1 Timothy 4:6-16)

December 3

A Good Goal

Q: Why did Paul tell Timothy to work hard?
a. to receive God's approval
b. to build a larger church
c. to be remembered after he died

If you were writing a close friend a good-bye letter knowing you'd never talk to him or her again, what would you say? Would you talk about the good times you'd had? Would you give your friend advice to follow? Would you send words of encouragement?

The book of 2 Timothy was Paul's last message to Timothy because Paul was imprisoned in Rome and facing death (see 2 Timothy 4:6). Paul had served God well and had given his all to the work of spreading the gospel. He'd been rejected, beaten, stoned, shipwrecked, and imprisoned more than once.

Everything Paul did and said centered around Jesus. Paul said, "Yes, everything else is worthless when compared with the infinite value of knowing Christ Jesus my Lord. For his sake I have discarded everything else, counting it all as garbage, so that I could gain Christ and become one with him" (Philippians 3:8-9).

Paul encouraged Timothy to work hard at studying the Scriptures so he would be able to explain them to others and earn God's approval. That was Paul's goal too. He wrote, "I focus on this one thing: Forgetting the past and looking forward to what lies ahead, I press on to reach the end of the race and receive the heavenly prize for which God, through Christ Jesus, is calling us" (Philippians 3:13-14).

For You

Do you, like Paul, live your life so that God will be pleased with you? Why not memorize Philippians 3:13-14 to remind yourself of your true goal in life?

Answer: a
Work hard so you can present yourself to God and receive his approval. Be a good worker, one who does not need to be ashamed and who correctly explains the word of truth. 2 Timothy 2:15
(The Whole Story: 2 Timothy 2)

December 4

Serving in Crete

Q: What young man did Paul leave in Crete to finish the work Paul had started?
a. Philemon
b. Titus
c. Timothy

Paul was a great missionary and preacher. He also took time to train younger men to be pastors and leaders. The previous devotions talked about Timothy, a young man who traveled with Paul and was also a pastor.

Titus was another young man who traveled with Paul on part of his journey and went to the church in Corinth to straighten out problems there. Titus traveled with Paul to Jerusalem and to Crete, a small island in the Mediterranean Sea. There was a large population of Jews there, some of whom may have been in Jerusalem when the Holy Spirit came 30 years before Paul wrote his letter to Titus.

Paul and Titus traveled together to Crete to visit the churches. Paul wanted to appoint leaders in each church who would teach the truth, help guide the church members, and set a good example. Paul had to leave before he was done appointing leaders, so Titus stayed to finish the job.

Paul gave Titus a list of qualifications the leaders should have. The qualifications didn't concern the training or knowledge they had, but how they lived. Paul said, "An elder must live a blameless life. . . . He must not be arrogant or quick-tempered . . . or dishonest with money. . . . He must love what is good. He must live wisely and be just. He must live a devout and disciplined life. . . . He will be able to encourage others with wholesome teaching and show those who oppose it where they are wrong" (Titus 1:7-9).

These are good qualifications not just for church leaders but also for everyone who is a follower of Jesus.

For You

Reread the list above. Do you see these things in the lives of your church leaders? How many of these qualities do you see in your own life? Try to live each day so that they are evident in your life.

Answer: b

I am writing to Titus, my true son in the faith that we share. May God the Father and Christ Jesus our Savior give you grace and peace. I left you on the island of Crete so you could complete our work there. Titus 1:4-5
(The Whole Story: Titus 1)

December 5

Philemon's Slave

Q: What was the name of Philemon's slave who stole from him and ran away?
a. Onesimus
b. Zenas
c. Epaphras

The book of Philemon is a short, personal letter to Philemon, a wealthy member of the Colossian church, which met in his home. Slavery was common in the Roman Empire, and Philemon owned a slave named Onesimus. Onesimus stole from Philemon and ran away to Rome. Once there, he met Paul and heard the gospel message. Onesimus became a believer.

Paul wrote to Philemon to ask him to take Onesimus back, not just as a slave, but also as a fellow believer. Slave owners had the right to kill runaway slaves, so Onesimus feared for his life. But Paul appealed to Philemon's goodness. Paul offered to pay any money Onesimus owed his master.

In many ways, what Paul did for Onesimus is a picture of what Jesus did for us. Just as Onesimus was a slave to Philemon, we are slaves to our sin. Paul interceded, or pleaded, with Philemon for Onesimus, just as Christ intercedes for us with God. Onesimus was forgiven just as we are forgiven in God's sight through Jesus. Paul offered to pay Onesimus's debt just as Christ paid the debt for our sin on the cross.

Philemon, Paul, and Onesimus provide a picture of the work Jesus did in freeing us from sin and making us part of God's family.

For You

Have you allowed Jesus to free you from sin? If not, talk to someone about doing that today. If you have, thank God for his gift of salvation through Jesus. Take time this week to read the short letter Paul wrote to Philemon.

Answer: a
I appeal to you to show kindness to my child, Onesimus. I became his father in the faith while here in prison. Onesimus hasn't been of much use to you in the past, but now he is very useful to both of us. I am sending him back to you, and with him comes my own heart. Philemon 1:10-12
(The Whole Story: The book of Philemon)

December 6

Hall of Faith

Q: What two men does this verse talk about? "It was by faith that _____ brought a more acceptable offering to God than _____ did."
a. Abraham and Lot
b. Abel and Cain
c. Jacob and Esau

Hebrews 11 contains the "Hall of Faith." It's a list of people who pleased God through living by faith and trusting him. Many people in the Hall of Faith have been discussed in previous devotions, but let's spend a few days reviewing how they showed faith.

Here's the background: God created Adam and Eve, placed them in a beautiful garden, and walked and talked with them. But when Adam and Eve sinned, they had to leave the garden. Their lives changed. Eve gave birth to two sons—Cain, who became a farmer, and Abel, who became a shepherd. Both boys grew up hearing stories from their parents of what life had been like when Adam and Eve walked with God in their garden home. Yet Abel was drawn to God and Cain wasn't.

Abel's faith in a God he couldn't see was shown in his offering of a perfect lamb given with a correct attitude toward God. Cain's offering failed to do that. (See January 7th's devotion.) The Hebrews Hall of Faith passage says, "Abel's offering gave evidence that he was a righteous man, and God showed his approval of his gifts." Abel had a heart for God, and God approved of him. Abel is an example of a man who lived by faith.

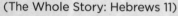

For You

There are many things you can give to God—your time, your talents and abilities, your money. Do you offer God the best you have with a right attitude? You do that when you willingly use your talents to help another person, give a little extra in the offering at church, or cheerfully help at home. What other ways can you give to God today?

Answer: b
It was by faith that Abel brought a more acceptable offering to God than Cain did. Abel's offering gave evidence that he was a righteous man, and God showed his approval of his gifts. Hebrews 11:4
(The Whole Story: Hebrews 11)

December 7

Going, Going, Gone

Q: What man does this verse refer to? "It was by faith that _____ was taken up to heaven without dying—'he disappeared, because God took him.'"
a. Noah
b. Elisha
c. Enoch

Enoch is another man mentioned in the Hall of Faith who we don't know much about (see yesterday's devotion). Genesis 5:21-24 says, "When Enoch was 65 years old, he became the father of Methuselah. After the birth of Methuselah, Enoch lived in close fellowship with God for another 300 years, and he had other sons and daughters. Enoch lived 365 years, walking in close fellowship with God. Then one day he disappeared, because God took him."

Enoch lived at a time when the world was becoming wicked, before God destroyed everything with a flood and started over. Enoch stood out because he walked with God. This doesn't mean that he literally walked with God but that in Enoch's 365 years on earth, he learned to love God and have a close relationship with him. Perhaps it was the influence of his great-great-great-great-grandfather Adam, passed down through the generations. Enoch may have grown up hearing stories about life in the Garden of Eden and about Cain, Abel, Seth, and others in Adam's family line.

Because Enoch pleased God, he didn't face death. The Bible doesn't say exactly how God took Enoch. One day he was just gone because God took him.

Enoch walked with God by having a close relationship with him each day. Because of that, he pleased God. Walking with God isn't just for those who lived in Bible times. It is important for us to walk with God today, too.

For You
There are many ways you can walk with God. You can read your Bible each day. You can pray throughout the day and include God in your problems and decisions. You can pay close attention in Sunday school and church. Can you think of more ways to walk with God?

Answer: c
It was by faith that Enoch was taken up to heaven without dying—"he disappeared, because God took him." For before he was taken up, he was known as a person who pleased God. Hebrews 11:5
(The Whole Story: Hebrews 11)

December 8

Saved by Faith

Q: What man does this verse speak about? "It was by faith that _____ built a large boat to save his family from the flood. He obeyed God, who warned him about things that had never happened before."
a. Jonah
b. Moses
c. Noah

Many years after Enoch went to heaven, God saw that the people on earth were getting more and more wicked. He'd created humans to worship him and to walk with him, but that's not what was happening. Everyone was doing evil, except for one family—the Noah family. Noah, Enoch's great-grandson, was a light of right living in the darkness of wicked living around him.

God decided to start over with just the Noah family. He decided to flood the whole earth and save Noah and his family. Here's the thing: It had never rained before, so no one knew that rain could fall from the sky and flood the land.

Because it had never rained before, God explained to Noah how rain would fall from the sky and flood the earth. Then he gave Noah instructions for building an ark. Noah must have had extraordinary faith to believe what God said. But Noah did believe God, and he got to work building the ark that saved his family. (You can read more about that in the January 11–13 devotions.)

It was important that Noah had a faith that allowed him to believe and obey God about something he'd never seen. Noah's faith led to obedience, which led to salvation for his family.

For You

Noah's faith allowed him to obey God without asking questions. Do you have the kind of faith that allows you to listen to God prompting you to do things and then do them? If not, ask God to build up your faith, then practice following God in faith each day.

Answer: c
It was by faith that Noah built a large boat to save his family from the flood. He obeyed God, who warned him about things that had never happened before.
Hebrews 11:7
(The Whole Story: Hebrews 11)

December 9

A Giant of Faith

Q: Eight verses in the Hall of Faith in Hebrews 11 talk about what Old Testament man?
a. Isaac
b. Abraham
c. Joseph

There were many men and women in the Bible who had a strong faith in God. Some of them are mentioned in Hebrews 11. Among the men and women listed, there is one who definitely stands out as a giant of faith. There were many circumstances in his life that required faith:

- He packed up and followed his father to a new country.
- After his father died, he journeyed farther without even knowing where God was leading him.
- He believed God would bless him with a son even though he and his wife were long past the age when they'd be able to have a child.
- He believed God's promise to give him many descendants, even before he had a son to carry on his family line.
- He was willing to offer his only son as a sacrifice to God.

You've probably already figured out that the man is Abraham. There were many situations that required Abraham to act in faith, believing God would keep his promises about his plan for Abraham's life. Because of Abraham's faith, God was able to bless Abraham with a large family that would play a big part in Jewish history. (You can read more about him in the January 15–21 devotions.)

God still blesses those who step out in faith and follow him even when things seem too painful or impossible to do.

For You

Sometimes we try to put our limitations on God, but he's above limitations. Don't be afraid to trust him during difficult or seemingly impossible situations. And don't be afraid to seek out the counsel of a godly man or woman to help you with hard times.

Answer: b
It was by faith that Abraham obeyed when God called him to leave home and go to another land that God would give him as his inheritance. He went without knowing where he was going. Hebrews 11:8
(The Whole Story: Hebrews 11)

December 10

Choosing the Hard Life

Q: The following verses are talking about what Bible man? "It was by faith that _____, when he grew up, refused to be called the son of Pharaoh's daughter. He chose to share the oppression of God's people instead of enjoying the fleeting pleasures of sin."
a. Moses
b. Samuel
c. Gideon

What is faith? According to Hebrews 11:1, "Faith is the confidence that what we hope for will actually happen; it gives us assurance about things we cannot see." The heroes of the faith listed in Hebrews 11, and many others who aren't named, believed what God promised them would happen even when they couldn't see obvious answers or rewards.

That kind of faith led them to be able to do things that were hard or didn't make sense at the time. It allowed them to follow God while being able to see only a small part of his plan.

Faith played a role in Moses' life from his birth. His parents are also listed in the Hall of Faith in Hebrews: "It was by faith that Moses' parents hid him for three months when he was born. They saw that God had given them an unusual child, and they were not afraid to disobey the king's command" (Hebrews 11:23).

Faith led Moses to leave his life of luxury in the Egyptian pharaoh's palace and join his own people. He traded what was familiar and comfortable for a hard and sometimes dangerous life. (You can read more about Moses in the February 8–23 and March 5–22 devotions.) Faith leads people to take the right road whether it's the more difficult road or not.

For You

Moses walked away from the easy life to follow God. Are you willing to step out for God even if it means making hard choices or standing alone? Ask God to help you to be able to do the right thing even when it's the harder thing to do.

Answer: a
It was by faith that Moses, when he grew up, refused to be called the son of Pharaoh's daughter. He chose to share the oppression of God's people instead of enjoying the fleeting pleasures of sin. Hebrews 11:24-25
(The Whole Story: Hebrews 11)

December 11

A Sign of Faith

Q: To whom does this verse refer? "It was by faith that _____ the prostitute was not destroyed with the people in her city who refused to obey God. For she had given a friendly welcome to the spies."
a. Rahab
b. Rachel
c. Rebekah

The Israelites had to wander in the wilderness for 40 years because they didn't have faith that God would help them defeat the Canaanites and take the land (see Numbers 14). After that time, they were ready to trust God.

The Israelites saw God miraculously cause the Jordan River to stop flowing when the priests carrying the Ark of the Covenant stepped into it (see Joshua 3). The Israelites crossed over on dry land. Then they saw God cause the walls of Jericho to tumble to the ground because they had the faith to follow his plan (see Joshua 6).

The Israelites weren't the only ones with faith. A woman named Rahab had faith too. She lived in Jericho and would have been killed when the Israelites conquered the city. But after she saved the Israelite spies, they promised to spare her if she hung a scarlet cord in her window. Rahab knew that the Israelite God was real. She knew her city would be destroyed. And she had faith the spies would spare her as promised, so she hung the cord out the window.

The scarlet cord was a sign of Rahab's faith, and that faith saved her and all of her family who were gathered in her house when the city fell. (You can read more about Rahab in the March 23, 24, and 27 devotions.)

For You
Rahab hanging the cord out the window was a sign of her faith. In what ways do you show your faith each day? What things have you done to make your salvation known to others?

Answer: a
It was by faith that Rahab the prostitute was not destroyed with the people in her city who refused to obey God. For she had given a friendly welcome to the spies. Hebrews 11:31
(The Whole Story: Hebrews 11)

December 12

The List

Q: Whose name is missing from this verse? "It would take too long to recount the stories of the faith of ____, Barak, Samson, Jephthah, David, Samuel, and all the prophets."
a. Daniel
b. Paul
c. Gideon

There are many names that could be listed in Hebrews 11 but aren't. How did God decide who would be listed and who wouldn't? We don't know. (This list in Hebrews 11 is known as the Hall of Faith, which we started discussing on December 6.) Many people are listed by name, and others are listed by their accomplishments.

Can you think of the Bible characters who fit the descriptions given at the end of Hebrews 11? "By faith these people overthrew kingdoms, ruled with justice, and received what God had promised them. They shut the mouths of lions, quenched the flames of fire, and escaped death by the edge of the sword. Their weakness was turned to strength. They became strong in battle and put whole armies to flight" (verses 33-34).

The people mentioned in Hebrews 11 are there because of their faith in God, but each showed their faith in a different way. Some followed God to foreign lands, stood up to ungodly leaders, believed God could do the impossible, and pushed on in the face of danger.

If God made a new Hall of Faith today, whom might he choose? The athlete who gives God the glory for his talent? The doctor who prays before performing surgery? The missionary who goes into a hostile country? How about you? Would your name be on the list?

For You

Would your name be on God's Hall of Faith list? You don't have to be an adult to live by faith. You can do it each day as you choose to be honest when taking a test, as you stand up for the girl who's being bullied, as you invite classmates to church, or as you help someone in need.

Answer: c
How much more do I need to say? It would take too long to recount the stories of the faith of Gideon, Barak, Samson, Jephthah, David, Samuel, and all the prophets. Hebrews 11:32
(The Whole Story: Hebrews 11)

December 13

Run with Endurance

Q: According to Hebrews 12, what helps you have endurance in your Christian life?
a. keeping your eyes on Jesus
b. going to church
c. reading the Bible

Long before our modern-day Olympics, there were competitions held in Greece. The New Testament authors were familiar with these, and Hebrews 12 compares the Christian life to a long-distance race. It gives the keys to running the race well.

The first key to running the race well is to get rid of any extra weight, especially the sins that trip you up. No runner wants extra weight. Some runners train with weights strapped around their ankles, and then when they take the weights off, they run even faster. But no one wears the weights during the race. In the Christian life, different people are tripped up by different sins. One person might struggle with honesty while another struggles with anger. Those are weights that slow them down as they live for Christ.

The second way to run the race well is to keep your eyes on Jesus. Have you had field day at your school or with your homeschool group? If you run in one of the races, you don't win by looking around and being distracted by other activities or by what your friends are doing. You keep your eyes on the finish line and head straight toward it as fast as you can.

Jesus is the example of how to run the race with endurance and not become distracted. He knew his path led to the Cross, and he never forgot why he was on earth. With each step he took as he taught others, healed the sick, rebuked the hypocrites, and made disciples, he kept his eyes on the finish line—his death and resurrection—in order to give us salvation.

For You
What things distract you from the race God has set you on? What do you need to do about them?

Answer: a
Since we are surrounded by such a huge crowd of witnesses to the life of faith, let us strip off every weight that slows us down, especially the sin that so easily trips us up. And let us run with endurance the race God has set before us. We do this by keeping our eyes on Jesus, the champion who initiates and perfects our faith. Because of the joy awaiting him, he endured the cross, disregarding its shame. Now he is seated in the place of honor. Hebrews 12:1-2
(The Whole Story: Hebrews 12:1-13)

December 14

Look in the Mirror

Q: According to the book of James, we shouldn't just listen to God's Word but also

a. preach it to others.

b. do what it says.

c. commit it to memory.

Imagine you are getting ready for school. You get dressed, brush your hair, and check yourself out in the mirror. If there's hair out of place, you fix it.

The book of James compares hearing the Bible with using a mirror: "For if you listen to the word and don't obey, it is like glancing at your face in a mirror. You see yourself, walk away, and forget what you look like." You may hear or read the Bible in church, during family devotions, or during your own quiet time. But if you hear and then forget, it's not very helpful.

Listening to Bible truths, remembering them, and obeying them will make a difference in your life. Perhaps you read from Colossians 3 and learn that God wants you to clothe yourself with tenderhearted mercy, kindness, humility, gentleness, patience, and love so you can live in harmony with others (see Colossians 3:12-15). But a few minutes later you go to watch your favorite television show and find your brother watching a ball game. You ask to watch your show, but he doesn't budge. You shout at him, throw the remote, and stomp out of the room. You may have read Colossians, but you didn't apply it, because you were angry.

When you read God's Word and obey it, it will change your heart. That will change your actions and attitudes.

For You

Sometimes God's Word shows us there are changes we need to make in our lives. If we seek to obey and live out the Word, God promises we'll be blessed (see James 1:25). As you read the Bible this week, let it soak into your mind and heart so you can live it out each day.

Answer: b

Don't just listen to God's word. You must do what it says. Otherwise, you are only fooling yourselves. For if you listen to the word and don't obey, it is like glancing at your face in a mirror. You see yourself, walk away, and forget what you look like. James 1:22-24
(The Whole Story: James 1:19-27)

December 15

Tame Your Tongue

Q: James says the tongue is a
a. flame of fire.
b. fountain of wisdom.
c. well of great depth.

The book of James, written by Jesus' brother James, is a practical book that shows us how to live the Christian life. James confronts sin, challenges the believer to do the right thing, and calls on Christians to be committed to God.

You might expect James to tackle what people consider the big sins, but he doesn't. One thing he speaks about is the tongue. Using the tongue in wrong ways—gossiping, cutting others down, being rude, talking back—might not seem like a big deal, but it is. A spark in dry grass can quickly spread into a wildfire that destroys everything in its way. The tongue is the same. The spark of an unkind or untruthful word can quickly build and destroy friendships, trust, and self-esteem.

Words can wound a person, and the damage can't be undone. Words can't be taken back or unsaid. You can apologize to a friend for saying something unkind during an argument, but the harm is done, and you'll both remember what was said.

It's better to stop and think before you speak. If you do speak during an argument, your words should focus on how you feel ("I'm upset because . . ." or "I feel hurt because . . .") rather than accusing the other person ("You always . . ." or "You're such a . . .").

Words can hurt, but they can also heal, encourage, teach, and inspire. Use your words for good today.

For You
Make it a point today to encourage someone with your words. A few well-spoken words can make the day for another person.

Answer: a
The tongue is a flame of fire. It is a whole world of wickedness, corrupting your entire body. It can set your whole life on fire, for it is set on fire by hell itself.
James 3:6
(The Whole Story: James 3:1-12)

December 16

Growing in God

Q: What does the book of 1 Peter say Christians should crave?
a. more of the Spirit
b. pure spiritual milk
c. healing from sickness

Did your parents keep a baby book for you? If so, it probably includes a growth chart that shows your height and weight at different ages and maybe even how you compared to the average baby of the same age. The book tells when you started eating baby cereal, fruits, and vegetables. It also shows when you sat up, crawled, and walked. It's amazing to see how much you've learned and grown.

When you accept Jesus as your Savior, you become a spiritual newborn. You need spiritual milk to begin your life in God. The sad thing is some Christians never get past the newborn stage. Years after they accept Christ, they are no farther along in their faith walks than at the beginning.

When you're a new Christian, you begin learning the truths about God, Jesus, and the Bible. You learn how God wants you to live, and you begin trusting him to guide you each day. You listen for God's prompting to make the right choices.

As you mature in your faith, you get deeper into the Bible. You begin learning harder concepts about God, Jesus, sin, and how to live the Christian life. The Holy Spirit reveals more to you as you allow him to.

Growing in God is a process just like going from scooting to crawling to walking is. And like with a baby, it happens one step at a time. Don't get stuck in the scooting or crawling stage. Move on in your Christian walk.

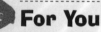

For You

Are you stuck in the newborn stage? If so, be faithful in your devotions. Take time to read "The Whole Story" Scripture passages for extra understanding. Listen carefully in church, and write down the things you understand. You will grow a little more each day.

Answer: b
Like newborn babies, you must crave pure spiritual milk so that you will grow into a full experience of salvation. Cry out for this nourishment, now that you have had a taste of the Lord's kindness. 1 Peter 2:2-3
(The Whole Story: 1 Peter 1:13–2:3)

December 17

Victorious Christian Living

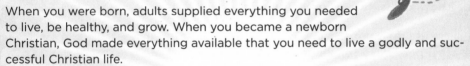

Q: According to 2 Peter, God has given Christians everything they need to do what?
a. start a church
b. be a missionary
c. live a godly life

When you were born, adults supplied everything you needed to live, be healthy, and grow. When you became a newborn Christian, God made everything available that you need to live a godly and successful Christian life.

Sometimes people search for something more. They want something that will make them feel good inside. But they don't need something more when it comes to living the Christian life. They can tap into God's power available to them when they turn their lives over to him.

Maybe you've gone to a Bible camp. You had fun playing games, doing skits, and swimming with your friends. The chapel services were exciting, and it seemed every word was meant for you. You were determined to go home and live a much better Christian life.

When you arrived home, things didn't go as planned. You missed your camp friends and the inspiring songs and messages. Reading your Bible and praying wasn't the same at home either.

That's because you were on a spiritual high at camp. The camp atmosphere was exciting and emotionally charged. But that doesn't mean you can't live for God just as well at home. God has already given you what you need to do that. But it's a day-by-day walk as you turn your own goals and feelings over to God and ask him to replace them with his own.

For You

If you don't feel as close to God now as you have at other times in your life, maybe it's time to tap into his power. As you focus more on what God wants for you and less on your own desires, you'll find yourself living a more victorious Christian life.

Answer: c
God has given us everything we need for living a godly life. We have received all of this by coming to know him. 2 Peter 1:3
(The Whole Story: 2 Peter 1:3-11)

December 18

The Sign of a Christian

Q: What word family fits in all the blanks? "Dear friends, let us continue to _____ one another, for _____ comes from God. Anyone who _____ is a child of God and knows God. But anyone who does not _____ does not know God, for God is _____."
a. see/see/sees/see/seeing
b. love/love/loves/love/love
c. know/know/knows/know/knowing

People use the word *love* in a lot of ways—not just to express their care for another person. You might hear, "I love chocolate." "I just love that new movie star." "Don't you just love that new store?" Do you truly love a food, movie star, or store? Not really. You might enjoy eating certain foods more than others, enjoy watching a certain person in movies, or like the clothing choices at a particular store. But you probably don't love them in the way that John tells us to love each other.

The book of 1 John says love is the mark of a genuine Christian. John is talking about *agape* love, or God's love. This kind of love seeks the best for others, even those who are hard to love, because that's the way God loves. Love is more than a feeling. It's a choice. Sometimes showing love means doing something difficult. After all, God is the source of love, and his love led him to sacrifice his own Son for us.

It's not enough to love only those who love us or those who deserve our love. Which of us really deserves God's love? But through God's strength, we can love those who are unfriendly or who don't love us in return. It's that kind of love that will draw others to Jesus.

For You

It's normal to find it hard to love those who are unkind to you or ignore you, but that's what Jesus asks you to do. Those people don't have to become your best friends, but you can love them because God created them and Jesus died for them just as he did for you. Ask him for extra help in loving the unkind people around you.

Answer: b
Dear friends, let us continue to love one another, for love comes from God. Anyone who loves is a child of God and knows God. But anyone who does not love does not know God, for God is love. 1 John 4:7-8
(The Whole Story: 1 John 4:7-21)

What Does Love Mean?

Q: Love means
a. caring about everyone.
b. doing what God says to do.
c. attending church faithfully.

The book of 2 John was written to "the chosen lady and to her children." Bible scholars don't know if that means this was a specific lady and her children or a church. Either way, the book was written to answer questions about God's truths. Sometimes leaders would claim to speak for God, but they were really speaking lies.

John says that the qualities of truth and love should be evident in every sincere believer's life. Love for each other is a mark of a true believer. But John also says that love means doing what God says to do. While on earth, Jesus said the same thing when he told his disciples, "If you love me, obey my commandments" (John 14:15).

When we truly love God, we do what he wants us to do. We obey his Word because we trust God to do the best thing for us. He can even use the bad things that happen to us and our mistakes for his own good to make us into the people he wants us to be.

God loves you no matter what you do, but he wants your obedience. And he wants you to love others because of his love for you.

For You

You truly love others when you accept everyone, including those with physical or mental differences. Your love is real when you reach out to those who are difficult to love. So, is your love real?

Answer: b

Love means doing what God has commanded us, and he has commanded us to love one another, just as you heard from the beginning. 2 John 1:6
(The Whole Story: The book of 2 John 1)

December 20

God's Children

Q: Fill in the blanks: "Those who _____ _____ prove that they are God's children."
a. do good
b. pray often
c. attend church

Do you offer some of your treats to friends? Do your parents invite people to your home for a meal? Do you ever have an overnight guest? If you or your family reach out to others and invite them to share what you have, you are showing hospitality.

The book of 3 John was written to a man named Gaius to show approval of the way he displayed hospitality and kindness to others, especially those who were traveling. Sometimes Gaius didn't even know the people he helped. In his letter to Gaius, John said, "Dear friend, you are being faithful to God when you care for the traveling teachers who pass through, even though they are strangers to you. They have told the church here of your loving friendship. Please continue providing for such teachers in a manner that pleases God."

Gaius knew that the Christian workers, both those in his home church and those who traveled, needed to be cared for physically. That's why he opened his house to them and offered them food and a place to sleep. They also needed to be cared for spiritually by being encouraged in their faith.

John heard of Gaius's good deeds, but he also heard of Diotrephes, who wanted to control things in the church but refused to do good for others. Diotrephes tried to stop others from doing good too. John told Gaius to follow only what was good because that would show he was one of God's children.

John wasn't saying that people's good works make them right with God. He was saying that when you are living for God, you just naturally do good works.

For You
Do the things you do each day show others that you are living for God? In what ways can you reach out to others and do good?

Answer: a
Dear friend, don't let this bad example influence you. Follow only what is good. Remember that those who do good prove that they are God's children, and those who do evil prove that they do not know God. 3 John 1:11
(The Whole Story: The book of 3 John 1)

December 21

Build Yourself Up

Q: What is one way Jude told believers to build each other up?
a. stay faithful in church
b. do good to all men
c. pray in the Spirit

Like James, Jude was Jesus' brother. He wrote the letter we know as the epistle of Jude in order to challenge Christians to stand strong in their faith against people who taught wrong things. False teachers were saying it was okay for Christians to live however they wanted without worrying about God's punishment. This false teaching was leading people away from the truth. Jude reminded believers that Jesus is Lord and that God does punish the wicked.

Jude urged Christians to take action. He wanted them to build up their own faith through praying, staying close to Jesus, helping others, and turning away from sin.

This letter could be written to Christians today, too, because there are many people who teach that it's okay to live the way you want. But it's not okay. God cares about the choices you make each day. He cares about whether you study for a test or do your homework. He cares how you talk to your parents and treat your siblings.

Romans 12:2 says, "Don't copy the behavior and customs of this world, but let God transform you into a new person by changing the way you think. Then you will learn to know God's will for you, which is good and pleasing and perfect." God wants you to live as his child so that you can discover his plans for you.

For You

People may tell you it doesn't matter if you do wrong things, but God's Word says it does matter. God has a wonderful plan for you, and you'll only be able to live out that plan as you try to please him each day.

Answer: c
You, dear friends, must build each other up in your most holy faith, pray in the power of the Holy Spirit, and await the mercy of our Lord Jesus Christ.
Jude 1:20-21
(The Whole Story: The book of Jude)

Book of Prophecy

December 22

God Reveals His Ultimate Plan

Q: To whom did God reveal the things written about in the book of Revelation?
a. Jesus
b. Paul
c. John

The author of the book of Revelation was first a fisherman, then one of the 12 disciples. After Jesus was resurrected and he returned to heaven, the author of Revelation was one of the original 12 apostles (the new name given to disciples after Jesus' ascension to heaven). In fact, tradition says he was the only original apostle who was not killed for his faith. The Romans exiled him to the island of Patmos in the Aegean Sea for preaching about Jesus.

So, who is the mystery author of Revelation? John. In addition to Revelation, the apostle John also wrote the Gospel of John, and 1 John, 2 John, and 3 John. At the beginning of Revelation, John explains that a voice told him to write down the things he saw in a vision and then send his account to seven churches.

First God gave John a specific message for each of the seven churches telling them what they were doing well and what they needed to change. After that, God showed John things that will happen in the future. People will become more evil, and one man will take over as the leader of the whole world. God will send different judgments to the unbelievers on earth, and Christians will be taken up to heaven. In the end Satan will lose, and Jesus will win.

For You

The book of Revelation may seem hard to read, but it's an important book because it shows that Jesus will triumph over evil and we will be part of his Kingdom forever. Even though Revelation talks of many judgments, it's a book of hope for those who believe.

Answer: c
This is a revelation from Jesus Christ, which God gave him to show his servants the events that must soon take place. He sent an angel to present this revelation to his servant John.   Revelation 1:1
(The Whole Story: Revelation 1)

December 23

The First and Last

Q: Jesus used what two Greek letters to describe himself?
a. *alpha, omega*
b. *alpha, delta*
c. *delta, omega*

Three times in the book of Revelation, Jesus says he is the Alpha and the Omega. Alpha is the first letter of the Greek alphabet, and omega is the last. Jesus isn't really talking about letters, though. He's talking about the fact that he has always existed. He was here in the beginning, and he will be here in the end.

In John 1:1, Jesus is called "the Word," and John tells us, "In the beginning the Word already existed. The Word was with God, and the Word was God." Jesus has always been. That's hard for us to understand because we are used to things that are created or made, or things that are born and die. But Jesus has always been.

Jesus was there when the world was first created, and nothing exists that he didn't make. If it's hard for you to understand that no one made God, and there is no time that God didn't exist, that's okay. Our minds aren't used to working that way, but perhaps one day in heaven God will allow us to understand it.

Jesus is also the beginning of our new life in God. Because Jesus died for our sins and rose again, he can offer us eternal life. John 1:12 says, "But to all who believed him and accepted him, he gave the right to become children of God." When we accept Jesus as Savior, we begin a new life as part of God's family.

Have you started a new life in Jesus?

For You

Jesus was present at the creation of the world. Everything has its start in him. Your salvation also begins with Jesus. Because of his death on the cross and his resurrection, you are part of God's family, and when the final showdown between Jesus and Satan takes place, you'll be on the right team.

Answer: a
"I am the Alpha and the Omega—the beginning and the end," says the Lord God. "I am the one who is, who always was, and who is still to come—the Almighty One." Revelation 1:8
(The Whole Story: Revelation 1)

December 24

Jesus Wins

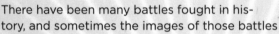

Q: Jesus rides what color of horse in the book of Revelation?
a. brown
b. black
c. white

There have been many battles fought in history, and sometimes the images of those battles are depicted in paintings or early photographs. You might have seen one of the many portraits of George Washington riding on his white horse. In one picture he's holding a sword, as though he's getting ready for battle. It's a picture that's easy to understand. There's a war being fought, and General Washington is planning to win.

The apostle John was given a clear picture of a battle yet to come. God revealed the future to John by allowing him to see visions. In Revelation 19 heaven opens, and John sees a warrior on a white horse. The battle lines between good and evil have been drawn, and both armies are preparing to meet in battle at Armageddon in the land of Israel. The armies of heaven are riding white horses and are dressed in fine white linen.

As the vision of the battle unfolds, John sees that the enemy has been defeated and the wicked leaders have been thrown into a lake of fire. Satan has been thrown into a bottomless pit. Sin is defeated, and Jesus reigns.

For people who don't believe in Jesus, the Battle of Armageddon will be a time of death and destruction. But for those who follow Jesus, it will be a time of victory.

For You
In John's vision of Jesus on the white horse, the words "King of kings and Lord of lords" are written on his robe. Jesus truly is King and Lord over all. Is he King and Lord in your heart today?

Answer: c
Then I saw heaven opened, and a white horse was standing there. Its rider was named Faithful and True, for he judges fairly and wages a righteous war.
Revelation 19:11
(The Whole Story: Revelation 19)

December 25

Happy Birthday, Jesus!

Q: Matthew records Jesus' family tree. Who is the first person in the list of names given?
a. Abraham
b. David
c. Boaz

Happy birthday, Jesus! Today we're taking a break from Revelation to celebrate Jesus' special day. Birthdays are important because they connect us to a family and remind people of the day we were born. But Jesus' birthday was even more important than that.

Each of the four Gospels records Jesus' life, but they do it in different ways and for different audiences. Matthew wrote especially to the Jews. Beginning his Gospel with Jesus' family tree, Matthew showed that Jesus was a descendant of Abraham and of David and, therefore, was Jewish.

The Old Testament prophesied that a Messiah would come. Hundreds of years passed, and the Jews were still waiting for their Messiah. The shepherds and the wise men recognized Jesus as the Messiah, but many Jews didn't because they were looking for an earthly king who would deliver them from Roman control.

Jesus didn't come to earth to set up a kingdom here, though. He came to live a sinless life. That way he could make salvation available to everyone. Jesus' birth brought hope and joy, but many of the Jews who lived at that time missed out on it.

Today people around the world celebrate Christmas, but for some it's just another holiday. For Christians it's much more. Although it's not Jesus' actual birthday, it's the day we celebrate God's plan for salvation was set in motion on earth through Jesus' birth.

For You
Read the story of Jesus' birth from Matthew 1 and Luke 2 as a reminder of why we celebrate Christmas. Share that story with someone else today.

Answer: a
Abraham was the father of Isaac. Isaac was the father of Jacob. Jacob was the father of Judah and his brothers. Matthew 1:2
(The Whole Story: Matthew 1)

December 26

Jesus' Plan

Q: In the book of Revelation Jesus says, "I am making everything ____."
a. big
b. new
c. gold

One day the earth we know will no longer exist because Jesus will set up his Kingdom on earth. He will make a new heaven, a new earth, and a New Jerusalem where God will dwell with his people.

John saw a vision of that New Jerusalem. The city didn't have a temple, because God himself lived there, so there was no need for a temple. There was no need for light because God was the light. The city gates were never shut, because there was no night, and no evil ever entered it.

John witnessed all the events in Revelation and wrote them down to encourage the churches of his time that were facing persecution and to tell Christians centuries later that someday we will live with God forever.

The Bible began in Genesis with the account of God creating the world and filling it with light and life. The Bible ends with the book of Revelation, where God creates a new heaven and a new earth. The beautiful Garden of Eden was destroyed when sin entered it, but there will be no sin in the paradise God will create, a paradise where he will dwell among men and women again.

The book of Revelation shows that no matter what happens on earth, God is always in control. We can keep living for God when times are tough, because we know that he is Lord over all.

For You

When things get difficult, and it's hard to stand up for what you believe, remind yourself that Jesus is Lord over all. He has a plan to carry out his work on earth until he returns, and you are an amazing part of that plan. Ask God to show you what he wants you to do each day to live out the special plan for your life.

Answer: b
The one sitting on the throne said, "Look, I am making everything new!" And then he said to me, "Write this down, for what I tell you is trustworthy and true."
Revelation 21:5
(The Whole Story: Revelation 21–22:6)

December 27

Goal for the New Year: Spend Time with God

Q: The psalmists compare their desire for God to
a. a rabbit running a race.
b. a lion hunting prey.
c. a deer longing for water.

January, the first month of the year, got its name from the Roman god Janus, who was considered the god of beginnings and endings. Statues of Janus show a god with two faces looking in opposite directions so he can see both forward and backward at the same time. What a fitting name for a month when people look both forward to a new year and backward to the year that's past.

Do you look both forward and backward at the end of a year? You might look backward and think of all the things you did in the past year. And you might look forward and resolve to do some things better or to start new habits in the new year.

One goal you might have is to spend more time with God in the new year. If you're reading this devotion, then you are spending time with God already. But you might resolve to spend extra time reading your Bible and praying in the coming year.

The psalmists said, "As the deer longs for streams of water, so I long for you, O God." More time with God is a good thing to desire, and you don't even have to wait until January 1 to start. You can spend 10 minutes reading your Bible today. Start with the book of John and read about Jesus, or read a chapter a day from Judges and see how God used ordinary people to do his work. Spend more time talking to God, telling him about the things that are really important to you and asking for his help.

For You
Set a goal for yourself of what you will do to spend more time with God in the coming year. Write it on a note card and stick it on your mirror so you'll remember it each day.

Answer: c
As the deer longs for streams of water, so I long for you, O God.   Psalm 42:1
(The Whole Story: Psalm 42:1-2)

December 28

Goal for the New Year: Know God's Word

Q: The psalmist says that God's Word is more desirable than what?
a. gold
b. honey
c. precious jewels

Yesterday's devotion talked about spending more time with God as a goal. Reading your Bible is part of that goal. But it might be time to do more than just read your Bible. It might be time to start digging deeper in God's Word.

You might feel like you're too young to study the Bible, but it's not too early to start. It may be as simple as choosing a specific passage to read in the Bible and finding out more about it. When you do that, you build yourself up against sin and temptation (see Psalm 119:11 and Ephesians 6:17). You earn God's approval (see 2 Timothy 2:15). And you grow in your faith (see 1 Peter 2:2-3).

There are many ways you can begin learning more about God's Word. You can pick one book of the Bible to focus on. There are good study Bibles that will tell you when and why the book was written and the person who it was written to. That will give you background information to help you understand what you read. You may want to start with an epistle such as Philippians or James.

You can pick a topic such as love or patience and find all the verses you can about it in the Bible. A Bible concordance will help you do that. It's an alphabetical list of words like you'd find in a dictionary, but instead of giving you a definition, it gives you Bible verses that use that word.

These are just three ideas for getting started in learning more about the Bible. Talk to a parent, Sunday school teacher, or youth pastor for other ideas.

For You

Set a goal of becoming a beginning Bible scholar this coming year. What books of the Bible would you like to learn more about? What topics can you think of that you'd like to read about from God's Word? Don't wait for the new year. Choose one and get started today.

Answer: a
[The laws of the Lord] are more desirable than gold, even the finest gold. They are sweeter than honey, even honey dripping from the comb. Psalm 19:10
(The Whole Story: Psalm 19:7-11)

December 29

Goal for the New Year: Pray for Others

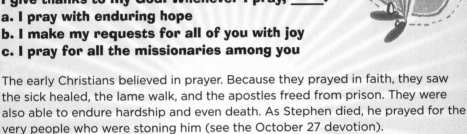

Q: Finish the verse: "Every time I think of you, I give thanks to my God. Whenever I pray, _____."
a. I pray with enduring hope
b. I make my requests for all of you with joy
c. I pray for all the missionaries among you

The early Christians believed in prayer. Because they prayed in faith, they saw the sick healed, the lame walk, and the apostles freed from prison. They were also able to endure hardship and even death. As Stephen died, he prayed for the very people who were stoning him (see the October 27 devotion).

Many of Paul's letters to the early churches tell them that he's praying for them. Romans 1:9 is an example of that. Paul said, "God knows how often I pray for you. Day and night I bring you and your needs in prayer to God, whom I serve with all my heart by spreading the Good News about his Son."

The early believers had the right idea about prayer. They prayed throughout the day, and it was as natural as breathing to them. God wants us to pray in the same way. It should be a normal part of our day.

If you aren't used to praying, there are many ways to get started. You might want to keep a list of people who need prayer. Then divide the list into days of the week. Perhaps you could pray for all the church leaders on Sunday, the government leaders on Monday, missionaries on Tuesday, school teachers and staff on Wednesday, and so on. You could pray for those who are sick or have immediate needs every day.

Or perhaps you could pray when you switch subjects at school or at home-school. It doesn't really matter how you remember to pray. The important thing is that you take time to pray for yourself and others every day. And don't forget to thank God for the things he's already done for you.

For You
Think of five people who need your prayers. Pray for them today.

Answer: b
Every time I think of you, I give thanks to my God. Whenever I pray, I make my requests for all of you with joy. Philippians 1:3-4
(The Whole Story: Philippians 1:3-6

December 30

Goal for the New Year: Share Your Faith

Q: If someone asks you about your faith, what should you do?
a. invite that person to church
b. give him or her a Bible
c. always be ready to explain it

The early believers were quick to share their faith with others, but they didn't all do it the same way. Peter and Paul were outgoing. They both spoke in front of large groups and also confronted people face-to-face. They didn't back down.

Andrew, on the other hand, was less direct but no less sincere in sharing his faith.

Andrew brought people to Jesus one by one. He brought his own brother Peter to Jesus, and he brought the boy with the lunch that Jesus used to feed the 5,000 (see the September 21 devotion).

The Samaritan woman whom Jesus met by the well quickly went and told her friends and family about the things Jesus had done and said (see the September 2 devotion). They followed her to the well to meet Jesus for themselves.

Dorcas shared God's love through the sewing she did for widows and the poor (see the October 30 devotion). She shared her faith through her good deeds.

These are all good ways to share your faith with others. Like Peter and Paul, you can spread the gospel: share verses from the Bible such as John 3:16 and Romans 6:23 that explain that Jesus died for our sins, rose again, and offers salvation to anyone who asks. Or like the Samaritan woman, you can tell how you met Jesus and how he changed your life. Or like Dorcas, you can get involved in ministries that reach out to others and share God's love that way.

There are many ways to share your faith, and you may be more comfortable with some than others. The important thing is that you share the Good News with as many people as you can no matter how you choose to do it.

For You

In what way can you best share your faith? Plan to share a Bible verse or something about Jesus with at least one person once a month or more in the coming year.

Answer: c
You must worship Christ as Lord of your life. And if someone asks about your Christian hope as a believer, always be ready to explain it. 1 Peter 3:15
(The Whole Story: 1 Peter 3:15-16)

December 31

Goal for the New Year: Stand Strong

Q: How does 1 Corinthians say you should work for the Lord?
a. carefully
b. prayerfully
c. enthusiastically

God created you with a plan in mind. He's given you the personality and talent to do the special job he's chosen for you. There are some things God has planned for when you're an adult, but there are other things to do right now. There may be someone only you can reach for Jesus because of a shared hobby or experience. Or there may be a student or teacher who needs the encouragement or help only you can give. There might be someone who struggles in an area you are strong in. God may plan for you to be the one to coach him or her in this weak area.

God might use your love for baseball, chess, Spanish, or math to reach others. The important thing is that whatever you do, you do it enthusiastically for the Lord and don't give up. For instance, you might sign up to tutor a student who has never learned to read. It may be fun at first, but then as time passes the task becomes more difficult because of the commitment it takes. It's tempting to quit and do something else instead. But you might be the best person not only to teach that student to read but also to help him or her to find a relationship with the Lord.

You have a new year in front of you to learn more about the Bible, grow closer to God, and reach out to others. Eagerly grasp the opportunities God places in your path.

For You
Ask God to show you what he wants you to accomplish in the new year. Take one day at a time and listen for him to speak to your heart.

Answer: c
So, my dear brothers and sisters, be strong and immovable. Always work enthusiastically for the Lord, for you know that nothing you do for the Lord is ever useless. 1 Corinthians 15:58
(The Whole Story: 1 Corinthians 15:35-58)

Scripture Index

About the Author

Katrina (Kathy) Cassel is the author of *The Christian Girl's Guide to Being Your Best, The Christian Girl's Guide to the Bible, The One Year Devotions for Girls Starring Women of the Bible,* and several other books for the teen/tween audience. Katrina has a BS degree in elementary education from Grace College, Winona Lake, Indiana, and an EdM with a reading specialty from the University of North Dakota. Katrina has worked with children of all ages in a variety of educational and church settings. She and her husband have eight children and live in Panama City, Florida.